Literature of the 1940s

The Edinburgh History of Twentieth-Century Literature in Britain
General Editor: Randall Stevenson

Published:

Vol. 3 *Literature of the 1920s: Writers Among the Ruins*
        Chris Baldick
Vol. 5 *Literature of the 1940s: War, Postwar and 'Peace'*
        Gill Plain
Vol. 6 *Literature of the 1950s: Good, Brave Causes*
        Alice Ferrebe
Vol. 9 *Literature of the 1980s: After the Watershed*
        Joseph Brooker

Forthcoming:

Vol. 1 *Literature of the 1900s: The Great Edwardian Emporium*
        Jonathan Wild
Vol. 4 *Literature of the 1930s: Border Country*
        Rod Mengham
Vol. 8 *Literature of the 1970s: Things Fall Apart, Again*
        Simon Malpas

Literature of the 1940s

War, Postwar and 'Peace'

Gill Plain

EDINBURGH
University Press

© Gill Plain, 2013, 2015

Edinburgh University Press Ltd
The Tun – Holyrood Road
12 (2f) Jackson's Entry
Edinburgh EH8 8PJ

www.euppublishing.com

First published in hardback by Edinburgh University Press 2013

This paperback edition 2015

Typeset in 10.5/13 Adobe Sabon by
Servis Filmsetting Ltd, Stockport, Cheshire,
and printed and bound in Great Britain by
CPI Group (UK) Ltd, Croydon CR0 4YY

A CIP record for this book is available from the British Library

ISBN 978 0 7486 2744 8 (hardback)
ISBN 978 0 7486 2745 5 (paperback)
ISBN 978 0 7486 3151 3 (webready PDF)
ISBN 978 0 7486 8936 1 (epub)

Contents

Illustrations   vi
Acknowledgements   vii
General Editor's Preface   ix

1   Introduction   1

I. WAR

2   Documenting   39
3   Desiring   74
4   Killing   111

II. POSTWAR

5   Escaping   149
6   Grieving   177
7   Adjusting   206

III. 'PEACE'

8   Atomising   239

Works Cited   273
Index   287

Illustrations

Figure 2.1 'It All Depends On You': The burden of the 'people's war'. Image © Imperial War Museums (Art. IWM PST 14374).   48

Figure 3.1 'Don't take the Squander Bug when you go shopping!': The dangers of irrational femininity. Image © Imperial War Museums (Art. IWM PST 15457).   80

Figure 3.2 'Keep Mum – She's Not So Dumb': The dangers of duplicitous femininity. Image © Imperial War Museums (Art. IWM PST 4095).   81

Figure 3.3 'Hello Boyfriend!': The dangers of female sexuality. Image © Imperial War Museums (Art. IWM PST 0800).   82

Figure 4.1 Aristocrats? Keith Douglas pencil drawing, leaf torn from lined notebook. Reproduced with the permission of Leeds University Library.   118

Figure 4.2 Pencil drawing, soldiers with tank. Keith Douglas. Reproduced with the permission of Leeds University Library.   130

Figure 7.1 One of the lucky ones? *A Diary for Timothy*, Humphrey Jennings, 1945. Courtesy of the British Film Institute.   216

Figure 7.2 'And Now – Win the Peace' The rhetoric of war continues. The Art Archive/ Bodleian Library Oxford, C. P. A. General Election, 1945.   223

Figure 8.1 Martins (Joseph Cotten) and Calloway (Trevor Howard) face up to the postwar world in *The Third Man* (1949). Courtesy of STUDIOCANAL Films Ltd.   249

Acknowledgements

My debt to Jackie Jones is, as ever, immense. For more years than I care to remember her insights have enriched my work, and her thoughtful approach to publishing has made Edinburgh University Press a pleasure to work for. I am also indebted to Randall Stevenson whose encyclopaedic knowledge of twentieth-century literature has energised the series.

I first started thinking about this project back in 2007, and I'm very grateful to Professor Stephan Kohl for the invitation to participate in his 'After the War' Seminar at the Universität Würzburg. Further stimulus came from the 'Femmes, Conflits et Pouvoir' meeting at the Université Toulouse-Le Mirail in 2008; from WAR-Net seminars and conferences; from the World War Two and Popular Culture conference held in Brighton in 2011; and from Ina Habermann's seminar on the middlebrow at the Universität Basel. Many thanks are due to Robert Lethbridge, the Fellows and staff of Fitzwilliam College, Cambridge who made me welcome during my Visiting Fellowship in Michaelmas term 2009–10. I was promised privilege without responsibility, and this was greatly appreciated! Also integral to the completion of this book were Cambridge University Library and the National Library of Scotland. The digital age has made much available at the click of a mouse, but a significant amount of the 1940s remains accessible only in paper form. Time was the other essential, and this was even harder to come by, which makes me all the more grateful to the Hosking Houses Trust, whose award of three-month residency in spring 2011 facilitated the completion of two chapters. I acknowledge and am deeply grateful for their support.

I wouldn't have been in Cambridge or Stratford without the support of Lorna Hutson and Andy Murphy, Heads of School past and present. Their kindness is much appreciated, as was Andy's persistent faith in the project. I'm enormously grateful to the many people who read sections of the book or listened to me talk about it, in particular Kate McLoughlin,

James McKinna, Petra Rau, Susan Sellers and Victoria Stewart. The fact that Petra's feedback usually came with tasting notes and suggestions for further drinking is a contribution that cannot be underestimated. Similarly, the companionship of planning WAR-Net events with Kate has made the business of working on war, death and misery altogether less lonely. Important thanks as well to Richard Dyer – without whom Dorothy Whipple would have passed me by – and Susan Manly, whose unexpected interest in the 1940s has been a valuable source of reading suggestions. For suggestions and conversations thanks also to: Tim Barringer, Nora Bartlett, Ian Blyth, Robert Crawford, Christoph Ehland, Alice Ferrebe, Lisa Griffin, John Goodby, Sue Grayzel, Laura Marcus, Lucy Noakes, Ravenel Richardson, John Wells and Jonathan Wild. Last, but most definitely not least, the students on my 'Reading the 1940s' module, whose responses forced me time and again to look afresh at my particular versions of the decade.

I am grateful to Faber and Faber Ltd for permission to quote from the works of T. S. Eliot. Some material from this book has appeared in different form in my contributions to Petra Rau, *Conflict, Nationhood and Corporeality in Modern Literature* (Palgrave, 2009) and Maroula Joannou, *A History of British Women's Writing, 1920–45* (Palgrave, 2012).

This book was begun in unpropitious circumstances, and could not have been written without the support of friends both at St Andrews and elsewhere. In addition to the readers already mentioned, enormous thanks to Frances Andrews, Helen Boden, Louise Bordua, Gordon McMullan, Rhiannon Purdie, Berthold Schoene (all grammatical errors are hereby acknowledged as my own), Emma Sutton, Ben 'Sapper' Winsworth, and the Mid-Wolders, in particular Clare Collins and Lawrence Green, who continued to ask after the book, despite periods of interminably slow progress.

By far my greatest debt is to James, for living with the 1940s, and for living with me living with the 1940s. The book couldn't have been written without him. It is dedicated, though, to my mother, Prim Plain, who died in 2008. She never forgave the Second World War for finishing before she could join the WAAF and escape from Brecon. Or so she said. But that, too, might be a myth of the Blitz.

University of St Andrews
February 2013

General Editor's Preface

One decade is covered by each of the ten volumes in *The Edinburgh History of Twentieth-Century Literature in Britain* series. Individual volumes may argue that theirs is *the* decade of the century. The series as a whole considers the twentieth century as *the* century of decades. All eras are changeful, but the pace of change has itself steadily accelerated throughout modern history, and never more swiftly than under the pressures of political crises and of new technologies and media in the twentieth century. Ideas, styles, and outlooks came into dominance, and were then displaced, in more and more rapid succession, characterising ever-briefer periods, sharply separated from predecessors and successors.

Time-spans appropriate to literary or cultural history shortened correspondingly, and on account not only of change itself, but its effect on perception. How distant, for example, that tranquil, sunlit, Edwardian decade already seemed, even ten years later, after the First World War, at the start of the twenties. And how essential, too, to the self-definition of that restless decade, and later ones, that the years from 1900–1910 *should* seem tranquil and sunlit – as a convenient contrast, not necessarily based altogether firmly on ways the Edwardians may have thought of themselves. A need to secure the past in this way – for clarity and definition, in changeful times – encourages views of earlier decades almost as a hand of familiar, well-differentiated cards, dealt out, one by one, by prior times to the present one. These no longer offer pictures of kings and queens: King Edward VII, at the start of the century, or, briefly, George V, were the last monarchs to give their names to an age. Instead, the cards are marked all the more clearly by image and number, as 'the Twenties', 'the Thirties', 'the Forties' and so on. History itself often seems to join in the game, with so many epochal dates – 1918, 1929, 1939, 1968, 1979, 1989, 2001 – approximating to the end of decades.

By the end of the century, decade divisions had at any rate become a firmly-established habit, even a necessity, for cultural understanding and analysis. They offer much virtue, and opportunity, to the present series. Concentration within firm temporal boundaries gives each volume further scope to range geographically – to explore the literary production and shifting mutual influences of nations, regions, and minorities within a less and less surely 'United' Kingdom. Attention to film and broadcasting allows individual volumes to reflect another key aspect of literature's rapidly changing role throughout the century. In its early years, writing and publishing remained almost the only media for imagination, but by the end of the century, they were hugely challenged by competition from new technologies. Changes of this kind were accompanied by wide divergences in ways that the literary was conceived and studied. The shifting emphases of literary criticism, at various stages of the century, are also considered throughout the series.

Above all, though, the series' decade-divisions promote productive, sharply-focused literary-historical analysis. Ezra Pound's celebrated definition of literature, as 'news that stays news', helps emphasise the advantages. It is easy enough to work with the second part of Pound's equation: to explain the continuing appeal of literature from the past. It is harder to recover what made a literary work news in the first place, or, crucially for literary history, to establish just how it related *to* the news of its day – how it digested, evaded, or sublimated pressures bearing on its author's imagination at the time. Concentration on individual decades facilitates attention to this 'news'. It helps recover the brisk, chill feel of the day, as authors stepped out to buy their morning newspapers – the immediate, actual climate of their time, as well as the tranquillity, sunshine, or cloud ascribed to it in later commentary. Close concentration on individual periods can also renew attention to writing that did *not* stay news – to works that, significantly, pleased contemporary readers and reviewers, and might repay careful re-reading by later critics.

In its later years, critics of twentieth-century writing sometimes concentrated more on characterising than periodising the literature they surveyed, usually under the rubrics of modernism or postmodernism. No decade is an island, entire of itself, and volumes in the series consider, where appropriate, broader movements and influences of this kind, stretching beyond their allotted periods. Each volume also offers, of course, a fuller picture of the writing of its times than necessarily-selective studies of modernism and postmodernism can provide. Modernism and postmodernism, moreover, are thoroughly specific in their historical origins and development, and the nature of each can be usefully illumined by the close, detailed analyses the series provides. Changeful, tumultuous and challenging, history in the twentieth-century perhaps pressed harder and more variously on literary imagination than ever before, requiring a literary history correspondingly meticulous, flexible and multifocal. This is what *The Edinburgh History of Twentieth-Century Literature in Britain* provides.

The idea for the series originated with Jackie Jones in Edinburgh University Press, and all involved are grateful for her vision and guidance, and for support from the Press, at every stage throughout.

Randall Stevenson
University of Edinburgh

Chapter One

Introduction

There are many '1940s'. For some it is and always will be the decade of the Second World War, and that conflict overshadows all other aspects of the period, not least because while hostilities ceased in 1945, the impact of the war continued to be felt – psychologically, emotionally and economically – in the state of the nation, the grief of its inhabitants and the pain of readjustment. For others, the 1940s is a beginning, not an end: the Cold War, immigration, the inception of the welfare state and the transformation of Britain as an imperial power. Yet the multiplicity of these 1940s is most often distilled into the crude division of 1945 and after. Studies of the century, whether literary or historical, concur with Jay Winter's argument that 1945 is the 'real caesura in European cultural life' of the twentieth century (1995/1998: 228).[1] This book at once agrees with and challenges that assertion. Undoubtedly 1945 is a catastrophic year, etching European cultural memory with the indelible scars of the atomic bomb and what would later be termed the Holocaust. Nonetheless, the literary manifestation of such a 'break' is harder to pin down – it is a more diffuse production, the product of a nexus of temporal, historical, subjective and pragmatic considerations. The horror of 1945 is both anticipated and avoided by literature. For some, writing stopped: physical and psychological survival took priority over the concrete crafting of a response to the unthinkable destruction of war; others, by contrast, sought a public voice, bearing witness both to the horror and to the quotidian business of living in uncharted territory; other writers looked inward, retreating to the personal as the only ground of certainty in a world in which all limits seemed to have been annihilated. For literature, then, 1945 is an arbitrary caesura, just as in many respects, the decade is an arbitrary organising concept imposed on the complex fluidity of public events and private imagination. For understanding the shaping forces of culture in the mid-century, 1933–45, for example, might be seen to form a more coherent period, or

1939–56. Yet we nonetheless habitually think through decades, and in the case of a period such as the 1940s, the exercise of refusing 1945 as a limit point enables a fruitful and necessary opening up of war's hinterland, and a better understanding of the relationship between literature and its contexts. The period 1939–51 takes Britain through a series of seismic cultural and political shifts: to what extent was literature able, or willing, to respond?

According to Angus Calder, the response was limited. In *The People's War* he suggests that 'few memorable works of fiction or drama emerged during the war itself', adding that the 'theatre had long suffered from a dearth of native talent which the war did nothing to remedy' (1969/1992: 513). Amongst those few writers Calder thinks worthy of mention – Nigel Balchin, Joyce Cary, Henry Green, Graham Greene, Evelyn Waugh – all are men and only Balchin comes as anything of a surprise. *The People's War* remains one of the most valuable cultural histories of the war years, but it perhaps goes without saying that Calder's verdict on the literature of the period is limited. But he is not alone in finding the 'literary' decade evasive. In an attempt to explain 'what happened to writing in the 1940s', Malcolm Bradbury concludes that this was 'a period less of major arts than of fundamental redirections' (1987: 72); in short, there was a great deal of activity in the decade, but no lasting legacy. The writers of the late 1940s ground to a halt in a haze of despair and a perverse nostalgia for a war now valorised as 'a time of common purpose when writing had mattered' (85). Bradbury's difficulties with the decade emerge in part from the critical reaction of the 1950s. In poetry in particular the backlash against war writing and the innovations of the so-called 'New Apocalypse' was devastating, and the gradual process of reconstructing the literary landscape has been a long time gathering momentum. A first staging post was the appearance in 1977 of Robert Hewison's *Under Siege: Literary Life in London 1939–1945*. I am greatly indebted to Hewison, but as he himself admits, his book is not an exercise in literary criticism (1977/1988: xii). His concern is with the factors 'that shaped the creative climate of the times' (xii) and the focus of the book is metropolitan. London here comes to represent the nation in microcosm, rather as it had done in the propaganda of the war itself. Hewison had, however, set something in process, and his lively survey was followed by substantial acts of recovery such as Linda Shires's *British Poetry of the Second World War* (1985) and A. T. Tolley's *The Poetry of the Forties* (1985), which not only runs the gamut from Apocalypse to Austerity and from surrealism to verse drama, but also departs from the metropolis to consider Welsh, Scottish and Irish poetry of the decade. These in turn were followed by Andrew Sinclair's

War Like A Wasp: The Lost Decade of the Forties (1989), which builds its case on the career of Julian Maclaren-Ross, whose *Memoirs of the Forties* (1965) are described as 'the indispensible Baedeker of the place and period' (1989: 295). Through MacLaren-Ross and the culture that surrounded him, Sinclair argues for the short-lived coherence of an 'artistic London coalesced around the pubs and drinking-clubs of Fitzrovia, Soho and Chelsea' (1989: 286). Although later 'condemned for its excess', he argues, 'it produced a feverish body of work that characterized its time' (286).

The 1990s saw a change of critical focus, and the fog of bohemianism was replaced by a resurgence of interest in the war. Adam Piette's influential *Imagination at War* (1995) set about dismantling the myth of war as a generator of creativity, arguing that the 'gigantic energies and complexities of the war-machine enervated and outclassed the private imagination, enmeshing it into the network of its fabrications, enforcing complicity in the double-dealing of its rhetoric' (1995: 2). Thematically exploring writing from the desert and the Blitz, and providing detailed studies of Alun Lewis and Evelyn Waugh, Piette's book builds a persuasive case for the war's 'violent dismantling of ordinary ideas of home and private life' (7). Jenny Hartley's *Millions Like Us: British Women's Fiction of the Second World War* (1997), by contrast, was more optimistic, arguing that women writers 'were moving in the opposite direction to their male contemporaries' (1997: 9). Exploring writers as diverse as Rosamund Lehmann, Betty Miller, Elizabeth Taylor and Virginia Woolf, Hartley finds evidence of a nuanced engagement with the 'meaning and implications of war' (1997: 15). 'Even when it is critical,' she concludes, 'this is a literature of commitment and citizenship' (15). Hartley's 'middlebrow', anti-metropolitan focus was a valuable corrective, as was Phyllis Lassner's emphasis on the political energy of writers such as Storm Jameson, Naomi Mitchison and Phyllis Bottome. In the work of these women, still largely absent from canonical considerations of the war, Lassner detects a complex and ambivalent process of bearing witness, the writing of which emerges as 'an epic of moral clarification' (1997: 23). In these studies, and the work of Plain (1996) and Schneider (1997), it became clear just how much remained to be done in recovering the literature of war, never mind the literature of the decade as a whole.

Further studies emerged in the new millennium, many of them questioning the stability of concepts such as memory and modernity, and opening up new writers to critical scrutiny: Mark Rawlinson's *British Writing of the Second World War* (2000), Kristin Bluemel's *George Orwell and the Radical Eccentrics* (2004), Victoria Stewart's *Narratives of Memory* (2006), Marina MacKay's *Modernism and World War II*

(2007) and Lyndsey Stonebridge's *The Writing of Anxiety* (2007).[2] Each of these works complicates and develops critical understanding of the war years, but they do not bring us any closer to a recognisable 'literature' of the 1940s. This difficulty might in part be attributable to the changing mediation of war. Unlike 1914–18, the Second World War has not, habitually, been seen as a 'literary' conflict. The 1940s were, rather, a 'golden age' of British cinema, that opened with the rise of the documentary feature under the auspices of directors such as Humphrey Jennings, Charles Frend and Alberto Cavalcanti, encompassed the considerable creative talents of Anthony Asquith, David Lean, Carol Reed and the Archers (Michael Powell and Emeric Pressburger), and ended with the triumph of the Ealing studio comedies. British cinema in the 1940s absorbed and reconstituted literary creativity: playwrights such as Terence Rattigan saw their work adapted or themselves wrote screenplays, while Noël Coward wrote everything – including the music – for the enormously successful morale booster *In Which We Serve* (1942). Graham Greene's stories and novels were adapted for the screen, and the construction of *The Third Man* (1949) was a collaborative effort between himself and director Carol Reed. J. B. Priestley wrote propaganda films, as – more improbably – did Dylan Thomas, while the documentaries of Humphrey Jennings, in particular *Listen to Britain* (1942), have justifiably been described as visual poetry. The literature of earlier eras also found its way onto the screen, most notably in adaptations by David Lean of Dickens's *Great Expectations* (1946) and *Oliver Twist* (1948) and in Laurence Olivier's Shakespeare films: *Henry V* (1944) and *Hamlet* (1948). Less elevated, but more successful, were the melodramas adapted by Gainsborough studios from popular historical novels. *The Wicked Lady* (1945) might not have won any critical plaudits, but it and Gainsborough fellows such as *The Man in Grey* (1943) and *Fanny By Gaslight* (1945), ensured that British cinema in the 1940s was a massive box office success.[3]

In popular memory, then, it is cinema rather than literature that is the characteristic form of the 1940s, and new media was similarly dominant in the reporting of war and its aftermath. Groups gathered around the wireless in family homes, canteens and service messes; audiences absorbed their information as much from Pathé news as from conventional newsprint. And they had a lot to take in: the events of the 1940s were simply too big, too diffuse and too varied for a homogenous literary response to the war or to its shocking and complicated aftermath. The immense scope of the conflict might also explain the tendency of critics to focus on London as a representative microcosm, even though life in the city was far from typical. The majority of the population spent the war in the provinces, in rural areas, or despatched overseas, recruited to industry or agriculture, or – in the case of non-'mobile' women – working in the profession of housework, made newly demanding by rationing, shortages and the billeting of evacuees. But another explanation of the absent decade might be found in post-1940s' critical habit. A significant reason for the disappearance of these years is the long-ingrained practice of reading the twentieth-century through the formal trajectory of modernism and after, into which the 1940s disappear as afterthought or hiatus. James Joyce and Virginia Woolf died in 1941, while T. S. Eliot had long since left *The Waste Land* behind him, and Ezra Pound had departed for Italy to produce anti-Semitic propaganda for the Fascist government. These endings, though, are deceptive and recent work on the 1940s has revived discussion of the modernist impulse. In analyses of 'late' modernism (Miller 1999; Esty 2004), 'intermodernism' (Bluemel 2004) and 'modernism and ...' (MacKay 2007; Mellor 2011), there is an urge to give cultural legitimacy to the work of a group of writers who do not 'fit' by evoking the century's most powerful literary term, even as it is qualified and resisted. There is no doubt that many writers continued to be influenced by a modernist aesthetic, but this book suggests that 'modernism' is a distraction for the 1940s, and its deployment risks obliterating the very diverse voices and literary developments of the period. The Second World War really does change everything. Perversely, it brings homogeneity of purpose while fracturing established literary coteries, generating new confluences of influence and fresh discursive modes. For this book, then, modernist writers and their texts will sit alongside the equally disputed and contentious categories of the popular and the middlebrow, and by works of literature – such as the baroque world of Mervyn Peake's *Titus Groan* (1946) – that resist any such categorisation.

The focus of *War, Postwar and 'Peace'* is on texts rather than personalities, and it tries to escape from the habit of seeing the decade as an almost entirely male story built around Fitzrovia at home and the forces abroad. The book seeks to provide both breadth and depth, using longer case studies of representative or remarkable work to convey the tone and texture of writing in the period. The downside of this approach is, of course, what gets left out. It goes without saying that this could have been a longer book. The more I read, the more amazed I became by the forgotten pleasures of the decade – and by the possibilities opened up by seeing familiar writers from a new angle. It is important to stress, then, that *War, Postwar and 'Peace'*, is *a* literary history of the 1940s, not *the* literary history of the 1940s, and it is one that focuses as much on work that was popular at the time as on that which has become part of the 'canon' of British literary studies. I hope that in bringing together literatures seldom considered in conjunction (or, indeed, not considered at all) it will be possible to evoke something of the spirit of the time (1939–51) and the place (Britain), and that this will in turn prompt the production of further histories and critical studies of what is to me the most fascinating of twentieth-century decades.

Navigating the 1940s I: War, Postwar and 'Peace'

As I suggested above, the 1940s are seldom examined as a coherent 'decade', not least because the almost unimaginable scale of the Second World War casts a shadow over the period's later years. Yet these years cohere as a period of unprecedented social and political change that marked the emergence of 'modern' Britain. The decade witnessed the end of a mode of national being and a fundamental transformation in the way the nation saw itself and was seen. The war introduced previously discrete classes and communities to each other, it imposed unprecedented controls on people's movements, and it gave rise in 1945 to a landslide election victory for the Labour party. From its ironically authoritarian democracy the concept of the welfare state emerged, and in its aftermath the rebuilding of Britain saw the expansiveness of the colonial imperative replaced by mass immigration and the dilution of the nation's long-cherished insularity. The war also bankrupted the nation and exposed the vulnerability of Britain's status as a world power, setting in train events whose repercussions would not fully be felt until the 1960s. But, as Robert Colls observes, in the 1940s, few were aware of the 'end' of Empire, or the imminent demise of a mode of national self-perception (2002: 4, 143–4). Rather, optimism and the possibility of building anew jostled uncomfortably with nostalgia for a lost pre-war world, and a post-traumatic uncertainty about the future. The literature that emerged from such a context is predictably heterogeneous, and the book's subtitle, *War, Postwar and 'Peace'*, reflects the problems of 'organising' the period.

War

The Second World War began on 3 September 1939 and ended on VE Day, 8 May 1945, unless you had the misfortune to be in the Pacific theatre of war, in which case the conflict finally ended on VJ Day, 15 August 1945. These dates, though, cannot be seen to demarcate the historical parameters of a war that had been anticipated, by some, as far back as the signing of the Versailles Treaty in 1919. The Second World War not only generated an anxious discourse of anti-war and anti-fascist writing in the late 1930s, culminating in the abortive false start of the 1938 Munich Crisis, it also continued to shape literary production long after hostilities had ceased. From the practical impact of continued rationing, to the psychological impact of grief and the post-traumatic shock of combat, blitz and rocket attacks, the war lived on in the mind of the nation even as many looked forward to the prospect of a new Britain.

The ambiguous boundaries of the conflict find their parallel in the difficulty of defining war writing in the 1940s. This was the war that exploded once and for all the hierarchy dividing combatant and non-combatant. As Sonya Rose has noted, until the middle of 1944 the war 'had produced more deaths among civilians in Britain than among those who were in the fighting services' (2003: 1). Yet, more than this, as many writers acknowledged at the time, the sheer immensity of the conflict – its geographical extent, political complexity and human scale – resisted interpretation or summation. While the press called for liter-ary mobilisation, repeatedly asking 'Where are the war poets?', writers themselves were left disorientated and uncertain, asking what, after the First World War and the Spanish Civil War, could possibly be left for the writer to say? (Calder 1969/1992: 517–18; Hewison 1977: 9–12). Equally uncertain was the question of how it should be said. Keith Williams observes that the question 'Where Are the War Poets?' is 'best answered' not by focusing on combatant poetry, 'but on the writers mobilised in the biggest exercise in mass-communications ever under-taken by a British government' (1996: 182). With writers as diverse as Graham Greene, George Orwell and William Empson recruited for the cause of cultural propaganda, the 'literature' of the Second World War was, perhaps inevitably, destined to take more unconventional form.

The necessity of rethinking the parameters of 'war writing' is perhaps most clearly articulated by Elizabeth Bowen. The Preface to *The Demon Lover* (1945) captures both the necessity of writing and the 'hallucina-tory' quality of the lived experience from which such writing emerged (Bowen 1945/1950: 49). In Bowen's analysis, the war permeated lit-erature, and texts bore the imprint of conflict even as they consciously turned from its direct representation. Writing became a mode of resist-ance and a release, the consolatory fantasies of the imagination permit-ting an assertion of self in the 'stupefying' climate of war. In a context in which what 'was happening was out of all proportion to our facul-ties for knowing, thinking and checking up', individual writers could not hope to be representative (49). Rather, the fragments of prose and poetry produced in this period acquire complex cumulative meanings as incremental parts of a much larger, communal narrative of war. Describing her own short stories, Bowen suggests a mode of writing as possession, a colonisation of what Adam Piette terms the 'private imagination' (1995: 1):

> The stories had their own momentum, which I had to control. The acts in them had an authority which I could not question. Odd enough in their way – and now some seem very odd – they were flying particles of something enormous and inchoate that had been going on. They were sparks from experience – an experience not necessarily my own. (Bowen 1945/1950: 47)

Piette argues that the drive to transform 'private imagination into public spirit' had a devastating impact on British culture (1995: 2), and in many cases, Bowen's short stories seem to confirm the self-annihilating dimension of the war. As Kate McLoughlin has indicated, the history of war writing is littered with rhetorical statements of its own impossibility. In every form, from the direct statement that the acts of war are indescribable, to metaphorical conceits of impossible reversals and unimaginable juxtapositions, there is an epic history of writers' acknowledgement that war defies representation. McLoughlin writes: 'Frequently encountered in conflict literature is the proposition that war defeats language, as though words themselves have been shot down or blown up' (2009: 20). In Bowen's story 'Sunday Afternoon', for example, Henry, visiting the neutral space of Ireland, attempts to answer his friends' questions about the bombing of London. The task defeats him, and he concludes that 'One's feelings seem to have no language for anything so preposterous' (Bowen 1983: 617). This short example encapsulates what, with hindsight, can be recognised as the dominant tone of British responses to the war. Henry's words speak to a detachment from self – an alienation and refusal of emotional engagement – and a profound reliance on understatement. War is a 'preposterous' experience, by implication absurd and topsy-turvy, rather than a fundamental threat to life. The self-consciousness of Henry's disclaimer categorises his statement as an instance of 'adynaton', a rhetorical trope described by McLoughlin as 'the mother of all diversionary tactics' and a mode of writing about war that makes 'not-writing its very subject' (2011: 152). Yet Henry's response is also characteristic of gender, class and nation; it speaks to the qualities of understatement and reserve that had come to form the bedrock of British, middle-class masculinity. This mode of being, which Alison Light argues had in turn been claimed by middle-class women of the interwar period, is post-traumatic in character: in the aftermath of the First World War, the British middle classes were 'incapable of speaking the language of romance' (1991: 108). Here, though, what is customarily seen as destructive – the repression of emotion – can be recognised as a self-preserving strategy distancing the predominantly middle-class characters of wartime fiction from the traumatic impact of combat, bombing and bereavement. For male homosocial communities, similar work was undertaken by 'banter'. Described by Anthony Easthope as 'a way of affirming the bond between men while appearing to deny it' (1992: 88), banter is another crucial 'diversionary tactic' of the Second World War, permitting the expression of emotion under the guise of attack. It is a coded language simultaneously acknowledging and denying the powerful emotions generated by the proximity of death.

Yet while nation and class seemed to prohibit the possibility of war stories, Bowen's preface suggests that war finds its inscription in more diffuse and uncertain forms. Her perception of a 'war-climate' opens out the concept of war writing, suggesting that it need not be confined to combat, but might instead embrace a more nebulous and inclusive concept of cultural dislocation. Such a reconfiguration is singularly appropriate for the so-called 'People's War', a conflict that rewrote the rules of engagement and was, in Annemarie Tröger's phrase, a 'war against civilian populations' (1987: 285). This relocation of the battlefield was consolidated by the rhetoric of writers, journalists and film-makers that merged the identities of soldier and civilian into a democratic national body. This public dimension of war reminds us just how much life changed for the British public during the war years. The process of mobilising a nation for total war ensured that – through evacuation, conscription and rationing – citizens experienced an unprecedented loss of autonomy: freedom of choice was radically curtailed. Beyond this disruption of the infrastructure of everyday life came the events of the war itself. Catastrophe was expected from the outset of hostilities, but it failed to materialise, giving rise to the psychologically exhausting period of the 'phoney war'. Firemen sat unoccupied in their stations, evacuees drifted back home to the cities. It was not until the spring of 1940 that the war began to fulfil its dreadful promise: German forces invaded Norway and Denmark in April, moving on in May to attack the Netherlands, Belgium and France. By the end of May, the British Expeditionary Force (BEF) – deployed in 1939 to supplement the defence of the Franco-Belgian border – was surrounded, and the consequent evacuation of troops from the beaches at Dunkirk (26 May–4 June) became the first propaganda triumph of the war, as military defeat was reinscribed as a miraculous, morale-boosting victory.

The events that followed Dunkirk – the Battle of Britain and the

Blitz – have come to epitomise national jeopardy. From the summer of 1940 to the spring of 1941, British cities were subject to sustained aerial attack. London was the main target, experiencing 57 nights of continuous bombardment, but industrial and military targets such as Birmingham, Glasgow and Portsmouth were also attacked. It was not until Hitler's decision to focus German resources on the invasion of the Soviet Union (Operation Barbarossa), starting in June 1941, that the threat of invasion eased a little. Yet, although diaries bear witness to the strain of living under constant physical and psychological threat, anxiety was not the entirety of British experience in the early war years. For people outside the cities, in rural communities, war meant social disruption and a more mundane but nonetheless demoralising sense of difficulty. Simultaneously, for those quite literally under fire, the structures of the quotidian did not collapse, and abnormal destruction was more or less self-consciously normalised as part of a 'business as usual' rhetoric. The first chapter of the 'War' section consequently traces the urge to document that was the pre-eminent feature of these early years. This was a literature that strove for transparency, assuming the duty of bearing witness to momentous historical events, but in the process inevitably revealing the limits of both articulation and imagination in the face of war's violence. Chapter 2, by contrast, explores the symbolic contours of conflict, examining the inescapable formations of gender and sexuality that could not help but shape the literature of the period. The section ends with an examination of killing, the exemplary experience of wartime and a subject of abject fascination to writers across the decade.

Postwar

Wars do not simply end with the signing of an armistice: the social, psychological and logistical 'hangover' of conflict can continue for years after hostilities have officially ceased. Similarly, we might note that the 'postwar' does not wait for the signing of a treaty, and that the cultural symptoms of war's end are manifest in advance of its actual conclusion. This phenomenon is particularly marked in the case of the Second World War. In the aftermath of 1942's decisive victories in North Africa there came the realisation that the war could, and eventually would, be won – and this relaxation in the perception of jeopardy had a range of significant consequences. For those on the home front, imminent threat mutated into a concept of duration, the prospect of an ending making the remaining unspecified 'sentence' of war all the harder to bear. For servicemen and women the distinction was not quite so clear, and in many ways the early onset of the postwar is specific to the home front. But, as is so often the case with the Second World War, the boundaries between the two 'fronts', and between combatant and non-combatant, can be difficult to discern. The repatriation of POWs began with the wounded in 1943: their wars over, they found themselves adrift in a domestic environment still in the grips of the mechanisms of conflict, a world that bore little resemblance to the 'home' they had left (Rolf 1988: 131–5). An equally disorientating sting in war's tail was the onset of rocket attacks in June 1944, returning London to a state of threat all the harder to bear for its arbitrariness and military futility. '[H]ow can they affect the outcome of the war?' asked George Beardmore, a writer and housing officer dealing with the fall-out of a new round of destruction: 'The answer is, not at all. They are senseless' (15 November 1944; 1986: 184).

While Beardmore catalogued the intense cold of a winter beset by fuel shortages in which even potatoes were scarce (1986: 187), soldiers in Europe were experiencing a series of demoralising setbacks. Hopes for a speedy conclusion to hostilities after the D-Day Normandy landings (6 June 1944) were dashed by the failure, in September 1944, of Operation Market Garden – the airborne assault on Arnhem designed to get Allied troops across the Rhine. This setback was followed by a dreadful hiatus in which German troops launched a major counter attack in the Ardennes (the 'Battle of the Bulge') between December 1944 and January 1945. Thus, on the home front and the battle front, the winter of 1944–5 proved a time of bleak ambivalence. Europe had been invaded, but was far from liberated, and Allied casualties were heavy. Britain itself was sufficiently safe to disband the Home Guard, but could do little to protect its citizens against hunger, cold, exhaustion and flying bombs.

Paradoxically, though, the origins of the 'postwar' precede not only the grim torments of the war's endgame, but also the decisive shifts of 1942. As early as March 1940, Cyril Connolly's *Horizon* could be found entertaining the idea in R. F. Harrold's optimistic article 'Peace Aims and Economics'. 'It must be in a chastened mood that one approaches the post-war problem', writes Harrold before mapping out his vision of a 'sort of inverted Federal Unionism' (*Horizon*, Vol. I, No. 3: 155; 161). Stephen Spender was also thinking ahead, asserting the need for 'remedies and plans and cures' after the collapse of Germany in an article for the *New Statesman* in July 1940 (Sutherland 2004: 268). Less than a year later, but from a very different post-Blitz perspective, *Picture Post* published its 'Plan for Britain' issue (4 January, 1941). Boasting articles on work, social security, town planning, land use, education and health, the special issue was rounded off by a contribution from J. B. Priestley entitled 'When the Work is Over'. Priestley, distrustful of the word 'leisure', warns against 'passive mechanical' entertainment and the 'wrong kind of enjoyment', advocating instead a postwar future where everyone has time and energy to be creative (1941: 39). These interventions might be seen as a strategic distraction: to imagine or plan a future is one way of ameliorating the difficulties of a current situation; but even so the optimistic belief in the perfectibility of society could not survive the war. Indeed, enthusiasm for planning and earnest self-improvement faded as the war dragged on, to be replaced by a taste for distraction epitomised by the meteoric rise of Gainsborough studio melodramas. Yet this transition should not be overstated. In spite of the popularity of documentary modes, the desire to escape the war had been present from its earliest years, as was evident from the on-going popularity of detective fiction and the remarkable revival of the nineteenth-century novel. Angus Calder records that, as the war progressed, the 'thirst for classics was impossible to slake' (1969/1992: 511), with Jane Austen, in particular, enjoying a significant renaissance. This was, notes Jenny Hartley, a mode of fiction that took readers out of the chaos of wartime and enabled them to 'assemble their scattered selves' (1997: 3). This trend in reading was regarded with suspicion by the influential critic, F. R. Leavis, who was motivated, at least in part, to construct his 'Great Tradition' out of concern at the indiscriminate 'vogue' for the Victorian age (1948/1972: 9). Leavis's narrative of the novel's development prioritises the inward over the outward, asserting categorically that the 'great English novelists are Jane Austen, George Eliot, Henry James, and Joseph Conrad' (9). In his discussion of why these figures achieved their pre-eminence, however, are several telling asides, not least of which is the footnote which condemns Sir Walter Scott's allegiance to 'the bad tradition of eighteenth-century romance' (14).

In the 1940s, then, the genre of historical fiction and the habit of retreating to the past were subject to a degree of critical opprobrium, but this did not impact upon their considerable popularity, and for this reason the literature of escape – both highbrow and popular – forms the subject of Chapter 4. Chapter 5 turns to the inescapable: the literature of grief and bereavement, tracing the struggle to memorialise the often nebulous and indeterminate losses of wartime. If articulating grief was to prove a problem in the postwar world, however, a counter-current of 'adjustment' proposed the answer. The final chapter of the postwar section explores the literature of reconstruction, an outward-looking discourse that finds words not to express but to cover over the psychological and social wounds of war. This impetus permeates postwar culture, but it is also integral to what might be seen as a signifying absence of this book: the Holocaust. The elision of the Holocaust and its implications from British literature of the postwar perhaps more than anything speaks to the impossibility of understanding or articulating the final solution – particularly at the immediate point of its full revelation. In her acutely observed postwar novel *A Summer to Decide* (1948) Pamela Hansford Johnson suggests that Britons were too busy worrying about ration books to fear the onset of World War Three, and much the same insularity is evident in responses to the Holocaust. People were shocked: people forgot; or, worse still, they refused to believe (Stafford 2007: 157). Yet Bryan Cheyette cautions against reading backwards from the Holocaust in an attempt to understand the constructions of anti-Semitism and 'the Jew' circulating in pre-war and wartime Britain (1993: xi, 5). His analysis instead focuses on what Artur Sandauer terms 'allosemitism' (8): the perception of the Jew as inevitably, foundationally, other. This is not to fix the Jew into a single mythic identity, but rather to recognise instability at the heart of representation, a paradox of 'liberal inclusiveness' that can allow the Jew in British national discourse to be constructed as both 'the embodiment of a transformable cultural heroism and, at the same time, as an unchanging racial "other"' (1993: 5–6).

The pervasiveness of allosemitism and its impact on Jewish lives is powerfully conveyed in Betty Miller's *Farewell Leicester Square*, a novel about the failure of assimilation whose publication history acts as a disturbing endorsement of the narrative's central thesis. Written in 1935 and dispatched to her usual publisher, the Jewish firm of Gollancz, the novel was rejected and remained unpublished until Robert Hale issued it in 1941, when events in Europe presumably made the novel's hard-hitting account of the corrosive psychology of otherness seem, if not welcome, at least topical. The book follows the career of Alex Berman from his teenage expulsion from the family home to his eventual return some 17 years later. In between he becomes a successful film director and makes a 'mixed marriage' to the daughter of the film magnate who gave him his first break in the industry. Yet this is no rags to riches story: although the film world makes him welcome and rewards his talent, Alex remains painfully self-conscious of the Jewishness that ensures he cannot, with any certainty, be said to belong to the country of his birth. While Alex, relaxing with his friend Lew, is able to ridicule the hyperbolic excesses of European anti-Jewish rhetoric (1941/2000: 179–80), he despairs of combating the insidious force of British 'toleration', a form of perpetual probation disguised as acceptance:

Some of my best friends are Jews. . . . They always said that. And one was supposed to be humbly grateful, quite bowled over, in fact, by the astonishing thing. *Jews*, just fancy! Some of my best friends are chimney sweeps, performing seals. Oh, Lord. Their tolerance. Their damned shallow self-satisfied *tolerance*! (Miller 1941/2000: 108)

The Holocaust had little or no impact on Jewish 'probationary' status, as Tony Kushner has demonstrated in his account of the unwelcome implications of Jewish suffering for the construction of a narrative of heroic British exceptionalism (1998: 229). The importance of the Second World War and its myths to postwar constructions of British national identity ensured that 'until at least the 1970s, what we now call the Holocaust made very little impact on British society and culture' (228). This point is made painfully evident by the disappearance from cultural memory of the riots of 1947. These manifestations of anti-Semitism (at their worst in Manchester, Liverpool and Glasgow) erupted in response to news reports of the retaliatory murder, in Palestine, of two British sergeants by the Zionist *Irgun*. The riots were, though, more complex than this obvious trigger point suggests. Inextricably linked to the economic pressures of austerity and unemployment, they represent a fresh instance of the familiar stereotyping of Jews as profiteers: a prejudice that had survived unscathed from the interwar period (McKibbin, 1998: 55–6; Kushner, 1996: 150).

'Peace'

'Peace' is the shortest section, and placed in inverted commas on account of its provisional status. The concept, though much anticipated, never really materialised, either literally or metaphorically. What peace was possible after the invention of a weapon that could annihilate a city not just for now but for generations to come? The atomic bomb dropped on Hiroshima on 6 August 1945 met with an ambivalent response. Mass Observation's pamphlet *Peace and the Public* (1947) was the result of a survey undertaken for 'The New Commonwealth', a society that lobbied for the creation of an 'International Police Force' that could dispense justice equitably across the world. The findings of the study suggested that few believed the bomb would facilitate such a dream, indeed for many it seemed as likely to presage the end of the world as the end of war (1947: 8). The survey reports stories of London children chalking up the slogan 'Shoot All Scientists' and tells of a woman who 'retired to bed for a fortnight feeling that nothing was worth while any more' (8). But beyond these extreme reactions there emerges a creeping depression and a pervasive current of pessimism. This loss of hope is not simply attributable to the destructive capacity of the atomic age, but to an unexpected nostalgia for the 'purposefulness' of conventional war. 'Worst of all' suggests a mother interviewed for the study, 'the friendly spirit of common burdens and real goodwill has vanished in a flash. We are now neck and neck again after money, job, power, favour . . . Peace means to me the return of old evils' (10).

If peace of mind was beyond the reach of the 1940s, so too was the more literal concept of peace as an absence of armed conflict. From terrorist attacks in Palestine, to the bloody partition of India, to the outbreak, in June 1950, of the Korean War, international politics gave little impression of a brave new world. Peace was also absent from the home front, where establishment resistance to reform – the BMA, for example, fiercely resisted the implementation of the National Health Service – combined with frustration at the slow pace of reconstruction and a significant wage freeze, to generate both middle-class and working-class discontent (Sissons and French 1963/1986; Morgan 1990: 37–9, 97–9). Meanwhile, the foundations of a new ideological conflict were laid with the arrival in June 1948 of the *Empire Windrush*, carrying some 492 Jamaicans eager to exploit the opportunities offered by their country of citizenship. What they, and the thousands who followed them, discovered was the paradoxical coexistence of competing communities of Britishness: in short, their arrival crystallised the Orwellian realisation that, as far as British nationality was concerned, some citizens were more equal than others. Kathleen Paul attributes the concretisation of a racialised understanding of British identity to the complex circumstances facing the postwar Attlee government, which sought to balance the demands of domestic reconstruction with the resources required to assert Britain's ongoing significance as an international power. Such an assertion was dependent on the vitality of the Commonwealth, and as a result, Paul argues, the 1948 British Nationality Act, which granted citizenship to all members of the British Empire, was not designed to attract colonial immigration, no matter how much Britain needed the manpower. Rather, the Act aimed:

> to maintain Britain's unique position as a metropolitan motherland and to demonstrate to the world that the United Kingdom was still the center of a great commonwealth of nations, even as certain parts of the commonwealth began to assert their independence. (Paul 1997: xii–xiii)

The *Windrush*, then, was the unexpected outcome of a political gesture, and was immediately configured as a problem. The passengers were British citizens who had been 'encouraged to think of Britain as home' (114); the Colonial Office and Ministry of Labour, by contrast, immediately categorised them as 'other', on the basis of their skin colour and their presumed unsuitability for the work available in Britain (116–24). The result was a situation in which Britain actively encouraged the recruitment of Irish workers and European refugees – in spite of their alien status – while withdrawing any official assistance from West Indian migrants arriving after December 1948.[4] The paradox of immigration was further compounded by the encouragement of emigration. 'British stock' was needed in the dominions, and this drain was to be counterbalanced, according to the recommendations of the Royal Commission on Population, by an energetic policy of pro-natalism.

While these political developments ensured that by the end of the decade 'Britishness' was a concept under stress, it would be a mistake to imagine that it was necessarily more coherent during the war years. As Sonya Rose has demonstrated, Britain 'both historically and contemporaneously was less a nation and more an empire' (2003: 238), and the uneasy relationship between hegemonic English authority and the 'regional' nations of Scotland, Wales and Northern Ireland was keenly felt during the conflict – not least as a result of the 'frequent verbal slippages between England and Britain made by the BBC and Government representatives' (2003: 218). Yet Rose suggests that the failure to articulate a coherent national identity does not mean that the British were not unified: 'They understood themselves as being members of the nation, even if they could not agree on how the nation was constituted . . . Being British and living in the United Kingdom, regardless of what Britishness meant, was enough' (2003: 290). This statement of the provisional nature of national identity and, paradoxically, of its remarkable cohesive power, also suggests a fluidity in national belonging precipitated by the unpredictable allegiances and loyalties of war. Britain in the 1940s was home to writers and broadcasters from across the globe, their presence on the island a statement of at least a provisional investment in the nation. The nation paid host to Americans, such as the poet H. D. and the journalists Quentin Reynolds and Edward Murrow; West Indians, including the cricketer Leary Constantine and the broadcaster Una Marson; Indians, including the novelist and critic Mulk Raj Anand; New Zealanders, in particular the writer and historian Dan Davin, and – from Ceylon – the entrepreneurial M. J. Tambimuttu, stalwart of Fitzrovia and editor of *Poetry London*. In the light of such (inter) national flux, Rose's definition of the limit point of belonging, 'living in the United Kingdom', has also been this book's, and for this reason the Hungarian Arthur Koestler plays a larger role than the British W. H. Auden. The fact of war, its psychology and the limits it placed on movement inevitably made Britain more insular in the period 1939–45: it also, paradoxically, made the nation more diverse.

Perhaps unsurprisingly, then, the final chapter of the book is entitled 'Atomising', a concept suggesting the fragmentation of the discourses and structures that had, however contingently, held sway during the war and postwar years. But 'Peace' did find some more optimistic symbols as Britain inched slowly towards the so-called 'age of affluence' that would follow the age of austerity. Before the Festival of Britain in 1951 came the London Olympics of 1948, an improbable spectacle the government agreed to support in the hope of generating hard currency for a bankrupt nation (Hampton 2008: 25). The Fourteenth Olympiad, the last to feature a poetry competition, took place in a deeply troubled international context: the aftermath of Indian partition, the heightening of Cold War tension encapsulated in the blockade of Berlin, the intro-duction of apartheid in South Africa. Yet in spite of an initial public lack of enthusiasm, the enormous transport difficulties facing compet-ing nations, and the lousy rations available for British sportsmen and women, the event – cobbled together in a wartime spirit of make-do and mend – was a considerable popular success. This appeal can perhaps be attributed to the opportunity the Games provided to recapture that 'friendly spirit' and common purpose mourned by the contributors to *Peace and the Public*; or perhaps, like the Gainsborough melodramas, it provided welcome distraction from the drab reality of austerity Britain. That the opening ceremony of the 2012 London Olympics should have chosen to highlight the achievement of the National Health Service, however, speaks to a significant legacy (Hennessey 1992: 174–5). The election victory that brought Clement Attlee to power in July 1945 set in process a radical reconstruction of national infrastructure: that a substantial portion of the British electorate wanted this reconstruction, and were prepared to endure a brutal austerity programme to get it, is illustrated by Labour's 46 per cent share of the vote in the election of February 1950 (Morgan 1990: 84). In spite of redrawn constituency boundaries and vocal middle-class dissent, the Attlee government sur-vived. What also survived, though, were the intransigent boundaries of a class society. Morgan notes that while the nation was a 'uniformly richer community' (79), a pattern of 'social segregation' (82) reasserted itself. Ross McKibbin, meanwhile, observes that 'on the whole, those who had authority in 1918 still had it, more or less, in 1951' (1998: v). But nonetheless, the Britain that emerged from the 1940s was differ-ent from the nation of the 1930s. The world beyond Britain had been similarly transformed. It is not that 1945 serves as a tidy dividing line in the twentieth century, but rather that the 1940s as a whole changed the limits of imaginative possibility. The decade opened with a heightened awareness of self and society, with Britain and everything it stood for facing an unparalleled threat. It ended in exhaustion, facing the possibility that winning the war had been achieved at the cost not only of imperial power and international authority, but also of any coherent sense of a national identity.[5] Celia, the melancholic protagonist of Stevie Smith's *The Holiday*, succinctly summarises this profound uncertainty in her lament: 'It is the war, I say, and the war won, and the peace so far away' (1949/1979: 155).

Navigating the 1940s II: Literature in Transition

The attempt to impose some sort of critical order on the culture of the 1940s was first undertaken in the decade itself. Between 1946 and 1947 the British Council published a series of pamphlets, *The Arts in Britain*, surveying national culture under such headings as *Drama since 1939*, *Films since 1939* and *The Novel since 1939*. The series ran to eleven volumes, including Ian Finlay's *Scottish Art* and Wyn Griffith's *The Voice of Wales*, but these more generalised offerings were not amongst the eight chosen to form the attractive two-volume compendium, *Since 1939* (1949). These are elegant publications, printed on quality paper with photographic plates, and they represent an effort to categorise the inchoate artistic developments of the war years. The writing is unashamedly subjective, and the coverage far from comprehensive, but they nonetheless provide valuable insight into critical attitudes of the time. The literary contributors – Robert Speaight on drama, Henry Reed on the novel, Stephen Spender on poetry – take very different approaches to the task, but one curious commonality emerges. In a consensus that exposes the difference between understanding the 1940s in the 1940s and the perspectives that have emerged in the years since, all are agreed that whatever is of value in the poetry, drama and fiction of the war years could have little if nothing to do with the war (1949: 29, 89). 'What is furthest from my intention', writes Spender, 'is to produce the impression that the poetry written in war-time is different, as poetry, from the poetry written at any other time' (109); yet, as the following surveys of literary production in the decade suggest, such a pure distillation of art from politics would be very hard to sustain.

Drama

That war would be 'bad' for the theatre – an art form that depends upon large numbers of people gathering nightly in buildings all too vulnerable to enemy attack – might seem obvious but, in fact, the 1940s were renaissance years for the *infrastructure* of British theatre. The departure of evacuated companies to the provinces, the emergence of professional touring companies such as the Pilgrim Players, the funding and organisation provided by government initiatives through CEMA (the Council for the Encouragement of Music and the Arts; from 1946, the Arts Council), ABCA (the Army Bureau of Current Affairs) and ENSA (the Entertainments National Service Association); all of these factors contributed to an energetic wartime performance culture. The 1940s also saw the concretisation of the Old Vic's status as a National Theatre in all but name and, under the creative control of John Burrell, Tyrone Guthrie, Laurence Olivier and Ralph Richardson, the company produced a repertory season that critic Peter Noble was moved to describe as 'the most important single event in the wartime theatrical scene' (1946: 133). The desire for some form of 'national' theatre was not confined to London. Similar developments were afoot in Scotland, where James Bridie (Osborne Henry Mavor), a popular dramatist who enjoyed interwar success on the London stage and with the Scottish National Players, became the first chair of the Scottish committee of CEMA. Although Bridie has 'fallen out of the story' of twentieth-century drama, he remained an important player throughout the 1940s, most significantly contributing to the foundation, in 1943, of Glasgow Citizens Theatre (Carruthers, in Bridie 2007: ix). At the same time, the Glasgow Unity Theatre was flourishing. Founded in 1940 on the principles of the wider Unity Theatre movement (London Unity Theatre was founded in 1937), Unity brought together a wide range of left-wing workers' theatre groups to perform both conventional plays and experimental political theatre. The company invested in Scottish writing, and in 1946 had a huge success with Robert McLeish's *The Gorbals Story*, which earned £100,000 in three years, toured extensively across Scotland and enjoyed a West End run in 1948 (Stevenson, in Findlay 2008: xv–xvi).

The Gorbals Story is an understated 'slice of life', ahead of its time in its capacity to create a poetry of the mundane. Its diverse cast of characters include the gentle Highlander, Hector; the pragmatic survivor, Peggie; an Indian pedlar; an Irish family, and the Mutries, a couple whose quick-fire dialogues turn them into a pair of 'cross-talk' comedians. These characters eat, drink, plan and find emotional sustenance in the face of unremitting poverty and a world where there is, quite literally, no room at the inn: over the course of the play two desperate couples come to the tenement seeking a room. It falls to Peggie to stress a resentment felt far beyond Glasgow in the postwar housing shortage:

PEGGIE: . . . men just talk about logic. They condemn honest folk tae live three or four in a room and they gie a burglar a room tae himself. Aye, ye can laugh. But you mark my words, Hector. Women chained themsels onto lamp-posts tae get the vote. One o' these days a woman will chain herself onto an empty house.

HECTOR (*Smiling*) And where would they find that?

(McLeish, in Findlay 2008: 5)

The crowded tenement is a space of desire and of violence: men fight and get drunk and, off-stage, a mother dies in childbirth. Yet there is no melodrama; the confrontations subside, two couples are united and the climax comes not in tragedy but in the irony of a winning, but unposted, football coupon. This is a long way from the polished dialectical theatre of Bridie, whose plays look back to Shaw rather than forward to the 1950s, but although Glasgow Unity and Glasgow Citizens were divided by politics and aesthetics, both were fundamental to the radical transformation of Scottish theatre. It seems therefore appropriate that both were present at the birth of an event whose impact cannot be in doubt: the Edinburgh Festival. Bridie was involved in the establishment of the International Festival, working with Tyrone Guthrie and Robert Kemp to produce a 'landmark' production of Sir David Lyndsay's *Ane Pleasant Satire of the Thrie Estaitis* (Carruthers 2007: x). Unity, by contrast, can arguably be seen to have founded the Edinburgh Festival Fringe, performing unofficially in the Pleasance, 'despite the hostility of the Arts Council and the Edinburgh Festival Society' (Stevenson 2008: xviii).

Much then was at stake on the stage in these years, but it is harder to define a legacy of new writing. Robert Speaight, the man charged with summarising the decade for the British Council, brutally concludes that 'no new figures of outstanding importance emerged among the war-time playwrights' (1949: 29), and turns his attention instead to the established figures of the interwar years: T. S. Eliot, J. B. Priestley, James Bridie, and Sean O'Casey, somewhat uncomfortably colonised on the grounds that 'our native theatre has continually been fertilised by Irishmen' (33). Eliot, to Speaight's mind, is by far the most important of these figures, and a reader could justifiably leave his essay under the impression that the chief legacy of the decade was the ongoing revival of verse drama. Poetic drama had been revitalised in the 1930s through the efforts of Eliot, W. H. Auden and Christopher Isherwood, and there is no doubt that the success of Eliot's *Murder in the Cathedral* continued to resonate throughout the 1940s. The play toured Britain during the war, under the direction of Martin Browne, impresario of the high-brow Mercury Theatre, and its influence was felt not only in the revival of poetic drama, but also in the confident resurgence of religious subject matter. The end of the war saw the production of Norman Nicholson's *The Old Man of the Mountains* (1946), Anne Ridler's *The Shadow Factory* (1946) and Ronald Duncan's *This Way to the Tomb* (1946). Nicholson's drama sets the story of Elijah in modern Cumbria, Ridler's presents a conversion narrative in a factory, and Duncan retells the legend of St Anthony through a Jonsonian masque and anti-masque structure, a formula that proved surprisingly popular with West End audiences. All three writers attempt to find a verse form that could express spiritual concerns on the contemporary stage, and all are profoundly anti-modern in outlook (Tolley 1985: 191). This postwar religious revival on stage, though, has a fascinating 'modern' counterpoint from earlier in the decade: the controversy surrounding Dorothy L. Sayers' radio drama *The Man Born to Be King*. Commissioned in 1940 by the BBC's Director of Religious Broadcasting, J. W. Welch, this twelve-play cycle on the life of Christ was first broadcast between December 1941 and October 1942. What made the drama so controversial was Sayers's decision to write in demotic prose. Her aim in so doing was to reassert the contemporary relevance of the story: 'God was executed by people painfully like us, in a society very similar to our own . . . He was executed by a corrupt church, a timid politician, and a fickle proletariat led by professional agitators' (Sayers 1943: 23). In her opinion, 'the swiftest way to produce the desirable sense of shock, is the use in drama of modern speech and a determined historical realism about the characters' (23). When this decision was reported, Sayers and the BBC were accused of everything from vulgarity to blasphemy: for some, the 'impersonation' of Jesus was an unacceptable violation of Christian principle. As a result of the outcry, questions were asked in the House of Commons, and Church leaders were assembled to decide the fate of the plays. Recognising the value of high-profile popular broadcasting, they were unanimous in their support for the project, which went ahead without further complication, and was a considerable popular success. No such qualms, it should be noted, surrounded the representation of the devil. He turned up, in the guise of a Highland minister, in James Bridie's *Mr Bolfry*, one of the London successes of 1943.

A counterblast to the highmindedness of *Since 1939* is provided by Peter Noble's usefully encyclopaedic *British Theatre* (1946), not least because, unlike Speaight, Noble is willing to engage with the work of the two most successful playwrights of the decade, Noël Coward and Terence Rattigan. Noble is no fan of Coward, who he feels 'stands for all the things which the war has brought to an end', but acknowledges his 'impeccable' skills and hopes he will 'adjust himself' to the postwar world (1946: 174). Rattigan's enormous wartime success, *While the Sun Shines*, meanwhile, is acknowledged as 'the best – or the worst – example of the successful West End commercial play' (73). Noble provides an invaluable survey of what was popular in the war years, detailing the appeal of Sheridan and Congreve revivals and the enormous appetite for Shakespeare manifest in the repertory seasons of Donald Wolfit, the Old Vic and the John Gielgud company. Noble also reminds us of the popularity of Welsh writer, actor and producer Emlyn Williams, whose London successes included *Druid's Rest* (1943) and *The Winds of Heaven* (1945), and of the presence of women amongst a predominantly male playwriting community. Mary Hayley Bell enjoyed success with *Men in Shadow* (1942) and *Duet for Two Hands* (1945), while Daphne du Maurier divided critical opinion with *The Years Between*, first performed in Manchester in 1944. Unlike the critics, the public loved du Maurier's play – a study of war's impact on gender roles and relations – which went on to enjoy a run of 617 West End performances in 1945. In the irreconcilable needs of the newly public woman and her returning soldier husband, the play articulated 'the difficulties and personal tragedies many Britons faced, which no propagandist fanfare could blast away' (Habermann 2010: 199).

Women, including Hermione Gingold and Diana Morgan, also enjoyed success as writers and performers in a very different theatrical mode, the revue, producing a variety of witty, gender-bending and irreverent sketches (Morgan 1994). Revue culture made West-End stars out of Gingold and the actor Sid Field, but somewhat unexpectedly, it was the London Unity Theatre that produced the first topical political revue of the conflict, writing and producing *Sandbag Follies* 'within forty-eight hours of the commencement of hostilities' (Noble 1946: 13). London Unity went on to success with Ted Willis's slum-boy redemption narrative, *Buster* (1943), and its story of the music halls, *Winkles and Champagne* (1944), but it was not the only 'people's theatre' to do well on the London stage. Experimental dramas, such as J. B. Priestley's *They Came to A City* (1943), were underwritten by CEMA, while his *Desert Highway* (1944) was produced by the ABCA Play Unit. Critics at the time observed the growth of a 'Penguin-educated' audience that was 'prepared to work for its enjoyment' (Hewison 1977/1988: 183), and this appetite for engagement contributed to the success of one of the most innovative productions of the period: *Exercise Bowler* (1946), written by William Templeton and produced by Alec Clunes for the radical Arts Theatre Group. The play begins as a conventional representation of the pieties of war, but before it can progress beyond the opening clichés, the cast are interrupted by three uniformed men who invade the stage and insist on deconstructing the script. These idealistic men are then obliged to put their beliefs to the test in the task of reconstruction, and inevitably fall prey to complacency. It is, in Speaight's words, 'not a very subtle play, but it is, from start to finish, theatrically alive' (1949: 40).

As the decade progressed towards its close, there were few theatrical surprises. Christopher Fry and J. B. Priestley enjoyed success with *The Lady's Not for Burning* and *An Inspector Calls*, as did the indefatigable Bridie, whose *Daphne Laureola* (1949), an unexpected fable about the frustrations of female emancipation, provided a meaty role for Dame Edith Evans. Lesley Storm's critically admired *Black Chiffon* (1949), meanwhile, provided an equally satisfying role for Flora Robson, as the mother whose inability to cope with her son's forthcoming marriage manifests itself in shoplifting (see Morgan (ed.) 1994). Glasgow Unity also enjoyed further success with plays such as Ena Lamont Stewart's unremittingly bleak *Men Should Weep* (1947), George Munro's *Gold in His Boots* (1947) and Benedick Scott's *The Lambs of God* (1948). But while new names flourished in Scotland, the London stage belonged predominantly to familiar figures, leaving Noble and Speaight in unexpected agreement: while English theatre of the 1940s is possessed of 'some of the greatest actors and finest producers in the world today' it is singularly devoid of fresh dramatic writing (Noble 1946: 191). It is hard to disagree: the hit of 1941 was *Blithe Spirit*, a drawing room comedy about adultery, spiritualism and death by Noël Coward. The cause célèbre of 1949, where it premiered at the Edinburgh Festival, was *The Cocktail Party*, a verse drama about adultery, spirituality and martyrdom by T. S. Eliot. Brittle people, stylised dialogue, middle-class mores, and no sign as yet of the angry young man.

Fiction

In spite of the war's disruptive influence, the decade produced some rich and rewarding fiction. As with drama, continuity of personnel can be observed, with significant work emerging from established authors such as Elizabeth Bowen, Graham Greene and Evelyn Waugh. But this is not to suggest that the 1940s can seamlessly be assimilated into accounts of career-long development. Writers changed direction in the decade, diverted by events and by the difficulty of sustained critical concentration in wartime. John Heyward summarises the impact of logistical challenges from paper shortages to community obligations:

Certainly those who succeeded somehow in putting pen to paper could not reasonably be expected to have either the time or the resources to make any extended contribution to prose literature. Their modest and occasional efforts tended to take the form of lyrics, short stories, and incidental reporting of current events, and were published in magazines and anthologies, notably in *Horizon*, *Penguin New Writing*, and *Poetry (London)*. (1949: 180)

The strongest trend in the novel of the 1940s, then, was its abbreviation, and it is the short story that demands to be recognised as the characteristic 'form' of the decade. The story was ideal for wartime production and consumption, its success facilitated by the magazine culture that developed to sate a powerful demand for writing new and old. Journals such as *Penguin New Writing* and *Lilliput* combined poetry, prose, non-fiction and, in *Lilliput*'s case, decorative young women, in user-friendly formats easily tucked into pockets or bags. That the story was a critically regarded as well as a pragmatic form is evident from Henry Reed's contribution to *Since 1939*, which identifies Elizabeth Bowen's *The Demon Lover* (1945) as the exemplary fiction of wartime England: 'there is no story in the book which does not convey that feeling of the deterioration of the spirit which, when the tumult, and the shouting, and the self-deception subside, is seen to be war's residue' (1949: 79).

Bowen's wartime writing is integral to an understanding of the creative climate of the 1940s. In the Preface to *The Demon Lover* she describes her stories as fragments of 'the particular' through which 'the high-voltage current of the general' must pass (1950: 52), and this image encapsulates the potential of the form to evoke the uncanny strangeness of local life in an unprecedented global conflict. Bowen's stories can be set alongside those of Rosamund Lehmann and William Sansom, both of whose work is permeated with an impressionistic modernist sensibility; Alun Lewis, whose stories combine lyrical prose with acute observation of a frequently tawdry world; Julian Maclaren-Ross, whose work captures the cynicism and absurdity of service life; Mollie Panter-Downes, creator of psychologically astute and witty stories of domestic life, and Elizabeth Berridge, whose deceptively simple narratives detail the painful, often inarticulable, cost of survival. 'Taken singly', writes Bowen, stories 'are disjected snapshots – snapshots taken from close up' (52), but together they create a powerful sense of the psychological climate of war. They also, of course, amuse and entertain, and this was clearly the remit of one of the first collections of short fiction to emerge at the outbreak of war, Jan Struther's *Mrs Miniver* (1939). These vignettes from the life of a middle-class mother in many ways set the tone for the public discourse of the conflict. Mrs Miniver, who first appeared in 1936 as a column in *The Times*, recounts her adventures, from hosting dinner parties to fitting gas masks on her children, with an unflappable good humour that is both reassuring and instructional, not least in its repeated emphasis on the distinction between the Nazi government and the German People (1939/1989: 61, 115, 122). This fundamental imperturbability would be a keynote for documentary writing, as would the emphasis on 'us' rather than 'them'. As Petra Rau has noted, 'in the novels of the Second World War the Germans are conspicuous by their absence. They seem a mere abstraction, sometimes realized as a *projection* of a home-grown malaise' (2009: 186).

Yet few writers were able to share Mrs Miniver's equanimity, and much fiction of the 1940s conveys, directly or indirectly, the dislocating impact of war on self and society. Fragile, fragmented selves abound in novels as diverse as Graham Greene's *The Ministry of Fear* (1943), whose protagonist is briefly rendered happy by a memory loss that annihilates his adult life; Patrick Hamilton's *Hangover Square* (1941), whose pitiful schizophrenic hero is symbolically torn between responsible citizenship and pathological, murderous desire, and Henry Green's *Caught* (1943), peopled by characters fundamentally damaged by class and sexual trauma. Hamilton's *The Slaves of Solitude* (1947), by contrast, depicts a claustrophobic domestic fascism parasitically drawing strength from denuded boarding-house lives. Henry Reed, writing of the great quantity of fiction set in or emerging from the war, concludes that 'war is a quotidian nightmare' (Speaight et al., 1949: 89), a phrase which, while not intended as praise, nonetheless encapsulates the broader approach taken by fiction to the almost unrepresentable global catastrophe of war. It also speaks to the significant redefinition of 'war-writing' discussed earlier in this Introduction, and to the difficulty of distinguishing fictions *about* war from fictions *of* war such as Virginia Woolf's powerfully allusive *Between the Acts* (1941). In the case of Woolf's final novel, the violence of war permeates the text at the level of imagery and through the parodic reinscription of history, raising fundamental questions about how conflict might be imagined. Violence, then, presents itself in unexpected forms – from the psychological wounds of Balchin's *The Small Back Room* (1943) to the physical trauma of F. L. Green's Belfast-set *Odd Man Out* (1945) – but it remains a keynote of the decade. Indeed, writing of Graham Greene and Ivy Compton-Burnett, Reed observes a 'return to the sense of evil' (73), implicitly suggesting that the war would prompt an ethical as well as an aesthetic transformation in British prose.

Yet in contradistinction to these adult concerns, Reed argues that perhaps the most potent thematic preoccupation of the war years was the trope of childhood. Novelists retreated *en masse*, either to the remembered childhoods of the Edwardian or interwar period, or to the point of view of a child, distancing themselves from current conflicts, or allegorising modernity through semi-comprehending 'innocence'. In *The Shrimp and the Anemone* (1944) L. P. Hartley does both of these things; the Edwardian era he evokes is shadowed by death. Nancy Mitford's depiction of the interwar period initially seems a lighter treatment of childhood, a female *bildungsroman* with an impeccable comic touch, but the deadly force of a world at war cannot, ultimately, be evaded. There is a similar sense of the half-glimpsed, semi-understood threat of the adult world in the limited point of view of Rosamund Lehmann's *The Ballad and the Source* (1944), in which a child attempts to assemble the 'truth' of a woman's life from the competing narratives that mythologise her. The impact of war on children was also addressed directly, providing fodder for fiction across the decade from Joyce Cary's *Charley is My Darling* (1940) to Rose Macaulay's *The World My Wilderness* (1950). Amongst the most impressive of these encounters is Noel Streatfeild's *Saplings* (1945), a painful demonstration of the psychological damage caused to children not so much by the violence of the outside world, as by the insecurity that comes from a war-induced collapse of family structures.

A range of thematic preoccupations can be identified to supplement Reed's categories; in the case of this book, a selection might be seen to map onto the chapter headings. In the 1940s, fiction variously documented, desired, killed, escaped, grieved, adjusted and finally went its separate ways in a complete breakdown of any (illusory) wartime consensus. In literature as in public life, the 1940s brought ways of reading into unexpected new conjunctions, and left a legacy of fiction that cannot be squeezed into the ill-fitting categories of modernism, the middlebrow and the popular. Nonetheless, it is important to acknowledge the breadth of fiction produced across genres and brows within the decade, and what follows might be seen as an indicative survey. Not all will be the subject of detailed analysis within this book, in some cases because they have already been treated in detail elsewhere, in other cases because of the pressure of space. I suggested earlier that this is but one possible history of the decade: here, in embryo, are many, many more.

The decade saw fiction, variously best-selling or critically acclaimed, by Mulk Raj Anand, Alexander Baron, Norman Collins, Monica Dickens, Neil Gunn, Patrick Hamilton, Malcolm Lowry, Somerset Maugham, Compton Mackenzie, Stevie Smith, Rex Warner and Dennis Wheatley. It gave rise to works of moral and religious complexity from Greene's *The Power and the Glory* (1940) to Waugh's *Brideshead Revisited*

(1945), and to baroque imaginings such as Mervyn Peake's *Titus Groan* (1946). It witnessed the last novel of Virginia Woolf, the first of Elizabeth Taylor, and the first and last of Philip Larkin, who published *Jill* in 1946 and *A Girl in Winter* in 1947. Henry Green was prolific, producing four novels in less than ten years; J. B. Priestley even more so, publishing at least five novels alongside his plays, *Postscripts* and auto-biography.[6] Naomi Mitchison, by contrast, took ten years to produce just one, her monumental historical saga, *The Bull Calves* (1947). Olaf Stapledon and C. S. Lewis wrote science fiction, as did George Orwell, whose *Nineteen Eighty-Four* is arguably the best-remembered prose work of the decade. Crime remained the province of Agatha Christie and a school of clue-puzzle detective writers: Margery Allingham, Nicolas Blake (who, as Cecil Day-Lewis also published fiction for children), Christianna Brand, John Creasey, Edmund Crispin, Cyril Hare, Michael Innes, Gladys Mitchell and Josephine Tey. The resolvable micro-climate of crime fiction would provide a welcome relief from the much larger, irresolvable crime of war, and fantasies of individual agency were also produced by thriller writers such as Eric Ambler, Peter Cheyney, Helen McInnes and Nevil Shute. Romance and historical adventures, while subject to critical condemnation, remained enormously popular in the hands of seasoned practitioners such as Georgette Heyer and Margaret Irwin, while family sagas emerged from Naomi Jacob, C. P. Snow and Howard Spring. The family took more disturbing form in the works of Ivy Compton-Burnett who published her regulation three volumes for the decade. Children, the subject of so much adult fiction in the period, were catered for by, amongst others, Elinor M. Brent-Dyer, Richmal Crompton, W. E. Johns and Enid Blyton, who initiated several of her most successful book series in the decade: *The Twins at St Clare's* (1941), *Five on a Treasure Island* (1942) and *The Island of Adventure* (1944). While some fiction for younger children, such as Gwynneth Rae's *Mary Plain in Wartime* (1942), directly addresses the events of war – in this case through the energetic, plucky and usually catastrophic assistance of a 'first-class' talking bear – Blyton's novels keep the conflict at a distance. War is not a major motivator of plot (spies being necessary adjuncts to adventure and not confined to times of conflict), it is not a source of anxiety; but it nonetheless permeates the narrative, reshap-ing the imaginative possibilities of the text. *The Island of Adventure*, for example, features working mothers, scarcely habitable housing, the threat of violence and the adventure of relocation. The most famous evacuation adventure of the period, however, would set the trend for a new decade: C. S. Lewis's *The Lion, the Witch and the Wardrobe*, published in 1950.[7]

Poetry

Where perhaps most changed was the world of poetry. This was a decade in which both the form and purpose of poetry became a battlefield, but as suggested earlier, criticism has not been particularly kind to the writers who fought in this conceptual conflict. Bernard Bergonzi nails his colours to the mast: 'Many poems were written during the war, but most of them were quickly forgotten. The outstanding exception is T. S. Eliot's *Four Quartets*, the major poetic work of the early 1940s' (1993: 54). While *Four Quartets* undoubtedly stands out as a lasting poetic achievement of the war years, Bergonzi's generalisation disguises an altogether more complicated poetic landscape. As A. T. Tolley has observed, the tendency to dismiss the poetry of the 1940s is largely the result of the 'derision' heaped upon the period by the Movement poets and critics of the 1950s (1985: preface). It also emerges from what Jonathan Bolton has described as the 'dialectical pattern of action and reaction with which literary history is often reconstructed' (1997: 3). Consequently, the 1940s are seen as a decade of reaction against the 1930s, in which the public political voices of the Auden generation were supplanted by an inward-looking neo-romanticism that sought 'to shut out the real war' (Piette 1995: 201). This distinction is not without substance, but it should not obscure a more complex network of affiliation and influence. Continuity rather than change was evident in the still powerful presence of the 'survivors' of the thirties – John Lehmann's *Penguin New Writing* and Cyril Connolly's *Horizon* ensured steady exposure for such stalwarts as Cecil Day-Lewis and Louis MacNeice (Hewison 1977/1988: 125) – while, as many critics have observed, the 'new' romantics were not altogether new. Their origins can be traced back to surrealism and the work of writers such as George Barker, David Gascoyne, D. H. Lawrence and Dylan Thomas in the 1930s, but the movement nonetheless found its most intense articulation in the wartime anthologies of the New Apocalypse. The second of these anthologies, *The White Horseman* (1941), edited like *The New Apocalypse* (1939) by J. F. Hendry and Henry Treece, included an introductory essay by G. S. Fraser that offers one of the more lucid accounts of the project. Apocalyptic poets, argues Fraser, are creators of myths, opposed to the 'false objectivism' and 'rationalizations' of the times (1941: 6). They are sceptical concerning political thought and the systematic manipulations of the 'state machine'; in politics they venerate the human, and in poetry, they work through a concept of the 'image' that Fraser compares to cinematic montage (10). The Apocalyptic poet, he concludes, is 'a sane man, who accepts dream and fantasy and obscure and terrible desires and energies, as part of his completion' (15). If war could not be stopped and political change effected, the least the poet could do was experience the horror to its full, a conclusion that leads John Goodby to argue that 'apocalyptic' is 'both a legitimate response and an accurate description of forties poetry and ... it is high time that the poetic canon was expanded to include the best of it' (2010: 860).

Beyond the 'old romantic-classical contest between artistic expression of self and artistic submission to collective values' (Esty 2004: 145) was the failure of poets to fit tidily into either of the dominant categories. Hewison attempts to catalogue the diverse poetic voices of the decade by distinguishing between the home-front factions, in his chapter punningly-titled 'Poetry (London)' after M. J. Tambimuttu's romantically-inclined journal of the same name, and the poetry of the services, gathered under the title of Keidrych Rhys's 1941 anthology, *Poems from the Forces*. He also suggests, in response to the ubiquitous search for 'war poets', that the boundary between 'war poetry' and 'poetry in wartime' is necessarily blurred by the Second World War (1977/1988: 133). This is not simply the result of the breakdown in the clear distinction between civilian and soldier, it is also a product of geography. As Stephen Spender notes, 'this war, with all its terrors, has been adventurous and expansive, more likely to produce agoraphobia than the claustrophobia of the war of 1914–1918' (Speaight et al. 1949: 121). Further complicating the conception of a homogenous 'war poetry' or a single narrative of literary 'action and reaction' is the presence in Egypt of a 'chance culture' that in its hybrid agglomeration of soldiers, civilians and exiles from across Britain and Europe created a 'near microcosm of the literary life in London' (Hewison 1977/1988: 138).

The familiarity – and otherness – of this microcosm is the subject of Jonathan Bolton's *Personal Landscapes: British Poets in Egypt during the Second World War* (1997), which complicates assumptions regarding the poetic fault-lines of the period and the national integrity of literary responses to war. Focusing on the magazine *Personal Landscape*, edited by Lawrence Durrell, Bernard Spencer and Robin Fedden, Bolton argues that 'there was in fact a significant development in British verse in the 1940s, but ... it had occurred far from Fitzrovia' (1997: xii). *Personal Landscape* published, amongst others, Keith Douglas, G. S. Fraser, Hamish Henderson, Olivia Manning and the influential Greek poet George Seferis, producing a 'lyric total' that welcomed diverse responses to the experience of exile and war (Bolton 1997: 14). In Olivia Manning's terms, these poets in exile became 'cosmopolitan' (*Horizon*, Vol. X no. 58, October, 1944: 271), and as such they resist categorisation within the dominant paradigm of public versus private.

Ideologically, the *Personal Landscape* poets had some sympathy with the Apocalyptic manifesto, but not to the exclusion of all else. Indeed, they remained alert to political developments, leading Bolton to suggest that their response 'was not one of reaction but of assimilation' (5); a 'middle ground' that was profoundly shaped by the 'spirit of place' (6). The triangulation of both personal and public through the palimpsestic contours of place would prove a resilient development in 1940s poetry. Albeit in very different contexts, amongst those new voices emerging in the latter half of the decade were John Betjeman, the chronicler of suburban England, and R. S. Thomas, witness to the bleak and brutal beauty of rural Welsh existence.

Other poets too resist easy categorisation. Edith Sitwell, for example, having been largely dormant in the 1930s, made a triumphant return to prominence. Responding to the Blitz in symbolic, incantatory verse, she captured the mood of the moment as far as the poetry-reading public was concerned:

> Still falls the Rain
> In the Field of Blood where the small hopes breed and the human brain
> Nurtures its greed, that worm with the brow of Cain.
>
> (Sitwell 1942: 1)

The imagery here is typical of Sitwell's wartime writing: blood, rain, sacrifice, and, later in the poem, 'the baited bear' and 'the hunted hare'. The poem ends on a note of Christian redemption, but the predominant tone of Sitwell's *Street Songs* (1942) was – like much apocalyptic verse – coloured by a visceral relationship to corporeality and death, negotiating repeatedly the relationship between corruption of the flesh and persistence of the spirit. Sitwell's poems and prose were popular and critical successes throughout the 1940s, as was her brother Osbert's monumental five-volume autobiography, to the extent that *Horizon* dedicated an issue to the family output in July 1947 (Glendinning 1981/1993). Her work, though, like that of the Apocalyptics, has for the most part been dismissed in the ensuing years. Bergonzi, for example, compares Sitwell with Dylan Thomas (whose career she supported enthusiastically), concluding that 'both went in for the high style, with rich images and biblical sonorities, and both were described as great poets. In neither case has time endorsed this judgement' (1993: 69). Time in turn has not endorsed this judgement, with Thomas in particular enjoying a critical renaissance; but Bergonzi's comments nonetheless usefully demonstrate the distinction between the 1940s' view of itself and the fluctuating opinions of posterity.

Stephen Spender, whose evolution in the decade saw him turn increas-

ingly to the criticism of poetry, attempted to chart a diplomatic course
through the minefield of influence and affiliation. In 'Poetry for Poetry's
Sake and Poetry Beyond Poetry' he attempts a technical solution,
drawing a distinction between the transparent and the opaque:

> Some younger critics call this kind of writing, in which language is used with
> the greatest precision in order to express a movement of thought . . . the 'new
> classicism'; and they call a more recent tendency in poetry, in which objects
> are created without a thoughtful meaning behind them, the 'new romanti-
> cism'. I think these terms are confusing, and it would be more valuable to
> draw a distinction between *transparent* poetry and *opaque* poetry. Eliot and
> Auden use language transparently; Dylan Thomas, Edith Sitwell, Vernon
> Watkins, use it opaquely.[8] (*Horizon*, XIII, No. 76, April 1946: 227)

In his contribution to *Since 1939*, by contrast, he argues for a unify-
ing concept of 'disintegration': the war years have seen the rejection
of 'movements' and the re-emergence of the individual, poets and
poetry should be taken on their merits (Speaight et al. 1949: 157). Not
everyone was able to produce such an equitable response to poetry's
retreat from the political – or to its opacity – as is demonstrated in the
decade's response to the work of W. H. Auden.

Auden left Britain for America in 1939 and stayed there for most of
the 1940s. Whatever the reasons behind his decision to turn a visit into
residency, and – in 1946 – citizenship, his departure was read as symbolic. Michael Roberts, reviewing *Another Time* (1940), the first of four
new volumes of verse produced by Auden in the decade, is scathing in
his response:

> This book gives the impression that Mr Auden used up all his emotional
> energy in treating the Spanish Civil War as a crusade, and cannot now bring
> himself to form anything but a cynical and pessimistic judgement on a world
> in which the cause of honesty and justice is tainted with dishonesty and injus-
> tice. (*Spectator*, 26 July 1940, quoted in Haffenden 1983: 302)

Not all critics reacted so vehemently to Auden's departure, and his critical reception in America was warm, with *For the Time Being* (1945) in
particular attracting praise for the poet's craftsmanship, and the 'beautiful flights' of imagination attendant on his reimagining of Shakespeare's
Tempest (Mark Schorer, in Haffenden 1983: 329). Yet projects such
as *For the Time Being* indicate that Auden, even in America, was not
immune to the changing 'atmosphere' of poetry; his writing became
increasingly symbolic, imbued with mythology and religion, and while
his imagery was far from apocalyptic, for many of his reviewers in
Britain it shared those writers' opacity. Certainly, 'transparent' was
not the first descriptive term that would have occurred to Desmond

McCarthy, who exploded with frustration in a *Sunday Times* review that despaired of explaining what, exactly, Auden was trying to say. Defeated, he concludes that 'the chariot of [Auden's] verse is again and again dashed to pieces by cutting too fine the corner of nonsense' (Haffenden 1983: 336).

Auden receives more positive treatment in *Since 1939* where Spender describes him as 'a great intellectual poet of our time' (130), before moving on to paint an impressively broad picture of the poetic landscape of the decade. Although detecting in poetry 'the haunting presence of a lament which is really for the lost and neglected freedom of emotion and imagination' (Speaight et al. 1949: 113), Spender argues that much has been achieved in English poetry of the 1940s (Spender, like his collaborators, uses 'English' to refer indiscriminately to writers from across Britain). Beyond the 'outstanding' legacy of *Four Quartets*, he finds much to admire in the work of 'elder generation' writers such as Edmund Blunden, Robert Graves and John Masefield, whose *Land Workers* (1942) is described as 'perhaps the crown of his achievement' (122). Spender dedicates sections to, amongst others, Edwin Muir, Louis MacNeice, William Empson and the 'word-intoxicated' school of Thomas, Barker and Gascoyne (144), before coming to the difficult matter of selecting those promising figures who have emerged since the war began. Roy Fuller, Henry Reed and Vernon Watkins are his first choices, with Watkins described as a poet capable of 'changing the world of experience into beauty and permanence' (150). In another indication of the difficulty of contemporary judgement, Keith Douglas – now perhaps the best-known poet to emerge from the war – is absent, but other poets receiving honourable mention include Laurie Lee, Alun Lewis, Sidney Keyes and F. T. Prince. This is, as with the theatre, a very male list. Edith Sitwell is the only woman to get a section to herself, but Spender also acknowledges the work of Kathleen Raine, Anne Ridler and E. J. Scovell. A more substantial effort to acknowledge the contribution of women was made by Catherine Reilly's anthology *Chaos of the Night* (1984), which includes work by writers such as Valentine Ackland, Wrenne Jarman, Patricia Ledward, Ruth Pitter and Sylvia Townsend Warner. The reputation of the Welsh-Argentinian writer Lynette Roberts has also been revived by renewed scholarly interest and the publication of her *Collected Poems* (Mellor 2011: 109–15), but it remains the case that the search for women writers of the 1940s is most likely to be rewarded in prose.

This brief account of poetic diversity reinforces Spender's perception of 'disintegration' as the keynote of 1940s' poetry. Movements dissolved and multiplied, writers changed direction, the perception and subjects of poetry were destabilised. The critic Maurice Bowra shared Spender's sense of fragmentation, but in 'The Next Stage in Poetry' he articulated a hope that war, while not obviously creating a poetry of value, might nonetheless create the conditions, in peace, for a new poetic sensibility:

> Modern war is no friend to poetry. The vast mechanized effort which it demands of everyone is too exacting and too exhausting to allow creative work, and the violent sensations of battle dull and stun the poetical sensibility. But the experience which war gives, the extension of horizons and the new knowledge of human nature which it brings, sooner or later touch poetry and give it a new direction. (*Horizon*, XIV, 79; 1946: 10)

The Movement poets, self-proclaimed agents of the new direction, would no doubt have agreed; but Bowra is too modest. From the brief but intense achievement of Keith Douglas to the reinvigoration of T. S. Eliot, the 'vast mechanized effort' of the Second World War had a remarkably revitalising effect on British poetry.

War, Postwar and 'Peace': Literature in an Age of 'lucid abnormality'

At the heart of the culture of the 1940s is an amorphous entity called the 'postwar'. It takes hold, as a vision, almost the moment that hostilities are declared; it becomes a state of mind as the war progresses through its interminable, deadly grind; it shapes a literature of the aftermath, traumatic and troubled; it limits the possibilities of recognising, let alone building, a concept of 'peace'. By the end of the decade, a new modernity was emerging. It would be welcomed by some and loathed by others, and it would generate new possibilities in fiction, in poetry and on stage; it would also, slowly, permit the articulation of the trauma generated by the decade's unprecedented technologies of destruction. But these are stories for another book. The 1940s stand alone in the twentieth century, cut adrift from what came before by an accident of historical timing, and able only to lay the seeds of what might follow. It is Elizabeth Bowen, identified earlier as a spokesperson for the creative mind of the period, who offers a language for understanding this era when she writes of the war as a 'climate' (1950: 48). This image can be extended, and it is as a 'microclimate' that we might begin to understand the 1940s' position within modernity's century: they represent a period when the conditions of life and the creative imagination were radically disrupted – a point when the continuity of literary development is fragmented – giving rise, in Bowen's terms, to a series of 'strange growths' that resist easy categorisation (48). The 1940s do not tell a story of modernism or postmodernism; they are uncannily familiar, and yet impossibly different. 'We all', writes Bowen, 'lived in a state of lucid abnormality' (48), and in this succinct diagnosis we might begin to understand what constitutes the literature of the 1940s.

Notes

1. For example, Arthur Marwick, *British Society since 1945* (1982); Kenneth O. Morgan, *The People's Peace: British History 1945–1990* (1990); D. J. Taylor, *After the War: The Novel in England since 1945* (1993), and the Palgrave 'Transitions' series, where Jane Goldman's *Image to Apocalypse* (2004) ends and John Brannigan's *Orwell to the Present* (2003) starts in 1945. Although pervasive, the boundary is, nonetheless, porous: Peter Hennessey prefaces *Never Again: Britain 1945–1951* (1992) with a fifty-page chapter on the war years.
2. Stewart and Stonebridge valuably embrace the 1940s as a whole, while Bluemel attempts to disrupt conventional categories of analysis through the identification of a network of influence and affiliation linking the writers Mulk Raj Anand, Inez Holden and Stevie Smith to George Orwell. Other innovative approaches include Sara Wasson's *Urban Gothic of the Second World War* (2010), Leo Mellor's *Reading the Ruins: Modernism, Bombsites and British Culture* (2011) and Stonebridge's study of the postwar period, *The Judicial Imagination: Writing After Nuremberg* (2011).
3. The individual creative talent of British cinema showed no sign of diminishing in the late 1940s, but the industry suffered setbacks, the most significant of which was an American film boycott brought about by the chancellor Hugh Dalton's decision in 1947 to impose a duty of 75 per cent on American films distributed in Britain (Forster, 1963/1986: 272–3). This had a crippling effect on J. Arthur Rank, then the most powerful man in British cinema, and the man whose organisation had provided a generous creative umbrella under which independent producers could flourish. Cut adrift from the protected environment of wartime film production, and facing a new threat in the revival, from June 1946, of BBC Television, film-makers would increasingly take refuge in the security of genre.
4. Jewish European refugees were also considered undesirable: 'A clear strategy was developed in the acceptance of immigrants based essentially on their ability to assimilate' (Kushner 1996: 160).
5. As suggested earlier, the extent to which the weakening of Britain's international authority was recognised by 1951 is debatable. The signs of change were undoubtedly present, however, in the presence of nationalist agitation in Africa, threats to Britain's authority in the Middle East, and the precarious nature of the 'special relationship' with a bellicose and unpredictable America.
6. Priestley's *Postscripts* were a series of Sunday evening radio talks that ran from June–October 1940. Immensely popular with listeners (if not always

with government), they caught the mood of the time in their down-to-earth documentation of the nation's response to crisis.

7. An exhaustive survey of children's literature is provided by Owen Dudley Edwards, *British Children's Fiction in the Second World War* (2007).

8. A statement seemingly contradicted by Spender's assertion in *Since 1939* that the 'difference between trying to explain a poem by Eliot, say, and one by Auden is like that between trying to explain a crime with and one without an apparent motive' (1949: 133).

I
War

Chapter Two

Documenting

I am going to keep a journal because I cannot accept the fact that I feel so shattered that I cannot write at all. ... Words seem to break in my mind like sticks when I put them down on paper. (Stephen Spender, 'September Journal', *Horizon*, Vol. 1, No. 2, February 1940: 102)

Oh, if only I had the composure and self-detachment to write of all these things. But everything is fluid in me, an undigested mass of experience, without shape or plot or purpose. And it is as well to let it be so, for it's a true reflection of this Now we scramble through. (Alun Lewis, Letter, 15 January 1944; 1948/2006: 67)

September 1st, 1939.–Enquire of Robert whether he does not think that, in view of times in which we live, diary of daily events might be of ultimate historical value to posterity. He replies that It Depends. (E. M. Delafield, *The Provincial Lady in Wartime*, 1940/1984: 373)

While most pronounced at the beginning of the war, the urge to document, to bear witness and, in the process, make sense of the conflict was a persistent feature of 1940s writing. Yet, as the epigraphs to this chapter suggest, the war resisted straightforward inscription. In part this was a problem of scale: as Elizabeth Bowen observes in *The Heat of the Day*, global war was 'uncontainable', it 'ran off the edges of maps' (1948/1962: 308). There were no fixed lines of battle, and shifting alliances destabilised the certainties of preceding decades. But it was also a problem of *déjà vu*. Vera Brittain, haunted by the memory of 1914–18 and frustrated by the failure to secure a lasting peace, wrote that the life of her generation felt 'like a recurring decimal in which the grimmest experiences are repeated again and again' (1941: 57), while the poet Keith Douglas was forced to admit the anxiety of influence: 'Rosenberg I only repeat what you were saying–' (1978/2000: 108). Douglas's frustration articulates the fear that the writers of the First World War had somehow had the last word on the horror of war, but this sense of inevitable repetition was accompanied by an equally pervasive sense of obligation. There might be nothing left to say, but something nonetheless had to be said. For both soldiers and civilians, then, the onset of hostilities raised the question of how writers might function in relation to the public event of war.

The initial response, however, appeared to be that the writer was superfluous. In one of the decade's earliest 'war' novels, E. M. Delafield's *The Provincial Lady in Wartime*, the Provincial Lady is assured that writers will be needed, but no-one can determine when or in what capacity. Rebuffed by the BBC and the Ministry of Information, she is obliged, like everyone else of her acquaintance, to 'Stand By' (1940/1984: 402). But while Delafield debunks the idea of a cadre of eager war writers, Cyril Connolly is bemused by their absence. His 'Comment' in the May 1940 issue of *Horizon* notes how little space the war has so far occupied: 'No contributor has yet expressed a wish to beat the Germans; nor been provoked into writing about the black-out, the blockade, the *Graf Spee* or Scapa Flow. The bomber, which played such a large part in pre-war poetry, is no longer mentioned . . .' (Vol. I, No. 5, 1940: 309). Connolly is concerned by this lack of engagement, arguing that 'intellectuals recoil from the war as if it were a best-seller' (313), and he ends his editorial with a plea for energetic cultural production (314). This plea was reiterated a year later in the publication of 'Why Not War Writers?', a short manifesto arguing that good war books were needed now and that officially-sanctioned war writers should be appointed in parallel with war artists (Vol. IV, No. 22; 1941: 236–9). A month later, however, Connolly seemed to be regretting such calls to arms. In an editorial demonstrating how difficult it was to agree on what, exactly, war writing might be, he attributed the total absence of poetry in the issue to a war-induced surfeit of 'Puritan verse' (Vol. IV, No. 23; 1941: 299). As these examples suggest, Connolly's editorials are consistent only in their contrariness; by 1942 he was comically asserting that all 'writers who feel that they are in the war and responsible for winning it should be excused literary activity, and even forbidden it' (Vol. V, No. 29; 1942: 298).

From the outset, then, critical opinion floundered on the issue of what war writing might be and what – if anything – it could achieve. This anxiety was exacerbated by the experience of the 1930s. The Second World War began at the end of a decade of urgent political activity, in which powerful polemical writing, such as Virginia Woolf's *Three Guineas* (1938) and Naomi Mitchison's *The Moral Basis of Politics* (1938), was accompanied by a spate of dystopian 'next war' novels. Storm Jameson's *In the Second Year* (1936), Katherine Burdekin's *Swastika Night* (1937) and Frank Tilsley's *Little Tin God* (1939) were just three of the fictions to imagine a fascist future. Poetry, meanwhile, addressed the Spanish civil war, convinced that poets could exert influence on the political landscape. This belief was short-lived: the collapse of the Republican cause suggested that such interventions were futile, and disillusionment haunted writers – such as Stephen Spender and George Orwell – who had invested hope and belief in the cause. Orwell, writing for *Partisan Review* in January 1941 reflects on this transition, concluding that the intellectual had become redundant, his visions of influence exploded by the technocratic dimension of 'all-in modern' war (Orwell 1941/1970: 71). Spender, by contrast, found new purpose. After the creative paralysis described in 'September Journal' he entered an enormously productive phase. He completed his first novel, *The Backward Son* (1940), and found his poetic voice stimulated by the spectacle of destruction. The poems of *Ruins and Visions* (1942), which move from 'personal breakdown, through public cataclysm, to personal re-integration' (Sutherland 2004/2005: 291–2), were accompanied by an increased fascination with the process of poetry, and the production of critical studies such as *Life and the Poet* (1942). Here, and in a later article for *Penguin New Writing*, Spender articulates his new belief in apolitical detachment, arguing that 'the extraordinary merit of poetry lies not in its power to transform the world but in its power to endure' (*PNW*, 19; 1944: 135).

Nonetheless, as Kristin Bluemel has argued, the writing of political engagement did not go away, and it is possible to trace, in the work of writers such as Inez Holden, a continuity of purpose and expression that links the 1930s to the Labour election victory of 1945 (2004: 132–3). Inevitably, though, this mode of writing became newly self-conscious, existing as it did in a climate of constant debate as to its value. Again the Provincial Lady puts her comfortable middle-class finger on the problem in her question about the need for a 'diary of daily events': bearing witness to 'history' is easier said than done. Yet diary-writing was a widespread activity, undertaken sometimes out of a desire to record the unprecedented progress of a truly global war, and sometimes, in the case of writers such as Frances Partridge, out of a need to make sense of events and emotions. Partridge, a committed pacifist and Bloomsbury group writer, treats her diary as a space for uninhibited expression: writing for herself, she does not need to censor her doubts, fears and frustrations.[1] In this sense, the diary becomes an exemplary form of the war years, bearing witness, while also – in its intimacy and privacy – encapsulating writing's retreat from the political. Its paratactic construction similarly took away the expectation of form and consequence. Diaries do not order experience, and they speak to the pressures of war as much through what they fail to record as through what they include. Partridge's diary, for example, devotes far more attention to abstract ideas than to the pain of loss. Throughout the published text, death is marginalised, placed in footnotes, or given expression through the fears of her young son Burgo. This might be an act of editorial self-protection, but these omissions stand in stark contrast to the imagery of the text, which, as the war progresses, turns increasingly towards disease and decay. The war is 'a hole in a tooth' (175), those living through it 'like people in the waiting room of a hospital' (192): images of gnawing anxiety that expose the threat not just to the individual, but to a whole civilisation.

Yet, while the private form of the diary answered well to the needs of writers, it could not satisfy the media demand for a new war poetry. Instead, the tension between the need for expression and expression's seeming impossibility was met by the rejuvenation of the short story. In this allusive, fragmentary form, the inarticulable could be hinted at, gestured towards, the story becoming – in Elizabeth Bowen's formulation – both a snapshot 'taken from close up' and a conduit for something more substantial that exceeds the boundaries of individual experience (Bowen 1950: 52). The impossibility of capturing the 'real' of conflict was also evident in the persistent vitality of modernist tropes in literature. Amongst the most powerful accounts of the Blitz are those found in Bowen's *The Heat of the Day* (1948), James Hanley's *No Directions* (1943) and Henry Green's *Caught* (1943). All these writers adopt elements of modernism's subjective, suggestive methodology to create the sense of a world in which time and space are distorted, and human relations dislocated from the comforts of convention. While Bowen struggled with the composition of a novel that she wanted to be 'comprehensive' (1950: 47), the novels of Hanley and Green were completed during the conflict, as was Virginia Woolf's *Between the Acts* (1941) and William Sansom's *Fireman Flower* (1944). Sansom's stories typify the modernist legacy, and their nightmarish qualities speak allegorically to the pressures of wartime living. Each story focuses around an intense sensory image: a paranoid fireman leaps, or is propelled, into a malodorous sea of burning coffee beans; a penal colony in a steel rectangle attempts to wring dry a monstrous sheet while warders stand by with hosepipes; a civilisation snips endlessly through a maze, seemingly unaware of the confines of their existence; a gardener is half-strangled by his peach trees, a General fully 'throttled by his own tent' (1944: 96); a village worships 'the *idea* of the lighthouse' (29), which functions in their community as a tangible manifestation of psychoanalytic symbolism: like the force of desire, its compelling totemic power evaporates when its foundations are finally reached. Even those stories that strive less ostentatiously for symbolic effect are filled with a sense of desolation, as in 'Difficulty with a Bouquet', where Seal's spontaneous gesture of giving flowers falters at the dawn of self consciousness (60).

The heady atmosphere of Sansom's stories comes to a climax in 'Fireman Flower', a hallucinatory Odyssey, in which the eponymous fireman is tested by uncanny visitations and multiple realities in his search for the 'true kernel' of the fire (138). This overheated story is typical of a preoccupation with fire as fact and symbol in wartime writing. Adam Piette, discussing the prevalence of the trope, compares interpretations of the Blitz by writers as diverse as Louis MacNeice, Herbert Read, Wilfred Gibson, David Gascoyne and James Hanley. Piette categorises these responses as variously 'conservative theological, Marxist revolutionary and psychoanalytic surreal' and argues that:

> all posit the Blitz as apocalypse, and all, significantly, defuse the bombardment as Luftwaffe action. The bare fact of real German bombers dropping sticks of bombs on real Londoners is translated into solitary politics and aesthetics, as though the enemy did not exist. (1995: 46)

While Piette's analysis of the tendency towards abstraction is acute, this does not necessarily translate into a denial of the enemy. Readers were perfectly aware of who was dropping the bombs – the challenge for writers was to make sense, or in some way to capture, the extraordinary nature of the experience: the heightened senses attendant on danger, the impossible juxtapositions of the familiar and unfamiliar, the advent of the unprecedented.

Documentary writing cannot be divorced from more ostentatiously creative literary production, or from recourse to topics seemingly beyond the remit of 'war'. In her 1940 essay 'Thoughts on Peace in an Air Raid' Woolf describes the psychological impact of bombing, suggesting it paradoxically annihilates and liberates creativity. The act of destruction must give way to the creative impulse, as this alone can restore the threatened individual and liberate the young man 'from the machine' (1942: 157). However, for Woolf, creation comes not from war but from the memory of peace, the saving 'other' of war:

> The bomb did not fall. But during those seconds of suspense all thinking stopped. All feeling, save one dull dread, ceased. [. . .] The emotion of fear and of hate is therefore sterile, unfertile. Directly that fear passes, the mind reaches out and instinctively revives itself by trying to create. Since the room is dark it can create only from memory. It reaches out to the memory of other Augusts – in Bayreuth, listening to Wagner; in Rome, walking over the Campagna; in London. Friends' voices come back. Scraps of poetry return. (Woolf 1942: 157)

Documenting transgresses the boundaries between public and private, historical and quotidian. Indeed, the global complexity of the Second World War ensured that for most writers and readers, the public and historical could only be comprehended through the lens of the personal, with the result that, from the ennui of the phoney war to the crisis of the Blitz and the longueurs of the long haul, the conflict's documentary record was a profoundly domestic affair. War's impact was refracted through personal relations and the incremental minutiae of daily life.

The All-Important Foreground: Reconciling Disparate Worlds

> . . . the frightful accounts in the papers of arctic warfare in Finland and of the Turkish earthquake – war, cold, fire and blood – all combine to turn one in upon one's nipped and frozen self, and fasten powers of satisfaction on to small sensual things, pots of cyclamen, the shine on holly berries and cats' fur, the texture of materials. The foreground has in fact become all-important, leaving the vast grim background to fade into chaos. (Partridge 1978/1996: 21; 3 January 1940)

The events of the first two years of war – evacuation, the German advance across Europe, the fall of France, the Battle of Britain, the Blitz – were such that understandings of 'normality' were subject to constant revision. After the strange hiatus of the 'phoney war', the fall of Norway and the Netherlands in May 1940 suddenly brought the threat of invasion into the heart of the domestic sphere. Looking back on events from the relative security of 1941, Margery Allingham observes that 'ordinary people were thinking extraordinary thoughts just then and were preparing for extraordinary deeds' (1941/2011: 176), albeit with the curious self-consciousness she attributes to the English national character. The dramatic advance of the Nazis also changes the tone of Frances Partridge's diary. Partridge spent the war at Ham Spray House in Wiltshire, with her husband Ralph, a conscientious objector, and although the couple refused to participate in the conflict beyond the requirements of civil defence, they nonetheless could not divorce themselves from the drama: a situation described by Ralph as comparable to having all your money put – against your will – on a horse in the Derby: 'We may hate horse-racing, disapprove of it even – yet we still want that horse to win' (1978/1996: 37). In spite of her best efforts to focus on the foreground, then, Partridge is pulled into the 'mad [world] of events' (3 April 1940; 1978/1996: 35). Writing after the invasion of Holland, she exclaims: 'So the blitzkrieg has begun at last! . . . it's almost a relief, as if one had lain for ages on the operating table and at last the surgeon was going to begin' (38–9; 10 May 1940). Here again is Partridge's tell-tale imagery of disease, and her sense of liberation is accompanied by the calm contemplation of suicide, imagining it as perhaps the only agency available (40).

As these conflicting emotions suggest, a pervasive sense of dissonance becomes evident in writers' responses to the crisis. The war remains inconceivable, even as it gathers momentum and force. In part this feeling of war's unreality emerges from ill-advised propaganda – both Allingham and Partridge record the absurdity of being warned against parachuting nuns – but it also has its roots in an ideology of the inviolate island and its timeless beauty. J. B. Priestley's *Postscript* radio talk of 9 June 1940 begins with the disjuncture between nature and war:

> I'll swear the very birds have sung this year as they never did before. Just outside my study, there are a couple of blackbirds who think they're still in the Garden of Eden. There's almost a kind of mockery in their fluting. I think most of us have often felt we simply couldn't believe our eyes and ears: either the War wasn't real, or this spring wasn't real. One of them must be a dream. (Priestley 1940: 5)

Priestley's *Postscripts* were phenomenally popular, and his words here are typically effective, evoking Britain as an earthly paradise at the same time as he mocks the conceit. Priestley's self-consciousness is a strategy well suited to the national reluctance to articulate powerful emotions, but not all attempts to harness the uncanny power of the land shared Priestley's nuanced humour. Vera Brittain, for example, concludes that the 'essence' of the nation lies not in politics, people or buildings, but in the abiding countryside:

> Those who call themselves our enemies may obliterate buildings, annihilate monuments, assassinate men and women; they cannot eliminate the flowers, the trees, the grass, the moist sunny air, the quiet inviolate spirit, of a whole countryside. Cities may vanish in a red fury of smoke and flame, but no conqueror by his bombs and aeroplanes can wholly remove the marks which immemorial centuries have laid upon our land. Whatever the future may bring of hope or despair, of sanity or suffering, of peace or war, the villages of this country will be England for ever. (Brittain 1941: 258)

The limits of such a vision as shorthand for the nation are not difficult to discern, and propaganda films such as Priestley's *Britain at Bay* (1940) are at pains to achieve a greater inclusivity by uniting village England with the nation's industrial heartland through an idea of national character. This recourse to a homogenising concept of Englishness is integral to popular constructions of community but, as Sonya Rose has noted, the frequent metonymic use of England and Englishness for the wider British nation was a source of considerable tension (2003: 197, 218–38).

Nonetheless, both land and character were mobilised to create the construct of a national family and from this assertion of belonging and shared purpose, described by critics as variously energising (Hartley 1997: 15) or enervating (Piette 1995: 2), came countless narratives detailing the events of the Blitz, Dunkirk and the Battle of Britain. Hewison describes narratives such as Basil Woon's *Hell Came to London* (1941) and John Masefield's *The Nine Days Wonder* (1941) as 'urgent and overcharged' (1977/1988: 42), but not all accounts quite fit this description. *Return Via Dunkirk* by Gun Buster, published in November 1940, scarcely six months after the evacuation, strives for exactly the opposite effect, its banter and camaraderie emphasising a phlegmatic, resilient Englishness. There are moments of overcharged imagery in its attempt to metaphorise peace, but the ending is – intentionally or otherwise – utterly bathetic. The returning soldiers, thrilled by the sight of Ramsgate, want nothing more than a bed to sleep in, a conclusion that simultaneously celebrates the quotidian and serves the propaganda purpose of encouraging calm in the face of potentially demoralising bombardment. But however such events were mediated, this intensity of engagement could not be sustained indefinitely. Hewison reports that by May 1941 'there was a marked decline in people's interest in the news' (60). Up until the Battle of El Alamein in November 1942, there had been little for the Allies to celebrate; while on the home front, supplies of food and fuel became increasingly restricted (60–1). This was the beginning of the 'long haul', a period characterised by hard, monotonous labour, shrinking horizons and a stultifying, insidious boredom. The transition is powerfully evoked in Partridge's diary:

> I have no desire whatever to write anything in this diary, and my only reason for doing so is to show that I am still alive, and not unhappy I might even say. But I have never in my life been less aware of my surroundings, got less pleasure from the visible world, nor felt more completely insulated from thrills of excitement. (13 February 1942; 1978/1996: 126)

Against her explicit assertion, this statement of sensory numbness is a confession of deep unhappiness, and the failure of writing to insulate the self against war's dislocations. The forces of consolation are insufficient, and the diary repeatedly reiterates the numbing imposition of war.

Such alienation is equally evident in fiction. *The Slaves of Solitude* (1947), Patrick Hamilton's bleak depiction of boarding-house life in late 1943, finds the perfect image for the transition from crisis to attrition, observing that the war, 'which had begun by making dramatic and drastic demands, which had held up the public in style like a highway-man, had now developed into a petty pilferer' (1947/2006: 134–5). Elizabeth Bowen, meanwhile, captures the contraction of self attendant upon this psychological and material depletion: 'you used to know what you were like from the things you liked, and chose. Now there was not what you liked, and you did not choose' (1950: 49). The attenuating impact of war was further exacerbated by the diminishing returns of propaganda. Diana Murray Hill's fictionalised account of her time in a factory records that not only was the war worker 'browned-off', a condition defined as being 'so bored that nothing has any significance to you but being bored' (1944: 51), he or she was also subject to insidi-ous pressure emanating from a climate of surveillance and a pervasive discourse of guilt:

> Other devices to bring us to account for waste of time were the cheerful or sinister posters and slogans with which we were surrounded continually, which could be relied upon to warn us with a stab of guilt whenever we felt like letting the nation down.
> The slogan 'It all depends on me' was chief offender. (1944: 58)

In such a context it is not surprising that the Ministry of Information approved the production of Frank Launder and Sidney Gilliat's *Millions Like Us* (1943), a film designed to reassure women that life in the fac-tories was not as bad as it seemed. The film is a well-made example of a documentary realist feature film, and as such it has a 'group hero'. Rather than focusing on individual achievement, it charts the progress of a disparate group of women who together represent the nation in micro-cosm. The group comprises an educated Welsh woman from a deprived area in the Valleys, a good-time girl from London, a working-class lass from the North and timid, lower-middle class Celia (Patricia Roc), who carries the story most clearly designed to further the propaganda purpose of the narrative. In a comic montage sequence, Celia fantasises about joining one of the women's services. Appearing in a range of attractive uniforms, she is wooed and won by a commanding male figure. Much to her horror, though, she is sent into industry and, typically, the necessity of her deployment is couched in personal rather than political terms: 'There's nothing to be afraid of in a factory. Mr Bevan needs another million women, you know. And I don't think we should disappoint him at a time like this.' Thereafter the narrative works to reassure, and Celia finds new confidence, love and a short-lived marriage to a Scottish RAF sergeant (Gordon Jackson). Significantly, the conclusion of the film is communal rather than individual in focus. The widowed Celia is shown back in the factory group, tentatively re-joining the community as they

Figure 2.1 'It All Depends On You': The burden of the 'people's war'. Image © Imperial War Museums (Art. IWM PST 14374).

sing together. Yet the film is not as straightforward as this summary might suggest. The story includes a second couple, London upper-middle class Jennifer (Anne Crawford) and Yorkshire upper-working class Charlie (Eric Portman), whose romance ends in debate rather than death (Babington 2002: 65). In representing a more mature cross-class couple, the film supplements its narrative of national belonging with an acknowledgment of uncertainty.

However, beyond *Millions Like Us* and *Went the Day Well* (1942) – a film produced to warn against complacency in the public's attitude towards invasion – much cinema and fiction of the mid- to late-war period turned away from documentary towards more escapist material, a transition that will be discussed in Chapter 5. In what follows, I examine three contrasting manifestations of the documentary impulse in wartime writing: the fragmentary glimpse of the short story; novels focusing on the social and psychological upheaval of evacuation, and the representation of factory work. The Blitz is a constant in all of these sections, but as one of the few aspects of the war to have been subject to significant critical analysis, I have not made it a central focus.[2] Instead, the chapter ends with a consideration of the wider context surrounding Britain's documentation of itself. Paralleling the almost obsessive self-examination of the home front was an anthropology not of ourselves, but of the 'other': writing that looks beyond the boundaries of the island in an attempt to understand not only what was happening, but why it had happened.

Everyday Horrors: 'War' Stories, War Selves

To survive, not only physically but spiritually, was essential. People whose homes had been blown up went to infinite lengths to assemble bits of themselves – broken ornaments, odd shoes, torn scraps of the curtains that had hung in a room – from the wreckage. In the same way, they assembled and checked themselves from stories and poems, from their memories, from one another's talk. (Bowen 1950: 50)

Alun Lewis's *The Last Inspection* (1942) and Julian Maclaren-Ross's *The Stuff to Give the Troops* (1944) encapsulate the paradoxes of the war's early years. Here is what Paul Fussell terms 'chickenshit': the boredom, the inanity, the petty authoritarianism and mindless bureaucracy of army life (1989: 88). Maclaren-Ross's largely autobiographical vignettes are prosaic demonstrations of the extent to which the left hand of the army machine does not know, and indeed often actively resents, whatever it is the right hand is doing. But while Maclaren-Ross stays firmly rooted in a mode of detached and comical understatement, Lewis's stories are not afraid to negotiate emotional pain, nor to draw attention to the awful inversions of a war initially more hazardous to the home than the battlefront. In a radical revision of the preoccupations of the First World War, this is a 'soldier poet' writing about civilian jeopardy. 'They Came' epitomises this irony, its taut, spare prose and matter-of-fact tone gradually unpeeling to expose a brutal account of war's arbitrary destructive force. Significantly, the key events of the story are not directly presented: rather, they are narrated by the survivor, whose difficulty in speaking, and resort to formulaic banalities, bears witness to the inarticulable horror of aerial bombardment.

The story begins, however, with the mundane routine of the military, a routine permeated by a squalid domesticity that renders army life tawdry and absurd: 'The unit did its squad drill in the hotel yard, kitchen maids watching flirtatiously through the windows, giggling, and the lavatory smelling either of disinfectant or urine' (1990: 167). There is nothing heroic about this spectacle, and throughout the story, Lewis uses images of the feminine or the domestic to expose weakness and venality. The sergeant of the guard, a self-serving parasite 'sucked and scraped the officers . . . zealously carrying out their orders with the finicky short temper of a weak house-proud woman' (172). Taffy, the soldier at the centre of the story, is more sympathetically treated, but is nonetheless first depicted through the iconography of a quotidian peace, dragging his legs 'like an old clerk going home late' (166). But this is also an image of burden: the 'young chap' is metamorphosed into an old man by the 'heavy greatcoat and equipment' that hampers his movements as he 'trudge[s]' to his billet under a 'curdling' sky. At the imperceptible boundary when day becomes night, the returning soldier once again exchanges his Welsh past for an English present. In camp – at war – the story suggests, is to be in a transitional state; distant from self, in limbo: 'None of us are ourselves now, the Welsh boy sat thinking; neither what we were, nor what we will be' (169). This indeterminacy – a sense of the soldier's uncertain becoming – was a significant trope of the early war years. In 'A Sentimental Story' Maclaren-Ross writes that you 'can tell yourself that the uniform does not matter that you are the same underneath but it does matter and you are not the same because the attitude of others makes you what you are' (1944: 128). Paul Scott sees this transition as self-annihilation, noting in his poem 'Tell Us The Tricks' that the 'soldier's here – the man is not' (Gardner 1966/1999: 32). In comparison, John Manifold's 'The Recruit' is optimistic about this reconfiguration of self: 'Pried from the circle where his family ends', he finds fellowship across 'Nation and region, class and craft'. The poem ends with a new subject emergent, 'a point where circles intersect' (1966/1999: 31). Lewis's work resists an absolute division between the soldier and the man, but nonetheless suggests a threat in military life's capacity to expose human nature, the glimpse of power afforded by uniform bringing out the worst in men.

In 'They Came' war's unspeakable impact is normalised through mundane rhetorical ritual. Four times Taffy engages in a banal exchange of pleasantries, responding as formula expects to the question 'Had a good leave?': 'Yes, thanks ... except for raids. The first night I was home he raided us for three hours, the sod' (167). The personalising of the enemy, and the reduction of the Nazi threat to an individual malign force, would become a commonplace of documentary writing, but here Taffy's mindless repetition is a marker of repression, a normalising strategy designed to make living possible in the face of a loss that scarcely can be articulated, let alone accommodated. As the story progresses, we learn that Taffy's 'cushy' job as a soldier has left him 'safe as houses' – a bitterly inappropriate metaphor – while his wife has been horrifically maimed in an air raid, mutating into a barely recognisable lump of flesh that will not die. Gwyneth's state of limbo reinforces Taffy's sense of powerlessness, and reiterates the story's preoccupation with transitional states. Taffy wants his wife to die, but her wordless death leaves him with nothing that can help him make sense of his loss. Telling the story to his friend, the Cockney outsider Nobby, enables what in the story passes for resolution: the construction of a narrative that must cover over the absence of meaning in Gwyneth's death. Nobby renders the relationship uncanny, dissolving the boundary between life and death to suggest the lovers 'belong to each other for keeps, now' (175). As Taffy sees his beloved, the past once more invades the present, the permeable boundaries of memory suggesting both sustenance and denial. Through inhabiting the past, the unthinkable future recedes.

Yet Lewis's deployment of the past is far from nostalgic and offers only limited consolation to the reader. A powerful sense of political irony pervades the story as Taffy's memories extend beyond the intimacy of his relationship with Gwyneth to a world riven with poverty. Remembering going hungry to save for a college book, he reflects bitterly on war's perverse abundance in which 'everything is free but freedom, and the doctor and dentist and cobbler send you no bills' (170). Here are the roots of the 'unspoken humanity of comradeship' that unite him in friendship with Nobby. Conscripts with no investment in military advancement, they have the perspective to see the system for what it is, but they also represent another key trope of wartime experience: the homosocial bond. Their friendship does not need articulation, and Nobby's value lies as much in his listening as in any of the euphemisms he manages to utter. As an audience, he legitimates the narrative, and gives back to Taffy at least the vestiges of a selfhood destroyed by the raid. He resurrects the ghost of Gwyneth as a constitutive other, while simultaneously representing such an other himself. In this sense, the army comes to form a duplication of the domestic, setting up in its necessary bonds of friendship a parallel structure of identity formation.

The need to speak, the impossibility of articulating that which must be spoken and, in some cases, the impossibility of being heard are equally central to Elizabeth Berridge's stories. Published in anthologies such as *English Story* before being collected in 1947, Berridge's fiction is fascinated by the difficulties of communication and the failure of speech. 'Tell It to a Stranger' typifies her concern, focusing on the process through which the dislocated selves of wartime 'assembled and checked themselves from stories' (Bowen 1950: 50), and the recognition of war's paradoxical capacity both to regenerate and destroy the subject.

'Tell It to a Stranger' begins as a social comedy in which Mrs Hatfield, finding her London house ransacked, rehearses how she will tell this dramatic story to her friends at Belvedere, a coastal guest house housing a community keen to avoid the impact of war (2000: 53). Mrs Hatfield has, ironically, been reborn by the conflict. She feels 'a happier woman, more alive than she had ever been' (55). Freed from the constraints of a crushing conventional marriage, she cherishes her new life, thinking of Belvedere as 'home' and enjoying the war as a mode of vicarious entertainment: 'She had something to tell this time. Here was some real news, directly touching her, and through her, every person at Belvedere. The war had at last affected them personally' (57). As so often with Berridge's stories, though, there is a sting in the tail: an abrupt reversal that exposes the complacent assumption that war can be enjoyed as a spectator sport. Mrs Hatfield returns to find Belvedere bombed – her community destroyed – a traumatic discovery that destroys her fragile new subjectivity. The new self brought into existence by her status as storyteller evaporates without an audience, and her loss exceeds the possibilities of verbal representation. Instead, as she is dragged from the ruins, the loss of her friends – her constitutive others – is displaced and condensed into a banal lament for property. 'My lovely wine glasses' (59), the final words of the story, become a suitably inappropriate epitaph for the totality of Mrs Hatfield's grief.

The fate of Mrs Hatfield – her self-constituting narrative unheard – finds a very different formulation in another of Berridge's stories: 'To Tea With the Colonel'. Here the focus is on class, and the geographic and generational fault lines exposed by the conflict. Berridge sets the metropolis against the provinces in her depiction of Miss Morton's alienation from the county town in which she has taken refuge from the Blitz. Conscious of her outsider status, Miss Morton longs for the 'blessed anonymity of a London bus', but as the story progresses, she unexpectedly finds friendship with another woman who bears 'the mark of spinsterdom upon her' (2000: 90, 94). However, the gendered commonalities of the two women cannot breach the gulf of Blitz experience. Miss Morton, experiencing a sudden cathartic urge to speak, describes the horror of waking to find 'what should be outside on the roof' invading the imagined 'invulnerability' of private space (93). As she reaches for words, her friend Miss Lumley recoils from this unwelcome exposure:

> She looked uncomfortable, almost hurt. Weren't Londoners supposed to be like the R.A.F.? Not mentioning things like actual death and mutilation. Of course it was to be expected that a near-miss should make people voluble. The relief, of course. *Another second, and . . .*
> 'How dreadful for you,' she said. (93)

The polite banality of Miss Lumley's response encapsulates the chasm of incomprehension opened up by bombing, but Berridge's story is equally concerned with the more fundamental division of class. The Colonel of the title is Miss Lumley's father, a relic of a past age, whose deafness symbolises his insulation from the realities of a changing world. Asked to provide the Colonel with his tea, Miss Morton obliges to please her friend, but once alone in the house she feels 'the ghost of a parlourmaid's panic' (99). Her class resentment and her 'hatred for people who had never known the nightly horror of sirens' (98) coalesce into the story's second cathartic outburst, and she voices the frustrations of a life of dependency in a bitter attack on the privileges of the gentry. The unhearing Colonel is oblivious, but responds with a courtesy that simultaneously relieves and crushes Miss Morton: she is freed by her outburst, but reduced to tears. The story ends on this tableau, and Berridge offers the reader no insight into the complex emotions behind Miss Morton's tears. They are, we conclude, born of trauma, resentment, frustration and guilt; her moment of rebellion undone by the impenetrable conventions of middle-class politeness.

Miss Morton is an adult evacuee, uprooted from the familiar and forced into an unwelcome encounter with an 'other' Britain. Such disorientation was a pervasive feature of documentary writing and wartime 'middlebrow' fiction, both of which worried about the fundamental ideological and social disparities exposed by this collision of worlds. The result was an anxious preoccupation with the impact of war upon a generation of children.

Save the Children: Class, Culture and Displacement

> There are some curious people – optimists, I suppose – who heralded evacuation as something that would bring new life to the poor children of the cities. They could not see evacuation as a great tragedy, so they looked to it as one of the hidden blessings of war. But it could never be a good thing to take children from their ordinary decent homes. And by home, you know, I do not mean a lovely house with all the modern conveniences. By home I mean the room or two that has become associated in the child's mind with mother and father, and the other children, and the cat. (D. W. Winnicott 1945/1984: 50)

In Nevil Shute's *Pied Piper* (1942), John Sidney Howard, an old man frustrated by his superfluity and grieving for his lost pilot son, travels to France seeking the regenerative distraction of spring in the Jura. Yet Howard's timing leaves much to be desired. France falls and he becomes the 'pied piper' of the title, leading a motley assortment of European children across occupied France to safety. He is assisted in his task by a French woman, Nicole, who had loved his son, and who – in the absence of a lover – demonstrates an admirable sense of national purpose (1942/1943: 211, 222). For both Howard and Nicole, action is a mode of grief work (166). The text is an adventure with a clear villain, but the brutally efficient Germans are not without a reassuring element of self-doubt. Howard's eventual escape is achieved through his acceptance of a final child: the niece of a Gestapo officer, a German girl whose mother 'was not wholly Aryan' (265).

Shute's novel is uncompromising in its depiction of Europe under Nazi occupation, and his children represent a curious combination of national stereotype and humanitarian indictment. The refugees comprise Ronnie and Sheila, two middle-class English children; Rose, a patient, maternal French girl; Pierre, a silent, orphaned French boy; Willem, a traumatised Dutch boy found in a gutter, and Marjan, a viciously angry Polish Jew, who is an adult at ten, and knows exactly what fate has befallen his parents and will befall him if he is captured by the Germans. In the depiction of Marjan, Shute attempts to show war's brutalising impact; the child has internalised the destructive logic of war:

> It would only be by great good luck that I could kill a German now; even if I could creep up to one in the darkness and rip him open with a sharp knife, I should be caught and killed. But in a few years time I shall be able to kill many hundreds of them, secretly, in the dark streets. That is much better, to wait and to learn how these things should be managed properly. (213)

Shute is unusually explicit in his inclusion of a Jewish refugee and his acknowledgement of their fate, but there is no doubt that Marjan is depicted as racially and ethically 'other', a repository for the violent impulses of war that Shute is unable or unwilling to attribute to the more 'civilised' children of western Europe. Further limits to Shute's vision become apparent in the concluding pages of the novel, where the hitherto resourceful and active Nicole mutates into a symbol of passive womanhood. Her agency is understood as something exceptional, the product of war, and necessary only for war's duration. When she imagines the future, it is a world in which Ronnie, or Willem, or Pierre will do great things. Civilisation will not be rebuilt by women, nor it would seem, by Jews (269).

For all its flaws, Shute's novel about saving children engages with a major preoccupation not only of documentary prose and fiction, but also of contemporary psychology. In a study published in 1942, Dorothy Burlingham and Anna Freud stress that exposure to war's violence may excite primitive destructive impulses in the child, attracting rather than horrifying or traumatising it (1942: 29–31). The writers' work was based on the observation of children in a residential war nursery in Hampstead. The children who came to them, all under the age of ten, were too disturbed for regular evacuation, and the nursery acted as a clearing house enabling them either to return to their families or be found billets elsewhere. The study's stated aims were to repair damage already done, prevent further damage where possible, and to disseminate knowledge concerning the psychological needs of children (11), and its findings are disturbing, not least because they conclude that the war poses an insoluble problem in terms of healthy child development. Obviously children cannot be left in the way of physical harm: they should be removed from areas likely to be bombed. But equally, the evidence suggests that evacuation is emotionally damaging in the rupture it causes to the family unit (41). To remove children abruptly from their parents can be a source of considerable confusion for the developing child, especially if it is billeted with foster parents significantly different in 'social and financial status' (41–2). The combination of primitive destructive excitements and a lack of emotional stability has potentially devastating consequences:

> War conditions, through the inevitable breaking-up of family life, deprive children of the natural background for their emotional and mental development. The present generation of children have therefore little chance to build up their future psychological health and normality which will be needed for the reconstruction of the world after the war. To counteract these deficiencies, wartime care of children has to be more elaborate and more carefully thought out than in ordinary times of peace. (Burlingham and Freud 1942: 11)

The fiction and prose writing that emerges from this context is curiously double-voiced. Novels such as Phyllis Bottome's *London Pride* (1941), Noel Streatfeild's *Saplings* (1945), and Barbara Noble's *Doreen* (1946) all use children as focalisers for the discussion of adult fears regarding social change and class miscegenation. Adult anxieties are displaced – or rather, an adult conservatism is translated – into a narrative of child welfare. Yet there is nonetheless significant common ground between psychologists and fiction writers in their assertion of the child's need for stability. Burlingham and Freud observe that children whose parents stay calm in potentially traumatic situations will not be unduly troubled by bombing (28), concluding that 'the quiet manner in which the London population on the whole met the air raids is therefore responsible in one way for the extremely rare occurrence of "shocked" children' (38). What is much more difficult for children is seeing their parents exhibiting extreme anxiety or being cut adrift from the secure referents of everyday life: but this is precisely the fate greeting the Wiltshire children in *Saplings*.

Noel Streatfeild's disturbing novel begins with the familiar security of British middle-class family life. Father Alex embodies rational common sense, his charming wife Lena is all sensibility (1945/2000: 57). Yet Lena's patriarchal conditioning verges on the pathological, leaving her self-destructively committed to the belief that woman's function is to worship a man (50). Lena insists that she is 'first a wife and, a long way second, a mother' (235), an attitude that causes few problems while the level-headed Alex is alive, but which results in a spiral of despair after his death in an air-raid. As Lena collapses into drink and an animal dependency upon various more-or-less suitable replacement men (213), the novel charts the impact of her decline on the four Wiltshire children: Laurel, Tony, Tuesday and Kim. Their different personalities ensure that each will encounter different problems in the aftermath of the family's dissolution, but what Streatfeild's novel stresses throughout is the fundamental need for stability. This is evident even before catastrophe strikes. Tony, we are told, 'liked, without knowing it, to believe in things going on as they had always done' (35), while anxious Laurel finds reassurance in her father's calm explanation of impending crisis (59).

It is the older children, the adolescents Laurel and Tony, who will suffer most as a result of the family breakdown, losing much of their ability to form friendships at school and being singled-out as 'problems' by the adults they encounter. The adults, in turn, persistently do the wrong thing for the right reason: part of the pain of Streatfeild's novel is the sheer quantity of good intentions gone astray. When Lena announces a second marriage to the bumptious and wealthy Charles, he fully accepts responsibility for the children. Unfortunately, in utterly disrespecting the fragile surroundings to which they cling, he alienates them all. Here is the desperate need, identified by Bowen, to cleave to the self-constituting fragments of a once-coherent past:

> By the end of the holidays the children had banded together and were atrociously rude to Charles. They did not resent so bitterly his adoption of their mother, as the way he treated their home. It was the only home they had possessed since Regent's Park and was peculiarly theirs, to the last bush. Charles was always outraging their sense of possession. (1945/2000: 335)

The concept of home, as Winnicott suggests, is fundamental to the wellbeing of the child, and the Wiltshire children – shuffled between incomprehending relatives – yearn for manifestations of normality. Yet the collapse of their home environment is not solely to be laid at Lena's feet, and Streatfeild's anatomy of parenting is accompanied by a demonstration of war's collateral damage. Staying with their grandparents, the children discover a falling-down cottage, which together they turn into a recreation of home. Here, the children feel 'invulnerable', and the adult world, 'where people whispered about how difficult you were', becomes 'a shadow' (116). This homemaking seems a conventional and reassuring representation of child's play, but only a short while later, its mimetic relationship to the adult world will disturbingly expose the damage of war. While the Wiltshires understand little of the conflict, they are hypersensitive to its repercussions, and their middle-class conditioning collapses to reveal the primitive excitement anticipated by Burlingham and Freud. Together with a pair of evacuees who have seen what war can do, the children enact in microcosm the destruction of the adult world:

> Albert threw a stone. It cracked through the glass in the window. Ernie climbed on to the window ledge and pulled at a tile. Several slid off the roof. There was a second when the Wiltshire children were about to stop them, then suddenly they joined in. It was an orgy of smashing. All the pent-up excitement of the world around them came out. (1945/2000: 132)

Albert and Ernie, Streatfeild's two working-class evacuees, are depicted as fundamentally damaged by war. However, their mother, in a perverse mirroring of Lena, cannot bear to be without her children, and insists on their return to London. Both are killed, and while their deaths are a footnote within *Saplings'* anatomy of psychological trauma, the dilemma that prompts it is central to the work of both Phyllis Bottome and Barbara Noble.

In the case of Noble's *Doreen*, a self-sacrificing mother eventually chooses evacuation for her beloved only daughter, while Bottome's Mrs Barton makes the opposite choice, unable to part with her favourite child, Ben. Bottome, an Adlerian psychologist, clearly subscribes to the belief that family context shapes the child's relationship to war. The unflappable Mrs Barton dismisses war as male excess, 'they don't none of them know when they've 'ad enough' (1941: 14), leaving Ben ironically secure in an acceptance of external threat as 'an ordinary and senseless subject' (14). Similarly, Mr Barton's warm, protective embrace is enough to reassure the child after his first experience of the violent disorientation of bombing (55). Ben's family are presented as respectable, resilient and essentially moral. Both parents are employed – Mrs Barton is a char and Mr Barton a docker – and they bring up their children with an understanding of morality based on a community ethic and a somewhat crudely parodied Communism. This, combined with the book's dominant focalisation through the innocent eyes of Ben, makes the narrative deeply reassuring. Arguably, reassurance might also be behind Bottome's decision to approximate Cockney dialect, not just in conversation, but also in free indirect discourse. The resulting plethora of dropped consonants and absent vowels is simultaneously infantilising and romanticising: these figures are 'other', but unthreateningly so, and their actions work to underline this message. When his community is threatened, Mr Barton's Communist sympathies yield to archetypally British patriotism, and his potentially threatening class hatred is diffused by its utility in calming his vulnerable son: 'What, he exclaimed contemptuously, were a few bombs dropped compared to class warfare' (54). The value of the Bartons is also demonstrated in comparison with their neighbours, the Corrigans. Ben, although a child of the slums, understands moral codes, but his friend Em'ly Corrigan is revealed to have no moral capacity beyond self-preservation. Brought up by her family to steal whenever opportunity presents, Em'ly finds unprecedented opportunity to develop her criminal skills in the chaos of the Blitz. She is punished by serious injury, caught in an explosion that leaves her hospitalised and powerless, 'crucified like Jesus Christ' (124). Em'ly, however, gets off lightly. The rest of her family, too drunk to hear the siren, get 'blown ter bits' (134).

The use of a child's perspective is, though, a powerful mode of documentation. As the book progresses, Ben becomes a witness, first to the bombing of the docks, and then to the awe-inspiring conflagration of the John Lewis department store in Oxford Street. The horror of the air-raids is made more disturbing by the child's limited understanding: 'There was nobody in the street near by. Most of the doors were open; and some people were lying flat on the pavement so that Ben had to step over them; but it was quite easy because they never moved' (50). Death is defamiliarised, while horrific injury is chillingly normalised in Em'ly's assertion that the nurses will not notice Ben's secret visit thanks to the squeaking of the burned children who surround them (142). In this context, Ben's understanding of mortality grows ahead of his years, but he remains a fundamentally secure child because of the proximity and stability of his parents. In the end, it is only the cumulative force of repeated jeopardy that forces his mother to let him be evacuated. Bottome makes clear the pain of separation from a secure environment (43), but she also depicts the fear that makes evacuation such a challenge for adults. Visited by the evacuation 'Lady', Mrs Barton expresses her fear that evacuated children will turn up their noses at their original homes: 'Let yer children go away onct–an' they come back strangers!' (26). *London's Pride* works hard to allay such fears, reporting the benefits of the countryside and the kindness of Ben's Cornish foster parents, but this resolution cannot wholly outweigh the considerable and well-grounded fears of Mrs Barton. It is these fears that form the basis of

Doreen (1946), Barbara Noble's subtle and disturbing examination of the class anxieties permeating wartime Britain.

Doreen differs from *London Pride* in its emphasis on mutability. Bottome's novel was not unsympathetic to the working classes, but her depiction of an emergent national community leaves Mrs Barton and her family in a position of dependency. The evacuation 'Lady' becomes 'the Vision' who has opened her house to the wounded, and facilitated the temporary transplantation of the city to the green fields of hope, where weary Londoners are tended by angels of mercy (189–90). *London Pride* cannot and does not look beyond this utopian ideal: it assumes that the normality of a deferential class structure will reassert itself. *Doreen* by contrast challenges this complacency in the ultimate refusal of both Mrs Rawlings and her estranged husband to accept the appropriation of their daughter by the well-meaning middle-class Osbornes. The book works hard to present both sides of an unprecedented emotional crisis emerging directly from the war.

Doreen begins when Mrs Rawlings finally admits to herself that Doreen, her only child and intimate companion, must be evacuated. In confessing this decision to the middle-class Helen Osborne, she instantly loses control of the situation, as Helen offers to send Doreen to live with her childless brother and sister-in-law. The tenacious Mrs Rawlings' fears about evacuation are powerful and prescient, and not least of them is her belief that a 'child could almost forget you in a year' (1946/2005: 2–3). Francie Osborne, meanwhile, is longing for a child. An insecure woman with love to spare, she believes that by making her evacuee happy, she will appease the ghost of her own unhappy childhood (17). Her husband Geoffrey, a solicitor, is a kind man made excessively self-critical through the experience of impotence: his asthma makes him unfit for military service (19–22). Doreen, when first encountered, is a silent child who looks more scared 'of the haven that awaited her than of the bombs she was leaving behind' (23). When the narrative enters the child's consciousness, her mind is a tumult of anxious questions concerning the rules and customs of the new world that awaits her: already compliant, she prepares to assume new levels of self-control (26–7). Nonetheless, Doreen settles successfully into the spacious Osborne household, delighting in a room of her own, conversing with Geoffrey and fitting neatly into Francie's template for a child (48). But Doreen's successful integration is the product of intelligence and effort, and Noble is at pains to resist any suggestion that class barriers can easily be overcome:

> At the end of the first week, the Osbornes congratulated each other on the fact that Doreen had completely settled down – giving half the credit to themselves and half to her. [. . .] Since their standard of living and behaviour was

an unconscious one, it did not occur to them that there could be anything for Doreen to attain. [. . .] They did not remotely suspect the state of tension in which Doreen lived from hour to hour or the watchfulness which lay behind her ready acquiescence. But Doreen watched and imitated and laboured to conform the whole time. (1946/2005: 49)

In the process, exactly that which Mrs Rawlings had feared is coming to pass. Doreen, relieved of the need to protect herself from a harsh environment, is growing in confidence and, inevitably, becoming attached to the people who are able to give her attention and space.

In an excruciating sequence, Mrs Rawlings spends Christmas with the Osbornes, and while Doreen is blissful, the adults spend the time in an agony of self-consciousness regarding the monetary value of gifts, the patterns of meal times and issue of parental authority (81–2). A battle has begun for possession of Doreen that will continue throughout the novel, and Doreen's estranged father makes the conflict explicit by kidnapping his daughter and returning her to London in a blitz. His actions are ill-judged but, Noble suggests, not without insight. He sees Doreen's infatuation with her foster parents, recognising that her newly enhanced horizons threaten his wife's authority and promise disappointment for his daughter. He and his wife find slender common ground in the immutability of the class system, with Mrs Rawlings bleakly concluding, 'She's got to live the life she was born to' (161).

Through this framework, class in the novel comes to approximate a developmental model and one that complicates the process of individuation. With her mother, in working-class Dakers Place, Doreen remains in a state of arrested development. Irrespective of age, she is bonded to her mother and wholly subject to her authority:

Unconsciously, she wanted to relax in the atmosphere of absolute security which Mrs Rawlings radiated for her. Dearly as she loved the Osbornes, their attitude towards her, with its scrupulous regard for her importance as an individual, was subtly more fatiguing than her mother's downright yea and nay. (1946/2005: 174)

This is a position of considerable security, but not one which will permit Doreen to develop into adult agency. Much the same could be said of her class position: where the middle classes, facilitated by financial resources and education, see change, her mother's life of unremitting drudgery has prepared her only to protect what little she has. As a girl in the 1940s, Doreen's situation is exacerbated: escaping class through education is a male fantasy. Yet while the Osbornes have the economic power, it is Mrs Rawlings who has the moral high ground of maternity. She and Geoffrey battle as equals (223), their adult needs obliterating those of Doreen, for whom going back to Dakers Place is 'like re-entering a box'

(229). Mrs Rawlings has triumphed in the battle for her only cherished possession, but she has been unable to recognise her daughter's capacity to hold irreconcilable forces together: to love both her mother and the Osbornes. As a result her victory is hollow. Doreen has seen too much, not only of middle-class possibility, but also of adult behaviour: 'Her child's face, still indeterminate in features, looked curiously shuttered and reserved. And watching her, Mrs Rawlings felt as though a hand had squeezed her heart' (238).

In this superficially simple story, Noble documents the complex cultural fault lines exposed by evacuation. Her focus on the irreconcilable psychological forces at play finds a disturbing counterpart in *A Friendly Hearth* (1946), the actress Norah Baring's non-fictional account of running a hostel in Wales for London evacuees. Baring suggests that not only is the gulf between working-class children and their middle-class carers unbridgeable, but also the gulf between urban Britain (of whatever class) and its rural counterparts. For all the differences dividing Baring from her charges – and these are considerable – she often finds herself more in sympathy with her variously angry, dishonest and dirty evacuees than with the hostile Welsh community that rejects and exploits them (92). A third term in this conflict is the force of bureaucracy: Baring struggles against petty regulations and arbitrary interventions from local authorities, while the evacuees' parents rail against 'The education', a faceless force 'held responsible for most of the small misfortunes that befell them, both in war and peace' (62). In the midst of this are the children themselves whose only weapons against a set of circumstances they do not understand are the abject forces of bodily waste. Traumatised and displaced, the evacuees take revenge through shit and piss (65–6).

The domestic battlegrounds of evacuation narratives convey more than anything the limits of community. The myth of national togetherness collapses into a provisional amalgamation of irreconcilable differences; and what was evident in village England was equally the case in the industrial heartlands.

Things Fall Apart: Work, Boredom and the Limits of Community

The extremes of fatigue brought about by long hours in the workshop and air bombardment could make an individual into another person, a half-conscious creature removed a little way from the things which were happening. All through this night people had been killed, buried, suffocated, made homeless, burnt and trapped beneath buildings, but as soon as the All Clear sounded all those no longer concerned with active civil defence work went to their beds and slept. Tiredness took over. (Holden 1941: 120–1)

In Inez Holden's *Night Shift* (1941) men and women inhabit a subterranean world of unremitting noise and mechanical labour, surviving at the limits of economic security. The workers support the war effort, but refuse the bland comforts of patriotic sentiment. Theirs is a personal war for survival fought against a set of personalised enemies, not all of whom are German. Air raids are the work of 'him', 'a personified god of evil', but 'he' is just a part of the problem:

> Besides this great 'He,' this fire-breathing, bomb-throwing, stinking jack-booted son of sweat there were a variety of smaller enemies called 'they,' only 'they' were much closer, always under foot or just around the corner; a set of empowered rats who built bad houses, muddled the insurance schemes, wilfully ignored the cost of living and were maliciously given over to making life more difficult. (Holden 1941: 108)

The alienating force of industrial labour emerges powerfully from Holden's novel, in which the workers exist only in their factory context, hermetically sealed from the wider world. Here, as in Diana Murray Hill's *Ladies May Now Leave Their Machines* (1944), the enclosed space and the force of physical and mental exhaustion combine to create a dehumanising environment that undermines the dominant wartime myths of community spirit and cooperation. Sara Wasson reads these factory spaces as uncanny manifestations of a repressed industrial past that is 'inimical to life' (2010: 103). Haunted by 'gothic, mechanised ghosts', the novels of Holden and Hill represent the wartime factory as a space of 'marginalization and dark cravings for death' (104). These are undoubtedly bleak books: both writers paint a stark picture of industry in which the propaganda ideal of the 'war effort' has become meaningless, usurped by petty rivalries and the more urgent needs of self-preservation (Hill 1944: 103). Hill's narrator Di observes that workers 'are too tired, or bored, or ill, to think' (104) and this state of numb existence is exacerbated by the brutality of management practice. There is no space for sympathy when bonuses are at stake, while the largely invisible bosses show their contempt for the workers in their cost-cutting cancellation of Christmas festivities (111–12). Holden's later novel *There's No Story There* (1944) paints a similarly grim picture. The workers are infantilised, subject to constant surveillance. There are, though, pockets of resistance in the form of non-compliance and comedy. Hill's frustrated workers play football with components (114), and while management resist demands for equal pay for women, the workers themselves give comprehensive support to the fight (124). Meanwhile, Holden's munitions workers, trapped in their hostel by a snowstorm, refuse the imposition of communal activities, complaining 'we'll be welfared down to nothing if it goes on like it' (1944: 157).

Holden and Hill combine explicit political commentary with innovative prose strategies. Both writers offer uncompromising depictions of gender prejudice, and Holden delineates the pervasive force of anti-Semitism through her depiction of the Jewish foreman Gluckstein (119, 127, 132), yet these issues, and the war itself, emerge through the fragments of unconventional narrative technique. In the aftermath of the raid at the end of *Night Shift*, for example, Holden creates a prose poem from the sounds of the Blitz: 'The penny whistle, the siren wail, airplane hum . . . the stones of a house falling in quickly, talk, ambulance bells, fire-engine bells, breaking glass, patter of shell splinter like fine rain, boots brave-walking along a street' (1941: 119). Holden's staccato list attempts here to capture the sensory dislocations of the Blitz experience, its briskness rendering it a more prosaic version of the monstrous animations that conclude James Hanley's *No Directions*. Here, as the impotent artist Clem rushes out into the Blitz, 'the city rock[s] with outrageous power': 'A great wall collapsing, a door hurling in the air like a demented sail, caught in a wind deluge, a falling girder' (1943/1990: 135). Where Holden focuses on sound, Hanley emphasises the intense visuality of Blitz, cascading image after image that cannot be reconciled, because they make no sense within the customary parameters of vision: 'And always the light sweeping past, as though blown by the great wind, a life lived to see this, a grey city rocking. Not what you felt, you couldn't even think, mind's doors closed up. It was what you saw' (135). Hanley's surreal narrative culminates in a white stallion dragging the artist inexorably closer to the fires of the burning city – an image that has led critics to link the book with apocalyptic late modernism – but the story ends with the quotidian. Just as Holden's unnamed narrator succumbs to the 'final blanket' of fatigue (1941: 126), so Hanley's artist walks, shaking, home to his wife. For both the drama will begin again tomorrow, as 'those people' come back again (Hanley 1943/1990: 99).

The writing of both Blitz and industry, then, invokes a crisis of plot. The workers in the factory and the civilians in the shelter are subject to a process of exhausting, and potentially deadly, repetition with variations. Agency is stripped from the protagonists, whose narrative must endure rather than progress. Writing of Holden and Hill's fiction, Sara Wasson draws attention to a 'lack of narrative coherence' (2010: 102): 'These factory texts yoke the passage of time to an imperative to repeat without change' (102). For Wasson, plot is impossible and the workers are trapped within the confines of a gothic modernity. For Kristin Bluemel, though, a writer such as Holden shifts the parameters of narrative, attempting 'to find plot when others saw random events, see heroes when others saw workers, create stories when others saw no story there' (2004: 134). Both arguments are persuasive: Holden writes into the record the customarily excluded voices of a marginalised working class, but these voices do not form a conventional narrative structure. Rather the books coalesce as 'pure' examples of documentary; not attempting to impose order on chaos, but simply recording it, breaking off abruptly into dissolution, in the case of Hill's alienated women, or death in the case of Holden's *Night Shift*. Holden's novel, like Hanley's, ends with death in the Blitz, and for both writers there is no ceremony to such passing. The body of Hanley's drunken sailor is dragged away by the wardens, while in *Night Shift* a group of bystanders watch the factory burn:

> A part of Braille's building crashed in and at this same moment a bird began to sing. The old lady in black looked at me in amazement. 'Did you hear that bird singing?' There was a second sound of falling stones, the note of the singing bird became more clear. 'That bird is really astonishing,' said the old lady. 'Fancy through all this, too.' (1941: 123)

The conclusion is characteristically muted and shockingly inconsequential. Destruction's ubiquity has robbed it of its power to disturb, and it is only fragments, such as the birdsong, that retain the capacity to intrude upon the war-numbed mind. The narrator falls asleep on the memory of her dead workmates, but their epitaph is prosaic: 'each one of them', she concludes, 'had been worth a second chance' (126). With the collapse of plot and the refusal of rhetoric, comes also the absence of sentiment.

Holden's conception of plot is a radical one – her novels offer glimpses of life rather than linked events or character development – and her work stands in marked contrast to two other factory novels of the long-haul period. J. B. Priestley's *Daylight on Saturday* (1943) and Monica Dickens's *The Fancy* (1943) are documentary hybrids, evoking the monotony of the factory environment, but imposing narrative order through conventional plot structures. Significantly, of all these factory writers only Priestley dwells on the dilemmas of men in authority, representing the burden of leadership through his paternalistic works manager Mr Cheviot. Although Holden's novels feature significant male characters, her emphasis is on the alienation of non-combatants: both men and women in her fiction occupy the 'feminised' subject position common to industrial labour. Priestley's non-combatants, by contrast, are much given to virility: real men, doing men's work in a new industrial technocratic world. Women workers are in evidence, but we see them argued over from above and constituted as a problem because of their essential unsuitability for skilled mechanical labour. In *Daylight on Saturday*, with a few exceptions, older women are Dickensian grotesques providing light relief through their incomprehension of the worlds of war and machinery, while young women are 'creatures', given to trembling like trapped animals or drooping like uprooted flowers (156). But although *Daylight* is significantly different in approach to the novels of Holden and Hill, not least in its inclusion of an optimistic cross-class love story, it nonetheless reiterates the women writers' preoccupation with alienation, fragmentation and boredom (194). *Daylight* is comparatively long, giving time to character development, but this does not create a sense of community or connection; rather, as each chapter enters a different consciousness, Priestley brings the reader to a cumulative realisation of the failure of communication. The gulf between external appearance and anxious interiority is vast, and the characters simply do not understand each other. Secret lives are revealed to the reader alone: the factory community offers no space for the negotiation of inner vulnerability, self-expression or desire. Yet this blow is softened through the reassuring presence of the benign Mr Cheviot and the upwardly mobile working-class engineer Maurice Angleby. In imagining an enlightened meritocracy, Priestley is at his most utopian, constructing a fantasy in which those in authority not only care about the workers, but listen to them too. This is a world in which 'it's all simple and sensible enough when you take a proper look at it' (198), and successful men triumph thanks to the support of women such as Mrs Cheviot, 'a comfortable little woman with no brains at all' (5). Priestley's romance plot works to further such gender reassurance. Angleby falls for the seemingly modern and independent Freda Pinnel – 'a fine, handsome creature' (110) – and proposes a future in which she stands by and helps him (301). She accepts with alacrity, especially once children have been mentioned.

Marriage gets a more prosaic treatment in Monica Dickens' *The Fancy*, which is, of all these novels, the one that comes closest to re-creating the morale-boosting properties of *Millions Like Us*. Through the structure of romance and considerable character-based humour, Dickens redeems the factory by making it a space outside time. The real business of life is conducted elsewhere, and in contrast to Holden and Hill, her characters have home lives that offer at least the potential for restoration. Indeed, the plot of the novel centres as much around rabbit breeding as aircraft manufacture, and with most of the characters' problems emerging from the private rather than the public sphere, the workbench becomes a nurturing micro-community. But *The Fancy*, like

Dickens's earlier documentary account of hospital work, *One Pair of Feet* (1942), is far from rose-tinted in its approach to human relations, gender and workplace dynamics:

> As he came off the track into the Inspection Shop, Edward's eyes went at once to his bench of girls. He was beginning to feel quite possessive about them. They were in his charge, and if the A.I.D. threatened to make trouble for one of their mistakes, Edward would cover up for them and make excuses and even put the blame on himself, if necessary. After all, you had to make allowances for girls. It was not like working with men. Girls had nerves, which were always playing them up. He knew that from Connie. (1943/1964: 78)

Dickens's third person narrative slides seamlessly into free indirect discourse, giving an intimate portrait of Edward at a carefully controlled distance. Edward, trapped in an unhappy marriage and anxious to do well in his newly promoted position, is one of the key figures in the novel, and the strategy through which we come to know him is replicated for other significant characters: Sheila, the middle-class girl who becomes infatuated with a self-centred journalist; Wendy, a woman so withdrawn and vulnerable that Edward comes to think of her as a rabbit; Kitty, the wartime bride, and Dinah, who acts as a benchmark of sanity in her 'common sense' approach to life. This central core of characters forms a typical 'group hero', which is supplemented by succinct portraits of less fully developed but representative characters: a mother who will lose her son; a woman who discovers that she and her husband have nothing in common; and Rachel, a comic embodiment of hyperbolic femininity who '[radiates] sex like a gas-stove radiating heat' (297). As the simile suggests, Rachel's vampishness is hardly seen as a threat to national security. Rather, danger emerges from beyond the factory in the figures of a bad wife, a tyrannical father and a distinctly dodgy estate agent.

The Fancy, then, depicts a wartime culture both reassuringly inclusive and plausibly realistic. Gentle comedy works to diffuse potentially disturbing situations, as does the broadly happy ending. Few characters think in terms of national goals, and the 'enemy' is conspicuously absent. For all that the women have become war workers, this is in essence a domestic novel: and it is here that tension becomes evident, as Dickens presents a telling indictment of the double burden placed on women. These impossible pressures are first articulated by a character known only as 'the pot hat' (52–3), and this comic presentation softens the brutal truth of her complaints about inadequate nursery provision and the logistics of looking after a family while working full time. Yet the novel goes on to reveal unchallenged double standards amongst the central characters: David, the journalist, expects Sheila to jump to his every whim (143–6), and even in the happy companionate marriage of Dinah and Bill, the domestic burden – the business of surviving on rations – falls entirely on the woman (268). Yet while *The Fancy* shows us a world of ingrained sexism, the unfairness of which must be evident even to the most obtuse of readers, the events of the novel suggest that reimagining women's roles is far from straightforward, even in the rupture of wartime. In choosing to 'live in sin' with David, Sheila might be seen to represent a challenge to sexual mores, but her romantic adventure brings her only unhappiness, debt and blackmail. When the estate agent, Dexter Bell, attempts to seduce her, his assault implicitly emerges from her indeterminate state: neither married, nor a virgin, she must inevitably be a whore. Living together outside marriage is not seen as a viable option for an adult middle-class woman, and Sheila must 'grow up' to respect her class and gender position.

A similar ambivalence is evident in the central romance of Edward and Wendy. While the father's death frees Wendy and her mother from bondage, the women emerge from their ordeal as helpless passive figures, rooted in conventional domestic values. The moral failings of Connie, by contrast, are symbolised by her absence of housewifely virtues. Pondering the inadequacy of his marriage, Edward wonders 'Why be married if you had to clean out the bath every time before you used it?' (309), a question which simultaneously invites us to laugh at Edward and understand that Connie has failed in the unquestioned duty of care that comes with marriage. In comparison, the newly liberated Wendy is revealed to be a domestic goddess:

> Wendy had told him only the other day how she had spent the whole week-end doing what she called 'Autumn cleaning'. Spring cleaning was such fun, she said, she didn't see why it should only be enjoyed once a year. (1943/1964: 310)

Arguably, Connie's departure with Dexter Bell is an entirely reasonable response by a woman who wants more from life than rabbits, but the text affords her no sympathy. Slovenly, humourless and equipped with bad teeth, she becomes physically repulsive to Edward, and what began as a reasonably balanced portrait of two people who should never have married, ends as an indictment of the woman who rejects her domestic role.

Postmortem: Arthur Koestler and Storm Jameson

The urge to document an imperilled domesticity was, for some writers, supplemented by an equally pressing need to make sense of the war as a European catastrophe. Pre-eminent amongst the questions raised by the conflict's early years was the collapse of France, and writers as diverse as Arthur Koestler and Storm Jameson anatomised the nation's failures through disturbing portraits of the French character. Koestler's *Scum of the Earth* (1941) is based on bitter personal experience: his imprisonment as an undesirable alien in the months leading up to the German invasion. Koestler, and countless other anti-fascist, Socialist, Communist and Jewish refugees, were arrested and dispatched to the internment camp at Le Vernet, an action by the French government that the writer describes as a gift to the Gestapo: 'Three hundred thousand pounds of democratic flesh, all labelled, alive and only slightly damaged' (1941/2006: 140). The mind-set that labelled the enemies of Fascism the 'scum of the earth', is seen by Koestler as symptomatic of a national 'suicide' (71, 239), a repeated trope within the book that metamorphoses from the figurative to the literal (244). *Scum of the Earth* categorically asserts that the French were complicit in their own downfall: France, as portrayed by Koestler, is complacent, insular, xenophobic and deeply anti-Semitic (48–9, 181, 237). This is a nation that fetishises a nineteenth-century, pre-industrial vision of the land and fears its own working classes more than the threat of German invasion (239); and this national decay is manifest not only in the betrayals of those in power, but within the heart of the bourgeoisie. Time and again, superficially pleasant acquaintances reveal a corrosive conservatism, as in the case of 'nice, motherly Mme. Brassard' and her niece, a pair of patriotic Catholics who turn out to subscribe to the Jewish conspiracy narrative. This betrayal hurts Koestler more than most:

> Sad – liked them so much. That kitchen with the shining pans was real France. Auntie and niece will go Fascist without noticing it. Behind each petty bourgeois idyll that lurking horrid grimace. (1941/2006: 181)

In Koestler's analysis, the French nation is too atrophied to resist a threat it secretly regards as the lesser of two evils, and it garners support for its complicity through the identification of scapegoats. Koestler suggests that the nation's aliens were an easy target for a xenophobia that was but a 'national variation' of German anti-Semitism (90): 'if there were any spontaneous popular feeling left in the apathetic masses of France, it was the feeling of hatred for foreigners' (89).

Scum of the Earth combines the immediacy of an adventure narrative with, in Jenni Calder's words, a 'strongly marked didactic intention' (1968: 75). The book is, simultaneously, both personal and impersonal, rejecting a sensational reality of escape stories, suicide attempts and relationship crises for a more intellectual drama: a story of 'unrequited political love' (Scammell 2009/2010: 200–1). Calder argues that in Koestler's documentary writing 'we are always conscious of his separation from the people and things he describes' (74), a detachment that, in *Scum*, emerges both from his status as a writer, with the contacts – eventually – to escape, and from a distinctive scientific precision in his writing. This clinical approach becomes a self-conscious method of bearing witness: a voice that condemns the 'scientific' rationalism of fascist logic through vicious satiric mimicry. In a world in which 'the measure of what a man can bear [has been] lost' (94), Koestler constructs his own mechanism for calibrating inhumanity:

> In Liberal-Centigrade, Vernet was the zero-point of infamy; measured in Dachau-Fahrenheit it was still 32 degrees above zero. In Vernet beating-up was a daily occurrence; In Dachau it was prolonged until death ensued. In Vernet people were killed for lack of medical attention; in Dachau they were killed on purpose. In Vernet half of the prisoners had to sleep without blankets in 20 degrees of frost; in Dachau they were put in irons and exposed to the frost. (1941/2006: 94)

Koestler's testamentary role did not end with his escape to Britain. Once released from Pentonville prison, 'the most decent jail I have been in so far' (249), his writing brought him to the attention of literary figures such as Cyril Connolly, George Orwell and E. M. Forster. The critical success of *Darkness at Noon* (1940), his devastating critique of Stalinism, ensured the swift publication of *Scum*, which in turn generated praise, contacts and a new level of celebrity (Cesarani 1998/1999: 183–5). Koestler became a contributor to *Horizon* and, in spite of his conscription into the Pioneer Corps, travelled the country lecturing to a British population he found disturbingly ill-informed (Scammell 2009/2010: 205–6). His writing generated controversy and stands, in hindsight, as ahead of its time in its understanding of the 'Nazi enterprise' (Cesarani 1998/1999: 208). His 1943 novel *Arrival and Departure* dealt unambiguously with the mass murder of Jews, but when the section 'Mixed Transport' was published by *Horizon* in October 1943, Koestler found himself accused of 'atrocity propaganda' by Osbert Sitwell and others (Scammell 2009/2010: 229–31). The challenge was vigorously refuted by Koestler, and he was not without support from writers such as Phyllis Bottome. However, the reception of 'Mixed Transport' is indicative of the scepticism with which the British establishment, and beyond it, the public, received news of Nazi atrocities (Piette 1995: 151–2).

In 'The BBC and the Holocaust', Jean Seaton discusses the much-debated questions of what was known, when it was known and by whom, while also addressing the issue of how the unbelievable comes

to be believed. Richard Crossman's response to Buchenwald is significant here: 'We had known in theory that they [the SS] were in favour
of extermination, but until we saw the concentration camps and the
gas chambers we only believed with our brain' (Crossman, quoted in
Seaton 1987: 55). This chasm dividing knowledge from belief is central
to 'On Disbelieving Atrocities', Koestler's considered response to the
accusation of atrocity propaganda. In this short article, first published
in *The New York Times Magazine* in January 1944, Koestler categorises himself as one of the 'screamers' trying to make the world listen
to the facts about the 'the greatest mass-killing in recorded history'
(Koestler 1945/1983: 90). Asking why photographs, books, lectures
and pamphlets have no discernable impact, he initially speculates that
Cassandras such as himself are the only sane figures in a world full of
neurotics unable to face the facts. Further reflection, however, brings
him to the conclusion that, while the 'matter-of-fact unimaginativeness'
upon which Anglo-Saxon cultures pride themselves is temperamentally
ill-suited to the business of absorbing horror (91), the scale of events is
also, quite literally, beyond belief:

> Distance in space and time degrades intensity of awareness. So does magni-
> tude. Seventeen is a figure I know intimately like a friend; fifty billion is just a
> sound. A dog run over by a car upsets our emotional balance and digestion;
> three million Jews killed in Poland cause but a moderate uneasiness. Statistics
> don't bleed; it is the detail which counts. . . . we can only focus on little lumps
> of reality. (Koestler 1945/1983: 92)

Koestler's perceptiveness is evident from the remarkable inadequacy of
responses once news of the extermination camps was definitively broken
to the British public in April 1945. Naomi Mitchison and Frances
Partridge were more articulate than most. Mitchison records an agonised
family debate about the German soul (15 April 1945), while Partridge
felt that the images of liberated camps indicated that 'the world's sanity
had received a fatal blow' (211). However, she goes on to note that for
Mrs C. in the kitchen it was easier to assimilate the individual tragedy
of a German mother's suicide (211–12), and other diarists seemed to
share this inability to absorb the concentration camp revelations. In the
case of George Beardmore, exhaustedly attending the funerals of rocket
attack victims, the news is distanced – a report of a report (26 April
1945; 1984/1986: 193) – while the diarist Vere Hodgson exemplifies
Koestler's distinction between knowledge and understanding. On 20
April she writes 'we are stricken with horror at the awful revelations
from the Concentration Camps' (1971/1999: 580). Three days later the
impossibility of comprehending the camps leaks through in a careless

aside: 'There are no soap flakes. I suppose they are all being sent to swab down those awful Concentration Camps' (23 April 1945; 582).

Koestler, then, had good reason both for his anger about unacknowledged atrocities, and for his earlier indictment of France as a nation that comfortably facilitated Fascism. But not all writers were as convinced of French culpability, nor as pessimistic in their attempts to understand the European predicament. In *Fair Stood the Wind for France*, H. E. Bates presents a martyred nation, symbolised by the virtuous and self-sacrificing 'girl', who restores the wounded to health while taking onto herself 'the agony of all that was happening in the world' (1944/2005: 255). The girl is both suffering pietà and source of hope, symbol of the essential goodness of a pastoral France. Bates's romantic vision is a complete antithesis to Koestler's condemnation, and might be seen as another example of how difficult it was to absorb the complexity of European politics. Such a struggle is painfully in evidence in *Cloudless May* (1943), Storm Jameson's attempt to portray a 'warts and all' vision of France that would somehow reconcile Koestler's anatomy of stagnation with a still potent idealisation of French civilisation. This was not an easy task. Koestler's description of France as a 'country of Bread and Wine, in an environment of Steam and Steel' (1941: 237) fits all too comfortably onto Jameson's morally atrophied landscape. Set in the comfortable Loire town of Seuilly, the novel depicts a corrupt and complicit community. There is an implicit decadence in this France where a defeatist ruling class struggles to suppress the ambition of selfish, brutal peasants, while lusting after ambitious women who – as so often in the literature of the 1940s – cannot see beyond the personal to wider political demands (1943/1945: 289–90). Jameson's France is split along generational and religious fault-lines. Her generals are still fighting the First World War and, like Koestler, she suggests that the nation – irrespective of its archaic defences – was too self-absorbed to resist the Germans. Men scheme for influence, betraying their nation in the hope of winning power over local rivals. The mayor, Labenne, is particularly repellent: a wealthy peasant of grotesque appetites that would put a Roman emperor to shame, he thinks only of securing his land and lineage.

From her account of pervasive anti-Semitism (86–7) to her depiction of an internment camp and its victims (400–1), Jameson covers much of the same territory as Koestler, but the style of her indictment could not be more different. For all the venality of her characters, this is a reasonably sympathetic portrait that seeks to distinguish between a nation betrayed by a decadent elite and a nation rotten to the core. This muted Francophilia is articulated through the virtues of the novel's soldier hero, the ascetic Colonel Rienne (228), who watches in despair as his childhood friend Emile Bergeot fails to mobilise Seuilly for total war (145, 190). Bergeot is an idealist undone by intellectual arrogance and ill-judged desire, his good intentions subsumed by his inability to break free from his ethically-compromised lover, Marguerite de Freppel. Rienne and Marguerite, symbols of public duty and private desire, conduct a battle for Bergeot's soul. Marguerite wins, but her triumph is short-lived: she is killed as the couple flee the advancing Germans. Rienne, however, escapes to England where, rejuvenated, he becomes a symbol of hope and resilience. And fighting alongside him will be a new uncontaminated generation – Bergeot's secretary Lucien and Marguerite's daughter Catherine – who will keep the idea of France alive in exile.

Cloudless May does not make easy reading. Jameson's style is over-explanatory: no motivation is left ambiguous, each dialogue is embedded in symbolism (105). The novel is drenched in a rhetoric of mystic dualisms that sets Nazi bodies against French minds (372) and male intellect against female instinct: or, in the case of the hapless Bergeot, internally manifest in his inability to reconcile public duty with private passion. That Bergeot should suffer in this way is a fatal flaw in his masculinity – an element of selfishness that Rienne describes as 'moral illness' (336) – but in the bigger picture of wartime characterisation, he was far from alone in his failure to negotiate the conflicting demands of passion and war. The construction of idealised masculine and feminine roles, and indeed the gendering of abstract concepts from belonging to betrayal, was a significant feature of wartime rhetoric, and the next chapter will explore the tensions embedded in writers' attempts to figure the desiring body both *as* and *against* war.

Notes

1. Partridge's diary, published as *A Pacifist's War* (1978), traces the conflict from January 1940 to May 1945, providing an eloquent account of the psychological impact of war. Her diary began, though, as a piece of private writing, in contrast to the diaries produced for Mass Observation, which straddle the public/private divide. Mass Observation – founded in 1937 by Tom Harrisson, Humphrey Jennings and Charles Madge – aimed to produce an 'anthropology of ourselves'. The organisation produced questionnaires gauging the public mood, published books, and recruited a national panel of diarists, including the novelist Naomi Mitchison. Writing for the record, some diarists undoubtedly responded to this sense of a semi-official audience (Sheridan 1990: 7–8). Excellent selections are available in Simon Garfield's two collections, *We Are At War* (2005) and *Our Hidden Lives* (2004), and in the earlier collections *Speak for Yourself: A Mass Observation Anthology*

1937–49 (Calder and Sheridan 1984) and *Wartime Women* (Sheridan 1990). Rare access to the thoughts of working-class writers can be found in Margaretta Jolly's anthology of letters *Dear Laughing Motorbyke* (1997).

2. See, for example, Hewison 1977; Piette 1995; Rawlinson 2000; Miller 2009; Wasson 2010; Mellor 2011.

Chapter Three

Desiring

Air-raids are a game for two or more players. (Balchin 1942/2002: 35)

Dorothy Whipple's *They Were Sisters*, published in 1943 and filmed in 1945, extolls the virtues of companionate marriage through its disturbing depiction of desire. While Lucy, the sister at the story's heart, marries late to a man who offers her 'companionable silence' within which to repair herself after an early life blighted by burdensome responsibility (1943/2004: 25), her sisters make radically different choices. Charlotte, the youngest, becomes obsessed with the bullying Geoffrey, abandoning her sisters, her children and eventually herself in a masochistic submission to conventional patriarchal power. Vera, the most beautiful sister, presents a case study of the other side of destructive heteronormative desire. With the power to attract every man, she cares ultimately for none – degenerating into a vulnerable narcissist exposed by the inevitable fading of her looks. Sexual desire, implies Whipple, is not to be trusted, and certainly does not represent a secure foundation for human relationships in peace or war.

Whipple's cautionary tale, while not a lone voice was, nonetheless, nostalgic. As with the later production of Noël Coward's *Brief Encounter* (1945), it acknowledged the force of physical desire while simultaneously rejecting it in favour of stable, rational conventionality. Whipple's fiction is emblematic of the 'conservative modernity' that characterises the interwar period. Hers is a world in which the ideal middle-class relationship is based on equality of esteem within the separate spheres of public and private responsibility (Light 1991: 121–4). Whipple imagines a modern world where women might go to university, and where maternity does not come naturally, but these insights do not form part of a revolutionary agenda. Rather they exist as possibilities subordinate to a dominant ethic of duty. For Whipple's sisters, liberation comes from the head not the heart, while in the case of Coward's

Laura Jesson, the pain of pleasure outweighs the gain. Once it reaches the point of consummation, she cannot enjoy her 'brief encounter', nor imagine extending it. Guilt overrides pleasure, and duty – as embodied in home, husband and children – becomes a safe haven from the threatening forces of desire.

Whipple's sisters are thoroughly modern women, products of the shift in social attitudes that followed the upheaval of the First World War, but their relationship to desire is nonetheless a conservative one that would be radically disrupted by a range of writers attempting to articulate the psycho-sexual impact of total war. For novelists such as Elizabeth Bowen, Henry Green and Mary Renault, the onset of a second world war disturbed such stable understandings of heterosexual relations, cracking open the repressive façade of British manners, to produce a curious and far from homogenous literature of desire.

That writers should negotiate war through a reconfiguration of desire is not entirely surprising. By 1939, British culture had been thoroughly permeated by psychoanalytic ideas, turning concepts such as repression, sublimation, and the Oedipus complex into a common – if debased – currency. The popular press, while sceptical, nonetheless adopted a language of complexes and neuroses, while writers as diverse as Phyllis Bottome, Arthur Koestler, Rex Warner and Virginia Woolf explored the possibilities opened up by the unconscious and its manifestations.[1] While Bottome made an Austrian refugee analyst the protagonist of *Within the Cup* (1943), Koestler submitted the hero of *Arrival and Departure* (1943) to a painful post-traumatic rebirthing. Warner and Woolf, by contrast, explored the conjunction of violence and desire: the fascist allegory of Warner's *The Aerodrome* (1941) is underpinned by an incestuous family drama, while Woolf's *Between the Acts* (1941) emphasises the atavistic violence beneath the surface of civilisation, and the intimate proximity of love and hate. The Oedipal story in particular hangs heavy over the fiction of the 1940s. In Neil Gunn's historical novel *The Silver Darlings* (1941), for example, a young man's coming of age in the emergent herring fisheries of Highland Scotland is figured in terms of conflict with the father and an ambivalent possessiveness towards the mother. Gunn's novel assumes that masculinity is formulated through a decisive break with the maternal: Finn must break away from the home if he is to become a man, but this process is complicated by the Oedipal triangle connecting him to his long-widowed mother Catrine and his surrogate father Roddie. When Roddie marries Catrine, Finn's violent resentment is sublimated into an entrepreneurial vision that marks the achievement of adult masculinity. Finn, possessed now of 'his own croft, his own house, his own boat' enters 'with clear consciousness upon the estate of manhood' (1941/1969: 502), and imagines his rival Roddie emasculated by domesticity (506). Yet Finn's acceptance of the wider patriarchal authority of the community heals the rift between the two, and through heroic labour their relationship becomes a homosocial ideal:

> It was a moment of communion so profound that Finn felt a light-heartedness and exaltation come upon him. This was where Roddie and himself met, in the region of comradeship that lies beyond all the trials of the world. (1941/1969: 513)

In Gunn's world, psychoanalysis gives a complex interiority to unquestioned structures of normative development; but this was just one facet of Freudian influence. Freud's *Three Essays on the Theory of Sexuality* (1905), described by Steven Marcus as fundamental to the 'understanding of how modernity – or the generally recognized modern point of view – came into being' (1984: 2), was first translated into English in 1910. The essays brought with them Freud's incendiary ideas, not only regarding infantile sexuality, but also the precarious nature of 'normal' heterosexual development. Here the 'aberrations' of masochism and fetishism were mapped out alongside the assertion that homosexuality was not a single concrete identity, but rather part of a spectrum of complex possibilities that cannot be separated out from 'the rest of mankind' (Freud, quoted in Marcus 1984: 27–9). 'No healthy person' argued Freud, 'can fail to make some addition that might be called perverse to the normal sexual aim; and the universality of this finding is in itself enough to show how inappropriate it is to use the word perversion as a term of reproach' (Freud 1905/1953: 160).[2]

Whether the ideas of Freud, or the other influential analysts of the interwar period, were accepted or rejected, they remain crucial to understanding the limits within which desire was imagined in the 1940s. This evolving language of psychosexual development was, however, supplemented by another entirely understandable psychological motivation for the lifting of inhibitions. As John Costello has noted, war is a potent aphrodisiac. Drawing on Freud's response to the First World War, Costello argues that 'the connection between violence and eroticism was evident in the collective tendency of a society in wartime to throw off the repressions that civilization has imposed on the human sex drive' (Costello, 1987: 3). With death a likely outcome for servicemen and city-dwellers alike, what was the point of restraint? Life had become newly uncertain, and needed to be lived to the full, even if the residual constraints of a prudish national culture made the comfortable satisfaction of desire somewhat challenging. Pepita and Arthur, the lovers in Elizabeth Bowen's 'Mysterious Kôr', have nowhere to go in a London whose interiors are bursting at the seams and whose exteriors are bleached by the light of a 'remorseless' searchlight moon (1980/1983: 728). Their only refuge in the physical world is Pepita's flat, presided over by the votive force of the virginal Callie, an 'unlit candle' whose desperate adherence to pre-war norms of social propriety ensures both her loneliness and the lovers' separation (735). A similar homelessness besets Gracie and her pilot, the lovers at the centre of Alun Lewis's 'Cold Spell', who find themselves taking refuge in a secluded cottage (1990: 144–5). But Gracie is less confident than Pepita, and her attempt to please by 'confirming the world their association had evoked' ends in tears that are the complex product of the lovers' inequality (147). Divided by class, and the double standard that ensures her innocence and his experience, she freezes into self-loathing. Gracie carries the burden of guilt in this story, becoming mistress to a man married not to a wife, but to his aeroplane and crew: 'Marriage wasn't in his mind. And how could it be when he didn't expect to live?' (147).

Gracie's self-protective withdrawal within a story permeated by frozen images is indicative of the complex gendering of war's disruption of convention. She wants her pilot, and gives herself freely, but must live in the knowledge that his over-riding emotional concern is the homosocial bond with his crew. As with 'Mysterious Kôr', pre-war and wartime are juxtaposed as irreconcilable economies of desire. Indeed, in Bowen's story values are inverted to bestow a curious innocence on sexual desire. At the story's conclusion it is Callie who awakens to a perception of guilt for her naïve belief in romance and her clumsy trespass into the lovers' space.

Nonetheless, these stories expose the social and cultural constraints that delimit the possibilities of expression. In the 1940s, all was not equal in love and war, and the writing of desire inevitably bears the imprint of a powerful set of gendered assumptions. Women were a 'problem', and the ways in which this problem was understood had significant implications for the representation of femininity, masculinity and sexuality. Consequently, the next section examines the anxiety that circulated around women, their roles and their bodies, for the duration of the war and beyond.

Problems with Women: Misogyny, Fear and the Limits of Desire

It seemed that women, having been surplus for twenty years, were suddenly wanted in a hundred different places at once. You couldn't open a newspaper without being told that you were wanted in the Army, the Navy or the Air Force; factory wheels would stop turning unless you rushed into overalls at once; the A.F.S. could quench no fires without you [. . .]

The Suffragettes could have saved themselves a lot of trouble if they had seen this coming. Men's jobs were open to women and trousers were selling like hot cakes in Kensington High Street. (Dickens 1942/1956: 7)

Monica Dickens' *One Pair of Feet*, a comic account of her wartime training as a nurse, opens with a list of career options which are then exposed as far from ideal. The services are rejected for their unflattering uniforms, while the AFS is undone by a lack of fires. A close encounter with a batch of evacuees ruins the WVS, and the Land Army is a dangerous illusion: 'One saw oneself picking apples in a shady hat, or silhouetted against the skyline with a couple of plough horses, but a second look showed one tugging mangel-wurzels out of the frozen ground at five o'clock on a bitter February morning' (1942/1956: 8). Only nursing, aided by a reading of Hemingway's *A Farewell to Arms*, retains its romance – which the book then remorselessly undermines. Nursing, like army life, is revealed to be beset by class divisions, petty regulations, bullying, prejudice and mind-numbing boredom. Yet for all the drawbacks Dickens exposes, the fact remains that the Second World War was a period of unprecedented movement for women: the war effort needed them, and culture suddenly imagined them capable of remarkably 'masculine' activity. Women could be soldiers, sailors and airwomen – admittedly without holding a gun, getting their feet wet or leaving the ground. They could take on traditionally male roles in industry, while 'women's work' became for some a newly dynamic occupation, with nurses seeing active service across the theatres of war. Yet the reality of wartime change was less profound than the bare facts of employment might suggest.

Women's public roles were wholeheartedly endorsed by government. Propaganda posters urged women into employment, while films such as *Millions Like Us* (1943) worked overtime to convince sceptics that life in the factories was a route to health, happiness and romance (see Chapter 2). Yet while women assumed previously unimagined roles in the public sphere, it was taken for granted that they would continue to occupy their traditional place in the home. Never for one moment did British culture imagine that a full-time job in a factory would interfere with women's capacity to cook, clean and queue, while also, of course, keeping themselves in tip-top shape for their returning menfolk. 'Beauty is your duty' trumpeted a range of advertisements, while magazines such as *Women's Own* offered dire warnings to women too exhausted to curl their hair:

Have you thought what it will be like if, after the war, men came home to wives and sweethearts who have let themselves go? If you let go now, you may not get the chance to pull up afterwards. Stay lovely. (Ursula Bloom, *Woman's Own*, 8 February 1941; Waller and Vaughan-Rees 1987: 80)

Embedded in such statements, and the culture from which they emerged is a mode of almost Orwellian doublethink. Margaret Higonnet encapsulates the problem:

[A]lthough wartime propaganda exhorted women to brave unfamiliar work, these appeals were contained within a nationalist and militarist discourse that reinforced patriarchal, organicist notions of gender relations. It stipulated that women's new roles were 'only for the duration' and that wives and mothers must make heroic sacrifices 'for the nation in its time of need.' Propaganda reminded female defense workers that they were not themselves – that is, not 'natural' – but behaving temporarily *like men*. (Higonnet 1987: 7)

This is a profoundly mixed message, and the uncertainty surrounding women's roles was exacerbated by the tendency of propaganda to use women as symbols of betrayal. Fundamental to stereotypes of femininity is the assumption that women struggle with abstract thought. They cannot understand concepts such as patriotism, they think with their hearts not their heads, and are loyal to men not nations. It is, then, at best unwise and at worst actively criminal, to entrust them with any secrets. Posters such as 'The Squander Bug' and 'Keep Mum' (Figures 3.1 and 3.2) suggest women to be both accidental and premeditated liabilities: the real danger embodied in the 'Keep Mum' woman is evident in her bold stare; she knows what she is doing. 'Keep Mum' also indicates that a large part of the problem resides in women's bodies. The *femme fatale* bewitches men, rendering them incapable of judgement. All three services are held in thrall to the potent force of a seductive female body. But the female spy was simply the tip of an iceberg of cultural anxiety, the excessive example that concretised an obsession with the control of women's sexuality. Every bit as dangerous to the nation as the *femme fatale*, was the mundane figure of the 'good-time girl', whose careless pleasure-seeking threatened to undermine the moral fabric of the nation. In her study of citizenship in wartime Britain, Sonya Rose identifies a class-inflected moral battle waged by the press and the church (73). 'Wartime' argues Rose, 'is an especially prime historical moment not only for demarcating the national self from that of the enemy, but also for identifying and excluding those who do not exemplify particular national virtues' (72), and in the 1940s, chief amongst those excluded were liberated young women (73, 79). In their failure to enact the 'sexual restraint and social responsibility' central to the myth

Figure 3.1 'Don't take the Squander Bug when you go shopping!': The dangers of irrational femininity. Image © Imperial War Museums (Art. IWM PST 15457).

of the nation as a quiet, good-humoured collective, these women were perceived as a threat to the body politic. Rose's argument grounds this anxiety in the transitions of the interwar period. She notes an on-going resistance to women's participation in politics and a pervasive 'apprehension that those who were newly enfranchised could not be trusted

Figure 3.2 'Keep Mum – She's Not So Dumb': The dangers of duplicitous femininity. Image © Imperial War Museums (Art. IWM PST 4095).

Figure 3.3 'Hello Boyfriend!': The dangers of female sexuality. Image © Imperial War Museums (Art. IWM PST 0800).

with the political rights of citizenship without instruction and control' (84).

The suggestion that selfishness, or indeed pleasure, is a mode of treachery gives some indication of how difficult it became to separate national and sexual betrayal in wartime. Rose concludes that 'libidinal women were an "internal other" against which the nation was defining itself', and these 'anti-citizens' became scapegoats for a wider range of social ills (92). The eroticised female body designed to cheer up the troops, was equally the diseased body that would kill them. In a powerful chain of association woman moves from vamp, to spy, to whore, to death incarnate (Figure 3.3). The concept of female betrayal embedded in such images is crucial to understanding the sexual tensions of the 1940s, and its paranoid force is exacerbated by the vulnerability of men in wartime. For all the iconic power of the soldier, individual enlisted men were, for the most part, simply small cogs in an alienating military machine, that threatened to bore, bully, maim or kill them. In a seminal essay on what she terms the 'blitz' on women, Susan Gubar identifies a powerful tide of resentment in the male literature that emerged from the Second World War, leading her to conclude that 'the degrading conditions of combat or the impersonality of military procedures and technology paradoxically led [men] to escalate the war between the sexes' (1987: 240).

The territory of desire, then, is riven with paradox. Women have for centuries been figured as symbols of home and hearth: they are the territory for which men fought, a national body to be defended as fiercely as Britain herself. In the fraught context of the 1940s, however, woman's symbolic function as 'home', and her status as possession, sit uncomfortably alongside her new-found economic independence and the suggestion that she represents a moral and political threat to the nation. Add into the mix the oft-repeated message that 'beauty is your duty', and a potentially explosive compound is created. Unsurprisingly, then, the literature of the 1940s was permeated with anxieties about women's roles, loyalties and sexual appetites, and it is this that underpins the astonishing misogyny of the decade's fiction.

Patrick Hamilton's quasi-allegorical 1941 novel *Hangover Square* offers a compelling conflation of death and desire distinguished by its portrayal of one of literature's most unpleasant female characters. Subtitled 'A Story of Darkest Earl's Court', the novel is set in 1939, the tense period between the Munich crisis and the outbreak of the war. Its protagonist, George Harvey Bone, is a kind, plodding and honest man, desperately in love with the seedy *femme fatale*, Netta Longden. Netta is a modern mythical monster who exudes an 'imprisoning field of radiance' (1941/1966: 33) that lures men to their doom, and her powers easily ensnare the doglike devotion of the vulnerable Bone. But kindly George is more complex than he seems. He suffers from a stylised literary version of schizophrenia, and the book is divided between his 'normal' moods and his 'dead' moods, in which his sole preoccupation is the murder of Netta. Unfortunately for George, he is the Hamlet of psychopaths, and it takes him 240 pages of torment and procrastination before he finally kills both Netta and her Fascist lover, Peter; an act, which, like the lancing of a political and sexual boil, coincides exactly with the outbreak of war. The novel is comical and affecting, but also disturbing. It is hard not to empathise with the exploited George, but the account of his travails is filtered through a narrative voice of pervasive misogyny. Netta is grotesque: she is attracted to power, she is beastly to George, she is stupid, greedy and self-serving. Although she looks like something out of Byron's verse, her thoughts 'resemble those of a fish':

> something seen floating in a tank, brooding, self-absorbed, frigid, moving solemnly forward to its object or veering slowly sideways without any fully conscious motivation. [. . .]
>
> Alternatively, she had become like a criminal. Lacking generosity she lacked imagination, and in her impassivity had developed a state of mind which does not look forward and does not look back, does not compare, reason or synthesise, and therefore goes for what it wants in the immediate present, without taking into account those considerations, moral or material, which are taken into account by non-criminal or normally provident members of the community. (1941/1966: 109)

Animal, criminal, outside time and beyond society: this, in Hamilton's novel, is woman. The only redemptive space of the book is the bond between George and his old schoolfriend Johnny, and this privileging of the relationship between men is typical of the period. In a central scene of the book, which promises a redemption almost immediately withdrawn by the return of Bone's dead moods, George finds succour when his company is chosen over that of Netta. He is asked to join a party of successful men who accept him in all his inarticulate strangeness, repairing his damaged masculinity through the assertion of women's expendability: 'they made him welcome, and gave him brandy and liked him, and thought she was a bitch!' (1941/1966: 234). Women, are constructed here as parasites, threatening the healthy homosocial economy, and this sense of danger is not confined to Netta. On Bone's first visit to Brighton he encounters 'a huge outing of violent girls down for the day from the "Lucky Tip" cigarette factory' (124). These screaming women, who look 'boldly, nastily' at the world around them (124), permeate the public spaces of Brighton, their presence on the sea front a 'brazen festival' of misrule (125). Singular or *en masse*, women are an alien force and Hamilton offers no hope of reconciliation between these fundamentally opposed economies.

Women's failure to understand men, the public sphere or the life of the mind – as symbolised by art – is central to a novel less obviously about war, but nonetheless a product of its environment, Joyce Cary's *The Horse's Mouth* (1944). This is the final part of a 'triptych', begun with *Herself Surprised* (1941) and followed by *To Be A Pilgrim* (1942), that tells overlapping stories from three different points of view. Each book is a master-class in unreliable narration. In the first we hear the voice of Sara Monday, a latter-day Moll Flanders who recounts the picaresque narrative of her life in a language of conventional pieties that invokes the forces of god and chance as active agents in her undoing. Cary, in a prefatory note, describes her as an 'essential' woman, and he exploits women's assumed unstable relationship to narrative and history to create a memoir that is entirely built around the domestic. Sara measures time through relationships and desire, not through the events of the public sphere, and the novel seems curiously timeless. Sara's domestic subjectivity is also manifest in the language of the text, which is enriched by a comic metaphoricity of the mundane. Describing a hot June day Sara enthuses that the 'sun was so bright as a new gas-mantle . . . and the sand so bright gold as deep-fried potatoes' (1941/1968: 90). A grey afternoon in London, by contrast, reveals 'a sky like a coal-hole ceiling' and 'roads like cold gravy' (154). In the second volume Sara's sensuous *weltanschauung* is replaced by the paranoid perspective of Tommy Wilcher, a wealthy miser and exhibitionist, who might have married Sara, but preferred to keep her as a mistress. The novel moves erratically through time, tracing Wilcher's life story, and obliquely suggesting his relatives' fight to inherit his property. The book is an acute dissection of possession and belonging, and charts a temporal transition from the Victorian to the modern, but Wilcher is an unpleasant character, whose pious meanderings make the novel hard going. *The Horse's Mouth*, by contrast, is filled with anarchic energy, abandoning religious hypocrisy for a priapic modernity.

The Horse's Mouth is narrated by Gulley Jimson, a dissolute artist addicted to painting but unable to stay within the lines of law or propriety. This Rabelaisian, picaresque fable is not unsympathetic to women: Cary's cast of female characters suffer gross indignities at the hands of men, and the narrative affords them both vigorous speech, and moments of exquisite revenge. The barmaid, Coker, pregnant and abandoned by her lover, curses the world for the misfortune of being born female (146), a refrain that grows in intensity until just before she gives birth:

'if I should have an accident with a bus or a traction engine, don't let anybody send flowers. Send along a pickaxe to bash my head in and make a good job of it. Put me in a sausage machine and can me into cat's meat and write Bitch, second quality, on the lid'. (206)

Coker spends much of the novel trying to recoup money owed her by Jimson, something she hopes to achieve through the sale of his paintings, which to her are a commodity that can be translated into financial security. Like all the text's female characters, she has no comprehension of painting as art: the conceptual and spiritual are completely closed to her, and the book proposes a parallel between women's corporeal suffering and man's artistic frustration. Jimson's problem is that he gets 'big ideas' (8) that lead him to paint enormous canvases or walls rather than commercially viable pictures, and over the course of the novel these Blakean visions are destroyed by the forces of conservative mediocrity. Coker's mother patches the roof with Jimson's 'Fall' (24–5), while the council demolishes his 'Creation' in the very moment of its production (372–3). In *The Horse's Mouth*, men make art and women destroy it, with the notable exception of Sara Monday who simply embodies it. Throughout the book, Jimson's creative lawlessness is paralleled by Sara's anarchic femininity. Like him, she cheats and deceives, retaining her voracious sexual appetite even as she ages into an 'old blancmange' (98). As Jimson's muse, Sara's is the body upon which his success is based, and she is also the only woman to appreciate his art. Her appreciation, though, is wholly narcissistic: she cannot but admire her own reflection (235). Women then are 'spiritual fodder' for the 'prophetic spirit' of man (58), and this mind-body dualism permeates the novel. Arguably Cary's text is characterised by misanthropy rather than misogyny, the book rendered farcical by grotesque characters, hyperbolic narration and absurd events. There is slapstick in Jimson's anarchic outbursts and something of the Punch and Judy show in Sara's capacity, after Jimson has pushed her down the stairs, to announce 'Oh Gulley. I never thought you would murder me' (330). Structurally, this is an appropriate ending: the war between male and female climaxing in an absurd fight over a painting, but it nonetheless makes uncomfortable reading. The final confrontation is narrated with characteristic self-deception ('I gave her a little tap', 330), and this understatement finally forces the reader to confront the absolute egotism of Jimson. Whether his pursuit of art is understood as obsession, vision, or anarchy, the destructiveness it unleashes is monstrous. The novel concludes, then, with both muse and Creation destroyed: an apocalyptic ending that, like *Hangover Square*, is set against the descent of civilisation into the barbarity of war.

However we read Cary's cast of grotesques, he at least accepts that women might take pleasure in their bodies without losing their humanity, which is more than can be said for Somerset Maugham. In *The Razor's Edge* (1944), Maugham exhibits an absolute horror of female desire that cannot be explained by recourse to comedy or archetypal form. The novel is narrated by a fictionalised version of Maugham, who watches as Larry, a young man seeking spiritual enlightenment in the aftermath of the First World War, rejects the trappings of both European and American culture, abandoning trust fund, employment and fiancée in favour of travel, book-learning and Eastern religion. Isabel, the fiancée, is the central female character, and her engagement to Larry collapses when she chooses financial security over unconventional adventure. Her reward for this failure of nerve is to marry a man who loses everything in the Wall Street Crash, but for the most part, she is treated sympathetically, and the Maugham character repeatedly asserts that he finds her a charming companion. That is, until the day when he notices her staring at Larry:

> Something in Isabel's immobility attracted my attention [. . .] Her eyes were fixed on the sinewy wrist with its little golden hairs and on that long, delicate, but powerful hand, and I have never seen on a human countenance such a hungry concupiscence as I saw then on hers. It was a mask of lust. I should never have believed that her beautiful features could assume an expression of such unbridled sensuality. It was animal rather than human. The beauty was stripped from her face; the look upon it made her hideous and frightening. It horribly suggested the bitch in heat and I felt rather sick. (Maugham 1944/2000: 202–3)

In revealing herself a desiring subject, the hitherto sympathetic character of Isabel becomes base and animal. This relegation of women to the non- or sub-human is a repeated trope of the book. If women's sexuality is not clearly deployed in the service of the male, then it becomes threatening and repulsive. Showing a superficially liberal disregard for such conventions as marriage, Maugham conservatively insists on an ethic of subordination so powerful it can redeem even adulterers and prostitutes. So, for example, Suzanne, an artist's model who has a 'career' as a professional muse, is a good woman, not simply a whore, because she provides a service to the men with whom she cohabits. She also understands her status as reward, asserting after Larry has been kind to her that he should ask for 'the return that is his right' (199). Ultimately Suzanne survives through her good business sense: she is a level-headed woman who knows her limitations, and has made a career out of her only asset, her body. Her reward is to be incorporated into bourgeois society by marrying a wealthy industrialist with the clout to rewrite her past. There are moments when Maugham shows a degree of awareness concerning the stereotypes to which he consigns his female characters – for example, when the drug-addicted alcoholic nymphomaniac, Sophie, announces she will not become Mary Magdalen to Larry's Jesus Christ (237) – but for the bulk of the book, he uncritically replicates the mind/body dualism of patriarchal culture. Men search for the absolute. They create, in literature, art or commerce. Women, by contrast, are creatures of instinct, seeking the male who will most adequately answer their financial and physical needs.

The representation of women as animal and instinctual permeates 1940s literature, as does their inability to grasp abstract thought. Examples span the decade: in Graham Greene's *The Ministry of Fear* (1943) the well-meaning heroine Anna enables her treacherous brother to escape, before explaining to the man she loves: 'I don't care a damn about England. I want you to be happy, that's all' (1943/2001: 201), while in George Orwell's *Nineteen Eighty-Four* Winston Smith's co-conspirator Julia is, we are told, only a rebel from the waist down (1949/1989: 163). Yet not all writers of the period confined the writing of desire to a replication of age-old binary oppositions, and a complicating example can be found in the theatre, where Terence Rattigan's *Flare Path* (1942) paradoxically disrupts and confirms the gendered assumptions of the period.

At the centre of Rattigan's enormously successful romance is Patricia Graham, an actress caught between desire for her old lover, Hollywood actor Peter Kyle, and her new husband, boyish RAF Flight Lieutenant Teddy Graham. The play takes place in the residents' lounge of the hotel where the air-force wives live and the aircrew come to relax, and it is into this intense wartime ecosystem, characterised by its own language of slang and understatement, that Peter Kyle comes to reclaim his lost love. As the play progresses, however, it becomes clear that Kyle represents the past. His heroic masculinity is outmoded, and his cultural capital belongs firmly to a time and space outside the conflict. As he begins to tell the initially star-struck Doris a Hollywood anecdote, she cuts him off 'sharply', instantly more concerned by the sound of an approaching aircraft (13). Kyle is 41, and his career is on the verge of decline, but more significant than physical aging is his position outside the new age, and psychology, of war. He has been deracinated by Hollywood and alone with Patricia he confesses his detachment from the conflict:

It's the war, you see. I don't understand it, Pat – you know that – democracy – freedom – rights of man – and all that – I can talk quite glibly about them, but they don't mean anything, not to me. All I know is that my own little private world is going – well, it's gone really – and the rest of the world – the real world – has turned its back on me and left me out, and though I want to get into the circle, I can't. (Rattigan 1953/2011: 57)

Radically, and unusually, Rattigan puts a man in the archetypally feminine position of prioritising private over public, while Patricia will ultimately reject Kyle's demands in favour of her duty to Teddy and, by extension, the war. She comes to this decision after Teddy has confessed his vulnerability, demonstrating both his new modern heroism and his desperate need of comfort. As the diminutive suggests, Teddy is simultaneously boy and man, and in choosing him over Peter, Patricia is reconfigured as both mother and lover. To achieve this, Rattigan moves back into more conventional territory. Patricia will give up her acting career to become a full-time wife: she will join Doris in supporting her man, serving the public cause through private sacrifice.

Rattigan plays throughout with the conceit of performance, comparing Kyle's identity, based on past screen performances, with the new performativity required of Teddy, who must both act the fool for the benefit of his crew, and perform a courage he no longer feels in order to carry a burden of responsibility beyond his 24 years. Patricia meanwhile moves from being outside the language community of the RAF to the role of an acolyte 'learning the old vernacular' (86). In this her subjectivity moves closer to that of Doris, the former barmaid now married to a Polish flyer, Count Skriczevinsky. Doris is an unexpected embodiment of idealised femininity, achieved by becoming one of the boys: she shares their banter, knows their aircraft and maintains an understated dignity in the face both of loss and redemption. Hers is the happy ending, when her beloved Count returns from bailing out, and her behaviour stands as the moral lesson that renders Peter and Patricia's desire unsustainable. Rattigan was criticised for this ending, but defended it staunchly at the time (Rattigan 1953/2011: xxxii–xxxiii); yet it nonetheless speaks significantly to the shifting mood of audiences, and to Rattigan's capacity to gauge this, that in his script for *The Way to the Stars* (1945) – which incorporates aspects of *Flare Path* – there are no such unexpected resurrections. The desperate optimism of the Count's reappearance was a product of a still-uncertain war: by 1945, grief could be acknowledged, even if, significantly, it was articulated through the silence, understatement and bantering displacement that characterise the expression of fear in *Flare Path*.

Rattigan, then, complicates the gendering of duty, but he does so within a framework that keeps desire entirely within the bounds of the social. For writers such as Elizabeth Bowen and Henry Green, by contrast, desire could not be so easily contained, emerging instead as a psychic force of violent intensity that comes to stand metonymically for the inexpressible conflagration of war. Desire, like war, threatens the annihilation of the self, while yet paradoxically offering the possibility of a physical intimacy that stands as the 'real' in a world cut adrift from the normative parameters of life and death.

'Distorted love': Elizabeth Bowen's *The Heat of the Day*

> Within the narrowing of autumn, the impulses of incredulous loneliness died down in her; among them that readiness to quicken which had made her look for her husband in other faces. True, she felt nearer Tom with any man than she did with no man – true love is to be recognized by its aberrations; so shocking can these be, so inexplicable to any other person, that true love is seldom to be recognised at all. (Bowen 1949/1962: 145)

Bowen's description of the relationship between Louie Lewis and her absent, later dead, husband Tom, while aberrant in conventional terms, has a straightforward relationship to loss that makes it a benchmark of logic and loyalty within a novel characterised by 'distorted love' (1949/1962: 142). Louie, yearning for the validation provided by her husband, attempts to replicate the relationship in the absence of the man. It is a form of truth, and the events of *The Heat of the Day* are such as to suggest that any more substantive ideal is impossible. True love, like a stable identity or a straightforward communication is simply not part of Bowen's landscape. In the words of Andrew Bennett and Nicholas Royle, she 'picks up, picks at, undoes assumptions of personal identity, and thus undoes the values of all constructions of the individual, social, political, erotic and ethical on which they rest' (1995: 89). *The Heat of the Day* then becomes 'a story about stories' (Piette 1995: 163) in which truth is subordinate to plausibility. Bowen's characters' lives are founded on lies – falsehoods actively or passively accepted – that have acquired through their persistence a patina of truth.

Within a shifting landscape of phantasmagoric imagery, *The Heat of the Day* tells a story of couples brought together and separated by war. Bowen's couples are odd ones: as Maud Ellmann has shown, they are persistently disrupted by shadowy thirds (2003: 152). Louie's relationship with her husband is haunted first by the lovers she takes to fill the void of his absence, and then by her friendship with the capable Connie, who in turn forms a couple with Tom's photograph to parent his haphazard wife (158). This odd-numbered coupling equally permeates the novel's central narrative of desire: the triangular relationship between Stella Rodney, her lover Robert Kelway and the enigmatic counter-spy

Harrison. Harrison, arriving at the start of the novel, but the middle of the story, tells Stella that Robert is a traitor and that he can withhold this information if Stella will let him replace Robert in her affections. Stella, unsurprisingly, thinks little of this bizarre proposal, but it nonetheless changes everything, shifting her relationship from a state of prelapsarian belief to one of watchful suspicion. The knowledge of Robert's lies becomes a third in their relationship, as Robert confirms when Stella finally confronts him: 'We have not then been really alone together for the last two months. You're two months gone with this' (191). Stella is pregnant with a truth that has been a cancerous presence within the relationship, yet as the book makes clear, the war has made Stella and Robert an odd couple from the outset: 'Their time sat in the third place at their table' (194).

For Bowen, wartime inexorably exposes the subjection of the individual to external forces, and nowhere is this more powerfully felt than in the relationship between Stella and Harrison. As a symbol of an unseen authority that invades the private space of the relationship, Harrison embodies the power of the state, but his authority is fatally compromised by his private desires. Yet the novel persistently refuses to define what it is that Harrison wants so much that he will jeopardise self and nation to acquire it. Stella, trying to explain this enigma to Robert, speculates 'I suppose he wants what he doesn't know' (283), and Stella embodies that unknown. There seems little passion in the mercantile exchange Harrison proposes; rather he seems drawn by a form of minimalist domesticity, and is cheered by the smallest tokens of intimacy: 'this evening when we came in and you changed your shoes everything began to be something like what it could be' (142). Ultimately, though, Harrison is less of a lover than a textual device, an anti-realist *deus ex machina* constructed by Bowen to expose the war's impact on constructions of the private. Indeed, as the narrative self-consciously observes, by 'the rules of fiction, with which life to be credible must comply, he was as a character "impossible"' (140). This impossibility is most profoundly felt at the point of Stella's eventual submission when Harrison, inexplicably, turns her down. Some clues as to Bowen's motivation, if not her characters', might be found in the setting. Stella's offer is made in a restaurant that appears as a distorting mirror of the one in which she first understood her love for Robert: as the final revelation of Harrison's first name – Robert – will show, the spies really are interchangeable. Ironically, at the end of the novel, it is Harrison that Stella desires: he becomes 'the last of Robert' (320), an uncanny status that once again displaces the character from the realm of the knowable. By contrast, for Harrison, it was Robert who made Stella attractive (283) and in his absence the possibility of gratification undoes Harrison's desire, rendering Stella worthless. It is, then, impossible to determine exactly what Harrison sought to achieve through his sexual blackmail, beyond a desire for desire, or a pleasure in planning (321), and Bowen insists upon this uncertainty to the novel's end. Harrison's response to the eventual revelation of Stella's impending marriage to an unknown Brigadier is telling: 'He paused, needing all he had to keep in command his features during their change, their change into the expression of a violent, fundamental relief' (321). The ambiguity here is immense. Is Harrison relieved or is he not? If his features express a *fundamental* relief, why had he needed to keep them in command? Is this relief a 'true' emotion, or merely one of the many unreadable surfaces of Bowen's study in emotional espionage?

Bowen has long been regarded as a clinical observer, her stylistic effects described as Brechtian by a number of critics (Plain 1996: 167–9; Ellman 2003: 152). Intensity, in Bowen, is reserved for the inanimate objects through which the self is constituted: human relations, of whatever sort, remain thus mediated as if suggesting a desire for the security of the concrete (Ellman 2003: 146). When Stella travels to Mount Morris, an old Irish estate unexpectedly willed to her son Roderick, she finds a space alive with personified objects, tangible conductors of the past that resonate within a denuded present: 'she carried the lamp to meet one of its own reflections in a mirror, and, lifting it, studied the romantic face that was still hers. She became for the moment immortal as a portrait' (1949/1962: 173). That the past might be more real than the distorted, war-torn present, and that ghosts might have more substance than the living, is a repeated trope of Bowen's work in the 1940s. In the Preface to *The Demon Lover* she suggests a new intimacy emerging from the proximity of death, 'walls went down; and we felt, if not knew, each other' (1950: 48), and this sentiment is reiterated in uncanny fashion by *The Heat of the Day*: 'The wall between the living and living became less solid as the wall between the living and the dead thinned' (1949/1962: 92). Small wonder, then, that love, like death, is understood through absence. With their first words lost to an explosion, 'the demolition of an entire moment' (96), the relationship between Robert and Stella only comes to signify as such when Stella awakens to an 'apprehension of loss' (97). From that point onwards, the lovers become both habit and habitat, existing alone, '[waiting] to live again till they were together' (99). Yet the intimacy of the relationship and the intensity of the 'deliberately outlandish' plot line (Piette, 1995: 165) are narrated with exactly the 'despairing, hallucinatory clearness' they describe (1949/1962: 93). Bowen does not simply avoid sentimentality, she annihilates it, in the process reducing desire to a detached textual voyeurism. 'Do you know much about love?' asks an incredulous Stella of the blackmailing Harrison, to which he simply replies, 'I've watched quite a lot of it' (43).

In this simultaneous creation and refusal of emotion, it is perhaps significant that Bowen sets the lovers' first meeting in the past. This is the intensity of the Blitz doubly displaced – by Stella's memory and by the gradual construction of the book itself – a process that took most of the decade. This is blitz not as chaos, but as art. Similarly, Stella's investigation of Robert's past works to detach the narrative from intensity and immediacy. Not only does her suspicion regarding Robert's present behaviour remain unvoiced, it is displaced by the much more pressing mystery of his genesis. Placing the lovers together at Holme Dene, Robert's man-eating childhood home, renders their relationship impossible. Robert warns Stella that his mother will refuse to acknowledge her individuality; yet her profound disinterest in both her son's lover and her actual son is countered by the obsessive attempt to inscribe what he should have been. A wall of photos establishes the ideal to which Robert, like his father before him, cannot conform. Robert's room stands as a terrifying manifestation of the performative instability of identity. Attempting to make sense of the space to Stella, Robert asserts that each time he enters the room he is 'hit in the face by the feeling that I don't exist' (117). Even more telling than this sense of obliteration is the claim that each photograph is an 'imitation' moment (118). Judith Butler's suggestion that the subject is compelled, from birth, to enact the gender roles prescribed by culture is made tangible in Robert's flawed performance as the ideal middle-class Englishman. Pointing at the images that attempt to fix him in his role, he observes, 'if to have gone through motions ever since one was born is, as I think now, criminal, here's my criminal record' (118). In this Robert lays the blame for his as yet unacknowledged treachery on the coercive forces of class and gender, and Holme Dene becomes the site of the novel's original sin: the emasculation of Robert's father.

Yet in terms of narrative construction, the trip to Holme Dene is simultaneously an act of detection and a red herring. The discovery of a phallic mother goes some way toward suggesting Robert's pathology, but the change of scene also acts as a delaying tactic in a book that cannot resist the bathetic. *The Heat of the Day* is a novel of interruptions, a comedy of unconsummated desire. Stella is saved from Harrison's initial predatory advances by the telephonic intervention of her son Roderick (44). Prior to this, Harrison's private contemplation of his own desire – his mental masturbation – had been interrupted by

Louie's artless manoeuvring. Louie's story has no logical connection to Stella's: they are simply two narratives that collide with consequences for both women, most significantly when Louie wanders into the restaurant where Harrison and Stella are meeting, cutting into their climactic encounter and becoming an uncomfortable third to their cryptic discussion. Here, for the first time, the women become a couple: two antithetical embodiments of femininity, divided by class, but also by a relationship to the body. Stella's poise and control, the characteristics that have led to her misreading as a *femme fatale*, are juxtaposed against Louie's clumsy corporeality: 'all over herself she gave the impression of twisted stockings' (235). The interruptions permeate the text, building suspense only to confound it with comedy, as when Stella returns from Ireland ready to confront Robert, only to find his sister Ernestine instead. The encounter generates a bizarre conversation about truth and deception that works once more to emphasise the self-consciousness of the book and its refusal of realism.

The most extreme interruption of all, though, is Robert's death – at which point the narrative itself breaks off in a very literal refusal of explanation. Believing himself about to be apprehended, Robert leaves Stella's flat via the roof. Neither Stella nor the reader is witness to his fall and his death generates no emotion. Rather it is immediately overwritten by war: 'That day whose start in darkness covered Robert's fall or leap from the roof had not yet fully broken when news broke: the Allied landings in North Africa' (291). Within his own story, Robert is pushed from the headlines, the bells ringing for battle becoming the novel's only lament for his passing. Emotion, once again, is displaced, this time onto Louie, who becomes a parodic Mrs Dalloway imagining the death of Septimus Smith: finding herself grasping the railings in Stella's street, she is 'struck, pierced' by 'an anguish, striking out of the air' (292), while Stella, in a remarkable assertion of routine, sets off to visit Roderick.

The restraint, bordering on alienation, that characterises relationships in *The Heat of the Day* finds an echo in another novel that refracts the Blitz through an economy of desire, Nigel Balchin's *Darkness Falls from the Air* (1942). This is a book in which two men spend a considerable amount of time debating which one of them has greater right to Marcia, the woman who loves them both. The first person narrator is Bill Sarratt, a man whose distrust of emotions makes him a typical Balchin hero. Marcia's lover Stephen, by contrast, is over-emotional and self-dramatising: a romantic who imagines his relationship with Marcia as something transcendental. Like *The Heat of the Day*, the book is structured through triangular encounters: either Bill and Marcia discuss Stephen, or Stephen and Bill discuss Marcia. In between, Sarratt attempts to negotiate a bureaucratic mire that undermines the self-congratulatory narrative of the people's war. Yet although its plot has all the ingredients for melodrama, *Darkness Falls from the Air* is a remarkably cool affair. Events are filtered through Sarratt's almost pathological detachment, creating brittle dialogues full of knowing cynicism in which the married couple reveal their modernity through their capacity to discuss her infidelity (61). In this sense the book is about a wounded hero and his remarkable phallic self-control. In comparison with Sarratt's restraint, Stephen is depicted as emotionally weak: indeed, after Marcia's death while working in an East End shelter, Bill lies to protect him, assuring him that Marcia did not suffer. The feminisation of Stephen is integral to Bill's self-worth: he makes sense of his wife's attraction to another man by reinscribing that man as subordinate. Stephen is not a man but a child, an association Sarratt makes explicit in an unusually overheated exchange:

> If she'd had any proper children you wouldn't have meant a thing. Marcia is nuts on lame dogs, crying children and binding up wounds. She also wanted to go on the tiles to see what it was like. Now she's got a nice lot of dogs, children and wounds down in Aldgate, and she's seen what the tiles are like, and that's that. (168)

Stereotypical gender assumptions here enable Sarratt to exculpate his wife, whose war work is reconstructed as hormonal displacement, and defuse the threat embodied by her lover; and indeed the text itself does not set out to condemn Marcia. Rather she is constructed in accordance with the archetype of the 1940s: entirely at the whim of her emotions and unable to construct a rational response to the conflicting demands of the two men. 'Women don't care a cuss about principles', argues Sarratt. 'They only care about people' (76).

The detachment through which Sarratt controls his personal problems extends to public crises. The book opens at the end of the phoney war, briefly sketched as a state of frustrated decadence in which danger has been rendered ridiculous; as Marcia notes, 'I keep having the last dinner I'm going to have' (10). Consequently, when the air-raids arrive they are greeted as entertainment. Mark Rawlinson suggests that Bill and Marcia 'cast themselves as tourists in the Blitz' (2000: 93): rich enough to buy safety and thus divorced from the implications of community and its loss. But Sarratt's narrative is more panoptical than this suggests, and while the lovers might be disturbingly self-absorbed, the first person voice coldly records a disturbing vision of London under fire. Balchin's book is sharply critical of complacent assumptions regarding the war: Sarratt, as a civil servant, spends his working hours fighting procrastination and self-interest (142); surging crowds ignore the wounded in their midst (100), and the wealthy congregate in the 'safest place in London' (159). In its depiction of Sarratt's public life, the book becomes a bleak portrait of one man's attempt to make a difference in a nation suffocating under stagnant leadership: a downbeat western, as reimagined by Whitehall. Bill Sarratt, the one good man, sticks to his principles and fights for the good of the community. He ends the novel in both public and private defeat, his scheme rejected and his wife dead. Yet the solitary hero endures, and the novel's final scene verges on the absurd as Bill, desolate and alone, rises from his torpor to drop a sandbag on an incendiary.

Balchin's novel, like Bowen's, refuses tragedy, and resists the emotional pyrotechnics threatening the self-contained masculine subject. Henry Green, by contrast, has no qualms about exposing the erotic currency that Balchin works so hard to defuse. Yet, although the two books differ profoundly in terms of style, plot and voice, they speak to similar anxieties about the construction of masculinity, and the central characters of *Caught* (1943) will find themselves disturbingly unmanned by the collision of desire and war.

'A daze of giving': Henry Green's *Caught*

> This was a time when girls, taken out to night clubs by men in uniform, if he was a pilot she died in his arms that would soon, so she thought, be dead. In the hard idiom of the drum these women seemed already given up to the male in uniform so soon to go away, these girls, as they felt so soon to be killed themselves, so little time left, moth deathly gay, in a daze of giving. (Green 1943/2001: 46)

'I can't help feeling that each moment may be my last, and as the opposite of death is life, I think I shall get seduced by Rupert tomorrow.' In this almost farcical juxtaposition of eros and thanatos Joan Wyndham bathetically encapsulates the erotic charge of the Blitz (1985/2001: 143–4). Her reduction of experience to a choice between bombing and seduction is naïvely articulated, but it nonetheless speaks eloquently to the logic of wartime desire, and absurdly summarises the web of erotic displacements that structure *Caught*. In this claustrophobic account of a fire station in the phoney war and the Blitz, bombing and seduction become synonymous. As one of the characters succinctly suggests, it is all about hitting the target: 'war, she thought, was sex' (1943/2001: 119).

In *The Writing of Anxiety*, Lyndsey Stonebridge argues that *Caught* 'gives poetic form and shape to the trauma, not of the told, but of the telling' (2007: 59), and this narrative self-consciousness is fundamental to a novel that constructs its supposed subject, the Blitz, as a temporal absence. *Caught* describes a period from the pre-war influx of Auxiliary Fire Service volunteers to the height of the London Blitz, but at no point does it narrate events from what might be termed the 'the real kernel of things' (Sansom 1944: 138). Rather, the conflagration, and the question of how individuals would respond to the 'test' of war, is narrated in anticipation or through memory. The fire is thus circumnavigated, and the anxious postponement of this public event is paralleled by the book's simultaneous deflection of a private trauma: the moment at which the lives of the two central characters first, catastrophically, intertwine. Middle-class, affluent Auxiliary Fireman Roe and working class, war-promoted Sub-Officer Pye first encounter each other before the war, when Pye's unhappy sister abducts Roe's son, Christopher. This incident is itself predicated upon unhealed wounds: the sister has been trauma-tised by a past sexual encounter, while Christopher has recently lost his mother. The boy is returned unharmed, but Pye's sister is sectioned. Pye's resentment of this injustice will haunt him throughout the text and render him fatally self-conscious in the presence of Roe who, by sheer mischance, is sent to Pye's station.

The narrative of the abduction begins the book, and forms the origi-nal 'sin' that will complicate the interpersonal dynamics, rumours and gossip of the text. This private narrative, told in fragments – disjointed leaps across shifting points of view designated by a welter of parenthe-ses – will find its parallel in the public spectacle of war, the attempted description of which concludes the book. In an uncanny re-enactment of narrative difficulty, Roe attempts to recount his experience of the Blitz to his sister-in-law, Dy. The parentheses – absent since the opening sections – return, complicating the process of Roe's narration and chal-lenging the veracity of his memory. He cannot find the words to convey the unreality of 'real' war, but the urge to speak is powerful and Dy, for all her failure to engage, grasps its necessity. Significantly, Roe's trau-matic speech ends with the memory – and defence – of Pye, bringing the book full circle, reinstating the private and concluding the unacknowl-edged mourning process for his wife, which has been bizarrely triangu-lated through his relationship with the Fire Service. His final words to Christopher, telling the child to leave him alone, mark the end of the sentimentalising process that had attempted to replace the lost object – his wife – with an ideal of paternity. These final words also represent the formation of an appropriately masculine carapace that covers the different wound of war.

The style of *Caught* makes the telling of this story almost wilfully

oblique, and this opacity is appropriate to a novel that is also fundamentally concerned with mis-communication. Throughout, utterances
miss their mark: nothing is ever correctly heard or understood. In the
case of Arthur Piper, the leaking ship at the centre of much of the novel's
inaccurate gossip, it is a matter of thoughtlessly repeating the last thing
said to him: a habit that causes disaster for Pye. More painfully, Pye is
incapable of expressing himself clearly, a combination of class anxiety
and pride making his speech needlessly circumlocutory. Considerately,
he offers to help the cook, Mary Howells, in the face of her family crisis,
but his good intentions backfire: 'Unfortunately for him she was too
upset to understand. If he had said straight out he would let her have a
paid holiday she would have understood' (81). Mary refuses his offer,
and Pye feels slighted, his authority undermined: two small incidents in
an incremental chain of events which will culminate in his suicide, an
event which might equally be described as death by mis-communication.
These scenes of misunderstanding are supplemented by passages of
memory that merge into the present of the text. There is little concrete
for the reader to hold onto beyond the occasional interventions of an
omniscient narrator (40, 45, 131) and the striking presence of the female
body. The contrast between a hazy psychic uncertainty and a concrete
corporeality is in part attributable to the dream state of the phoney
war within which the bulk of the novel is set. The 'Great Bore War', as
Evelyn Waugh dubbed the period in *Put Out More Flags* (1942), created
an impasse: a period of suspended animation in which an expected
catastrophe failed to materialise. Within this awful lacuna, the men of
the London Fire Service were 'caught', deprived of agency and eternally
waiting, unable to justify their status as heroes. The prospect of war
interpellated them as men: the first line of defence against the expected
cataclysm (47). The failure of war to materialise in turn emasculates
them (155), a conceptual unmanning anticipated in Green's fable by the
absurdity of the station's first call out: a shambolic encounter which sees
the firemen charging into the wrong house while the fire is extinguished
by 'one old lady on her ownsome' (79). In the absence of jeopardy,
flagging masculinity predictably turns to women for self-affirmation,
capitalising on the 'daze of giving' unleashed by the expectation of
apocalypse (46).

Thus it is that sex replaces death in this novel of the Blitz, and
becomes the sole anchoring reality of an unreal war. The ghostly bodies
of the past, Roe's wife and Pye's sister, cohabit with the tangible desiring bodies of the present, described – as so often in Green's work – with
a disturbing, visceral intensity. For example, Ilse, the Swedish woman
who has 'coldly begun to go to bed' with fireman Shiner Wright, is

described lying naked 'like a worm with a thin skeleton, back from a window, pallid, rasher thin' (142), while Richard's hands embracing Hilly are 'like two owls in daylight over the hills, moors, and wooded valleys, over the fat white winter of her body' (116). Hilly is a WAF with whom Roe begins a relationship that will be integral to the resolution of his mourning process, but in the context of the novel's dense textuality, it is worth noting the way in which their sexual encounter is formulated:

> What he had now, and had only held before when drunk, was so much to his contentment that he wanted nothing more. . . . He had no further questions. He had the certainty of her body in his arms. (Green 1943/2001: 117–18)

In a book of opulent colours and evasive exchanges, this is an unusually clear and definitive piece of writing that stands as a still point in the midst of chaos. It suggests the possibility of resolution and understanding, a possibility that the context of the passage immediately undoes. This paragraph sits embedded between an account of Mary Howell's wishful thinking and the spectacle of Pye, as uncanny other to Roe, sitting with his girlfriend Prudence 'in the half dark of that night club Richard had taken Hilly' (118). Pye's evening, like that of Roe before him, will end in sex, but it is the sex of prostitution bought by a combination of money Pye can ill afford and the Scheherazade-like recounting of 'such excitements as had come his way on peacetime fires' (118). The bathos of Green's juxtapositions echo an earlier image from the novel. In one of the text's flash-forwards to the Blitz, Roe enters a shelter to find a soldier and a girl obliviously locked in an embrace: 'man and girl were motionless, forgotten' (95). The couple are out of time, sex supplanting the threat of death, a spectacle that provides voyeuristic pleasure to the fireman Chopper who returns 'almost with reverence' as if from 'seeing a Prince and a Princess'. As with Richard's still moment of certainty above, Green cannot let such redemptive romanticism stand. The illusion collapses as the soldier totters out drunk: 'Would you boys like to 'ave a whip round, see, to raise me a shilling so I can 'ave another go?' (96–7).

Sara Wasson argues that Pye and Roe are variously captivated and tormented by hallucinatory women (2010: 46). Roe's lost wife haunts him, a tangible presence he tries desperately to preserve: 'He could not keep his hands off her in memory' (30), while Pye is destroyed by the traumatic recall of what might or might not have been an incestuous encounter with his sister (38). This repressed memory disrupts his consciousness with Oedipal force, but such psychic damage cannot be viewed outside the constraints of class, and the text contains a crucial third haunting: that of Pye by his class 'other', Roe. The novel remorselessly connects the two men. War brings Roe out of his class and into the fire station; it simultaneously elevates Pye out of his comfort zone and into authority. As has been noted by a number of critics, the two men are linked by their names: Pye and Roe forming two parts of a single, incendiary whole. In a Freudian reading of the text, Stonebridge suggests that the two characters exemplify opposing responses to trauma:

> Roe, the anxious fetishist, supplements the thought of death with a kind of compulsive citation of literary and painterly rose-coloured images that turn anxiety into desiring memory. Where Roe recollects pictures in order to collect himself, his anxious alter-ego, Pye, is subject to traumatic memory images which shatter meaning and identity by bringing desire and anxiety together. (Stonebridge 2007: 65)

Implicitly, then, Roe's survival depends on Pye's fragmentation. Certainly, they seem locked in an unholy symbiosis; and while Roe ends the novel suffering from war-induced nervous debility, Pye ends it with his head in a gas oven. This is a curiously gendered ending for the two men. Although 'blown up', war has made a man of the middle-class Roe, while the working-class Pye has been reduced to a peculiarly domestic demise. The past histories of the two men are not sufficient to explain this extreme disjuncture: attention must also be paid to the 'present' women of the text and their role in the constitution of the male ego.

Providing Pye's epitaph at the end of the novel, Roe concludes that 'it was sex finished him off' (196). Alongside the traumatic memory of his sister, Pye is caught in a contemporary embrace: he becomes addicted to the uniform fetishist, Prudence. This is a taste he can ill afford and his attraction is rooted in a class aspiration he outwardly disavows: 'He coveted her fingers because they had not worked' (121). He aspires to possess a symbol of what Roe, an auxiliary amongst the regulars, has as his birthright. Interwoven here are the conflicting forces of security and risk, literally embodied in the text by the figures of Hilly and Prudence. In Hilly, Roe gains a life raft denied to Pye. He does not just have sex with her, he also uses her therapeutically as a means of self-constitution. As part of his mourning process, he constructs a self-preserving nostalgia and an idealised image of his past life (91). Pye, by contrast, moves ever closer to the chasm of madness provoked by having no fixed referents in past or present. Pye's disorientation is rooted in the indeterminate incest dilemma, and the novel suggests a shared shame in the description of Pye's visit to his sister: he was, we are told, 'elated at his release from the asylum' (142). By the end of the novel Pye is wandering a moonlit London suffering 'a fit of rememberin' back' (167), an echo of Freud that clearly situates him as hysteric, but the events that drive him out into the moonlight also posit him as castrated (Gay 1989/1995: 598). Like the fireman earlier described as having his words 'scissored . . . off his tongue' (25) by a woman's legs, Pye is cut adrift by Prudence's rejection. The fate of the two men is thus linked to the stereotypes of female embodiment: Hilly, maternal and pragmatic, nurtures and restores Roe; Prudence, promiscuous and phallic, becomes the final female body in the destruction of Pye by his libido.

Green had been convinced that he would not survive the war, writing his memoir *Pack My Bag* in order to 'put down what comes to mind before one is killed' (1940/2000: 1). He was not alone in his pessimism, but as the war progressed people acclimatised and acquired a dual subjectivity in which death was simultaneously acknowledged and denied. Angus Calder's observation that a 'sensible fatalism made risks in pursuit of pleasure acceptable' (1969/1992: 177) obviously refers to the physical threat faced by cinema and theatre audiences, but it might equally be applied to writers. Not only did many make light of the danger, they also utilised the conflict as a means of textual liberation.

'Mild anarchy': Queer Possibilities and the Farce of War

> the country was tired of regulations and regimentation, and there was a mild anarchy in the air. In a sense our comedies were a reflection of this mood . . . a safety valve for our more anti-social impulses. (Balcon 1969: 159)

Michael Balcon's phrase was coined to describe the carnivalesque spirit of the postwar Ealing comedies, but it might equally be applied to the licensed mayhem of much wartime theatre, and to a number of fictions that resisted the comforts of romance. Desire in the 1940s was not confined to the apocalyptic union of sex and death, and indeed, in a number of theatrical productions it became a subject to be treated with a *sang-froid* reminiscent of the 1920s. Although the arrival of war had initially brought about a shutting down of possibilities – cinemas and theatres closed, radio programmes oscillated between the sepulchral and the mindless (Hewison 1977/1988: 9–12) – as the conflict progressed it became clear that more rather than less distraction would be needed. With the notable exception of *Flare Path*, and Mary Hayley Bell's thriller *Men in Shadow* (1942), war plays did not prove popular. Rather, the biggest theatrical successes of the war years were comedies, and these were made all the more anarchic by the circumstances of their performance. Dan Rebellato quotes Terence Rattigan's memories of wartime theatre:

At first it was the little blitzes . . . they *were* very, very noisy. The poor actors would have to shout their lines against the din, and the audience would laugh delightedly – not at the lines, which they couldn't hear anyway – but at the spectacle of the actors' purple faces, as they desperately tried to make their subtle comedy points by dint of yelling their lungs out. (Rattigan 1953/2011: xxxiv)

The conventional relationship between performer, writer and audience is here confounded. The play becomes something other than intended; it is not an opportunity for empathy and engagement, but a self-conscious attempt to proceed as normal in patently abnormal conditions. The audience's complicity is also a critical distance: they laugh at the hyperbolic performance, not the integrity of what is being performed. Going to the theatre becomes a shared act of bravado at the same time as it represents an escape from the boredom of war, creating an excess – specific to the time and not now accessible – in the contract between performer and spectator.

These exceptional circumstances undoubtedly shaped what was possible for writers and what audiences enjoyed. As noted above, plays about the war were not popular, and the mood of the time is more accurately captured by one of the most successful productions of the decade: Terence Rattigan's *While the Sun Shines*. This energetic farce, written in three weeks and first performed on 24 December 1943, ran at the Globe for 1,154 performances, surviving doodlebug raids and the total destruction of the next-door Queens theatre. *While the Sun Shines* plays the war for laughs, treating it as a space of liberation in which nations and classes are thrown together with chaotic consequences. It is also an engagingly queer play, opening with a teasing homoerotic reinscription of heterosexual farce. The play begins with two men in a bed, albeit off stage, an event made all the more absurd by the Wildean negotiation of the discovery. Lord Harpenden's butler Horton beats a hasty retreat from the bedroom, thinking he has encountered his employer's mistress on the eve of his Lordship's wedding. Lord Harpenden insists Horton return, look again and apologise, which he does, observing 'Funny, it looked just like Miss Crum' (2). This double misrecognition receives its punchline a page later when the strapping young American Lieutenant Mulvaney appears, semi-naked, at the bedroom door. From the outset, heterosexual and homosexual desire seem scarcely distinguishable – an impression heightened by Mulvaney's drunken conviction that Harpenden was his girl Dulcie (5). This confusion is revisited in Act II when it becomes clear that the men will be sharing a bed again:

HARPENDEN (*calling through door*). Use the side nearest the window. And don't take up all the bed, like you did last night. I spent most of the night squashed against the wall, struggling for breath.
(MULVANEY'S *head appears at the door.*)
MULVANEY. Last night I thought you were Dulcie.
HARPENDEN. Well, tonight you would oblige me by thinking I'm Hitler. (38)

The absent presence of the bedroom is a constant throughout the play, and by Act III it is playing host to three men: Harpenden, Mulvaney and the French Lieutenant Colbert, brought together, in classic farce style, through mistaken identities and competing desires.

Yet what makes the play so effective is not its timeless structure, but its contemporary bite. The wealthy Lord Harpenden is due to marry Lady Elizabeth Randall, daughter of the impecunious and randy Duke of Ayr and Stirling. Lord Harpenden, a man of 'rather frail' appearance, is a singularly inept sailor incapable of getting a commission. His titled fiancée is in the WAAFs and has just been demoted from sergeant to corporal after leaving the Station Defence plans in the toilet (16). Neither seem born to rule – indeed, the play is littered with references to the forthcoming revolution (57, 85) – and both embody a peculiarly British mode of desire, summed up by Elizabeth's eventual conclusion that 'white-hot burning thingummy is a mistake' (85). The lovers' peaceful progress to matrimony is disrupted, however, by the intervention of specifically national outsiders. While Harpenden rescues Mulvaney and offers him the company of his former mistress, the self-confessed 'trollop' Mabel Crum (83), Elizabeth confesses her innocence in love to the courtly Frenchman, Lieutenant Colbert, before offering him use of her fiancé's bed. The scene is set for the queering – the rendering self-conscious, and in this case absurd – of what might be termed national sexualities. Colbert and Mulvaney compete for Elizabeth, bringing all the weight of their resources – physicality, alcohol, passion and the language of love – to bear on the beleaguered English maiden. That Mulvaney begins by mistaking Elizabeth for Mabel, only reiterates and renders comic the unreadability of bodies that proved so lethal for fireman Pye. Yet ultimately Elizabeth rejects the hyperbolic sexualities of America and France in favour of the prospect of mutual extinction with the 'swooning lily' Harpenden (44, 85). In terms of gender and nation, order is restored. The only threat remaining is the incursion of working-class femininity into the body politic, and Mabel's fate acts as a pertinent reminder of the limits of imaginative possibility. Harpenden proposes, but she rejects him, an act that ensures she remains a sympathetic character, a tart with a heart who will not abuse the trust of a man 'too easy to cheat' (83). It also, of course, ensures her exclusion. Mabel remains outside conventional structures of respectability, and legitimacy remains the prerogative of a polite and asexual Britishness.

One of the few plays to enjoy even greater wartime success than *While the Sun Shines* was Noël Coward's *Blithe Spirit*. When the play opened in July 1941, Coward reported that the 'socially impeccable' audience 'had to walk across planks laid over the rubble caused by a recent air raid to see a light comedy about death' (Coward 1954: 205); or, to be more precise, a comedy in which death proves no impediment to jealousy, adultery and murderous desires. At the heart of *Blithe Spirit* is the battle fought over Charles Condomine by his current wife Ruth and his former wife Elvira – inadvertently recalled from the 'other side' by the shambolic psychic powers of Madame Arcati. Coward's comedy emerges from the juxtaposition of the supernatural and the quotidian: Elvira's resurrection is less a psychic phenomenon than a social embarrassment; she is an uninvited, adulterous house-guest with homicidal intentions. Aside from making trouble between husband and wife, Elvira plans to reclaim Charles by killing him, but her plan backfires, and it is Ruth who joins her in limbo. Charles, whose short romantic attention span had been evident in this pleasure at seeing Elvira again, is now conveniently free, and the play concludes with his delight at having thwarted all the demanding women in his life.

Coward's choice of subject matter was vindicated by the play's success. *Blithe Spirit* ran for 1,997 performances, finally closing in March 1946. The play was perfectly suited to the mood of the time, not only in its nonchalant approach to death, but also in its representation of women. Philip Hoare notes that the play has a touch of misogyny unusual in Coward's work (1995: 320), and indeed, Charles' final triumph leaves his two dead wives trapped in a perverse domestic haunting. As ever, man is granted agency, while women remain confined to the home; that the female ghosts want to kill Charles hardly seems to mitigate the imbalance. This, then, is a violent boundary-crossing desire appropriate to wartime; but for all its venom, it is far from melodramatic. Its tone, typical of the cynical banter of Coward's earlier work, resolutely refuses emotional intensity. As Ruth observes of her rival, it's all about style: 'If, since her untimely arrival here the other evening, she had shown the slightest sign of good manners, the slightest sign of breeding, I might have felt differently towards her' (Coward, 1941/1999: 70). In adultery, as in war, nothing is more important than keeping up appearances.

Fiction writers also made light of love, cynically re-evaluating the merits of desire. In Mollie Panter-Downes's 'The Hunger of Miss

Burton', the eponymous schoolteacher is tormented by her remorseless appetite:

> No more erotic visions of unknown or (even more embarrassing) known males flitted disturbingly through Miss Burton's slumbers. Instead, they were punctuated with good blowouts of dream food which never had any taste, which melted tantalisingly into the slow return of the chilly room and the school bell clamorously ringing. (1999: 123)

No food can satisfy her, and her life has become nothing more than a weary trudge from one inadequate meal to the next. Yet mysteriously, when her colleague's engagement to a Canadian soldier breaks down, Miss Burton's stomach experiences an epiphany: 'she felt a sense of utter, wonderful repletion, as though she had just had a satisfying meal that would last a long time' (130). The implication that love is not all it's cracked up to be, indeed, even borders on the grotesque, emerges strongly from Patrick Hamilton's *The Slaves of Solitude*. Here, the supposedly irresistible appeal of the GI is comically configured as the 'Lieutenant and the laundry', a future to which the novel's protagonist, Miss Roach, might have aspired if she had not, at heart, rather preferred peace and quiet, and if the Lieutenant had not been a serial seducer of women (1947/2006: 275–7). The disappointment occasioned by the Lieutenant is as nothing, though, to the humiliation Miss Roach suffers at the hands of the bully Mr Thwaites, a 'lifelong trampler through the emotions of others' (15), who makes increasingly vicious play on her unmarried – and therefore presumptively frustrated – status (237, 268). He is joined in his sadistic pleasure by Miss Roach's former friend, Vicki Kugelmann, who 'exquisitely Nazi' (176) in her worship of power, recognises Thwaites's dominance and joins him. Unlike Netta Longden, Miss Roach is a complex character – self-contained, intelligent – a woman not obviously resentful at her position outside the heterosexual matrix. She has a satisfying job, and a kind employer, and is genuinely liked by the other residents (109). She too needs to be liberated by war, not into desire or uninhibited emotion, but rather into self-determination, privacy, the integrity of the self. Leaving the Rosamund Tearooms and enjoying her understated triumph over Vicki (306), she finds her freedom not through a man, but through escape from a crushing economy of normative expectations. Finally free of Thwaites's bullying and of the guilty suspicion that she might have contributed to his death, she experiences 'that divine serenity of happiness which only relief, as opposed to mere joy or pleasure, can bring' (301). Returning to London, returning to war, Miss Roach, although still the slave of solitude, embraces life in all its danger.

The queer possibilities opened up in these stories of *schadenfreude* and heterosexual discontent remain just that – moments of instability, the gaps in which the 'naturalness' of heterosexuality is exposed – fleeting suggestions that desire is more complex than the straightgeist might suggest. For the most part, lesbian and homosexual desire in the 1940s could only be inscribed indirectly, or take place in the margins, as demonstrated by Arthur Koestler's *Arrival and Departure* (1943). Only at the end of the novel are we told that two women, Odette and Sonia, are involved in a relationship. The protagonist's response is a 'faint physical repulsion' (1943/1999: 164) as he imagines Odette, the woman he desired, 'drowned in the carnivorous flower's embrace' (165). A notable exception to this marginalisation, though, is provided by Mary Renault's *The Friendly Young Ladies* (1944), in which queer possibility is transformed into an affirmation of lesbian desire, and a damning indictment of the prescriptive forces of psychoanalysis and normative heterosexuality.

Undoing Gender: At home with *The Friendly Young Ladies*

The Friendly Young Ladies, my third [book], was written in the pauses of full-time hospital nursing. [. . .] I was seeing again terribly ill and dying and bereaved people [. . .] Looking around at the lot of these fellow creatures, I thought it becoming in people whose only problem was a slight deviation of the sex urge – not necessarily an unmixed tribulation – to refrain from needless bellyaching and fuss. (Renault 1944/1984: 281–2)

Despite the protestations of its author, the achievement of *The Friendly Young Ladies* (1944) should not be underestimated. Normalising difference was a balancing act not easily achieved in an age when the censorship of explicit sexual content was rigorous and homosexuality was variously criminalised or pathologised. Alison Hennegan, writing of Nancy Spain's postwar high-camp detective novel *Poison for Teacher* (1949), notes that the book has 'at least two audiences: a fairly uninformed heterosexual one which will enjoy Spain's high-spirited romp; and an altogether more sophisticated and knowing one with which Spain shares jokes and allusions based on insider, gay knowledge' (1949/1994: xiv).[3] While far from a direct analogue for Renault's work, the example of *Poison for Teacher* nonetheless emphasises the balancing-act required to write transgressive desire in the 1940s. Although Renault claimed that she had 'always been as explicit as [she] wanted to be' (1944/1984: 283) her novel is necessarily suggestive in its account of the ladies' sexuality; nonetheless the book is remarkable in its account of two women's happy indifference to the expectations of heterosexual desire.

The 'ladies' of the title, Leo and Helen, are an unflappable pair, going about their respective businesses – writing westerns and technical illustration – while cohabiting peacefully in a houseboat on the Thames. This river idyll is an Eden outside the constraints of heteronormativity. The women are welcome; their relationship is accepted. Renault suggests that the women live together for very different reasons: Helen is reacting against the impossible confinement of heterosexual relationships (219), while Leo is free to express her female masculinity. Having run away from her parents' miserable marriage and from the implications of her own non-conformity, she has never been, in any cultural sense of the word, a girl. Indeed, as she struggles to understand the interpersonal dilemmas brought about by the arrival of her foolish sister Elsie, Leo ruefully comments, 'I wish I understood more about young girls. It's a handicap never to have been one' (181). Leo's masculinity is similarly evident in her relationship with her neighbour Joe, a fellow writer with whom she enjoys a sustaining homosocial relationship. United by work and leisure, Joe, like Helen, accepts Leo as simultaneously both male and female. This is integral to the subtlety of the novel. Helen does not choose to live with Leo because she impersonates a man, rather she lives with her because she embodies a specifically female masculinity; a mode of being that does not replicate the suffocating power dynamics of patriarchal masculinities. The movement beyond binary gender demarcation is equally evident in the account of Joe and Leo's climbing expedition: they are placed outside gender by activity – understood as climbers, not man and woman – and Leo is accepted 'precisely as Joe was accepted' (183). Yet, while her gender is masculine, Leo also enjoys the performance of hyperbolic heterosexual and lesbian femininities, dressing up over the course of the novel to seduce both men and women. Gender in this novel, then, is fluid and protean, as is sexual desire. The ladies are bisexual, combining their stable, fulfilling lesbian relationship with recreational heterosexuality, using men for pleasure and discarding them when they become too demanding or dull. In this sense *The Friendly Young Ladies* operates not to comment on or even defend homosexuality, but rather to expose the unquestioned assumptions that regulate masculinity, femininity and the heterosexual 'norm'.

The prelapsarian state enjoyed by Leo and Helen is, however, disrupted by the arrival first of Elsie, and then of Peter, an egotistical doctor with a sideline in psychoanalytic interventions. These unlikely serpents together form the heterosexual matrix within the novel, bringing their conventional expectations to bear on the ladies' queer lifestyle. They also represent a comic attack on the conventions of psychoanalysis and romance. In Peter's case, his understanding of gender and psychology is rooted in a crude, patronising and selective Freudianism.[4] Obsessed by spinsters and their perceived lack, he thinks he is being scientific, when instead he has simply placed a veneer of modernity over traditional patriarchal attitudes (108). Peter is, we are repeatedly told, sincere and well meaning. However, his embedded attitudes are evident in the 'ghost of proprietorship' (190) which hovers over his relationship with his long-suffering girlfriend Norah, and the barely concealed aggression with which he approaches Leo: 'the desire to give Leo's psyche a helping hand had turned into something not unlike a desire to put it in its place' (187). The one person Peter has never analysed is himself, and his 'generosity' is utterly conditional. He gives only in the expectation of reward (32), and the act of giving contributes to his exaggerated sense of his own power (41). Peter's unquestioned faith in masculine supremacy is most clearly parodied in his encounter with Helen, who dismisses his attempt to map her relationships through a conventional paradigm: 'I think you must have read a lot of novels, or something. People don't live like that' (219). Predictably, Peter does not hear what Helen is saying: to him, her 'eccentricity' means simply that she 'wanted a man' (222).

Helen's criticism of Peter as having read too many books is all the more piquant for the taint of femininity it carries. In this it acts as a reminder of the character who really has read too many of the wrong books: Elsie. It is Elsie's consciousness that opens the narrative. Mouldering through her teenage years in a state of arrested development, she is prompted to run away from home by one of Peter's psychological experiments, but this is not the beginning of a female *bildungsroman*. Rather, Elsie's trajectory runs from reading romance to believing she is part of a romance, to disillusionment that is rapidly reinscribed as tragic romantic loss. While the self-loathing that briefly emerges from her recognition of Peter's deceit is distressing (254), she has resisted the dawning of consciousness (270–1), and in going nowhere she has also destroyed everything for everybody else. Her admittedly unpleasant parents have been driven from their home to refuge in the anonymity of London (which the self-absorbed Elsie sees as ideal for her new needs: cinema, shops, secretarial training), while Helen and Leo's mutually supportive long-term relationship has been dealt what may be a fatal blow. Not for nothing does Helen describe Elsie as 'our little Trojan filly' (269). By bringing Peter to the river, Elsie has operated as a destructive innocent, and in trying to save her sister from disillusionment, Leo's own strategies of self-protection have been painfully exposed. The damage centres around the construction of Leo's masculinity. While she has throughout the novel expressed both heterosexual and homosexual desires, these have not conflicted with her masculine gender identity. When she puts on her striking red dress she adopts a form of drag, performing an identity neither wholly alien nor innately natural. As she says to the 'open-mouthed' Elsie, 'It's me . . . up to a point' (123). Beyond this point is the Leo who lives through masculine modes of being, most specifically work. Leo's cowboy novels create for her the identity 'Tex O'Hara', but more importantly, they give her access to the homosocial: her friendship with Joe. This is fundamental to Leo's sense of self: she works because she is masculine, but equally, she is masculine because of her relationship to work.

All this falls apart when, at the end of the cascade of events triggered by the 'Trojan filly', Leo sleeps with Joe. The event, figured through a violent struggle in the river that acts as a perverse rebirthing, might seem to suggest that Renault, like Peter, ultimately conforms to a Freudian paradigm. Leo had simply been waiting for the right man to 'cure' her. This reading, however, cannot be sustained in the face of the novel's many ambiguities. When Leo realises that Joe is no longer seeing her as a man, her 'consciousness of being a woman' is described as 'a kind of sickness' (237). The equality they enjoyed has been radically compromised, and the reader is invited to ask whether the exchange of friend for lover is worthwhile. In the aftermath, Joe writes to Leo, acknowledging her duality, and using the male pronoun to discuss the friendship that has been lost (275). That part of the letter Joe writes to Leo as woman is, however, absent from the text. Rather, Renault opts to paraphrase here, leaving this seemingly indescribable possibility to the reader's imagination (275). The novel ends without resolving Leo's dilemma. She begins to pack, but a reminder of Helen stops her in her tracks: she cries, first like 'a beaten boy' (278) and then 'the tears of a woman' (279).

Renault's afterword bluntly describes the novel's ending as silly (281), basing her objection on the implausibility of Leo and Joe as a couple. And here perhaps lie the real roots of the novel's radicalism: its suggestion that there is no space within heterosexuality for two active subjects. If Leo is not to be lost in some mythic idea of woman, then her relationship to Joe must revert to the homosocial. That Renault sees the categories 'man' and 'woman' as fatally limiting is suggested in Helen's briefly sketched story. Her past male lovers had absorbed everything, denying Helen's subjectivity and the value of her work. In consequence, she now chooses potential partners by 'imagining them shut up with [her] in a three-room flat' (220). Leo's spectacular masculinity is, then, something of a red herring. What *The Friendly Young Ladies* demonstrates above all is that the coercive normativity of marriage is entirely incompatible with women's happiness and agency, irrespective of gender, desire or sexuality. The book, then, takes us back to the conflict with which this chapter began: the choice between a stable companionate relationship and the destructive pleasure of desire. In this Renault joins her contemporaries in exhibiting a profound set of anxieties around the desiring female body and its social status. That the war would also generate profound anxiety around the male body and its newly legitimate violence will become evident in the next chapter, 'Killing'.

Notes

1. Woolf's Hogarth Press published Freud in translation, but other analysts also exerted significant influence. Bottome published a biography of Alfred Adler in 1939, while Naomi Mitchison's diary records the impact of reading Carl Gustav Jung (1985/1986: 252).
2. Freud's work of the 1920s and 1930s involved a number of revisions to his formative theory, not least of which was his formulation of the 'death drive'. First posited in 'Beyond the Pleasure Principle' (1920), Freud's observations of traumatic neuroses and child's play suggest that 'there really does exist in the mind a compulsion to repeat which overrides the pleasure principle' (Gay, 1989/1995: 605). Peter Gay concludes that 'aggression . . . became from 1920 on the equal adversary of eros', but what might also be extracted from Freud's speculations is the significance of repetition for agency. Freud notes that in the *fort/da* game, repetition translates passive loss into a more active role (600). Translated to the context of war, the compulsion to repeat, particularly in contexts of desire, becomes a potent, if unstable, assertion of self in the proximity of death.
3. *Poison for Teacher* is set at Radcliff Hall School, an establishment that could rival St Trinians, and the detective is Miriam Birdseye, a character based on the popular revue star Hermione Gingold. As Hennegan notes, there is 'comparatively little overt homosexuality' in the novel. What is significant, though, is that '*hetero*sexuality is viewed through lesbian eyes, denied its usual privileges of "normality"' (xiii).
4. In 'Three Essays on the Theory of Sexuality', Freud proposes three types of invert: the 'absolute' invert, who exclusively desires sexual objects of their own sex; the 'amphigenic' invert, a 'psychosexual hermaphrodite' (1953/2001: 136) attracted to both sexes, and the 'contingent' invert who is capable of deriving pleasure from their own sex in the absence of a 'normal' sexual object (137). Peter is fixated on the final category: he believes the ladies' lesbianism is contingent, existing only due to the lack of a sufficiently compelling male object.

Chapter Four

Killing

... I keep thinking during a raid, when we are running over the target, just as we are going to release our bombs, I keep thinking to myself, shall I just jink a little; shall I swerve a fraction to one side, then my bombs will fall on someone else. I keep thinking, whom shall I make them fall on; whom shall I kill tonight.

Roald Dahl, 'Someone Like You' (1946/2010: 152)

'I think I am becoming a God'

Keith Douglas, 'Sportsmen' ([1943]1978/2000: 156)

'The characteristic act of men at war is not dying, it is killing' argues Joanna Bourke (1999: xiii), but arguably in wartime killing and dying cannot easily be divided. For the most part those doing the killing are equally likely to be dying further down the line[1] – an intimate symbiosis not lost on Keith Douglas, who concludes his 1943 poem '*Vergissmeinnicht*' with an image of lover and killer 'mingled': 'And death who had the soldier singled/ has done the lover mortal hurt' (1978/2000: 118). Yet this chapter is, nonetheless, called 'Killing': its emphasis is on the active rather than the passive, and on the complex relationship between that activity and the dominant discourses of man-making circulating during the war. As critics such as Mark Rawlinson have noted, the turn to killing reflects a significant change in the focus of combat literature from the canonical works of the First World War. Comparing Douglas's '*Vergissmeinnicht*' to Wilfred Owen's 'Strange Meeting' he notes that Douglas's work disturbs through its seemingly callous detachment (2000: 8). While Owen's 'Strange Meeting' acknowledges the parity of killer and killed, its concerns are sacrificial: the lives wasted, the unrealised potential. The poem exudes an extreme weariness, ending with the plea 'Let us sleep now' (Stallworthy 1994: 36). Douglas's 'How to Kill', by comparison, seems thrilled by the power mechanised warfare has invested in man: 'This sorcery/ I do. Being damned, I am amused/ to see the centre of love diffused' (Douglas

1978/2000: 119). Here, and in countless other poems, Douglas demonstrates an abstract fascination with death: he stands at a distance amazed by the contrasts – and, tellingly, the similarities – between living and dead, human and machine, desert battlefield and urban habitation. He is also fascinated by the idea of war and the men who fight it, both of which seem to him caught between the pragmatic modernity of mechanisation and the nostalgia of a chivalric mindset still potent for all the lessons of earlier wars.

This abstract fascination is not confined to Douglas. It permeates the literature of combat, both fictional and autobiographical, crossing the boundaries of class and service. Alexander Baron, a Corporal at the time of the Normandy landings, and initially distanced from the combat by his involvement with the Communist party, remembers that there 'was something going on around me that I did not want to be left out of any more' (Baron 1948/2010: x), while Richard Hillary's *The Last Enemy* records that war in the air 'promised a chance of self-realization that would normally take years to achieve' (1942/1997: 24). Douglas's memoir *Alamein to Zem Zem* similarly indicates that the poet saw conflict as an opportunity for personal development, 'an important test, which I was interested in passing' (1946/1992: 15). Douglas's phrase, like his poetry, suggests detachment, the gaze of the curious onlooker, only this time the subject is himself, and this self-consciousness is echoed in the diary of Alun Lewis:

> They [the soldiers of his regiment] seem to have some secret knowledge that I want and will never find out until I go into action with them and war really happens to them. I dread missing such a thing [. . .] When I was leaving Karachi, one of the instructors said to me, 'You're the most selfish man I've ever met, Lewis. You think the war exists for you to write books about it.' I didn't deny it, though it's all wrong. I hadn't the strength to explain what is instinctive and categorical in me, the need to experience. (30 September 1943, 1948/2006: 53)

While this emphasis on personal experience has been seen as axiomatic of 1940s poetry, Lewis's empiricism might also be seen as an instance of what James Campbell terms 'combat gnosticism': the belief that 'combat is a liminal experience that sets the veteran irrevocably apart from those who have not crossed the ritual threshold of war' (1999: 204). Such an ideology insists that war can only be understood through direct experience: fighting is the privileged signifier, the place from which authoritative speech is legitimised (209). To be outside combat is to be excluded from this archetypally phallic role: to be civilian, feminine and passive. Paradoxically, the First World War's protest poetry becomes not something from which to learn, but a knowledge accessible only to the initiate; it reiterates that war is the 'ultimate rite of passage':

> A definitive coming to manhood for the industrial age, in which boys become men by confronting mechanical horror and discovering their essential masculinity, perhaps even their essential humanity, in a realm from which feminine presence is banished' (1999: 204)

Thus, irrespective of the traumatic impact of mechanised warfare, within the cultural imaginary, war remains the pre-eminent mode of man-making. For the interwar generation, the shadow of war was equally that of their fathers: as survivors, sacrifices – or poets – this generation of men had been tested, and there was nothing that their sons could do to match up.

For the young men of 1939, then, war had acquired a new potency: it was an opportunity to answer the unasked questions of masculinity, to find a way of constituting masculine subjectivity that admitted no illusions, but nonetheless welcomed the challenge of mortal danger. It was to be an active critical encounter with the rituals of war, a literature not of passive suffering but of fascinated engagement.

How to Kill: Masculinity, Technology and the Experience of War

> [F]rom the air it must have looked less like a battle than the advance of a multitude of little worms across the face of the land. Every little file was the same: six, eight or ten tired men, more aware of the weight of their packs than of the enemy who awaited them; looking idly across the silent fields on either side with the lethargic unconcern of the early workman's bus [. . .] There was no drama, no earthquaking bombardment, no masses in conflict; only the ten men plodding along a lane in single file, tired and out of step, the ten men multiplied ten thousand times. (Baron 1948/2010: 123)

Alexander Baron's description of D-Day Plus One in *From the City, From the Plough* (1948) insists on a bird's eye view to make sense of battle. The advancing 'multitude of worms' together form an army; move any closer and this cohesion falls away to reveal a multitude of tired men 'plodding along' in 'lethargic unconcern'. Yet these men are indispensible cogs in a machine whose workings they cannot fully understand; as the climax of the narrative reveals, the individual and collective actions of each platoon build towards an end point none of them will see. It is an image replicated by Douglas in *Alamein to Zem Zem*: the British army is 'a city of ants', and its arrangement looks like 'a body would look to a germ riding in its bloodstream' (1946/1992: 17). Richard Hillary, the fighter pilot, imagines himself freed from this overwhelming complexity: the aviator is 'the duellist', 'cool, precise, impersonal', raised above the ground, 'privileged to kill well' (1942/1997: 97).[2] As these images suggest, the relationship between individual combatant, group identity and abstract cause is an uneasy one, and these three writers all work to expose the complexity of combatants' relationships with both the war machine and the machines of war.

From the City, From the Plough tells the story of the Fifth Battalion of the Wessex Regiment, a unit of military machinery welded together from the disparate lives of its personnel. In this it replicates the form of the 'group hero' discussed in Chapter 2, but Baron stretches far beyond the usual small core of characters. Indeed, it would be hard to say who are his protagonists. As Sean Longden has noted, the young boy most likely to be the subject of a coming-of-age narrative is abruptly dispatched within minutes of landing in France (1948/2010: 115–16). Beyond this, the cast is simply too large for a traditional group hero, and it is part of the skill of Baron's novel that he manages to engage the reader's concern for characters whose stories are sketched in barely one or two pages of prose. Certain key figures do recur, though: Colonel Pothecary, the amiable and well-liked Commanding Officer; Major Norman, his unlikely friend, a cynical upper-class aesthete; Lieutenant Paterson, a young platoon commander; Sergeant Shannon, tough on the outside, but acutely attuned to the complexities of the homosocial group; Charlie Venable and Dickie Crawford, leading lights of the Doggy Boys, a subcultural force of London wide-boys operating with impunity from the ranks; Private Smith, a 'swedebasher', more concerned with the harvest than the second front; boy-man Alfie Bradley, experiencing his first sexual encounter with the vulnerable Floss, and Scannock the Scouse, whose underclass origins in the Liverpool slums make him incapable of understanding the basic rules of social behaviour. Although much emphasis is placed on the fleeting moments of connection forged between these men, Baron's novel is brutally unsentimental. Whether characters die futile deaths or make heroic sacrifices, the narrative presses on with no space for mourning, or even for the ritual observances of death (116–17). Indeed, the dead must be erased from history, put beyond the serial present of the soldier's consciousness, if there is to be any hope of survival (149).

From the City never lets the reader forget the bigger picture, and as the book progresses, the army machine begins remorselessly to devour its individual components. Its unremittingly bleak conclusion achieves its impact not from the depiction of individual deaths, but through a demonstration of the complete evacuation of empathy necessary for the machine to function. This is not, though, a return to the First World War's depiction of complacent staff officers sending young men to their death, but a more complex recognition of the pitiless logic of war. Major Norman, commanding the battalion after Pothecary's death, desires acknowledgement of his soldiers' achievement. He needs praise to validate and ameliorate their suffering. But the Brigadier, who has 'hardened himself' to pass on the news that the men will now be sacrificed as decoys, gives him nothing. Receiving no hint of human recognition, Norman then turns this chilling lack of affect on Paterson. A chapter later, the scene repeats itself, but this time Baron does not show Norman passing on the news; indeed, we hear no more of the specific characters whose stories we have followed. In a final scene, tanks move across the village reclaimed by the survivors of the Fifth Battalion:

> Among the rubble, beneath the smoking ruins, the dead of the Fifth Battalion sprawled around the guns which they had silenced; dusty, crumpled and utterly without dignity; a pair of boots protruding from a roadside ditch; a body blackened and bent like a chicken burnt in the stove [. . .] The living lay among them, speechless, exhausted, beyond grief or triumph, drawing at broken cigarettes and watching with sunken eyes the tanks go by. (Baron 1948/2010: 189–90)

Baron does not tell which – if any – of the characters have survived. The novel is over, but the war is not, and this absence of certainty leaves the reader bereft of comfort.

From the City was based on Baron's experiences as an infantry-man during the Normandy landings, and the book was a critical and popular success from the moment of its publication (1948/2010: xv). This was attributable, at least in part, to its realism; it presented an utterly unromantic portrait of war. Yet while war was recognised as harsh and unglamorous, the men who fought it were nonetheless subject to a variety of mythologising processes. As Michael Paris has demonstrated, fiction for children insisted on the inherent superiority of British soldiers, sailors and airmen. The fundamental message that 'an Englishman can always out-smart a Nazi' (Paris 2000: 198) is conveyed through a combination of heroic adventure and comic representations of the enemy. Not surprisingly, W. E. Johns' invincible hero Biggles was deployed early in the conflict, variously dispatched to the Russo-Finnish war of 1939–40 for *Biggles Sees it Through* (1941) and commanding an eccentric squadron of rebellious officers in *Spitfire Parade* (1941). The structure of this second novel, in which unity is forged out of diversity to persuasive military effect, is typical of the emergent group hero narra-tive, but the presence of Biggles himself ensured continuity with earlier, more individualistic, models of heroism. The popularity of such types is evident from the War Office's request that Johns produce a new series of novels featuring a soldier hero comparable to Biggles. *King of the Commandos* (1943) introduced the nation's youth to 'Gimlet', a steely-eyed professional soldier of upper-class origins who proves distinctly modern in his approach to soldiering. Paris locates Gimlet within a structure of heroism that began to emerge in the aftermath of the First World War: 'These young men were just as patriotic, just as convinced of British superiority, but now they sometimes questioned their orders, employed unorthodox methods, and, if necessary, were prepared to bend or even break the rules in order to gain their objectives' (2000: 206). *King of the Commandos* also replicates the group structure, with Gimlet supported by a working-class ex-policeman, a French-Canadian trapper, and a sixteen-year-old boy, all of whom are skilled in the arts of unconventional warfare. Johns, at the behest of the Air Ministry, also created a female adventurer in *Worrals of the WAAF* (1941). Air warfare offered rare opportunity for women characters to escape the restrictive conventions of pre-war literature (209), and significantly, both Worrals and Dorothy Carter's aviator Marise Duncan – *Sword of the Air* (1941) – were presented as willing to kill for their country. Paris, however, notes an equally significant exclusion: 'Native troops were virtually excluded from fiction of the period, which portrayed the war as a largely European affair fought exclusively by the white race' (213).

The hybrid heroic formulation favoured by popular fictions was also evident in the cinema. Here, the influence of the documentary film movement on feature film production saw the emergence not only of a group hero, but also a democratised hero, and it is possible to trace a transition in heroic archetypes across the war period. As critics have observed, the war years saw the paternalistic archetype of leadership embodied by Noël Coward in *In Which We Serve* (1942) mutate into the ordinary working man: David Niven's Captain in *The Way Ahead* (1944), or John Mills's Pilot Officer in *The Way to the Stars* (1945) (Aldgate and Richards 1986: 214). These modern 'meritocratic' figures (Spicer 2001: 10) at home with technology and the demands of total war could not, though, wholly replace the archetype of romantic, chivalric heroism, and throughout the decade the representation of combat nego-tiates a tension between these emergent and residual forms.[3] The debate finds eloquent articulation in Michael Powell and Emeric Pressburger's *The Life and Death of Colonel Blimp* (1943). The film begins with the repeated phrase 'war begins at midnight' (war, in this case, being an exercise pitting the regular army against a Home Guard contingent led by General Clive Wynne-Candy VC, the eponymous Colonel Blimp) and the young army officer Spud Wilson's defining response is to abandon the cherished British concept of fair play, and steal a march on Blimp by starting early and surprising the Colonel in his bath. The fairy tale overtones of 'war begins at midnight' are thus replaced by remorseless pragmatism, and the film treads a delicate path between a nostalgic celebration of the values enshrined by Blimp – loyalty, friendship, fairness, honour, sportsmanship, courage – and the acknowledgement that modern wars will not be prosecuted in this way. The Nazis, implies the film, will not wait until midnight, and neither must the British. Nor must they be afraid to use whatever methods necessary to defeat an enemy defined as being without scruple. The film's most articulate character is a German, Theo Kretschmar Schuldorf, and it is to him rather than Blimp or the thinly-drawn Spud that the filmmakers give a seemingly definitive statement of purpose. Theo, now a refugee, tells Blimp that this is 'not a gentleman's war'; rather, it is a fight for existence 'against the most devilish idea ever created: Nazism'. Yet, as A. L. Kennedy has argued, the film is 'deeply ambivalent' about this new world order, and it demands respect for the values embodied in the Colonel (1997: 62–3). Blimp's ideals are mourned by the film, not simply rejected, and while the necessity of total war is accepted, the film spends much of its time demonstrating the values that are lost in adherence to such an ideology.

The debate enshrined in *Blimp* is echoed in *Alamein to Zem Zem*. Here, as in his poetry, Douglas depicts an outmoded Englishness at odds with the demands of modern warfare:

> [Guy] was fantastically rich and handsome, and appeared, as indeed he was, a figure straight out of the nineteenth century. He was charming. His ideas were feudal in the best sense – he regarded everyone in the regiment as his tenants, sub-tenants, serfs etc., and felt his responsibilities to them as a landlord. Everyone loved him and I believe pitied him a little. (1946/1992: 91)

Douglas was part of what had formerly been a Cavalry regiment – a body of soldiers in the process of transmuting from Gentlemen on Horseback to the rather more prosaic Men in Tanks – and he notes 'the unbridgeable gap between those who had been the original horsed officers [. . .] and the "odds and sods" who came to make up the regiment's officer strength when mechanization was complete' (1946/1992: 94) (Figure 4.1). The men in charge in many cases knew less than those under their command (95), but although this has echoes of Flanders, the experience cannot exactly be mapped as repetition (Piette 1995: 16–17). The aristocrats of Douglas's poetry are not safe behind the lines, and honour is of little avail in the indiscriminate assault of shellfire, as Douglas observes in the viciously ironic 'Gallantry'. Here, to the sound of personified weaponry 'overcome with mirth', the doomed boy meets

Figure 4.1 Aristocrats? Keith Douglas pencil drawing, leaf torn from lined notebook. Reproduced with the permission of Leeds University Library.

his fate: his 'perfectly mannered flesh fell/ in opening the door for a shell' (Douglas 1978/2000: 104). The boy's schooling has not prepared him for battle, rather it has rendered him precociously obsolete. 'Aristocrats' is still more explicit about the uncomfortable conflation of cavalry and tank, melding man and horse to create a noble but archaic figure, incongruously transplanted from his natural home in 'the shires'. Later in the poem, these men become unicorns, semi-mythical legends celebrated equally for their 'stupidity and chivalry'. The language is powerfully understated, matching the euphemism of Blitz rhetoric in its refusal of suffering:

> Peter was unfortunately killed by an 88;
> it took his leg away, he died in the ambulance.
> I saw him crawling on the sand, he said
> It's most unfair, they've shot my foot off. (1978/2000: 117)

Peter's words are hardly the stuff of epic. Rather they speak the language of the playground or the playing field. His lost leg has been 'taken away', confiscated almost, while his death, recorded as 'unfortunate' seems more of an embarrassment than anything else. The language is prosaic, and as William Scammell has noted, placing Peter's words after his death suggests the speech of a rather petulant ghost (1988:169).

Alamein to Zem Zem is at times brutally critical of army organisation, but this criticism coexists with a paradoxical pleasure in the adventure of desert warfare. Douglas the writer is not immune to the temptation to read battle as a game, and there is a romantic, 'sporting' relish in his descriptions of British tanks routing Italian convoys: 'The Crusaders, like enough to hounds, raced across the plain, bellies to the ground, and put up small parties of the enemy every few minutes' (62). The sense of freedom conveyed in this image is indicative of the ways in which the desert was mythologised as the 'perfect backdrop' for war. The desert is imagined as a tabula rasa, a bare stage that can be occupied by a pure body of fighting forces, miraculously divorced from ethical complexity. As Rawlinson argues:

> Tropes of isolation and marginality sustained the idea of the desert as a bat-tlefield possessing unprecedented transparency or legibility. [. . .] The urban-industrial scenarios of trench war and strategic bombing are displaced by what is considered, without irony, as a clear field for the play of military force and intelligence, uncomplicated by the (political) problems of occupation or the 'side-effects' of civilian death. (Rawlinson 2000: 115)

This is an attitude that imagines codes of honour can still exist in the face of overwhelming evidence to the contrary, and it gives rise to a conception of war as a spectator sport. Piette observes that Douglas 'returns again and again to theatrical imagery to describe the Eighth army' (17), and he notes that participants were acutely aware that they were being watched by those back home. For someone as well versed in literary tradition as Douglas, though, it was also a case of being watched by the past. The self-consciousness brought about by repetition works to distance Douglas from any 'authentic' emotional engagement with the horror he encounters. In his prose this is manifest as a 'business as usual' failure to acknowledge the substance of death, but the absence of emotional engagement is also a fundamental necessity of survival. Just as Baron's soldiers must forget their dead, so Douglas and his crew must refuse to acknowledge the abject horror of the battlefield. Nowhere is this clearer than when they acquire a replacement tank, which has not been cleaned since the previous occupants were killed inside it. The men accept this as a messy inconvenience, not a desecration, translating the visceral into the banal through a euphemistic process of normalisation: '"Bit mucky in the turret," said the driver, as though apologizing to an inspecting officer' (53).

The acceptance of detachment as a strategy for survival is evident throughout poetic responses to the Second World War. In Sidney Keyes's 'Advice for a Journey' the poet prescribes the occupation of a serial present: 'So take no rations, remember not your homes – / Only the blind and stubborn hope to track/ This wilderness' (Tambimuttu 1942: 85). Keyes proposes survival through a shutting down of sensory and intellectual processes, warning that 'The thoughtful leave their bones/ In windy foodless meadows of despair' (85). Henry Reed, by contrast, focuses on the evacuation of affect from military language. In 'Lessons of the War' he uses the discourse of the training ground to elide the body of both killer and killed:

Today we have naming of parts. Yesterday,
We had daily cleaning. And tomorrow morning,
We shall have what to do after firing'

(Selwyn 1995/1996: 10)

Against this barren ritual, Reed sets a natural world that variously stands aloof from, or comically parodies, the clumsy manoeuvres of the soldiers: 'The early bees are assaulting and fumbling the flowers:/ They call it easing the Spring'. The second part of the poem, 'Judging Distances', is more explicit in its statement of the alienating impact of military discourse: 'Not only how far away, but the way that you say it/ Is very important' (11), and the poet, schooled in technical euphemism and told that 'things only seem to be things', finds himself cut adrift by 'roughly a distance/ Of about one year and a half' from the lovers he watches through his scope (12). This distortion is echoed in G. S. Fraser's 'Apology of a Soldier', which distances the combatant from destruction through a cinematic image:

And I have seen films of war, bombs
Destroying the momentary profile
We call the wall of a house;
Smoking rifles destroying
The momentary identity we call a man.

(Tambimuttu 1942: 63–4)

The poem struggles to make sense of the war through an extended cancer metaphor, and the films of war are set against those of cancerous cells multiplying on a slide, a perverse image of life that is death, which can only be destroyed at the cost of the host body (63). The doctors, 'have not an answer', and the poet, in a telling instance of adynaton, concludes 'my rhymes have all run out' (65). The overwhelming impression is one of instability: objects lose their integrity, the human becomes transient and insubstantial. The conviction of contamination, of death infecting life, is typical of a poetic fascination with liminal states, and Fraser's 'momentary identity we call a man' evokes the central transformation of Douglas's 'How to Kill' in which Death, at the order of the sniper, magically makes 'a man of dust/ of a man of flesh' (Douglas 1978/2000: 119).

Elsewhere in Douglas's poetry, detachment takes more visceral form, with death figured as a mode of recycling. In 'Dead Men' once-human flesh becomes meat for scavenging dogs, much as in *Alamein to Zem Zem* the carcases of enemy tanks become resources to be looted by the pursuing army. Ethical considerations are a luxury, 'human virtue . . . a vapour tasteless to a dog's chops' (100), and the poem imagines contrasting strategies for evading the real of death: that of the lover, outside time, free of cynicism and reason (and war), and that of the dog, pragmatically eating meat wherever it can be found. Yet not all of Douglas's poetry aims for detachment. The sequence 'Landscape with Figures' begins at a distance, looking down on the detritus of the battlefield. The poet is figured as 'a pilot or angel looking down', far-off vehicles turn into 'beetles', and the whole landscape becomes a junk shop covered in 'useless furniture' (109). By the third poem, however, the poet has become hopelessly implicated in the landscape: 'I am the figure burning in hell' (111), a transition prefigured in the previous poem in which the approaching spectator comes close enough to 'trace' the figures of the dead and to become the 'figure writhing on the backcloth' (110). Here the theatrical imagery noted by Piette resurfaces: not only are the dead men mimes, but their blood is 'cosmetic'. This is Douglas's characteristic conflation of living and dead. In *Alamein to Zem Zem* a group of Italian soldiers lie 'like trippers taken ill' (54), their deaths strangely tawdry and unconvincing. While the term 'trippers' indicates the narrative's tendency to consider the Italians sub-standard soldiers, the image also emphasises the shock of death, its unexpectedness. In seeming so unmartial, the Italians bring the domestic to the battlefield, their quotidian death tableau simultaneously inscribing and refusing the reality of war.

Douglas's writing thus combines clinical detachment with voyeurism and a schoolboy pleasure in adventure, and his fascination with combat is shared by his close contemporary Richard Hillary (born within a year of each other, Hillary and Douglas went to Oxford in 1937 and 1938 respectively). Although the style of the two men's memoirs could scarcely be more different – Hillary's tendency towards anecdote, debate and mysticism is in marked contrast to Douglas's anthropological distance – they share an understanding that combat represents an opportunity for self-development. It is also the case that for Hillary the Air Force, to an even greater extent than the desert, represents a return to an idealised and 'noble' vision of war. As he explains to his pacifist friend, David Rutter:

> In a fighter plane, I believe, we have found a way to return to war as it ought to be, war which is individual combat between two people, in which one either kills or is killed. It's exciting, it's individual, and it's disinterested. I shan't be sitting behind a long-range gun working out how to kill people sixty miles away. I shan't get maimed: either I shall get killed or I shall get a few pleasant putty medals and enjoy being stared at in a night club. (Hillary 1942/1997: 15)

War, however, proved much less clear-cut, and Hillary was indeed maimed, receiving horrific burns to his hands and face after being shot down in September 1940. The extent of his injuries put Hillary in exactly the border zone he had hoped to escape. Neither killer nor killed, the wounded combatant acquires a liminal identity on the borders of conflict, and it is perhaps not surprising that Hillary sought a return to active duty, even though his injuries made flying an aircraft extremely difficult. In returning to 'combat' Hillary could once again occupy the safe identity of the fighting man, and the power of that identity in wartime is made clear in *The Last Enemy*. A later encounter with Rutter records: 'He was uneasy and I felt guilty: I had such an unfair advantage' (166). Hillary distinguishes between external and internal wounds, suggesting that 'the scars of [Rutter's pacifism] would be with him always' (167), and in so doing he conforms to the dominant understanding of masculinity as the conspicuous exhibition of agency.[4]

Yet while Hillary evidently believes that masculinity is rooted in proactive doing, a significant proportion of *The Last Enemy* records the combatant in a state of enforced passivity. In his account of his injuries, and the months spent in ground-breaking plastic surgeon Archibald McIndoe's 'Beauty Shop', Hillary draws on a set of particularly British masculine norms to achieve agency through endurance. His recovery is mapped through the distancing strategies of humour, modesty and the refusal of emotion. For the most part, pain operates as a signifying absence within the text, its seldom-stated presence a mark of Hillary's heroic stoicism. Significantly, this endurance is facilitated by homosociality. Before going into hospital for his reconstructive operations, Hillary has no eyelids and not much upper lip, infected eyes and exposed bone on his hands, but after an evening's conversation with a friend, he goes to bed 'content' (138). Importantly, the hospital operates as an extension of familiar environments: Hillary and his fellow patients behave like boys in a boarding school, or operational pilots in the mess. They tease the nurses, get drunk and smoke (143), using banter and bad behaviour to deny the impact of their injuries. In a telling scene, Hillary and a friend posture as old men, watching the dancers in a nightclub with fatherly eyes, claiming that their physical injuries have had the beneficial side effect of sparing them the pains of youth (149–50). This assertion of wholeness in the face of all-too-visible wounds is a manifestation of what Anthony Easthope describes as the 'masculine myth': 'Masculinity aims to be one substance all the way through. In order to do this it must control what threatens it both from within and without' (1990/1992: 166). The threat from within is the feminine, whether that be manifest in homosexual desire or displays of emotion; the threat from without is the power of women to 'wound' the male ego, through the acquisition of power or the denial of sexual access. In the nightclub scene, the men's repudiation of desire negates the threat of impotence or undesirability. Their loss cannot hurt them because they refuse to acknowledge it as such. In Easthope's formulation, the masculine myth is generally destructive, denying men the potential of emotional expression and oppressing those who fail to conform to its strictures. In the context of war, however, it becomes a fundamental building block of combat identity.

Hillary concludes *The Last Enemy* with a fictional epiphany in which, after pulling a dying woman out of a blitzed house, he recognises that clinical detachment is not possible. This leads him to assume a new identity as writer and memorialist: 'If I could do this thing, could tell a little of the lives of these men, I would have justified, at least in some measure, my right to fellowship with my dead' (178). Yet in this performative act of memorialisation, Hillary adds his voice to an already overdetermined mythologising process. As Martin Francis has demonstrated, it would be difficult to overstate wartime cultural investment in the pilot:

> The flyer could be imagined as a classless meritocrat, a tribune of the people's war, or he could be envisaged as an anti-democratic superman, rendered omnipotent by his ability to literally ascend above the rest of humanity. He could be an emblem of scientific modernity or a reincarnation of the chivalric heroes of a medieval past. (Francis 2008: 13)

The romantic power of this myth is evident from its penetration even into the pacifist world of Frances Partridge: when her young friend Rollo

Woolley visits in October 1940 she records that 'the effect of his air-force uniform was electric' (1978/1996: 64). Rollo gives the Partridges an account of 'young men living in the present or the near future' who fully realise the 'suicidal nature' of their careers (65). At the news of Woolley's almost inevitable death, Partridge's comment reiterates the chivalric, transcendent ideal: 'I felt no surprise. Rollo always seemed to have a doomed air, as if he knew himself not to be long for this earth' (11 January 1943; 155). Yet, as Francis suggests, the airman could just as easily be co-opted into an 'anti-democratic' mythography, and it is exactly this vision of a superman attaining mastery over self, society, the elements and history that forms the subject of Rex Warner's *The Aerodrome* (1941).

In Warner's satire, the Air Vice Marshall will let no emotion stand in the way of his vision of a world made 'clean' (1941/1982: 188). As the aerodrome comes to dominate the 'shapeless' form of the all-too-human village, the narrator, Roy, becomes infatuated by the Air Force's promise of freedom from the 'bondage of both past and future' (180). While Roy's disenchantment with family is understandable – he has recently discovered that his parents are not his parents and the man he thought was his father is a murderer – the appeal of becoming an airman is something more visceral, a physical transcendence enhanced by both the aeroplane and the machine of the organisation:

> We were set to exercise our brains, our nerves, our muscles, and our desires to one end, and to back the force of our will possessed the most powerful machines that have been invented by man. It was not only our dexterity with these machines, but the whole spirit of our training which cut us off from the mass of men; and to be so cut off was, whether we realized it or not, our greatest pleasure and our chief article of pride. (1941/1982: 224–5)

Not least of the irony of Warner's totalitarian dystopia is the eventual introduction of pilotless planes, able to replicate exactly those skills that had raised the pilot to a man amongst men. In rendering the pilot redundant, Warner sends him back to earth, deprived of the aviator's cyborg subjectivity.

This mode of self-fashioning permeates accounts of aviation, as the pilot – more than any other combatant – depends upon intimacy with the machine. In the air, as Roald Dahl's story, 'Death of an Old Old Man' suggests, pilot and aeroplane become one:

> ... the Spitfire was not a Spitfire but a part of his own body; the muscles of his arms and legs were in the wings and in the tail of the machine so that when he banked and turned and dived and climbed he was not moving his hands and his legs but only the wings and the tail and the body of the aero-

plane; for the body of the Spitfire was the body of the pilot, and there was no difference between the one and the other. (Dahl 1946/2010: 18)

Small wonder that Hillary was compelled to return to flying. The dual status of wounded hero and successful writer were not sufficient to reinstate the technologically-enhanced transcendent masculinity lost in his grounding. Nor were they sufficient to compensate for the appalling guilt he felt at having survived to enjoy the success of *The Last Enemy*. Indeed, in an influential essay of 1943, Arthur Koestler argues that Hillary was destroyed by the mythical status conferred upon him: 'We see in his letters as under a microscope how the hero-craving, symbol-eager expectations of his Time creep like microbes under his skin, penetrate the blood stream and burn him out' (1945/1983: 54). Koestler theorises that Hillary represented a class and generation defined by lack and nostalgic for a cause: 'we all more or less feel that we fight this war rather *in spite of* than *because of* something. The big words and slogans rather embarrass us, we don't like to be thought quite so naïve as that' (55). Patriotism and grand gestures belong to the last war, not to this one, which presents itself instead as pragmatic and reluctant. But the refusal of patriotic discourse disguises the fact that these men are, nonetheless, willing to die for *something*; and this suggests that Hillary's cultivated individualism might be seen as disingenuous, a front covering a chasm where the languages of belief, duty and patriotism used to be. Alternatively, Hillary might be read less as a symbol than as an object of desire, a prototype British 'Superman' offering a potent combination of human vulnerability and 'superhuman' achievement. In this context, Hillary's mythologisation emerges as a form of stardom, in which his capacity to convey an 'extraordinary ordinariness' becomes crucial (Dyer 1979/1998: 35, 43). *The Last Enemy* is complicit in this star-making discourse:

> Within one short year [the pilot] has become the nation's hero, and the attempt to live up to this false conception bores him. For, as he would be the first to admit, on the ground the pilot is a very ordinary fellow. [. . .]
>   The pilot is of a race of men who since time immemorial have been inarticulate; who, through their daily contact with death, have realized, often enough unconsciously, certain fundamental things. It is only in the air that the pilot can grasp that feeling, that flash of knowledge, of insight, that matures him beyond his years; only in the air that he knows suddenly he is a man in a world of men. (1942/1997: 42–3)

In the very process of challenging the myth, Hillary's writing reinforces it. In referring to a 'race of men' he imagines the pilot as a man apart, and the emphasis on ordinary characteristics is offset by the contextualisation of these qualities. The pilot becomes a mystical figure, from a different world, unable to speak the language of ordinary mortals. Hillary, then, protests too much. His pilot *is* a remarkable figure, and it is only in the surrounding narrative – the Oxford years, the training, the schoolboy banter – that these men appear as genuinely ordinary: of their time, not beyond or above it. These contextual features are crucial. They make Hillary typical of his generation, a man from a background familiar to middle-class imaginations and, consequently, available for identification to wide readership. Yet what Hillary could not have anticipated is that both his mythological status, and his stardom, ultimately emerges not from his potency in the air, but from the fact of his wounding. It is here – in the exhibition of extraordinary bravery, stoicism and endurance – that Hillary, rather than simply the icon of the pilot, becomes exceptional. In an ideal well suited to British propaganda, he triumphs as a wounded hero rather than a superman, and the fate that he inhabits becomes a site of abject fascination. In a war against civilian populations, many must have feared injury, and while Hillary was no everyman, his seemingly exceptional circumstances were the stuff of everyday nightmares.

This discussion of the airman began with the trope of detachment, a state facilitated by, but not confined to, technology. As Warner's ambivalent hero Roy recognises, the airman's state of mind offers a welcome insulation from time: from the weight of the past and the anxious hopes of the future. This serial present, which is also a numb denial of consequence, is another self-preserving illusion of combat lost by Hillary in the fact of his survival. The pilot is destined for a death as clinical as that effected by Douglas's sniper; he disappears into thin air, a transformation succinctly euphemised in *The Last Enemy* by the memorialising refrain: 'From this flight [. . .] did not return' (95, 97, 99, 108). Survival, by contrast, is messy. Not only did Hillary suffer dreadfully with the implications of outliving his generation – 'the survivor is always a debtor' (Koestler 1945/1983: 62) – he also found himself confronted by the problem of 'after'. This was a temporal state that runs profoundly counter to effective combat masculinities, as is demonstrated by Dahl's 'Death of an Old Old Man'.

Dahl's nameless pilot is remarkable for his longevity. He has been flying for four years, and with this unexpected duration has come not confidence but terror. The pilot is consumed by a fear that whispers to him: 'you are young [. . .] you have a million things to do [. . .] if you are not careful you will buy it [and when you do] you will just be a charred corpse' (1946/2010: 13). Significantly, the pilot reflects that four years ago it had been wonderful, 'because the waiting on the aerodrome was nothing more than the waiting before a football game or before going in to bat' (12). Here is the sporting fascination of Hillary and Douglas: an engagement with the world that depends upon a refusal of time and consequence. This a-temporality demands a rejection of self-consciousness, of desire, memory and self, in favour of an addictive, but ultimately destructive, physical inhabitation of the moment. To think about the future is fatal, as Baron demonstrates in the death of Colonel Pothecary, who walks in an 'exultant dream' through a hail of bullets, but falls at the point when 'the consciousness of safety, of survival' intrudes into his thoughtless invincibility (1948/2010: 178). The intensity of combat, of killing, creates an 'other' self that can only inhabit the present and which can only be sustained in times of extreme crisis. Beyond that crisis lies the mundane, the quotidian, the draining reality of surviving war.

Killing Communities: Group identities and the Uncanny Domesticity of War

As the previous section suggested, caring is a hopeless condition for killing, and also paradoxically, for survival – not least because it speaks to a temporality beyond the immediacy of battle. However, the literature and film of combat equally suggest that caring is essential for pre- and post-killing. Much of the bitterness at the end of *From the City, From the Plough* comes from the refusal of the Brigadier to show humanity, to give some indication that he cares about the Fifth Battalion. Although the army marches remorselessly on, the book implies that by refusing to recognise the group's achievement, the brigadier has deconstructed something essential to the success of the military endeavour. The soldiers' willingness to be subject to military discipline, and to go into battle, emerges from a contract, a balance of give and take. As Charlie Venable announces before going AWOL at the cancellation of his leave, 'No leaf, no soldierin'' (39). The unwritten laws of the military community have little to do with regulations, rather they are a conglomeration of etiquettes combining class distinction with an almost familial duty of care. The functioning of the army depends upon a homosocial environment, and those who threaten this community must be absorbed or expelled.

Absorption is the preferred option for the preservation of a healthy community, not least because the failure to absorb threatens the integrity of the community. Baron's Mad Major Maddison, whose failure to recognise the community is encapsulated by his reckless endangerment of his men and his admiration for fascist masculinities (61–2), is too powerful to be absorbed, and is ultimately shot by one of his own men. This lethal fracture of group ethics leaves the perpetrator in a state of terror, until he hears witnesses lie on his behalf (166). In that lie, the community repairs itself, having expelled the cancer of deadly fascist homoeroticism. Maddison's homosexuality is obvious and yet unarticulated. Baron suggests that the man himself does not recognise his feelings as desire (63), and he is pathologised more for his fetishisation of hard-bodied militarism, 'the mystic communion of soldiers' (63), than for his inarticulable desires. Significantly, Maddison's warrior status is constructed as both asset and liability: the 'best officer in the battalion' and yet a man to whom the Colonel cannot entrust his men (63). The problem is presented as national rather than sexual: Maddison's natural aptitude for killing makes him 'other' to a national body imagined as essentially peaceable. Colonel Pothecary despairs of turning his 'bumpkins' into a coherent fighting force. Country-boy soldiers slope off to work the fields, while urban contingents such as the Doggy Boys would rather gamble than wage war. Both culturally and sub-culturally, the British nation is constructed as resilient, but only reluctantly martial, skilled amateurs rather than trained professionals in the business of killing. It is nonetheless the case, though, that in killing Major Maddison, Baron's text simultaneously expels the homosexual, reassuring the reader that the many intimate friendships that remain are unproblematically familial.

In comparison, the examples of community reabsorption are many: Baron's Scouse Scannock is redeemed not just by his courage under fire, but by his eventual recognition of community. In stealing fags for the lads, he becomes, at last, one of them (132–3). A similar, but more painful, redemption is achieved by AB Triggs, the most useless seaman on board HMS Artemis, the community at the centre of C. S. Forester's *The Ship* (1943). Triggs, like Scannock, is described as drunken, dirty and 'incapable of grasping an order' (1943/2006: 167–8). Nonetheless, with the ship on fire, it is Triggs who burns his hands to the bone turning the wheel to flood the magazine (191–2). A similar dynamic is evident in Noël Coward's *In Which We Serve* (1942), although the censorship shaping cinema production ensured that rather than being drunk and stupid, the failed sailor is simply a small scared boy, played by a very young Richard Attenborough. When Attenborough's stoker panics, and leaves his post in battle, he is not expelled from the body politic, nor subject to brutal punishment, rather the Captain, as a responsible father figure, takes the blame upon himself. This holistic vision of the fighting unit has obvious propaganda value, but that should not detract from its importance as a feature of war narrative, and *The Ship* provides an exemplary case study of the 'group hero'. The book's similarities to Coward's film are many, with Forester echoing the rhetoric of a 'happy, efficient ship' (1943/2006: 50), and focusing on an interwoven set of stories detailing the disparate lives of men across all classes and ranks. As with Baron's community of soldiers, comradeship ebbs and flows: moments of intimacy and communication are achieved across boundaries of class, and then broken again on the rocks of custom. All of human life is present on Forester's ship, including the literary. The ship has a poet, Able Seaman Presteign, a working-class autodidact who has 'revelled in Shakespeare ... during some weeks of debauch, like some other sailor on a drinking bout' (1943/2006: 112). His genius is recognised by well-educated sub-lieutenant Jerningham who, drunk and temporarily uninhibited, introduces the orphanage boy to Keats. This cross-class encounter is echoed in *From the City* as literature almost becomes a currency through which Sergeant Shannon and Lieutenant Paterson can communicate (1948/2010: 136–7). Class inhibits the dialogue both men desire, and it seems also to inhibit the possibilities of *The Ship*. Presteign is blown to pieces with the port-side pompom gun (138), one of a disproportionate number of clever, ambitious working-class characters whose agency is limited to a heroic or dutiful death.

The male community is thus permeated with social distinctions that not even combat can erase. Douglas is acutely aware of this and his detachment dilutes the homosociality found in other fictional, filmic and autobiographical reminiscences. What *Alamein to Zem Zem* provides instead is an uncanny recreation of home. The book is suffused with references to physical and emotional comfort: the first provided by whatever resources can be looted from the detritus of the desert landscape, the second provided by books. In the most unyielding of environments, the men of the Eighth Army are depicted as persistent and effective homemakers. 'Books and flowers are invincible beautifiers' notes Douglas, describing the officers' Christmas decorations, 'I have often used them to make horrible surroundings habitable' (98). Yet, more than this, books in the text become the means through which the unthinkable can be repelled. Men read in their tanks in the midst of battle – the conditions of which are often as static and frustrating as the military training camp – and men injured take refuge in whatever reading matter can be found.

Yet more remarkable than the decoration of the mess tent is the extensive account of tank culture. In the process of crossing the desert, tank crews cooked for themselves, and Douglas reports that for any stop of more than two-days duration, whole kitchens were forged from

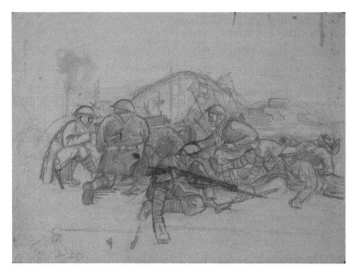

Figure 4.2 Pencil drawing, soldiers with tank. Keith Douglas. Reproduced with the permission of Leeds University Library.

petrol tins and vast ingenuity exerted in the construction of dishes of 'professional elegance and great variety' (104). This domesticity forms a significant counter-current to Adam Piette's insistence on 'loot' as the symbolic driving force of the narrative. Piette argues that the war in the desert 'bred a war mind peopled by boys playing at killing, men going to a "show" of made-up corpses and colourful maps' (1995: 33), and his argument is persuasive; but what are we to make of the simultaneous play of home-making that accompanies these boy's games? At one level, the reassertion of the domestic points to the self-sufficiency of the homo-social environment. Women are not simply absent from this landscape; they are superfluous. But beyond this virtue of necessity, the pervasive domesticity speaks potently to a memory of home that stands in opposition to the delusions of wartime 'sport'. This memory, or desire, receives no articulation beyond Douglas's assertion of the beautifying power of books, but the persistent drive to domesticate mechanical and military surroundings nonetheless speaks to a recognition of their lethal, life-denying qualities.

While the power to kill at a distance undoubtedly insulated combatants from the import of their actions, the desert undermined this insulation through its inability to 'bury' the dead. Derelict tanks and dead men littered the landscape, a persistent reminder of mortality, and men lived in intimate proximity both to death and the machines that enabled it. In the midst of this lay the complex duality of the tank, simultaneously war machine and mobile home:

Stacked around the sides of the turret were the six-pounder shells, nose downwards, hand-grenades, smoke grenades and machine gun ammunition [. . .] On the shelf, when we were in action, we usually kept also some Penguin books, chocolate or boiled sweets if we could get them, a tin of processed cheese, a knife and some biscuits. We were lucky enough to begin the battle with a tin of Australian butter as well. (Douglas 1946/1992: 24–5)

This is not equipment for the tank at rest: it is the tank at battle readiness. Outward force and inward nurturance take the same form, and the well-equipped mechanised soldier goes into battle with a shelf of Penguin books and a tin of butter. While the need for such comforts becomes evident in the repeated false starts and longueurs of the campaign, the tank remains, nonetheless, a site of radical uncertainty. On the border between human and machine, it is both clumsy automaton and enhanced flesh, home and its antithesis. Ironically, though, the most prominent and telling characteristic of the tank in *Alamein to Zem Zem* is not its potency, but its failure. This may be technologically-enhanced mechanised warfare, but as tracks break, gears seize, guns jam and engines overheat, Douglas's desert battlefield looks less like epic theatre and more like a vicious, disorganised farce (Figure 4.2).

Running Away: Eric Linklater's Picaresque Satire

Private Angelo (1946) surveys the war in Italy from the point of view of the eponymous Angelo and his patron the Count of Pontefiore. The book is darkly satiric, in places distressing, and often very funny, using Angelo's faux-naïve narration, and his assumption that all are as well-meaning as he, to expose the corruption and stupidity of the war. The plot involves its unlikely hero being conscripted into three different armies before finally killing a German, on whose body he finds enough money to enable his own domestic happy ending. Angelo, peripheral to structures of authority and, in spite of his innocence, very much a rogue as far as the rules of war are concerned, is a picaresque figure and also a very literal anti-hero. His defining characteristic is his cowardice, and his cheerful acknowledgement of this not only disrupts assumptions regarding masculine subjectivity and 'manliness', it also exposes the logic of war to a scrutiny it finds hard to bear.

The novel's challenge to customary assumptions regarding loyalty, belonging and 'right' is facilitated by Angelo's fluid identity. As the illegitimate offspring of the Count, his bastard inheritance makes him a common man who sees and hears far more than the average private. He is also aided in his ubiquity by his looks – he is at one point deployed as a 'homme fatale' – and his facility with languages. Angelo is useful to all sides, but belongs only to a timeless pastoral vision of Italy (241) that transcends the corruption of politics, invasion and war. His real loyalty is to beauty, as manifest in the body of his beloved Lucrezia and the art of Piero della Francesca, whose painting of the Adoration of the Shepherds comes to symbolise a peace transcending human concerns. Furthermore, in terms of Linklater's analysis of the war and its prosecution, the use of a 'foreign' protagonist facilitates a challenge to the unquestioned connection of manliness and war, and enables a detached examination of both fascist and British masculinities. Expected hierarchies of value are turned on their heads as Italian martial incompetence, a cliché familiar even from such contemporary writing as Douglas's *Alamein to Zem Zem*, becomes a matter of common sense. Crucially, Angelo's masculinity is not undermined by his entirely rational desire to save himself, nor does his refusal to accept the necessity of physical bravery exclude him from the male group. Rather it is the Germans and the British who come to seem either bad or mad, their masculine self-confidence a demonstration of childish immaturity, and radically flawed priorities.

In the case of the Germans, Linklater pulls no punches. They are greedy, self-absorbed sadists, and the text parodies the fetishisation of order and the lack of self-consciousness that go to create a belief in their own infallibility. When the Count is imprisoned without charge, and no-one can remember why he is there, General Hammerfurter simply responds that he 'is in a German prison. Therefore, of course, he is a criminal' (41). More disturbing is the portrait of Captain Schlemmer. Both an educated art critic and a manipulative sadist, he is temporarily undone by his own need for order and certainty. Finding himself in the same room as Piero's 'Adoration', he is tormented by not knowing whether the painting is authentic. Without this knowledge, he cannot categorise it, and thus finds it utterly unbearable. His response, typically, is violence: he opens fire on the painting (157) before destroying the castle and village that sheltered it.

The British, meanwhile, are depicted as schoolboys, friendly but reckless and haphazard, with no understanding of the damage they are inflicting. The central British character is the commando Simon Telfer, a man who operates on a system of 'useful Christian names' and whose rank fluctuates from Major to Lieutenant depending on a series of absurd bureaucratic decisions (107). Simon is improbably rescued by Angelo, and adopts him as an interpreter, but their friendship nearly founders when Angelo confesses to not having enjoyed the war in Libya (78–9). Angelo's horror of combat is utterly inexplicable to the British, and Linklater presents, in comic form, the already emergent mythology of the desert war:

> 'It's an ideal country for a war,' said the Intelligence Officer. 'You can't do any damage there, except to yourself and the enemy.'
> 'One had a lot of freedom in Libya,' said Simon, 'but the landscape needed colour to give it variety: that's where we began to wear chokers.'
> 'It's a pity we had to come into Europe,' said Michael. 'I enjoyed myself in the Desert.' (1946/1992: 78)

The Italians also live up to stereotype, being passionate, sybaritic and fundamentally corrupt. Here the satire benefits from frequent chapters using the Count as focaliser. The ultimate pragmatist, he begins the book as a friend of Mussolini and ends it infatuated with the American way of life. Yet the cynicism of the Count's relatively empowered point of view is persistently set against Angelo's first-hand experience. Throughout the book, Angelo's polite interventions expose not only the cost of war, but the linguistic distortions through which it is justified:

> 'I am not being unfriendly,' said Angelo in his most earnest voice. 'You must not think that, please. We are very grateful to you for coming to liberate us, but I hope you will not find it necessary to liberate us out of existence.' (1946/1992: 142–3)

Angelo's role as translator extends beyond the service he performs for the various armies: for the reader he translates the euphemisms of war back into the brutal reality of destruction. The text repeatedly emphasises the collateral damage of total war, a damage exacerbated by the fallibility of mechanised warfare. 'Do I, in any way, resemble Cassino?', asks Angelo, after being knocked unconscious by an indiscriminate English bombardment, and this point is reiterated with more gravity later in the text: 'a bomb has no political opinions and will explode in the wrong place quite as loudly as in the right place' (182).

Unsurprisingly, it is women who suffer in this game of war. In *Private Angelo* women are victims of what the poet Wrenne Jarman calls the 'rotted veils of man's misgovernment' (Bax and Stewart 1949: 136), and war is characterised as an inherently male pursuit, from which natural womanhood stands askance. But women's implied good sense is of little avail in a world where the boundary between private and public has collapsed, and where war has invaded domestic space. The powerlessness of Lucrezia, Annunciata and the Countess is paralleled by that of their men, who prove utterly incapable of defending them. Indeed, in a rare complication of the stereotype of women as unable to understand national loyalty, Lucrezia proves herself more politically astute than

Angelo. She warns him that allegiances mean nothing when it comes to the sexual politics of war, responding to his claim that the advancing Moroccan soldiers are 'on our side' with bitter realism: 'Not if you are a woman' (167). Rape is international, and Angelo's unloaded gun is of little use in protecting Lucrezia from this fate.

Yet in radically different ways, by the end of the book both the Count and Angelo have become new internationalists. The Count, having observed the machinations of power, comes to the conclusion that 'there is nothing international in the world but villainy' (218), and he survives by embracing a criminal enterprise that transcends national boundaries. Angelo meanwhile ends the novel in a parody of the conventional romantic happy ending. Returning from battle minus a hand, but with a mistress, he finds himself father to three children not his own. Initially offended that the 'polyglot forces of democracy' have left such an indelible mark upon his family, a moment's contemplation of the beauty of Tuscany turns him into an evangelist:

> ... I have a mission. I must demonstrate that all the peoples of the world – or four of them, at least – can make their home together in civilization. I shall bring up these children in such a way that they will have no obsession about their nationality, and that will be a very good thing indeed. For even the best of nations may have a bad influence on its subjects ... (241)

Angelo becomes a one-man embodiment of the United Nations, and Linklater, whose role as official War Office historian during 1944 gave him an intimate insight into the Italian conflict, crafts romantic reconstruction out of gratuitous destruction, while also boldly suggesting that the 'manliness' validated by war is a much over-rated construction.

'We've all got to die sometime!': Murder in Wartime

> A soldier sprawls in a muddy trench with machine-gun bullets crackling a foot or two overhead, and whiles away his intolerable boredom by reading an American gangster story. (Orwell 1944/1965: 71)

While it might seem counter-intuitive to read about the gratuitous death of strangers when living in fear of death, crime fiction remained as popular during the Second World War as it had been in the interwar years. As Stephen Knight has noted, standard accounts of the conflict dismiss the massive sales of popular writers such as Agatha Christie and Peter Cheyney, and in the process ignore the significant expression of cultural anxieties through what is, arguably, the most socially responsive of literary genres (1995: 161–2). Knight suggests that the wartime consumption of crime fiction cannot be dismissed as escapism, arguing that in the case of a writer like Christie, the dislocations of crime fiction symbolise, in manageable form, the alienating impact of war:

> Christie's wartime mysteries superintend contemporary battles from a distance and with an Austenesque pattern of radical displacement, not recognising the war as itself, but representing its effect in terms of disruptions to the normal balance of gender and social power. (1995: 163)

Unlike later critics, writers at the time were alert to the not-unproblematic intersection of crime fiction and culture. Graham Greene, in *The Ministry of Fear* (1943), has his persecuted protagonist Arthur Rowe describe the modern world to his dead mother, symbol of a lost Edwardian age of innocence. Real life now, he claims, is 'like a thriller', 'it's what we've all made of the world since you died' (Greene 1943/2001: 65). Greene suggests that life mirrors art, not so much through mimesis as through a process of becoming fantastical. The everyday world is rendered unreal by the encroachment of war's unthinkable violence: the body in the library finds its parallel in the bomb on the house. If one, why not the other? The parameters of plausibility are stretched by war and a new logic is required to make sense of unprecedented experiences. Greene found the generic forms of crime fiction and the thriller to be ideal for exploring this new 'paranoid reality' (Stewart 2006: 61); George Orwell, by contrast, feared that such narratives were as likely to generate as to explain the violence of war.

In 'Raffles and Miss Blandish' (1944) and 'The Decline of the English Murder' (1946), Orwell argues that the rise of fascism and the prosecution of the Second World War fundamentally devalued human life. 'Raffles and Miss Blandish' focuses on fiction's complicity in this process, and holds the hard-boiled novel to account for pandering to a 'cult of power' (Orwell 1944/1965: 76). James Hadley Chase's *No Orchids for Miss Blandish* (1939) is selected as a particularly pernicious example and denounced as 'a daydream appropriate to a totalitarian age' (78). In 'The Decline of the English Murder', by contrast, Orwell proposes that it is the transgression of the law that acts as an index of culture: the methods and motives of murderers are inextricably linked to national values. According to Orwell, the perfect pre-war English murderer 'should be a little man of the professional class – a dentist or a solicitor, say – living an intensely respectable life somewhere in the suburbs':

> He should go astray through cherishing a guilty passion for his secretary or the wife of a rival professional man, and should only bring himself to the point of murder after long and terrible wrestles with his conscience. [...]

The means chosen should, of course, be poison. In the last analysis he should commit murder because this seems to him less disgraceful, and less damaging to his career, than being detected in adultery. (Orwell 1946/1965: 11)

This intensely English mode of murder is compared to the actual wartime 'Cleft Chin Murder', the background to which 'was not domesticity, but the anonymous life of the dance-halls and the false values of the American film' (12). What disturbs Orwell about this case is its lack of premeditation. Elizabeth Jones and Karl Hulten did not know their victims and seemed to kill as much for the thrill of murder as for the meagre financial rewards of their crimes. Hulten was hanged, and Jones imprisoned – an act of leniency that led to a public outcry. This response provides the icing on the cake of Orwell's argument: 'It is difficult not to feel', he concludes, 'that this clamour to hang an eighteen-year-old girl was due partly to the brutalizing effects of war' (13).

The contrasting perspectives of Orwell and Greene give some indication as to why murder is a 'problem' in wartime. It is not simply the transgression that matters, but how that act is performed and how society responds to victim and perpetrator. Orwell's writing expresses his fear that readers exposed to the horrors of gratuitous violence will be attracted rather than repulsed, and that war will construct newly callous subjectivities. As the earlier sections of this chapter suggest, Orwell's fears were not without substance, and there is in his anxiety an echo of the ambivalence that permeates *Colonel Blimp*. In crime fiction, as in combat writing, a conflict emerges between the necessity of a total war ideology and the traditional, comforting myth of English sporting amateurism. Writers such as Christie and Margery Allingham adapted their fictions to suit the climate of threat, and these adaptations included both higher body counts and a willing embrace of the 'legitimate' murder of war. But while Christie and Allingham seemed comfortable turning amateur detectives into *de facto* combatants, Graham Greene was more willing to expose the ethical ambiguities of the genre. *The Ministry of Fear* (1943) is a remarkably bloodthirsty book, but like Powell and Pressburger's film, it undercuts its own adventure with persistent moral questioning. The popular fiction of killing thus represents both continuity and change in relation to pre-war generic templates, putting narratives of reassurance on a war footing, and making public and national what had once been strictly private concerns.

As Orwell's characterisation of the typical English murder suggests, interwar crime fiction focused predominantly on a middle-class milieu obsessed by respectability. Every character harboured a guilty secret and everyone was capable of murder in thought, if not in deed. It is, then, an illusion to imagine that interwar murder narratives depict a prelapsarian society violated by murder and restored to harmony by the detective. For all its tidy closures, this was a world in which 'nothing is sacred' (Light 1991: 67). Alison Light argues that the work of Agatha Christie can be read as a 'literature of convalescence' (69), facilitating the recovery of a nation traumatised by the First World War. In a world of determined superficiality, corpses go unmourned, and heroic masculinity becomes an object of ridicule. Yet interwar fiction is also characterised by the satisfactions of explanation. It is not so much that justice is done, as that bodies are fully explained. In the aftermath of a war in which bodies were quite literally annihilated, interwar detective fiction grants new integrity to the individual corpse. These bodies become the subject of multiple competing explanations and their deaths are given a surfeit of meanings. In reconstructing the corpse-as-signifier, interwar crime fiction also consoles its readership through the presentation of death as part of a rational pattern. Victims die for a reason explicable in terms of human desire; they are not simply the collateral damage of war's mass, mechanised slaughter (Plain, 2001: 33–4).

The desire to give meaning to individual deaths did not disappear with the advent of the Second World War, but in the early years of conflict at least, a new set of anxieties were addressed. Between 1940 and 1942, with the threat of invasion at its most intense, a number of crime writers responded by transforming their detectives into pro-active agents. Christie's Tommy and Tuppence Beresford and Allingham's Albert Campion mutated from amateur sleuths into semi-professional spy-hunters, struggling not to uncover the evidence of a past crime, but to prevent the prosecution of a future one. The body under threat in this prospective crime was neither wealthy heiress nor greedy landowner, but the vulnerable body of the nation itself. National security took precedence over individual concerns and the 'criminal' was configured as the 'enemy within', the fifth columnist whose misplaced loyalties corrupt the body politic. It says much about the flexibility of crime fiction that familiar detective figures could be mobilised to such 'national' ends, and it also indicates the extent to which readers now desired action more than explanation. Christie's *N or M?* (1941) opens with the middle-aged Tuppence's plaintive cry that 'It's bad enough having a war . . . but not being allowed to do anything in it just puts the lid on' (1941/1962: 6). Her sense of impotence, shared by her redundant husband Tommy, speaks to the war's disturbing removal of individual agency. In a world of conscription, evacuation and rationing, there seemed little that the individual could do to combat the vast impersonal forces that threatened to destroy self, community and nation. As Elizabeth Bowen observes, 'life, mechanized by the controls of wartime, and emotionally torn and impoverished by changes, had to complete itself in *some* way' (1950: 49), and the reading of crime fiction offers both vicarious agency and a fantasy of resolution in the face of almost unbearable uncertainty.

In *N or M?* the supremely ordinary Tommy and Tuppence save the nation from a fiendish fifth column plot being enacted in a seaside boarding house. Going undercover as middle-aged middle-Englanders, they must try to establish which of their fellow residents is a spy, and in consequence, much of their detection focuses on a reading of bodily signifiers. Who or what is archetypally British, and whose body bears the imprint of otherness? Christie plays on her readers' likely prejudices to throw suspicion on an Irish landlady and a German refugee; and in a sign of the shifting priorities of wartime detection, when a Polish refugee is murdered, her death receives only the most cursory of investigations (1941/1962: 125). Hers is, emphatically, a body that does not matter. She is simply collateral damage that helps Tuppence identify the more important body of the spy. In this, though, Christie's vision is far from reassuring. The 'German' turns out to be British, while one spy is discovered to be the bland, neurotic mother Mrs Sprot, and the other the blustering 'hearty Englishman' Commander Haydock. Captured by Haydock, Tommy experiences an epiphany: 'That jovial florid face [. . .] was only a mask. Why had he not seen it all along for what it was – the face of a bad-tempered overbearing Prussian officer' (144). *N or M?* gives with one hand and takes away with the other, suggesting that 'little' men and women can make a difference, while fundamentally challenging concepts of a clear and legible 'national' body.

A similar fantasy of agency is enacted in Margery Allingham's *Traitor's Purse* (1941). Again, the body in peril is that of the nation, and Allingham pulls no punches in her depiction of Britain's vulnerability: 'England was such a little place. It would take so short a time to fan the poison out all over her lovely petite body' (1941/1954: 168). The national body is equally a female one to be protected, and Albert Campion must save this damsel in distress from a man who thinks he alone knows what she wants: Lee Aubrey, the Principal of the Masters of Bridge. The Masters are a semi-secret society acting as a dictatorship within the body politic, and their existence, in the heart of England, implicitly raises uncomfortable questions about the constitution of the nation and its values. Aubrey is a megalomaniac who assumes that hereditary privilege should entitle him to absolute authority (203–5); he will save the nation from the Nazis by using their methods, not the supposedly 'British' techniques of fair play, muddle and improvisation. And here lies the reassurance of Allingham's text: while her readers might be disturbed by this vein of aristocratic corruption running through the nation, they will be consoled by the fact these fascist forces can be defeated by the familiar figure of the detective.

Yet here too Allingham adapts her text for the conditions of war: the detective, as well as the nation, is in crisis. Campion has lost his memory and his disability acts as another metaphor for Britain's imperilled state. That he survives, and succeeds, will be down to class and gender cooperation. Campion, and the nation, are kept afloat by the loyalty of his fiancée Amanda and man-servant Lugg. This is detection by a representative national body to save the national body in its hour of need (Plain 2003). And, consequently, the approach to mere individual bodies is, to say the least, utilitarian. At the end of the novel Campion is perched on a ledge above a cavern filled with lorries preparing to spread their criminal cargo around the nation. He is alone and unarmed, except for an experimental grenade. Up until this point the novel remains within the parameters of British sporting amateurism, but as Campion throws his grenade, a significant textual metamorphosis occurs: 'there was a sea of blazing petrol and paper and the fumes of smoldering sacks [. . .] Injured men swore and died under their lorries, while others fought each other in their attempts to clamber onto the ledge' (1941/1954: 197). In a scene of carnage far beyond the scale of any of Allingham's previous novels, it implicitly becomes clear that war both breaks down the detective's habitual detachment from the crime under investigation, and eases the prohibitions of the law. The men in the cavern were not simply criminals, they were working for the enemy, and their deaths do not count as murder.

In wartime, then, the detective is licensed to kill as well as detect. He becomes judge and executioner, as well as investigating agent. The most famous case of such executive power is undoubtedly Christie's *Curtain*, the final novel to feature Hercule Poirot, in which the detective solves the problem of an untraceable murderer by killing him. However, while it is undoubtedly significant that Christie imagined such an insoluble problem in the 1940s, the novel was not published until 1975. More pertinent for the reading public at the time was *The Moving Finger* (1943), which incongruously combines traditional village detection with a callous disregard for human life. As the novel ends, in typical Christie fashion with marriage and reward for the newly restored community, the narrator pauses for a brief moment of reflection:

> Just for a fleeting moment I thought of Mrs. Symmington and Agnes Woddell in their graves in the churchyard and wondered if they would agree [that everything turns out for the best], and then I remembered that Agnes's boy

hadn't been very fond of her and that Mrs. Symmington hadn't been very nice to Megan and, what the hell? we've all got to die some time! And I agreed with happy Miss Emily that everything was for the best in the best of possible worlds. (Christie 1943/1948: 189)

The refusal to mourn here is hyperbolic to the point of comedy, and it indicates that, for all the energy expended in identifying the murderer, the main concerns of the novel lie elsewhere. It is, as Knight has suggested, a novel that 'superintends' war from a distance. The narrator, Jerry, is an injured pilot sent to recuperate with his sister Joanna in a typical English country town, the peace of which is shattered by a series of poison-pen letters. While the investigators assume the writer to be a woman, and speculate fruitlessly on the manifestations of pathological repressed femininity, the community regresses into paranoia (65), seeking scapegoats in the non-conforming women of the village (44–5). In her depiction of Lymstock under siege, Christie is more than usually explicit in her suggestion that the idyllic 'English' community is a fragile construct. Perhaps in response to this vulnerability, the novel also demonstrates a considerable investment in the restoration of social 'norms', with the result that *The Moving Finger* is as much a fantasy of forceful masculinity as it is a detective novel.

In a culture of wounded masculinity, the marriage plot characteristic of crime fiction's resolution achieves a new significance, and *The Moving Finger* demonstrates just how far society has been destabilised by offering two romances: a background one in which Jerry's wayward sister is subjugated to the will of the dark and handsome local doctor, and a primary one in which Jerry restores his masculine agency through the god-like creation of woman. Twenty-year-old Megan seems devoid of femininity; without training in this socially necessary condition, she remains trapped in a pre-pubescent state. Neither masculine nor feminine, for much of the novel she is described as animal: 'She looked, I decided this morning, much more like a horse than a human being. In fact she would have been a very nice horse with a little grooming' (19). The absent femininity of Megan and the independent sexual power of Joanna act as metaphors for the war's disruption of female roles, and it is part of the novel's reassurance that both women are brought into alignment with heteronormative convention. Yet Christie struggles wholeheartedly to endorse the restoration of hegemonic masculinity, persistently undercutting events with comedy, to the extent that it is unclear whether she is making fun of the sophisticated Londoners, or whether she feels female agency must indeed know its limits. Either way, it is not the dead who matter. As Jerry's reflections suggest, no-one will mourn Mrs Symmington, while Agnes is debarred by her class from

signification. Far more important is the novel's assertion of communal health and gender normativity. *The Moving Finger* is designed to
assert stability in the face of change and to keep wartime trauma under
control: the brutality of its refusal to mourn psychologically putting the
civilian on a combat footing.

While Christie and Allingham respond to war by toughening up their
detectives within a context of generic reassurance, Graham Greene
undoes the comforts of genre by making them the subject of explicit
debate. At the centre of *The Ministry of Fear* is Arthur Rowe, a self-
confessed murderer who cannot forgive himself for the mercy killing of
his wife. Alone and unhappy, he wanders a London being blitzed beyond
recognition, attempting to avoid anything that might remind him of his
adult life. He is shaken from his guilt-ridden self-obsession by stumbling
into the midst of a fifth column plot to smuggle documents out of the
country. Beginning in a fortune-teller's tent that might have been 'an
impromptu outside lavatory' (1943/2001: 11) and ending with a suicide
in a public toilet (219–20), the book from the outset adopts a surreal
approach to the spy narrative. Not even the identity of the protagonist is
stable, as Rowe is temporarily reborn as a 'happy' man after losing his
memory in a bomb explosion. Renamed Richard Digby, the happy man
remembers nothing of his crime, nor of the war, which – once it has been
'gently broken to him' (119) – remains as unreal as schoolbook history
(116). In this paradoxical state of innocence regained, he acquires the
investigator's necessary detachment, and speculates with unwitting
irony, 'do you think . . . that by any chance I was a detective before this
happened?' (121).

By making his detective both a guilt-ridden murderer and an adventurer 'with the freshness of a boy' (169), Greene constantly foregrounds
questions of agency and responsibility, and he also sets in train an examination of the term 'murder' itself. Ironically annoyed that someone has
tried to murder him, Rowe approaches the 'Orthotex' detective agency
for help. As its name suggests, this is a deeply conventional business:

> Mr Rennit's calm incredulity shook Rowe. He said with resentment, 'In all
> your long career as a detective, have you never come across such a thing as
> murder – or a murderer?'
> Mr Rennit's nose twitched over the cup. 'Frankly,' he said, 'no. I haven't.
> Life, you know, isn't like a detective story. Murderers are rare people to meet.
> They belong to a class of their own.' (35)

Rennit links crime to the 'lower orders' (35) revealing a Victorian sensibility untouched by interwar crime's insistence that the killer must be
'one of us'. This is in marked contrast to the opinions of Willi Hilfe, the

novel's symbol of murderous modernity. For the ironically named Hilfe there is no such thing as a 'criminal class' (46):

> 'Your old-fashioned murderer killed from fear, from hate – or even from love, Mr Rowe, very seldom for substantial profit. None of these reasons is quite – respectable. But to murder for position – that's different, because when you've gained the position nobody has a right to criticize the means. Nobody will refuse to meet you if the position's high enough. Think how many of your statesmen have shaken hands with Hitler. (47)

This reiterates the dynamic described by Orwell in 'Raffles and Miss Blandish'. These people do not murder to preserve their respectability, they kill to achieve power and with it the respect born of fear. Murder, in this new world order, is not the 'English' variety – long-repressed desires mutating into an essentially romantic private scheme. Rather it is open, pragmatic and ideologically motivated (184). Superficially, then, Greene sets up his spy thriller along the established national lines of 'them' and 'us'. They commit murder without a qualm, we – at least in the form of Rennit – can hardly credit its existence.

However, the ethics of both murder and war are complicated by the introduction of Prentice, the 'surrealist' policeman (158). Prentice is a professional detective-agent, a symbol of British modernity to counter Hilfe, but also a policeman given to 'giggling', who does not know how to use a gun (165–8). This ambivalence is typical of wartime representations of British national identity. In film and documentary, the contrast between the British and the Nazis is repeatedly figured in terms of bathos. J. B. Priestley's *Britain At Bay* (1940), for example, juxtaposes goose-stepping Nazis in crisp uniforms against ramshackle British volunteers, drilling in baggy shorts and vests: it is a self-conscious deployment of the myth of the underdog, designed to make the Nazi war-machine seem absurdly overblown. Faced with the impossible efficiency of the enemy, the only outlet for anxiety is humour. As Mrs Miniver, benchmark of middlebrow attitudes to war, observes, 'one had to laugh', and to laugh at the enemy is, psychologically at least, to deny his power (Struther, 1939/1989: 63). Nonetheless, the war must be prosecuted in practical terms, and the character of Prentice demonstrates the contradictory forces that need to be yoked together to create a British 'agent'. He is both ruthless and infantile, merciless and gentle (160), and his introduction brings an urgency into the narrative that overrides Rowe's introspection. This is war, not 'just' murder.

Prentice and Rowe's adventure ends in 'a massacre on an Elizabethan scale', and like Allingham's exploding cavern, this is an ending appropriate to the excess of war. Yet the killing of the traitor Dr Forrester by his disciple, Johns, is genuinely shocking. It is one of the tonal shifts in this section of the book that sets Rowe's storybook understanding of war against a more brutal reality. It also foregrounds the moral impasse faced by the hero-worshipping but humane 'little man' Johns. Betrayed, deceived and made a passive accomplice to the murder of the innocent Stone, he can see no solution but to become himself a killer. His actions occupy a border zone between domestic murder and public war that is further complicated by the discovery of a 'body'. Jones, Mr Rennit's second in command, an insignificant figure who disappeared in the opening pages of the book, is eventually accounted for, but his disinterment refuses the comforts of explanation. This is not the restoration of the grievable body of interwar fiction, rather it is a return to the body annihilated by war. Absurdity and moral seriousness struggle for supremacy as Greene lists the component parts that constituted Jones: 'So is a poor human creature joined respectably together like a doll: take him apart and you are left with a grocery box full of assorted catches and buckles and buttons' (186). Yet Jones' absent body is not allowed to signify for long. Rather than becoming a disturbingly prescient symbol of war's atrocity, he is swiftly assimilated into the refusal to mourn characteristic of wartime narratives:

> 'What do you think they did to Jones?'
> 'I don't suppose we shall ever know. In time of war, so many bodies are unidentifiable. So many bodies,' he said sleepily, 'waiting for a convenient blitz.'
> Suddenly, surprisingly and rather shockingly, he began to snore. (188)

In this image, the war does not overwrite the domestic narrative of murder; rather, the massive destructive force of the Blitz is enlisted as an accomplice and a blessing in disguise for the contemporary murderer.

Greene's novel concludes in a characteristically ambivalent fashion: Rowe sacrifices the comforts of amnesia for the pain of knowledge. For many wartime readers, however, the opposite effect was desired, and as the conflict progressed towards its endgame, a significant transformation in public taste became evident. David Kynaston records an overwhelming desire to get back to normal, 'which in essence meant life before the war' (2007: 49). With subversive gardeners growing flowers instead of vegetables (49–50) and cinemas attracting record audiences, there also emerged a significant shift in reading patterns. Penguin 'Specials', designed to inform and educate, experienced a massive slump in sales, leading in 1945 to their temporary abandonment (55). Mass Observation's survey *Books and the Public* (1944) did much to explain why, revealing a populace with little energy for self-improvement and no appetite for war:

I like light fiction best, of the family story kind, and I prefer them to have a happy ending, even if it is highly improbable. There's enough tragedy in real life to want to read about it, and that's one of the reasons I *never* read a war book. (McAleer 1992: 95)

A similar trend was evident in the cinema, where the vogue for documentary realism gave way to the box office triumph of Gainsborough costume melodrama. Beginning in 1943 with *The Man in Grey*, Gainsborough brought lavish costumes and sets to the screen in narratives less concerned with historical verisimilitude than with emotional excess. This transition in public taste horrified the highbrow critics but satisfied a war-weary public seeking pleasure as an escape from the grey realities of too much work, not enough play and a miserable diet. This is the 'postwar': a period of intellectual and spiritual exhaustion in which writers nonetheless attempted to think beyond conflict and to imagine new possibilities, while the general public turned away from the serious business of planning the future, and delighted instead in melodrama's presentation of the past 'as a site of physical pleasure' (Harper 1994: 129). In this topsy-turvy time the absence of war proves stranger than its presence, and wartime diaries struggle to make sense of a period characterised by 'a horrible mixture of dread and longing' (Partridge, June 1944; 1978/1996: 186). After a surfeit of duty, cultural preference became one of the few arenas through which people could express the widely held perception that the nation deserved some reward for years of suffering and sacrifice (Kynaston 2007: 21), but superficial transitions in taste disguised the more disturbing legacies of war. This was also a period of mourning, readjustment and reconstruction in which people struggled to assimilate a world changed beyond all recognition. The postwar is thus a beginning rooted, psychologically, in the impossibility of an ending: a fearful ambivalence best captured by Stevie Smith in her unanswerable question: 'Shall we win the post-war, how does it go?' (1949/1979: 90).

Notes

1. As Petra Rau has noted, genocide represents an important exception to this statement (Rau 2010: 1).
2. Although a popular myth, the illusory quality of such representations of the aviator was recognised at the time. Behind the fighter pilot's duel stood the indiscrimination of strategic bombing, a point made by John Middleton Murry in his discussion of Hillary: 'The glory of the fighter-pilot grinds slowly and inexorably down to the shame of Bomber Command' (quoted in Rawlinson 2000: 66).

3. The group hero, while modern in construction, was not always forward looking in attitude. Nevil Shute's *Most Secret* (1945) is a blood-thirsty narrative which combines a defence of total war methods with attitudes to the enemy more typical of Great War popular fiction. A group of men united by a pathological desire to kill Germans orchestrate a morale-boosting flame-thrower raid on the French coast, satisfying their need for revenge by watching Germans burn to death (1945/2000: 141). When they decide to increase the potency of the weapon by using dirty oil, the narrator briefly pauses to consider the ethics of their actions, but the book seems satisfied with its assertion that 'if the Boche had thought of it first he'd have used it against us fast enough' (215). Shute's conviction that the end justifies the means might, however, have carried more weight had not one of the characters been avenging the death of his pet rabbit.

4. The difficulty associated with non-combatant masculinity in the war years is explored in the work of a number of women writers. In Barbara Noble's *Doreen* the asthmatic Geoffrey Osborne has learnt to 'conceal his self-contempt' (1946/2005: 42), while in Betty Miller's *On the Side of the Angels* Claudia, infatuated with a commando, suddenly recognises the social stigma of the civilian, a figure 'branded by the violence not committed' (1945/1985: 214).

II

Postwar

Chapter Five

Escaping

As we recorded some time ago the Swastika is doing a disappearing act. So too are stories allied to Nazi brutality, or to grim aspects of the war.
The time will come when great war stories will be screened again . . .
And those pictures will be welcome.
But at the moment the immediate feeling is: 'Let's get away from the Nazis.'
(Editorial, *Picturegoer*, 14 October 1944)

As the war entered its final stages, literature as well as cinema proved keen to get away from the Nazis, and indeed from the physically, emotionally and spiritually enervating landscape of wartime Britain. The literature of escape took many forms, and this chapter will focus on writing emerging from the later war or immediate postwar years that negotiates the conflict through avoidance, or challenges its shibboleths through comedy. These are fictions which turn away from the effort of the 'long haul' to focus on pleasure, offering frivolity as an antidote to war weariness; or which conjure up fantastic worlds, including the world of childhood, as an alternative habitus in the face of an inhospitable reality. Traces of the wartime context, though, are still evident in these works. As Diana Wallace has noted, while readers might be attracted to the richness of a past world, 'any historical novel always has as much, or perhaps more, to say about the time in which it is written' (2005: 4). These narratives, then, occupy a complex double space: both of their time and resistant to it, escapist yet critically engaged.

There are obvious advantages to setting fiction in the past, especially for writers wishing to appeal to a female readership that perceived itself excluded from the public narratives of nation and war. The past is both fixed and mutable: within the framework of a reassuring known resolution, all manner of fantastical interventions might be imagined. The past is also a site that enables the examination of contemporary issues through a safely distancing lens. Jenny Hartley argues that women historical novelists 'plunder' past wars for their fictions (1997:

151), their critical engagement with conflict shifting as the pressures of the contemporary moment changed. Writing of Daphne du Maurier, Hartley observes that while the Restoration setting of *Frenchman's Creek* (1941) offered a fantasy of agency, her 1946 novel of the English civil war, *The King's General*, instead became a 'vehicle for late and post-war weariness' (150). Another example is provided by Margaret Irwin's *Young Bess* trilogy (1944–53), which maps present anxieties onto the Elizabethan era, inserting both romance and a narrative of female power into a reassuring context of 'national continuity, stability and greatness' (Wallace 2005: 97). But the past could also be used more critically. Discussing Sylvia Townsend Warner's *The Corner That Held Them* (1948) and T. H. White's *The Once and Future King* (1958), Jan Montefiore observes that these writers' fictionalisation of the Middle Ages questioned 'the patriotic fantasy of an ideally unchanging England' (2009: 39). Naomi Mitchison also creatively politicised history, using it as a space through which to imagine 'an abstract future postwar', and to challenge the assumptions of patriarchal history (Plain 1996: 143–4; 154). Mitchison had good reason for choosing the past as a means of writing about the present. In a career of over seventy years, she wrote only one contemporary novel: *We Have Been Warned* (1935). The book, which deals with the politics of socialism was, admits her biographer Jenni Calder, 'uneven and unsatisfactory in many ways' (1997: 121), but it was its sexual explicitness that led to its rejection by Cape, Gollancz and John Lane. Its eventual publishers, Constable, then proceeded to cut the book at proof stage. 'It was probably no accident' concludes Calder, that Mitchison 'returned to the ancient world as a way of writing political fiction' (124).

The past was, then, the safest place for any writer wishing to engage with sexual politics and, for many popular writers, it became a space within which women's fantasies could be made explicit. Diana Wallace suggests that historical novels of the period exhibited 'an almost obsessive concern with transgressive and subversive femininities' (2005: 80), and it is not difficult to find examples to support her claims. Daphne du Maurier's Dona St Columb, the heroine of *Frenchman's Creek*, became a pirate, while Magdalen King-Hall's wicked Lady Skelton took to the road as a highwaywoman. King-Hall's novel was filmed as *The Wicked Lady* (1945), becoming one of the most successful of the Gainsborough Studio melodramas, and Wallace suggests that rebellions such as these appealed because they represented a reaction against the 'suppression' required of women in wartime (2005: 84). But not all the costume novels of the 1940s found their focus in explicit transgression, or in an assertion of women's place in the narrative of British history. Some fiction spoke directly to the 'postwar' moment, articulating a set of desires that resonated powerfully with the conflicted position of women at the end of the war.

A 'fantastic dream': Georgette Heyer's Double Discourse

> [A]lthough she would not for any consideration have acknowledged it, the prospect of being able to cast her burdens on his shoulders could not but attract her. [. . .] it was fatally easy to allow herself to be carried into a fantastic dream wherein she was only expected to do as she was bid. (Heyer 1946/2004: 35–6)

Elinor Rochdale's fantasy of submission is presented as the logical desire of a woman who has, like the wartime nation, experienced six years of disagreeable hardship. Reduced to penury by her father's ruin, Elinor's desire for security is understandable, but it coexists with an equally contemporary desire for independence. Indeed, she begins *The Reluctant Widow* (1946) by asserting that she would rather receive a wage for her labour than be dependent on the charity of her relatives (1946/2004: 23). Her narrative thus becomes a search for acceptable terms through which a woman can reconcile her desire for agency with the limited possibilities offered by her society.

In her heroine's dilemma, Heyer acknowledges the contradictory pressures placed on women in wartime: the demand that they contribute to the war effort, often through the adoption of male roles, while yet maintaining their traditional femininity (Higonnet, 1987: 7). The expectation that women maintain this double consciousness permeated the culture of the 1940s, but it was understood throughout as a temporary wartime measure:

> [R]epresentations . . . were designed to instil patriotic commitment while at the same time reassuring both women *and* men that, regardless of what it was women were doing during the war, their femininity would survive.
>
> Drawing upon a familiar melodramatic narrative, one frequently deployed theme promised that love and marriage would follow wartime service and sacrifice. (Rose 2003: 128)

At the end of the war, attitudes towards working women hardened. John Bowlby's work on adolescent criminality, published in 1946, identified separation from their mothers as a common denominator amongst delinquent youth, and women's magazines were wholeheartedly propounding a pro-natalist, domestic agenda (Kynaston 2007: 98). In this context, the 'rescue' of Elinor from a life of drudgery as a working woman places *The Reluctant Widow* firmly in line with contemporary ideology. Yet it would be a mistake to assume Heyer's total allegiance to the postwar cult of the housewife, or to imagine that a consistent message emerges from her fictions. Even without the conservative gender pressures of 1946, the conventions of genre insist that Elinor's narrative could only end in marriage. This is the shape of the formula, and the space of transgression lies not in the ending, but in the narrative crises that beset the heroine *en route* to her eventual happiness. *The Reluctant Widow* pushes few boundaries in this respect: the novel is a combination of detective story and gothic romance, with echoes of *Pride and Prejudice*. Indeed, in its concern with international intrigue and national security, the book looks back to an earlier phase of the war. Far more troubling, in terms of the 'subversive femininities' discussed by Wallace, and the particular tensions of the 'postwar', are the trials and tribulations that beset Hero Wantage, the protagonist of *Friday's Child* (1944).

Heyer's lively late-war novel is a Cinderella story that takes an oblique approach to social criticism. The book is based on the premise of a woman so naïve that she takes everything her husband says *literally*, thereby getting into great trouble, and at the same time exposing the hypocrisy and double standards of fashionable male society (228–9). Hero Wantage is not an entirely typical Heyer heroine, being utterly besotted with her husband and childhood friend, Lord Sheringham, who has married her in a fit of pique after being turned down by the 'incomparable' Isabella Milborne. Hero's conviction that her husband can do no wrong is presented as laudable loyalty, and the book demands that 'Sherry' grow up and become worthy of his teenage bride. The presentation of Hero, though, is more complex than this summary might suggest. Moving immediately from the schoolroom to the private house of marriage, and spending most of her time with Sherry's friends, Hero learns the language of male banter rather than that of female propriety; and in consequence, many of her problems arise from her inappropriate linguistic register. As Kathleen Bell has noted (1995), Heyer often makes use of cross-dressing heroines, but Hero represents a subtly different manifestation of this trope. She is, in effect, a linguistic cross-dresser: able to perform polite femininity when required, but much more at home in homosocial environments.

Hero's problems, which largely stem from behaving like a man when she should be acting as a woman, emphasise the extent to which femininity is a learnt condition. Hero exists outside the social codes policing polite behaviour, and her innocence enables Heyer comically to expose the cynical double standards of both Regency and contemporary society:

'It isn't Sherry's fault!' Hero said, firing up in defence of her free-spoken husband. 'He is forever telling me what I must not say! The thing is that I don't perfectly remember what I may say, and what I may not. I dare say I ought not to call that dancer a fancy-piece either?'

'Upon no account in the world!' Mr Ringwood said emphatically.

'Well, I must say I think it's very hard. What may I call her, Gil?'

'Nothing at all! Ladies know nothing of such things.' (Heyer 1944/2004: 124–5)

Hero's confusion highlights the impossible demands of performing femininity in the 1940s, and in other respects too the book offers insight into the preoccupations of wartime culture. The crises of the plot include the machinations of the unpleasant Lord Revesby, who has fathered an illegitimate child, and the question of whether Isabella, who has been exceptionally well-schooled in the performance of femininity, will put passion over status in her choice of husband. While Revesby's behaviour is another instance of sexual double standards, Isabella's choice of husband speaks to the anti-elitist leanings of what would become the postwar settlement. This being a Regency romance, her choice is between two aristocrats, but she finds herself repulsed by the chill decorum of her most wealthy suitor and opts instead for the warm-blooded 'people's' aristocrat, Lord Wrotham. In *Friday's Child*, as in the later *The Reluctant Widow*, Heyer is careful to stress the value of the social contract. A capacity for cross-class respect is always a sign of virtue in a character (1944/2004: 136).

Writing of Heyer's 1940 novel, *The Corinthian*, Kathleen Bell observes that the hero and heroine undertake a journey 'which introduces them to experiences not usually encountered by members of their class' and concludes that this can be related to 'a journey recommended to the British wartime population as a whole' (1995: 158). Hero's journey is of a very different order, and perhaps the novel is most manifestly a 'postwar' text in its extensive fantasies of conspicuous consumption (1944/2004: 44). Hero spends fortunes and, after years of living Cinderella-like with her ugly cousins, has more frocks than she can wear. Heyer's novels of the mid-1940s thus seem to present a twin fantasy of shopping and submission. Unlike Elinor Rochdale, Hero has no problem submitting to her husband, and in many ways seems to be living out the reward-contract described by Sonya Rose. Yet Hero is uncomfortable with the hyperbolic femininity of the fashionable set, and finds it difficult to let go of the language she shares with her male friends. Hero's marriage is thus an act of reassurance in which a boyish, energetic woman is willingly infantilised, not least through her husband's assertion that 'Hero is a nonsensical name for a girl' (40). Society sees heroism as the preserve of men, and in renaming his wife 'Kitten', Sherry deprives her of both age and agency.

Somehow, the Regency woman, like her post-Second World War compatriot, must navigate a path rigidly policed by the gender norms of a culture that prioritises a decorative role for women. The world created by Heyer offers the pleasures of familiarity and easy identification, while simultaneously translating its readers to a happier time in which crises and adventures are played out in a world of plentiful food, spacious houses and fantastic outfits. Beauty was, thus, still a duty but, in contrast to the world of the 1940s, the rewards were plentiful and guaranteed.

'Something was changing': The Distorted World of *Titus Groan*

'There should be no rich, no poor, no strong, no weak,' said Steerpike, methodically pulling the legs off the stag-beetle, one by one, as he spoke. 'Equality is the great thing, equality is *everything*.' He flung the mutilated insect away. (Peake 1946/1998: 291)

Not all alternative landscapes were as hospitable as Heyer's Regency world. *Titus Groan* (1946), the first instalment of Mervyn Peake's Gormenghast series, introduces a world of dust-encrusted tradition peopled by characters, such as the 'grey scrubbers', who are born into roles of inherited drudgery. The life of the upper classes is little better. Lord Sepulchrave, father to the eponymous Titus, spends his days in the endless reiteration of ritual, performing the ceremonies and observances accreted during the reigns of the previous seventy-five Earls of Groan. This is a richly imagined world, but also a grotesque and, at times, horrific one. Cruelty is built into the fabric of Gormenghast Castle, and its inhabitants are flawed, venal and, in Steerpike's case, sociopathic. Nonetheless, the book made a considerable impact, which Anthony Burgess attributes to the context of its publication: '1946, year of austerity, was very ready for imaginative feasts' (1946/1998: 9). Burgess goes on to suggest an absence of 'topical themes' (10) in the novel, arguing that Peake creates a world that resists a 'central sermon or warning' (9), but this seems a debatable conclusion, not least because the stagnant world of Gormenghast proves singularly ill-prepared to deal with evil and the changes it will force upon a fossilised society. *Titus Groan*, then, like so much literature of this period, both bears the imprint of its context, and seeks, through extravagant fantasy, to displace the known world.

The novel charts the Machiavellian rise of the youthful Steerpike from the castle kitchens to a position of power as adopted son of Barquentine, son of Sourdust, Lord of the Library; an elevation he achieves by playing on the vanities of those around him, and through the symbolic act of burning down Lord Sepulchrave's library. Steerpike's story is woven into the narrative of the royal family and their entourage: Sepulchrave, the melancholy, book-loving seventy-sixth earl; his monumental countess, Lady Gertrude, who spends her life surrounded by birds and a sea of white cats; the lonely Fuchsia, sister to the newly born Titus; her nurse, the diminutive Nannie Slagg; her aunts, the foolish twin sisters, Cora and Clarice, and the family's doctor, Prunesquallor, a man who never stops talking, but who nonetheless has sufficient perception to observe Steerpike's rise with concern. These are the insiders, and their necessary others are the dwellers beyond the castle walls, an archaic society of men who carve and women who grow old before their time. This semi-feudal world is constructed through a language alternatively comical and incantatory. There is something Lawrentian and apocalyptic in Peake's intense rhetoric, especially in the portentous account of Keda, an outsider from the dwellings who becomes wet nurse to Titus. On returning to her people, the two men she loves fight naked in the moonlight to possess her. Both die and she becomes an outcast, a crude symbol of suffering who wanders the earth:

> 'Keda,' she was saying, 'your life is over. Your lovers have died. Your child and her father are buried. And you also are dead. Only your bird sings on. [. . .] Beauty will die away suddenly and at any time. At any time now – from sky and earth and limb and eye and breast and the strength of men and the seed and the sap and the bud and the foam and the flower – all will crumble for you, Keda, for all is over . . . (355)

Yet this mysticism that typically figures women as creatures of intuition, bonded to the natural world, is leavened by episodes of comic absurdity (337–8, 385). Within the walls of the castle, Peake creates an ambivalent fairy-tale world, playing with traditional tropes to produce a world of dissonance and disquiet. Steerpike, for example, escapes from servitude in the kitchens in an epic climb across the roofs of Gormenghast, culminating in a Sleeping-Beauty-like battle with the ivy that leads to Fuchsia's attic retreat. But he is no prince, and Fuchsia understands nothing of romance: she awakens him by throwing the rotting dregs of a flower vase in his face. Yet while comedy and mysticism are combined to create a monstrous sense of place, Peake creates character through an almost Jamesian descriptive intensity:

> Making use of the miniature and fluted precipice of hard, white discoloured flesh, where Fuschia's teeth had left their parallel grooves, he bit greedily, his top teeth severing the wrinkled skin of the pear, and the teeth of his lower jaw entering the pale cliff about halfway up its face; they met in the secret and dark centre of the fruit – in that abactinal region where, since the petals of the pear flower had been scattered in some far June breeze, a stealthy and profound maturing had progressed by day and night. (150–1)

Steerpike eats as he lives, with an aggressive desire to penetrate secrets and Peake's imagery encapsulates the violence, effort and deceit of his anti-hero's journey. Yet for all the gothic monstrosity of both setting and language, the wider resonances of plot should not be overlooked. Gormenghast is both threatened – by Steerpike's machinations – and is itself threatening in its absolute denial of human subjectivity.

Titus Groan begins and ends in the echoing Hall of Bright Carvings, presided over by the caretaker Rottcodd. Like every other character in the book, Rottcodd has been born to a role, and he never leaves his sanctum, nor questions the emptiness of his hours. Yet, even in his intense isolation, at the book's end he intuits a new and pervasive sense of threat:

> And as he pondered he became aware of a sense of instability – a sensation almost of fear – as though some ethic he had never questioned, something on which whatever he believed was founded and through which his every concept filtered was now threatened. As though, somewhere, there was *treason*. (Peake 1946/1998: 500)

The growing sense of uncertainty that characterises the later chapters of the book is singularly appropriate to the post-atomic, Cold War world in which it was finally published. The ending, with its description of the 'Earling' ceremony through which the infant Titus becomes the seventy-seventh Earl of Groan, is sinister in its emphasis on surveillance: all the characters watch each other, made newly paranoid by the disturbing force of change. Yet the book looks backwards too for its terrors. Peake was traumatised by his military service (Stevenson 1986: 107; Wasson 2010), and irrespective of his intentions in creating the fantasy world of Gormenghast, there are aspects of the novel that uncannily revisit the ideological pressures of the conflict. Steerpike's manipulation of the greedy twins Cora and Clarice is particularly telling in this respect. In their desire for power and their perception of having been mistreated, they become a crude manifestation of the force of resentment: fickle masses in thrall to a dictator who alternately threatens them and promises them riches beyond imagination (254–61).

Yet it would be a mistake to read Steerpike simply as the serpent in the garden or the dictator in embryo. Gormenghast is no Eden, and its rigid hierarchies are depicted as oppressive and dehumanising. Each character's subjectivity is limited to their function, and the castle depends upon the unchallenged operation of this caste system. This is made most evident in the fate of Flay, first servant of Lord Sepulchrave. Flay's sense of self is entirely invested in his role – until absurd circumstances lead to his banishment from the castle. Yet, this catastrophic exile leads not to collapse, but to a tentative awakening:

> The prospect from the northern cave was unusual. It gave Mr Flay what he imagined must be pleasure. He was discovering more and more in this new and strange existence, this vastness so removed from corridors and halls, burned libraries and humid kitchens, that gave rise in him to a new sensation, this interest in phenomena beyond ritual and obedience – something which he hoped was not heretical in him . . . (443–4)

No longer interpellated as a servant, Flay sees the world differently, and takes pleasure in his self-sufficiency (441–2). The book thus suggests that it is only disruption that awakens people from the mindless repetition of ritual, the way things have always been. But the question remains: at what cost? Both stasis and rebellion have grim repercussions. Conformity dulls the senses, creating a cancerous self-absorption, but Steerpike's transgressive self-definition is only achieved through an equally selfish, and powerfully destructive, amorality.

Peake's fantasy, then, is a disturbing one, demonstrating the lure of power and the threat posed by free will to an ordered hierarchical society, while exposing that society as dehumanising and destructive. A rich imaginative feast, perhaps, but also a bleak and indigestible alternative even to the disturbing world emerging in the aftermath of Hiroshima and the Holocaust.

Thinking about Kôr: Elizabeth Bowen's Temporal Shifts

> This war shows we've by no means come to the end. If you can blow whole places out of existence, you can blow whole places into it. I don't see why not. (Bowen 1944/1980: 730)

First published in 1944, 'Mysterious Kôr' focuses on the strategies through which people protect themselves against war's emotional depredations. The vulnerable Pepita's imagination takes her outside the time and space of war-ravaged London and relocates her in the fantastical landscape of 'Kôr', 'a completely forsaken city, as high as cliffs and as white as bones, with no history' (Bowen 1980/1983: 729). Inhabited only by herself and her lover, Arthur, Kôr is a 'saving hallucination' (Bowen 1945/1950: 50), as real to Pepita as the hostile environment of London. Pepita's Kôr is blown into existence as a necessary strategy for surviving the pressures of wartime, and its logical inversion of the relationship between creation and destruction frees her from the pain of investing in the fragile here and now. Arthur, however, is not so sure about the viability of Kôr, initially responding with the gendered assumption that women's being is predicated upon a need for others. Pepita's response encapsulates the alienating impact of war: 'Think about people? How can anyone think about people if they've got any heart? I don't know how other girls manage: I always think about Kôr' (730). Pepita's room-mate Callie, by contrast, survives through an assertive process of normalising. As discussed in Chapter 2, she holds fast to pre-war notions of hospitality, chaperoning Pepita through the duration of Arthur's visit. As she waits for the lovers to return, the naïve Callie is mesmerised by the extraordinary brightness of the moonlit night: her 'saving hallucination' is a consolatory fable of romance (734).

For all the frustrations of 'Mysterious Kôr', Pepita's strategy seems a healthy mode of escape; but not all of Bowen's stories reveal such a controlled relationship between the present and the alternative spaces of imagination, memory and the past. Writing of *The Demon Lover* stories, Bowen notes that the past 'in all these cases, discharges its load of feeling into the anaesthetized and bewildered present' (1945/1950: 51). This image of wounding, of violent irruption, implies that the present can only be evaded at a cost. Escape seems often to be a double-edged sword, and Bowen acknowledges that many of her 'resistance fantasies are in themselves frightening' (50). In 'The Happy Autumn Fields', for example, Mary's hallucinatory inhabitation of a Victorian past amounts almost to a death wish. Mary is pulled into the past by a 'dangerous' box of letters and photographs; the residue of unknown lives. Yet these fragments have a visceral intensity that utterly absorbs her. Transported out of the dust of bomb-damaged London, she enters a state of profound otherness beyond the dangers of the Blitz and the relationships of the present. The pleasures of inhabiting her other self are such that, on returning to consciousness, she is frustrated at 'being saddled with Mary's body', and pushes away the concerns of her contemporary lover, Travis, who appears to her 'like a book once read [. . .] remembered clearly but with indifference' (677). Yet the past world to which she so eagerly returns is itself a painful one. While the family romance has a ravishing intensity that fills her with desire, her alter-ego, Sarah, is overcome by a sense of 'formless dread' (681). Nevertheless, this escape from fear into fear is a narrative Mary cannot bear to abandon, and its loss leaves her bereft:

> There being nothing left, she wished he would come to take her to the hotel. The one way back to the fields was barred by Mary's surviving the fall of the ceiling. Sarah was right in doubting that there would be tomorrow: Eugene, Henrietta were lost in time to the woman weeping there on the bed, no longer reckoning who she was. (683)

Neither Mary nor Sarah, the explosions leave her caught between two worlds: the emotionally authentic one of the past and the 'rot-dry' imitation of the present (683). Mary's refusal of the present is a critique of a modernity that cannot feel – we 'only know inconvenience now, not sorrow' (683) – but it is also an acknowledgement of what Bowen terms the 'desiccation, by war, of our day-to-day lives' (1945/1950: 49). But for all the value that Bowen places on hallucination, the story does not suggest that Mary can survive in the past, and the character's subjectivity is stabilised through the recognition of an 'other': the 'helpless white face' of Travis. This is a transition from what Julia Kristeva has termed 'women's time' – a time outside the remorseless linear progression of history – to the symbolic order of patriarchal society. While Mary has been lost in the sensations of her timeless other world, Travis has imposed order on the past, sorting the letters and determining the historical fate of her fantasy family. To survive, suggests Bowen, hallucinations must ultimately be contained.

The dangers of failing to reconcile past and present are at the heart of one of Bowen's most desolate short stories, 'Ivy Gripped the Steps', in which a middle-aged man turns back from a denuded present to the memory of a golden Edwardian era. Here in vivid nostalgic colour is a culture of warmth, vitality, effortless leisure and desire; the antithesis of a bleakly-evoked contemporaneity. The comparison is starkly realised. Southstone, declared the 'front line' in 1940, has been destroyed not by war's violence but by an incremental draining of purpose:

> It was now the September of 1944; and, for some reason, the turn of the tide of war, the accumulation of the Invasion victories, gave Southstone its final air of defeat. The withdrawal of most of the soldiers, during the summer, had drained off adventitious vitality. [. . .] And, within the very last few days, the silencing of the guns across the Channel had ended the tentative love affair with death: Southstone's life, no longer kept at least to a pitch by shelling warnings, now had nothing but an etiolated slowness. (Bowen 1980/1983: 687)

Southstone's identity has been irrevocably changed by war. The leisured self-sufficiency of a seaside past cannot be recaptured: ironically,

Southstone – a 'town without function' (691) – has lost its meaning. Bowen's evocation of a more richly textured past is, however, only deceptively nostalgic. Her alienated protagonist, Gavin Doddington, borders on the pathological in his obsession with the lost world of his mother's friend, Mrs Nicholson. The past is a site of painful memory, a betrayal that, Bowen suggests, arrested his development and rendered him incapable of feeling. Only the past is real to him, its appeal embodied not just in Mrs Nicholson's body, but also in the 'effortless' quality of her *rentier* existence (690) and her relation to the symbolic order. She is another example of a woman who understands only the personal: secure in a prelapsarian belief that 'civilized countries are polite to each other', she enjoys the happy belief that, in its Edwardian apotheosis, History has 'all ended happily' (690). That the inhabitation of timelessness is unsustainable is evident in the story's concluding images of the contemporary Gavin. His return to the past is a 'tour of annihilation' (708): he has become a living ghost whose dead eyes terrify a passing ATS girl (711).

Although the gothic undertones and Freudian preoccupations of 'Ivy Gripped the Steps' give the story an uncanny edge, it is nonetheless part of a group of fictions that configure the past as a locus of emotional intensity, a site of feeling in contrast to the impoverished, war-shocked present. These fictional pasts constitute a form of 'nostalgic pastoral', repositories of memory and meaning that facilitate escape while yet negotiating an ambivalent relationship to the present.

'The past is a foreign country': Virginia Woolf and L. P. Hartley

> It was a summer's night and they were talking, in the big room with the windows open to the garden, about the cesspool. (Woolf 1941/1978: 7)

One of the decade's earliest examples of 'nostalgic pastoral' is also one of its most ambivalent. Virginia Woolf's final novel *Between the Acts* (1941) utilises the immediate past – the final summer before the outbreak of war – to enshrine in memory a way of life that must already have seemed profoundly historical. Woolf composed much of the novel during the first year of conflict, and the book is not obviously therefore a late or postwar text. It is however a precedent: a fiction that reaches for the past to escape from the present, while simultaneously interrogating that past for its role in bringing about the unbearable now. *Between the Acts* is a comedy of manners among the propertied classes that forms the frame for an absurd rendition of English history in the shape of Miss La Trobe's village pageant, a mode of faux-naïve narration that both celebrates and undermines a familiar story of cultural 'progress'. Its depiction of Britain's confident golden ages, from the Elizabethan to the Victorian, lets slip the unexamined realities of imperialism, to which the audience – preoccupied, fragmented, dispersed – are oblivious. Yet the book also celebrates continuity and community. The pageant is an annual event momentarily uniting villagers and gentry, insiders and outsiders, cynics and believers: participants in a way of life that has persisted for centuries. The pageant, in this context, is less about a narrative than a performance, and the recognition of the performers for who they are and the lineage they represent. There is an element of carnival in the spectacle: the villagers, not the gentry, take centre stage, and community is consolidated through the act of assembly:

> Everyone was clapping and laughing. From behind the bushes issued Queen Elizabeth – Eliza Clark, licensed to sell tobacco. Could she be Mrs Clark of the village shop? She was splendidly made up. Her head, pearl-hung, rose from a vast ruff. Shiny satins draped her. Sixpenny brooches glared like cats' eyes and tigers' eyes . . . She looked the age in person. (1941/1978: 64)

Yet Woolf's evocation of the Domesday book (27) and maternal continuity coexist with a disturbing undercurrent of violence. Daniel Ferrer suggests the presence of a 'white noise' within the text, the voice of something inarticulable that can manifest itself only in textual disruption (1990: 119–22). This is a past, then, in which the present is uncannily proximate: the newspaper brings the violence of the public sphere into the consciousness of the novel's female protagonist, Isa. As she reads of the rape of a woman by a group of soldiers her poetic reverie is torn apart, and the novel opens up one of its many suggestive echoes; soldiers rape women as imperial nations rape the earth, a point made with calculated irony in the self-regarding language of the pageant:

> Thus encouraged Reason spoke out.
> *Time, leaning on his sickle, stands amazed. While commerce from her Cornucopia pours the mingled tribute of her different ores. In distant mines the savage sweats; and from the reluctant earth the painted pot is shaped.* [. . .]
> She paused. A long line of villagers in sacking were passing in and out of the tree behind her.
> *Digging and delving, ploughing and sowing* they were singing, but the wind blew their words away. (Woolf 1941/1978: 92)

While Isa is exposed to reality through the power of the printed word, her stockbroker husband Giles is confronted by the violence of the natural world. The boundary between man and animal has already been disrupted in the novel by old Mrs Swithin's confused reading of H. G. Wells' *Outline of History*. In a comical collapsing of time, she mistakes her maid for a mastodon, a 'beast in a swamp' (11), inadvertently aligning the violent primordial past and the 'civilized' present. Not surprisingly, then, when Giles encounters a snake choking on a frog, 'birth the wrong way round – a monstrous inversion' (75), the reader sees a symbol of war's futile, arbitrary destructiveness. Neither animal can be saved, and Giles the impotent bystander can only wreak further destruction. He resolves the situation by stamping on the creatures before returning to the community with blood on his shoes. It is an ominous, and yet faintly ridiculous, encoding of political impasse and patriarchy's habitual resort to violence.

Woolf's pastoral, then, is a blood-stained one. She escapes from the Blitz into the tranquillity of village England, but the traces of war cannot be obliterated. As would be the case with other wartime novels that take the interwar period as their focus – Patrick Hamilton's *Hangover Square* (1941); Nancy Mitford's *The Pursuit of Love* (1945); Julian Maclaren-Ross's *Of Love and Hunger* (1947) – it is almost impossible to write the 1930s without simultaneously inscribing the seeds of the Second World War. This observation returns us to Diana Wallace's argument that the historical novel is always also a contemporary one (2005: 4), and suggests that a temporal shift alone will not be sufficient to escape the pressures of the present. If location in the past, then, offers no respite, can escape be achieved through alternative modes of consciousness? Through nostalgia less for a time or a place, than for a way of occupying that space? Can childhood offer a return to innocence that effectively leaves the war behind?

L. P. Hartley's famous evocation of a sun-drenched Edwardian childhood, *The Shrimp and the Anemone* (1944), offers at best an ambiguous answer to these questions. Hartley's novel, the first of a trilogy completed by *The Sixth Heaven* (1946) and *Eustace and Hilda* (1947), is predominantly focalised through its sibling child protagonists, charting their growing awareness of a wider world and its complexities. However, from its opening scene on the beach at Anchorstone, when the world should be no larger than the rock-pool that fascinates Eustace, the book is permeated by death. Hartley's melancholic comedy progresses through the technique of presenting adult dilemmas through the defamiliarising eyes of children, and – in a surreal echo of the dilemma that confronts Giles Oliver in *Between the Acts* – the book opens with nature 'red in tooth and claw'. This time Eustace is the impotent bystander, debating moral options as the anemone slowly sucks a shrimp to its death. Lacking Giles's capacity for action, and already demonstrating an almost pathological dread of hurting others, Eustace calls upon his older sister Hilda, confident that her proactive personality will resolve the situation. The result is similarly reminiscent of Giles's intervention:

> The shrimp lay in the palm of Hilda's hand, a sad, disappointing sight. Its reprieve had come too late; its head was mangled and there was no vibration in its tail. The horrible appearance fascinated Eustace for a moment, then upset him so much that he turned away with trembling lips. But there was worse to come. As a result of Hilda's forcible interference with its meal the anemone had been partially disembowelled; it could not give up its prey without letting its digestive apparatus go too. Part of its base had come unstuck and was seeking feebly to attach itself to the rock again. Eustace took Hilda's other hand and together they surveyed the unfortunate issue of their kind offices. (Hartley 1944/2000: 3)

This inadvertent murder is the first of the novel's encounters with death. Before the book is over, Eustace will not only have experienced the reality of human death, as he holds the hand of his dying benefactor, Miss Fothergill, but also confronted the prospect of his own mortality. In an ironic commentary on the priorities of the adult world, Eustace's unexpected inheritance changes his status, translating him from sickly child to proto-adult. He becomes for the first time 'Master' Eustace:

> They looked at him differently and spoke to him differently, in prepared voices, he fancied, as though they had been in church. They fell in with his smallest whims, and even, as if disappointed that he had so few, invented for him small preferences and prejudices which, for fear of hurting their feeling, he did not like to disclaim. (1944/2000: 174)

Eustace misreads these signifiers and assumes that his much talked of 'going away' will be to the grave rather than to a now affordable school. Through this misunderstanding, Hartley constructs a parody of conventional pieties. Adapting to his 'posthumous existence' (174), Eustace prepares to divest himself of his worldly possessions and imagines himself a benefactor bestowing blessings on a newly dependent Hilda. This fantasy of self-assertion is, in turn, comically undercut by Hilda's complete lack of interest in his inheritance.

Yet Hilda's unselfishness is not merely comic: it is also an integral part of the complex gendered relationship between the siblings. For the most part, *The Shrimp and the Anemone* is a typical *bildungsroman* in that it is centred upon the boy's development. Hilda has already acquired adult characteristics and gendered expectations, and it is her brother whose emerging ego is most profoundly subject to the conflicting demands of the social order (1944/2000: 77). Yet, perhaps all the more powerfully for being consigned to the margins, the novel delineates the limits of female opportunity. Hilda, whose fierce intelligence has no recognised outlet, has instead dedicated herself to her brother's development (21). Living vicariously through Eustace, she is both one of the super-egos shaping his consciousness, and the 'other' excluded from the rewards of masculine subjectivity. Her quasi-maternal relationship to Eustace is a combination of pride and possessiveness: although she guards him jealously, she is not jealous of his privileged relationship to the public world. In forcing her brother to be polite to Miss Fothergill, Hilda effectively makes his fortune, but she makes no effort to capitalise on this, seeming entirely to have internalised an ethic of female servitude. That Hilda should be so successful in repressing her own desires (108, 211) is perhaps attributable to the paradoxes of the Cherrington household. Here the emergent 'I' of the male child, Eustace, is almost entirely shaped by unmarried women. Mr Cherrington, Eustace's father is, in comparison, an inconsequential figure, whose one attempt at patriarchal authority makes Eustace sick (116–17). 'The female element in Cambo' (149) both venerates and emasculates the male, and creates the context through which Hilda emerges as a simultaneously subservient and dominant figure.

At the end of this first novel, though, the children themselves remain on the borders of innocence, only partially aware of their emergent gender roles. Consequently, *The Shrimp and the Anemone* ends, much as it began, with an image of prelapsarian childhood happiness existing in the shadow of adult knowledge. Hartley's vividly evoked landscape has evaded the war, but not death. The relationship between innocence and experience is less firmly bounded in *The Pursuit of Love* (1945), Nancy Mitford's novel of childhood remembered. Here nostalgia achieves a critical voice, its hyperbolic deployment drawing attention to the problems as well as the pleasures of the past.

'They lived in a world of superlatives': Nancy Mitford's *The Pursuit of Love*

There is a photograph in existence of Aunt Sadie and her six children sitting around the tea-table at Alconleigh. The table is situated, as it was, is now, and ever shall be, in the hall, in front of a huge open fire of logs. Over the chimney-piece plainly visible in the photograph, hangs an entrenching tool, with which, in 1915, Uncle Matthew had whacked to death eight Germans one by one as they crawled out of a dug-out. It is still covered with blood and hairs, an object of fascination to us as children. (Mitford 1945/1986: 9)

Examining the role of memory in Second World War writing, Victoria Stewart contends that 'a memory plot can provide an element of escape tempered by a return to the present' (2006: 17). Although Stewart does not dwell on Nancy Mitford's work, this formulation seems highly appropriate for *The Pursuit of Love* (1945), a novel that begins with a nostalgic revisitation of the past and ends with shocking finality in the traumatic reality of the present. This duality is crucial to an understanding of this critically undervalued novel. Unlike many of the ambivalent escapes considered earlier in this chapter, it offers an uninhibited, almost joyful, evocation of a lost world, but the richness of this fantasy coexists with the complex depiction of a changing society. Linda's story, the distorted *bildungsroman* at the centre of the narrative, is shaped by the diffident background figure of her cousin Fanny, and from the intersecting lives of these two women there emerges an unresolved textual tension between a celebrated romanticism and a validated modernity. The book, then, is knowingly nostalgic, and while it permits the reader a frivolous escape to the past, it never suggests they would actually be better off living there.[1]

As the section epigraph indicates, from the outset Alconleigh is invested with almost religious significance. This is a site of continuity, a place of eternal verities suggested by the evocation of the Lord's Prayer: 'as it was, is now, and ever shall be'. But the image is deceptive. By the end of the novel, this 'world without end' has undergone fundamental changes and the table is occupied by the displaced refugees of a second world war, a dysfunctional extended family that has even accepted a foreigner into its midst. The opening juxtaposition of domestic hearth and barbaric violence also does more than simply evoke the memory of a lost world. Indeed, it introduces an ideology of Englishness that will be both embraced and subverted in the narrative ahead. The subversion begins almost immediately, pulling a war-weary readership into 'a world of superlatives' (15), a landscape of extremes in which the constraints of wartime are replaced by the torments of childhood. Fanny tells us that she spent her holidays at Alconleigh and, 'while some of them slipped by with nothing much to remember, others were distinguished by violent occurrences and had a definite character of their own' (1945/1986: 9). This is followed by a comic catalogue of excess, from Linda's attempted suicide over the death of her dog, to the tormenting of neighbouring children with the facts of life. In establishing the parameters of 'violence' through the tribulations of childhood, the book immediately achieves a fantastical sleight of hand. Memory brings back into focus not simply pre-war events, but also a pre-war frame of reference. 'Violent occurrences', a term that for the past six years can only have connoted the horrors of wartime, slides effortlessly back to an earlier, more innocent set of meanings. Time, and the calm control of Fanny's distancing narration, softens the impact. Violence becomes fun again.

Fanny's narration is crucial to the operation of *The Pursuit of Love*. Even as she speaks with warmth and fondness of Alconleigh, her point of view remains remorselessly modern. She is a pragmatist, not a romantic, and her tone is very much that of the 'modern age'. This is a novel, then, in which an adult voice remembers the romantic ideals of childhood, but it is noticeable that these are ideals which Fanny herself never fully shared. While her cousins declare how lucky she is to have 'wicked parents' (11), Fanny remains profoundly grateful for her surrogate mother, the unglamorous Aunt Emily, and the solid upper-middle-class education she provided. To her, the world of the Radlett family is somewhere for a holiday, not for 'real' everyday life. Yet even as her distance implicitly criticises the past as child's play, her indulgence of the Radletts encourages a nostalgia for a mode of living that cannot be recovered, and this nostalgia is central to the book's appeal. In its double-voiced discourse the book delights in the Radletts, while simultaneously celebrating the values of Aunt Emily. Yet here, perhaps, lies the book's real veneration of the past, for Emily's modernity is, paradoxically, a traditional one. Although far from middle class, she qualifies as an icon of what Alison Light has termed 'conservative modernity', an embodiment of traditional values within a newly 'feminine' form. According to Light, conservative modernity 'could simultaneously look backwards and forwards; it could accommodate the past in the new forms of the present' (1991: 10), respecting long-established national modes of being, such as self-control, reticence and stoicism, but deploying them within a newly domestic national context. Although the insular Britain of the interwar years seemed a radical departure from Victorian imperialism, it did not reject the fundamental values that created that empire. Emily, while the antithesis of Uncle Matthew, remains a reformer, not a rebel.

Above all, though, *The Pursuit of Love* is a novel about women's experiences and choices in the twentieth century. Its narrative drive comes from Linda and Fanny's negotiation of public and private worlds and, although focused on the story of Linda, it draws ongoing contrasts between the two women's lives based upon their upbringing and engagement with the ideological force of romance. While Fanny grows out of her adolescent fantasies, Linda is 'paralysed by her longing for love' (32), so permeated by the ideology of heterosexual romance that she can conceive of no other mode of being (44–5). The contrast with Fanny's common-sense perspective is clear, and from Linda's extravagant fantasies to Fanny's stable companionate marriage the cousins are distinguished by a contrasting relationship to the real. Simultaneously, however, the two are linked by their status as representatives of a 'lost' generation. Almost at the end of the novel, in an uncharacteristic moment of reflection, a feeling of obsolescence is articulated by Linda:

> 'It's rather sad,' she said one day, 'to belong, as we do, to a lost generation. I'm sure in history the two wars will count as one war and that we shall be squashed out of it altogether, and people will forget that we ever existed. We might just as well never have lived at all, I do think it's a shame.' (1945/1986: 147)

While it is odd that these words should be given to a character repeatedly depicted as living in a sort of eternal present (107, 113, 123), it is important to note Mitford's construction of the interwar years as a liminal space; a site of uncertainty and flux in which an entire generation feels itself in limbo. Not for nothing does Linda marry a crypto-Fascist and a Communist and fail to make sense of both relationships before finding happiness in a relationship outside time, as the mistress of a French aristocrat. Linda's first husband, Tony, is 'a perfect mountain of pomposity' (72) who thinks only of himself, while Christian, her second, 'was really only interested in mass wretchedness, and never much cared for individual cases' (92). Linda's retreat from the contemporary moment seems, in one sense, an admirably lucid response to this political impasse. And yet it is also, of course, deeply problematic. This flight into a nineteenth-century fantasy of decorative, sensual femininity (114–15) is one of the many events of the novel that exposes the limitations of Alconleigh as a fantastical space. With its fairy-tale ogres and medieval chaperonage (49), it facilitates the development of a mind-set that imprisons Linda, limits her horizons and roots her in an ultimately destructive gender binary. After her sojourn in Paris with Fabrice, we learn that Linda is finally 'fulfilling the promise of her childhood, and [becoming] a beauty' (125). The cost of this entirely passive becoming is a life without resources, and a subjectivity that functions only in relation to a male other (145).

Yet Linda, for all her romantic a-historicism, is also a significantly national figure. Described as 'instinctively and unreasonably English' (73), she and her aristocratic family function as hyperbolic embodiments of national resistance. In its representation of peace, the novel critiques the rampant jingoism of Uncle Matthew, preferring the calm understatement of conservative modernity. In its depiction of war, by contrast, it wholeheartedly endorses the roaring excesses of the Radletts, turning them into a people's aristocracy. From the outset, their world has been one in which hardships are endured in an uncomplaining manner, and the book implies that the life of the landed gentry ideally prepares you to be part of the 'people's war' (133). With Matthew's schemes for resisting invasion, and Linda's stoical response to bombing, the family comically enact the resilience demanded by propagandist myths of Englishness. Arguably, Mitford's depiction of the 'sacred' relationship between Matthew, his tenants and his land (64) turns the book into an apology for a way of life on the verge of redundancy, but it is one that feeds into cherished national ideas of eccentricity and community. Matthew would not dream of abandoning England in its hour of need, and his xenophobic prejudices are rewritten as a laudable loyalty, particularly in comparison with the middle-class villains of the novel, the complacent and inauthentic Kroesigs (74–5). A great admirer of Hitler, Sir Leicester Kroesig's only concern is capital, and his fear of the proletariat ensures his fundamental opposition to war on the grounds that conflict 'brings people together and opens their eyes' (73).

Mitford, then, is ruthless in her condemnation of those who do not endorse a traditional mode of instinctive patriotism, but the book is far from a straightforward piece of propaganda. Indeed, the novel's Englishness resides as much in its refusal of seriousness as in its active assertion of national values. *The Pursuit of Love* is a novel of escape not simply in its deployment of nostalgia, but also in its gleeful assault on the shibboleths of war. Seriousness is evoked, and almost immediately banished, for example in the novel's account of Dunkirk. In an unusually bleak paragraph, Mitford reports that 'London people cried openly in the buses, in the streets, for the English army which was lost' (124), before turning sharply around to announce that 'suddenly one day, the English army turned up again' (125). The juxtaposition represents a comic refusal to mourn that evokes the post-traumatic reactions of the 1920s. Alison Light's work on the interwar period suggests that the rise of the detective story is symptomatic of 'a loss of appetite for melodrama' and an absence of awe (1991: 70–1). These are books in which 'nothing is sacred', and they work 'more to relieve generalised anxiety than to generate strong emotion' (67, 71). Much the same could be said of *The Pursuit of Love*, and the novel utilises a characteristically British understatement – Alfred has had a 'fascinating time' at Dunkirk – to translate the horrific into something manageable. This bantering tone sets *The Pursuit of Love* alongside the cinema of the period in its use of litotes, euphemism and humour as modes of reassurance, but the novel also offers escape in a fantasy of plenty. Just as Heyer's heroines enjoyed a rich Regency world, *The Pursuit of Love* revels in Linda's lavish lifestyle as Fabrice's mistress (122–3). Here is everything absent from the shops of austerity Britain, a frivolous celebration of a scarcely recognisable mode of femininity.

Even more fantastical to a half-starved nation, though, is the magical appearance of Juan, the Spanish refugee. In a pantomime transformation he is revealed to be a remarkable cook, turning the inhospitable Alconleigh larder into an 'Aladdin's cave' (138), filled with the forbidden delights of black-market produce. In the pleasure of illicit consumption, the final chapters of *The Pursuit of Love* construct a comic nostalgia, conjuring up 'succulent birds, beasts, and crustaceans' for the vicarious delight of its readership (138). Yet crucially, this is a fantasy of plenty in the here and now: a vision of loaves and fishes for all the inhabitants of the little Britain that is Alconleigh at war – and this conservative modernity, while a long way from documentary realism, nonetheless sets the book apart from its more celebrated contemporary, Evelyn Waugh's *Brideshead Revisited*. Here the strawberries and champagne of memory are precisely that: something that can never be recovered, and certainly never shared with the debased community of postwar Britain.

'it was not as it had been': Evelyn Waugh's Romantic Self-Assertion

> There were few left in the mess now of the batch of volunteers who trained together at the outbreak of war; one way and another they were nearly all gone [...] and their places were taken by conscripts; the wireless played incessantly in the ante-room nowadays, and much beer was drunk before dinner; it was not as it had been. (Waugh 1945/1962: 11)

In late eighteenth- and early nineteenth-century writing, memory emerges as a mode of self-creation, fundamental to the process of 'anchoring a sense of individual continuity over time' (Ferguson, 1996: 509). Memories give cohesion to the otherwise fragmented self and, in the process of recollection, they have the power both to console and regenerate. Yet studies of 'romantic memory' also draw attention to the turbulent socio-political context framing these interrogations of individual subjectivity. Anne Whitehead, for example, argues that 'the central dilemma articulated within Wordsworth's poetry of this period becomes how to assimilate the rapid and pervasive historical transformations that were occurring, and which confounded available explanatory frameworks' (2009: 79–80). In such a context, the 'turn to lyric and pastoral writing' that characterised the period can be seen to represent a protective strategy – a 'virtual zone of safety' (Pfau 2005: 215) – that negotiates radical change at a carefully modulated spatial and temporal distance.

The pertinence of romantic memory to the scarcely assimilable excess of the 1940s is not difficult to discern. The consolations of both the recent and the more distant past, recalled and reimagined, have been central to this chapter, and, as John Brannigan has noted, the 'scenic mode' would become a feature of postwar British writing, particularly in the work of John Betjeman (2003: 17, 29). Yet for Evelyn Waugh, the elegiac tone of *Brideshead Revisited* (1945) represented a new departure, a mode of writing far removed from the contemporary satires with which he had made his name. Writing about the book in 1946, Waugh claimed that this transition emerged from a desire to 'represent man more fully, which, to me, means only one thing, man in his relation to God' (Stannard 1984: 250). Although undoubtedly sincere as a piece of self-analysis, the proselytising intent of *Brideshead Revisited* can only partially explain Waugh's turn to memory. What, then, is at stake in Waugh's new found lyricism? What does he seek to 'anchor' and commemorate in his extended exercise in nostalgic recollection?

At the outbreak of war, Waugh was an established writer of robust conservative opinions and a deep investment in the Roman Catholic faith to which he had converted in 1930. Although secure in his political and religious convictions, his attitude to the conflict was not unlike that of the much younger Richard Hillary, in that he initially saw it as an opportunity for personal development, joining up because 'nothing [would be] more likely to stimulate me than a complete change of habit' (Diary, August 1939, quoted in Patey 1998: 181). However, Waugh's early desire for heroic action was frustrated and his romance with the military was short-lived: his involvement in a number of chaotic commando raids and the abortive Battle of Crete (1941) left him utterly disillusioned, and this sense of betrayal is evident even in his first wartime novel, the satirical comedy, *Put Out More Flags* (1942). Featuring a cast of superficial characters caught up in the absurdities of the phoney war, *Put Out More Flags* is in most respects typical of Waugh's writing. Marina MacKay describes it as a high-spirited novel 'about how the British got off more lightly than their political leadership merited' (2007: 133), but this frivolous air fades as it progresses, to be replaced by a sense of disintegration and defeat (Hastings 1994: 432). *Put Out More Flags* was a popular success but, as was the case with Nancy Mitford's 'sitz-krieg' novel, *Pigeon Pie* (1940), as a war book it missed its moment. The pace of the Second World War presented an impossible challenge to the topical satirical novel, and Adam Piette has suggested that Waugh was driven 'out of time' both by the pressure of events and his own changing attitudes to the conflict (1995: 102).

This growing sense of cultural dislocation is crucial to *Brideshead*

Revisited, which displaces war to the margins and self-consciously constructs a 'virtual zone of safety' in the past. But memory is tantalisingly double-edged, and the 'enclosed and enchanted garden' of Captain Charles Ryder's memories is both a place of consolation and a site of loss (1945/1962: 32). There is mourning in process here, and denial: the inarticulable resentments of unfulfilled ambition and frustrated desire. Ryder's recollections, then, also become strategies through which the threatened male subject can 'anchor' himself against change, the unwelcome flood of modernity figured through the combined forces of women and mass culture. The further back the memories reach, the more distant these 'destructive' forces seem. The opening Oxford chapters, for example, assume a prelapsarian quality, acknowledged by Ryder's admission that 'I was in search of love in those days' (32). This early memory establishes an immediate contrast with the book's wartime prologue in which a jaded Ryder states that here, in the impotent anti-climax of mundane soldiering, 'my last love died' (11). Without the kudos of conflict, the identity of the soldier is insufficient to restore an emasculated masculinity depleted by the legacy of the First World War and the inescapable rise of 'woman', and Ryder's only consolation is the continuity of the 'small red flame' of faith (331). The dominant mood of *Brideshead Revisited*, then, is pessimistic and elegiac, but it nonetheless cannot quite escape the traces of its author's past: Waugh's 'serious' novel is riven with jokes, making the text uneven and unstable, haunted by the memory of its own satirical forebears.

Brideshead Revisited follows the development of its narrator, Charles Ryder, from youth to maturity through a series of love affairs. The sequence begins with his infatuation with his Oxford contemporary Lord Sebastian Flyte, continues onto Sebastian's sister Julia, absorbs her family and, most importantly, their houses, and ends with a final doomed homosocial bond, his love affair with the army. This final relationship represents the novel's clearest indication that escape is being sought, not from war, but from postwar, a concept that finds its apotheosis in the figure of the subaltern Hooper:

> In the weeks that we were together Hooper became a symbol to me of Young England, so that whenever I read some public utterance proclaiming what Youth demanded in the Future and what the world owed to Youth, I would test these general statements by substituting 'Hooper' and seeing if they still seemed as plausible. Thus in the dark hour before reveille I sometimes pondered: 'Hooper Rallies', 'Hooper Hostels', 'International Hooper Co-operation', and 'the Religion of Hooper'. (Waugh 1945/1962: 15)

As critics such as Edmund Wilson noted at the time, Waugh's snobbery breaks new ground in this book (Stannard 1984/1997: 246), and

Hooper is an easy target for the writer's prejudices. Within the terms of the novel, however, Hooper destroys Ryder's final sanctuary – the army – acting as a sort of cultural fifth column eating away at the edifice of the narrator's complacent hegemonic masculinity.[2] And yet Hooper, or the mass mediocrity for which he stands, is not ultimately to blame for the emasculation of Charles Ryder, or for the underlying debasement of a masculine cultural elite. Rather, at the heart of the novel's anxieties resides the figure of woman and the perceived feminisation of society in the aftermath of the First World War. From the outset, *Brideshead Revisited* depicts women as alien:

> Here, discordantly, in Eights Week, came a rabble of womankind, some hundreds strong, twittering and fluttering over the cobbles and up the steps, sight seeing and pleasure seeking, drinking claret cup, eating cucumber sandwiches; pushed in punts about the river, herded in droves to the college barges; greeted in the *Isis* and in the Union by a sudden display of peculiar, facetious, wholly distressing Gilbert-and-Sullivan badinage, and by peculiar choral effects in the College chapels. (1945/1962: 23)

So extreme is the otherness of woman that a whole new language is required to communicate with her. Conversation is impossible, only a 'distressing' badinage can deflect the unsettling impact of her penetration into the masculine spaces of university life. The association of woman with a sub-human mass culture is equally evident here. Like animals, women are 'herded in droves' to the barges, while their cultural debasement is evident in their appetite for sight-seeing. These are not tourists in the tradition of the grand tour, rather they are day-trippers, oblivious to beauty and concerned only with clichéd pleasures. Significantly, what is cherished in the memories of the opening section of the book is the homosocial and the homoerotic. Oxford, seen through the rosy glow of Charles' first love, Sebastian, is an Eden without women; and initially this Eden extends to Brideshead itself. On the lovers' first visit, the Marchmain family are not in residence and the house becomes a paradise. Unsurprisingly, it is a woman who will destroy this Eden: Lady Marchmain, the phallic mother, is a serpent whose intervention undermines Charles's intense dyadic relation with Sebastian. The idealised bond of the two men – beyond time, convention and society – is severed by the pressure of the social: family ties, structured religion and heterosexuality. In an inversion of Freudian norms, it is a woman who brings patriarchal law to bear on the child's idealised pre-social space, and Waugh punishes Lady Marchmain for her presumption by cursing her with statements of quite astonishing crassness, such as her claim that 'it is possible for the rich to sin by coveting the privileges of the poor' (122).

It is not entirely surprising, however, that Charles should be seduced by Lady Marchmain, her house and the whole Marchmain family, nor indeed that he should particularly cherish his time with Sebastian as a belated happy childhood (1945/1962: 45–6). Following the death of his mother on 'active' service with the Red Cross in Serbia, Charles's father retreats into the past, cultivating a studied eccentricity that masks his skilful misanthropic distancing of all familial contacts. In a parody of middle-class emotional restraint, Charles grows up in a world without women or affection, an experience that leaves him fascinated by other people's families (40–1). Embedded in this miserable upbringing, however, is the first of a number of discrete conflations of women and war that work to undermine male subjectivity. Here, comically, the hero loses his mother rather than his father in combat. By the end of the book, however, the wound will be deeper, as Waugh ironically dispatches both Julia and her sister Cordelia to war service overseas, while Charles is left mouldering in barracks (329). In between, the emasculating legacy of the First World War is exposed through Lady Marchmain's almost idolatrous worship of her three brothers, all of whom died heroic deaths in battle. It is impossible for the surviving men of her generation, or the next, to live up to these 'garlanded victims' (133–4). At this point in the narrative, though, Waugh seems curiously divided. On the one hand he constructs a scathing critique of women's romanticised yearning for an impossible male ideal, but at the same time his text subscribes to the lost generation myth. Suddenly Hooper intrudes once more into the narrative, as Ryder reflects that these heroes 'must die to make a world for Hooper; they were the aborigines [. . .] to be shot off at leisure so that things might be safe for the travelling salesman, with his polygonal pince-nez, his fat wet hand-shake, his grinning dentures' (134). From this horror of ordinary people emerges not only Waugh's loathing of modernity, but also his fear of cultural degeneration. The fetish of the lost generation is here reconstituted through class-based anxieties.

Yet Waugh's primary concern in his evocation of the First World War is its impact on masculine subjectivity. As Boy Mulcaster observes, with uncharacteristic insight, his generation 'were too young to fight in the war. Other chaps fought, millions of them dead. Not us. We'll show them. We'll show the dead chaps we can fight, too' (1945/1962: 198). Mulcaster's bravado leads to nothing more than a misdirected street brawl, and in the absence of heroic opportunity, the novel's gender anxieties find new focus in the figure of Charles's wife, Celia. Their courtship and marriage is not something Charles chooses to remember, beyond the pertinent fact that it was she who proposed, and by the time the reader encounters the relationship, it is already beyond redemption.

Celia manages Charles, viewing his art as a commodity and attempting to sell both it and her husband to fashionable society (220), and she is rewarded for her unwelcome female agency by being described in terms of sterile, artificial modernity. Her 'prettiness' is 'hygenic' (218), her tastes banal (221) and her appearance greatly admired by Americans (223). The text gives her no interiority, and her role within the book is purely symbolic. She is a caricature of superficial acquisitive modern femininity, and is designed to act as a mirror for the novel's validated model of womanhood, Julia Flyte. This is not to suggest that Julia herself is unproblematic: after all, in a disturbing recognition of the feminisation of society, it is she who will eventually inherit Brideshead. However, Julia is a fitting object for Charles' attention because she is artistically satisfactory. Through suffering, she has become a thing of beauty:

> That was the change in her from ten years ago; that, indeed, was her reward, this haunting, magical sadness which spoke straight to the heart and struck silence; it was the completion of her beauty. (1945/1962: 228)

Ryder, like his creator, has an intensely ambivalent attitude towards modernity, finding consolation in the art and architecture of the past. His strategy for asserting himself in the face of the disturbing modernity of women, is to subject them to a similar criterion of taste. Julia's beauty redeems her, and her status as *objet d'art* is heightened by the frequent descriptions of her stillness. Whether Charles is painting her or not, she sits for her portrait (295).

In its dealings with women and modernity, then, *Brideshead* emphatically seeks to escape the moment of its publication. It represents both a fantastical escape into a more richly textured past – a place of plovers' eggs, fine wines and baroque excess – and an elegy for the passing of that world. Its act of mourning, however, it is strangely insecure. Marina MacKay persuasively argues that *Brideshead* is about 'what, domestically, winning the war is going to mean for artists and for private individuals' (MacKay 2007: 126, 133), but what this interpretation cannot quite explain is the novel's simultaneous debunking of the artist. Waugh could not entirely abandon the habits of a lifetime, and *Brideshead* is on one level an entirely serious elegy for a lost world, and on another, a satirical anatomy of human venality.

This double narrative is embedded in the structure of the novel. Although Waugh had experimented with first person narration in the unfinished *Work Suspended* (published as a short story in 1943), *Brideshead* was the first of his novels not to enjoy the comforts of third person distance. The reader, as a consequence, only gains access to events through the distorting perspectives of Charles Ryder. Yet the text is littered with dissenting voices that destabilise Waugh's narrative. This is evident in the construction of Ryder's artistic career. Popular with the chattering classes, he peddles his nostalgic images of faded splendour to fashionable society, and the text's most compelling outsider, Anthony Blanche, correctly identifies him as 'an imposter': the paintings for *Ryder's Latin America* could have been produced in 'the corner of a hothouse at T-t-trent or T-t-tring' (1945/1962: 257). In his infatuation with the English aristocracy he can do nothing creatively except reflect this culture's faded grandeur (260). Yet to write of Ryder's infatuation is in some sense to ignore his complicity in the destruction of the Marchmain family. In the margins of the narrative, its dissenting voices, and the abandonment of Sebastian for the greater reward of his family, it becomes possible to recognise Ryder not as an acolyte, but as a parasite; a man who comes as a tourist to the stately edifice of the English aristocracy and effectively steals the silver:

> The financial slump of the period, which left many painters without employment, served to enhance my success, which was, indeed, itself a symptom of the decline. When the water-holes were dry people sought to drink at the mirage. After my first exhibition I was called to all parts of the country to make portraits of houses that were soon to be deserted or debased; indeed, my arrival seemed often to be only a few paces ahead of the auctioneer's, a presage of doom. (1945/1962: 216)

Ryder, then, is both the object of satire, and the controlling voice of the narrative, a combination that unsettles the novel's claims of dignity. As the unreliable quality of the narration slowly manifests itself, the value of its memorialised past is undermined, and the reader as day-tripper wonders quite what all the fuss was about.

Anne Whitehead has argued that 'the predominant voices of memory are male' (2009: 12–13), and perhaps this accounts for why *The Pursuit of Love*, a female memory novel and *bildungsroman*, is generally dismissed as frivolous, while the portentous *Brideshead Revisited* is invested with significance. Rose Macaulay was one of a number of critical voices at the time of the book's publication, noting in a somewhat damning *Horizon* review that *Brideshead* takes itself far too seriously: 'love, the English aristocracy, and the Roman Catholic Church, combine to liquefy a style that should be dry' (Macaulay 1946: 372). But nonetheless, *Brideshead* was a huge success that, somewhat ironically, brought Waugh an unprecedented popular following. Clearly the book offered something attractive to a postwar readership, and with hindsight, this might be seen not so much as a matter of content, but of tone. What stands out from *Brideshead Revisited* is its uncertainty about the future, and its pervasive note of personal and cultural mourning. As the next chapter will discuss, finding a voice for loss in the aftermath of war was not easy to achieve, and Waugh's escapism articulates, albeit through displacement, the multiple griefs and constitutive losses of 1945.

Notes

1. That Mitford caught the mood of the time with this paradoxically hard-edged nostalgia is evident in the novel's success. A Book Society Choice for December 1945, 200,000 copies were sold in the first 12 months, and it made Mitford more money than anything she had previously written (Hastings 1985: 168).
2. Hegemonic masculinity is a term used to describe whichever mode of masculinity is invested with cultural and political power within a given society. The term is historically contingent, and subject to considerable national variation (Connell 1995: 76–7). In 1940s Britain, hegemonic masculinity resided in a white, upper-middle class, private school and Oxbridge educated elite.

Chapter Six

Grieving

'I do not know,' he said, 'that we can bear not to be at war.' (Smith 1949/1979: 8)

This counter-intuitive assertion from Stevie Smith's *The Holiday* (1949) forms the keynote of the 'other' postwar, the one that finds no escape and which is abjectly bound to the destructive force of war. In this formulation, the postwar is a paradoxical space in which the absence of war proves stranger, and more disorientating, than its presence. For the nation, war's end signifies loss, not only through the pain of bereavement, but also through a loss of structure. The goal has been achieved, the war is, or is about to be, won, and the social, cultural and emotional energies that have for so long been directed towards one purpose must find alternative outlets. The wartime subject, similarly, is faced with fragmentation, as he or she is confronted by 'the bewilderment of a postwar consequence' (Smith 1949/1979: 184). If the war came to make what Rose Macaulay called a 'lunatic sense' (1950: 61), then its conclusion demanded a further logical readjustment. In the face of the Holocaust, the atom bomb, a landslide election victory for the Labour party, and the estrangement of coming 'home', society once again found itself up-ended, its points of reference and structures of signification undergoing perplexing transformations. This is a period of disappointment and uncertainty, in which the work of reconstruction is permeated by a necessary and painful negotiation of grief.

In the Introduction I discussed the problem of writing about war, a problem that manifests itself in a rhetoric of impossibility. The texts of the Second World War repeat time and again that war defies representation, its events are indescribable and an approximation of meaning can only be conveyed through metaphor, litotes and silence. In the space of what writers cannot say, we find an intimation of what was and is beyond representation; we apprehend the unspeakable. But war is not the only subject that exceeds the grasp of textuality. As William Watkin notes in his study of loss in modern literature, death too defies representation: 'When we speak of loss we always speak figuratively with no hope of actually communicating the truth of it' (58). In the loss of loved ones, structure and self, brought about by the transition from war to peace, we consequently find a crisis of expression. It is not that British literature did not write about readjustment, post-traumatic symptoms and death, but that it did so in a manner appropriate to the culture, and much of the fiction of the time worked energetically to police the unruly forces that threatened the stability of self and society. The postwar is, thus, a site of multiple losses, many of which strenuously resist the process of inscription.

As part of his analysis, Watkin distinguishes between bereavement, 'the raw emotion of loss'; grief, 'the work of loss' and mourning, which is a 'ritualised and communal activity' shaped by specific ideologies (26–7). This tripartite distinction, moving from the subjective to the public, usefully draws attention to a concept of transition, and this is equally fundamental to Judith Butler's anatomy of mourning. In her examination of post-9/11 America, *Precarious Life*, Butler suggests that 'mourning has to do with agreeing to undergo a transformation . . . the full result of which one cannot know in advance' (2004: 21). It is also the case, she suggests, that in experiencing loss, we cannot always know quite what it is that has been lost:

> When we lose certain people, or when we are dispossessed from a place, or a community, we may simply feel that we are undergoing something temporary, that mourning will be over and some restoration of prior order will be achieved. But maybe when we undergo what we do, something about who we are is revealed, something that delineates the ties we have to others, that shows us that these ties constitute what we are [. . .] It is not as if an 'I' exists independently over here and then simply loses a 'you' over there, especially if the attachment to 'you' is part of what composes who 'I' am. If I lose you, under these conditions, then I not only mourn the loss, but I become inscrutable to myself. Who am 'I', without you? When we lose some of those ties by which we are constituted, we do not know who we are or what to do. On one level, I think I have lost 'you' only to discover that 'I' have gone missing as well. (Butler 2004: 22)

In this suggestive passage Butler stresses that loss is not simply to be conceived as the loss of a person, but can also be understood as dispossession from a place or a community. The resonance of such a statement is enormous: in the postwar moment, a community, however flawed, has been lost, and a purpose, however resented, has been simultaneously achieved and displaced. A dominant 'fact' of life (the war and its prosecution) has gone, and its absence changes everything. Women who were part of the forces, who organised voluntary services, who worked in communal environments from canteens to munitions were part of a group. Similarly, men in uniform, in civil defence and in POW camps, were part of homosocial economies quite other to the normative structures of peacetime life: yet it was these 'other' social formations that provided sustenance and a sense of belonging in the face of the identity-shattering impact of conflict. While clearly not an unmixed blessing, these modes of communality constituted a range of provisional relationships, that for the duration of the war replaced the more conventional 'we' of the heterosexual dyad, the class-bound hierarchy of the workplace, or the isolated 'I' of the woman in the home. The loss of these constitutive ties is a feature of postwar writing, in particular women's writing, and the impact of war's end on women will be considered in greater detail below.

The ideas of Butler and Watkins help to conceptualise what is at stake in the postwar economy of mourning, and the literature of this section can be seen, directly and tangentially, to be engaged in 'the work of loss'. These are not public commemorative works; rather they are a literature of fragmentation that attempts to 'make sense' of the aftermath of war. In this they negotiate an ongoing and unresolved relationship with loss that is both individual and communal. The process of writing attempts to shape the inchoate emotions of grief into the manageable forms of poetry and prose. Yet the transition from subjective emotion to public monument is complicated in Watkin's analysis by his argument that 'emotion is primarily a social construct' (50). How emotion is experienced, let alone how it is articulated, is inevitably culturally mediated. Quoting Elaine Showalter's analysis of hysteria, Watkin draws attention to the 'symptom pool' of a given culture: those 'pains' that it is legitimate for a person to complain about as a means of communicating distress. The dominant culture of Englishness, and indeed Britishness, of the 1940s was, as has been noted in Part I, one of understatement, euphemism and repression. The language of complaint available to men and women was thus profoundly limited, as is evident from fictions of the combatant's return such as Nigel Balchin's *Mine Own Executioner* (1945). Here the traumatised and guilt-ridden pilot Adam Lucian, who has been tortured as a prisoner of the Japanese, describes his experiences in a register entirely appropriate to British masculinity: 'I had rather a sticky time in the war' (1945: 56). Yet not all fiction of the period co-operates with the cultural imperative of repression, and a number of novels stand out as exceptional in their attempt to articulate pain in excess of the 'symptom pool' of British literary culture. Similarly poetry, a more traditional home for elegiac impulses, negotiates a complex boundary between dignity and anguish, expression and repression. The following sections examine the tension between cultural repression and cathartic expression in the post-traumatic context of the 'postwar'.

A Literature of Lost Possibilities? Women Writers and the Return to 'Normality'

N. H. Reeve has coined the phrase 'uneasy homecoming syndrome' to describe a narrative 'so ubiquitous as to have become a virtual cliché' (Mengham and Reeve, 2001: 162). This story of a man's return to a changed world is the exemplary postwar fiction of male experience, but what is less obviously recognisable is the parallel account of women's postwar experience, a narrative that might be termed a 'literature of lost possibilities'. Victoria Stewart observes that:

> At the most mundane level comes the recognition that it will not be possible to simply switch back from one's wartime way of life to one's pre-war role; authors are often attentive both to the changes that active service has wrought and to how civilians have had to adapt and change. (2006: 136)

What accompanies these changes, though, and is at the root of much psychic difficulty, is the assumption that change can be undone: that there is a normality to which self and society can be returned. Postwar writing is fraught with anxiety precisely because it attempts to assimilate the fractured subjectivities and changed consciousnesses of wartime into templates of social and psychic organisation based on an outmoded 'normality' that – however much desired – was felt by few. This process was particularly significant for women because their experience of loss is less obviously visible. Because the majority of them do not make the journey of the returning soldier, they are assumed to be the benchmark of stability, the unchanged centre and symbol of 'home'. As earlier chapters have demonstrated, women's wartime lives were far from normative, but the fact of their symbolisation as such cannot be denied. British culture of the postwar effectively denies the radical changes taking place in women's lives, and women's literature struggles to articulate this experience in the face of the priority given to the returning soldier. Women's losses thus become a 'signifying absence' of the postwar, and the most potent of these absences is the representation of women in the public sphere. From Elizabeth Taylor's *At Mrs Lippincote's* (1945), in which Julia is trapped in an alienating marriage and a borrowed house, to Mollie Panter-Downes's *One Fine Day* (1947) in which Laura is exhausted by a domesticity she feels obliged to demonstrate in the face of her husband's return, the middle-class female protagonists of postwar fiction experience their dilemmas and mourn their losses within the confines of the home. Working women, when they appear, come to tend the wounded hero in romances such as Monica Dickens's *The Happy Prisoner* (1946), in which love blossoms between a bed-ridden soldier and his nurse. Even Elizabeth Bowen's *The Heat of the Day* (1949) concludes with the restoration of class and gender norms. We are told that Stella, the autonomous, gainfully-employed, single-mother protagonist will marry a nameless brigadier whose sole function in the novel seems to be to mark the end of her status as a desiring subject in the public sphere.

The cinema reveals a similar trend and provides a valuable context for the fiction of the period. Although not yet the all-out demonisation of women that would characterise British cinema in the 1950s, the late 1940s tends increasingly towards a normative domestic representation of women. *The Way to the Stars* (1945), for example, is notable for the absence of uniformed women from its landscape of war. A newly arrived American airman, keen to find female company, asks whether WAAFs are girls, to which the English hero replies doubtfully, 'I suppose so', implying in his hesitation that the woman in uniform ceases to qualify as female. The central character of *The Way to the Stars* is the hotel manageress Toddie, whose narrative trajectory is an archetypally feminine one. She marries a pilot, bears his child, mourns his death in stoic and appropriately muted fashion, and becomes a transcendental mother figure nurturing the fragile emotional lives of the other pilots. She represents the postwar imperative of continuance. Women are needed not in the factories, but in the home, building families and by extension, the brave new postwar world.

Other films carry similar ideological imperatives. *Brief Encounter* (1945), although set in the 1930s, nonetheless encodes a powerful narrative of postwar duty, demanding that romance and adventure be set aside for the familiar: the home, the husband, the children. *Brief Encounter* took its message of conformity to the middle classes; *The Wicked Lady* (1945), perhaps less obviously, dispatched a similar message to the working classes. Here, the audience is presented with two women, one domesticated and good, the other wild, ambitious and bad. Barbara, the wicked lady of the title, takes what she wants, respects no one, and has no time for community, church or civic duty. Having stolen her virtuous friend's wealthy fiancé, and become the lady of the manor, she finds herself frustrated, craving the excitement of the public sphere: 'I've brains and looks and personality' she cries, 'I want to use them instead of rotting in this dull hole.' Thankfully unfettered by any moral sense, she resolves this dilemma by taking to the road as a highwaywoman, where she cheers herself up with a diet of adultery, theft and murder. Inevitably, she is punished for her crimes, but notably, her punishment is private rather than public. While her highwayman accomplice is subject to the law and sentenced to hang, Barbara's punishment is to die alone, spurned by the man she loves. Caroline, the good girl, inherits her husband and her status. Duty has been rewarded, and the wayward woman who would continue to seek her pleasures in the public sphere has been punished for her failure to conform to gender norms. It is an unsubtle dichotomy, and as propaganda it has obvious limitations. Barbara's transgressive behaviour dominates the film, and the character's evident pleasure in the pursuit of her desires easily outweighs the reward given to Caroline for her patient, almost masochistic self-sacrifice.

The emphasis on family and duty evident in these films is also, significantly, a demand that women's loyalties – the source of so much anxiety in the war years – be shifted back from public nation to private house. No longer are women being asked to believe in their nation, now they must believe only in their man. Yet as fiction of the period makes clear, the 'home' is an ambivalent space, simultaneously desirable and oppressive, and haunted by the memory of its wartime reinscription. In Mollie Panter-Downes's *One Fine Day*, for example, Laura thinks back to a war spent sharing the house with other women and children. In this world, the gradual collapse of a domestic ideal did not matter. But with the return of a normality that does not feel normal, Laura begins to feel her value predicated upon her capacity to keep house. Watching a young man setting out on a day's walk, she reflects:

> He walks alone by choice [. . .] He walks with calm, manly decision, while my day is a feeble woman's day, following a domestic chalk line, bound to the tyranny of my house with its voices saying, Clean me, polish me, save me from the spider and the butterfly. It is so long since I measured out a day for myself and said, This is mine, I shall be alone. (1947: 55)

Laura's crisis seems largely to be resolved by taking an unscheduled walk and falling asleep on the grass. In a miraculous condensation of grief work, she weeps, sleeps and recovers her happiness. But it is hard to feel entirely confident in this optimistic resolution, as Laura's hillside nap gives Panter-Downes the opportunity to switch focaliser to her husband, Stephen, a man who exhibits an absolute horror of the disorder represented by women without men: 'He absolutely shuddered to think how she and Victoria had got along while he was away. Meals on trays, all the clocks wrong, and the worst of it would be nobody would mind in the least' (237). Stephen, like Laura, is experiencing a form of postwar class trauma, his sense of a lost world exacerbated by the absence of the servants, whose unseen and miraculous workings used to smooth over the gulf between his sense of order and his wife's vague distraction. *One Fine Day* ends on a note of hope, but its tone is conflicted. Ultimately, with its potentially disturbing interior monologues juxtaposed against comic character sketches and the cheery voice of common sense, the novel reads like a combination of *Mrs Dalloway* and *Mrs Miniver*. Within such a framework, Butler's dispossession is glimpsed rather than acknowledged, leaving the reader only with the certainty that 'prior order' has not been, and cannot be, achieved.

The loss of constitutive cultures and the possibilities they represent is made much more explicit in Elizabeth Berridge's 'The Prisoner'. The spinster Miss Everton, having decided to devote herself to her brother, finds her life rendered meaningless by his futile wartime death (149). Having turned instead to the village community as a means of self-constitution, Miss Everton is surviving, managing rather than overcoming the aching loneliness of her life:

> She found herself half turning to ask Humphrey about it, and his loss came once more as a bitter pain. She missed more than anything, now she was nearing fifty, not having anyone to whom she could say, 'Do you remember?' (Berridge 1947/2000: 147)

Miss Everton's existence is disrupted by the arrival of a working party of German POWs, one of whom befriends her in her search for some semblance of normality. Erich, the prisoner, possesses the 'bewildered, blunted mind of the uprooted peasant' (155), but the unlikely pair find sustaining companionship in a quiet domesticity. Miss Everton's role is quasi-maternal, feeding Erich sweet things 'as if her gifts could somehow assuage the times in which he had been born' (154), but the potential of their friendship is ultimately undermined by the constraints of class and community. Miss Everton cannot bring herself to invite Erich to spend Christmas with her because, 'when he had gone . . . She would have to continue to live among the villagers, who never forgot anyone's departure from their accepted code' (158). When the prisoners leave, she is bereft – 'it seemed to her that they were free, and once again she the imprisoned one' (164) – for the war has doubly wounded her. Not only has it robbed her of her constitutive other, it has, in the disruptive presence of the German prisoners, exposed the lost possibilities of her life. The glimpse of companionship, and of other worlds, represents the return of a knowledge repressed since the death of her brother.

The wound of grief is reopened to expose not just the original pain of bereavement, but also the fundamental melancholy of a previously unmourned loss: the 'physically and mentally' fulfilling life that had never been hers (149). Miss Everton knows that 'nothing would ever be the same again' (164); war has laid bare a loss so far beyond the possibilities of articulation as to be utterly irresolvable.

Although its canvas is considerably broader, Elizabeth Bowen's *The Heat of the Day* is equally a narrative of loss that struggles to negotiate the single woman. While Stella is fated to be reabsorbed into the socially acceptable structure of marriage, the status of Louie is altogether more uncertain. In losing her parents and her husband to the war, Louie discovers that she has 'gone missing' as well:

> There still was, however, some negative virtue in being outdoors. Indoors meant Chilcombe Street; here resided the fact of her being of meaning only to an absent person, absent most appallingly from this double room. (146)

Desperate to receive some confirmation of her existence, she takes to casual sex with soldiers who stand in for her husband, but the satisfactions of this displacement are easily overridden by the meaning she takes from the communities constructed by newspapers:

> Dark and rare were the days when she failed to find on the inside page of her paper an address to or else account of herself. Was she not a worker, a soldier's lonely wife, a war orphan, a pedestrian, a Londoner, a home- and animal lover, a thinking democrat, a movie-goer, a woman of Britain, a letter writer, a fuel saver, and a housewife? (152)

Louie's naïvety is a source of comedy for Bowen's novel, but the vivid image of a woman who has lost all the 'others' who give meaning to her life is nonetheless disturbing. As Chapter 3 suggested, Louie attempts to fill the void by variously attaching herself to the ideal woman, Stella, and to her flatmate Connie; but it is not this 'queer' companionship that restores Louie. Rather, her eventual salvation comes through maternity. The grief which she is unable to articulate is resolved, or at least overridden, by this new sense of 'no longer being alone' (325). For Louie, the dyad of mother and child enables a rediscovery of both 'you' and 'I'.

Bowen, then, depicts her characters conforming to the necessary pull of convention, repressing both pain and possibility. Her prose suggests the traumatic impact of war, but she seldom makes it explicit: that is rather the role of Stevie Smith, whose novel, *The Holiday*, represents a disturbing vision of social and subjective 'dispossession'. Written during the war but not published until 1949, *The Holiday* is a fragmented and evasive text; but it is also one of the most powerful literary representations of trauma to emerge from Britain in the 1940s.

'The Peace Goes Badly': Stevie Smith's *The Holiday*

> Everything in this world is in fits and splinters, like after an air raid when the glass is on the pavements; one picks one's way and is happy in parts. (Smith 1949/1979: 143)

The Holiday configures war's end as a void – a gap, a chasm, a desire for oblivion – characterised by lack of purpose and confusion. Its pervasive melancholy and repeated failures of articulation stand as eloquent testimony to a range of signifying absences, not least of which is 'peace'. Early in the novel, Smith sets the scene: 'It is a year or so after the war. It cannot be said that it is war, it cannot be said that it is peace, it can be said that it is post-war; this will probably go on for ten years' (13). Smith's postwar is a state of cultural and psychological exposure: a site of mourning and a locus of impossible desires, both personal and political. Such a 'condition' might be seen to act as a potent metaphor for what is commonly known as the 'age of austerity', but Smith's construction is a somewhat disingenuous one. The novel was originally written during the war, but could not find a publisher – a situation perhaps attributable to its characters' enervating states of despair and suicidal melancholy – and it was not until Smith went through the manuscript inserting 'post' before each war reference, that the book was accepted. The technique might seem crude, but it works surprisingly well: 'How long will the post-war last', asks Celia, 'shall we win the post-war, how does it go' (90). As the economic crises of the period demonstrate, Britain, or at least the concept of the British nation that had shaped the pre-war years, certainly did not 'win' the postwar. But the ironic interchangeability of war and peace has disturbing implications, and underlines the extent to which the Second World War cannot be contained within the temporal limits of 1939–45. Psychologically, the war far exceeds these boundaries, and Smith's dysfunctional characters are, like nation as a whole, haunted by its repercussions. The novel also, however, conveys a disturbing sense of disempowerment that emerges from its characters' loss of direction, and from its underlying concern with two key tropes of women's postwar writing: mourning and repression.

The book is structured through conversation, argument and tears. Celia, the protagonist, craves death and attempts suicide by drowning (103), but between these outbursts of melancholy she works in her office at 'the Ministry', goes to parties and discusses the pressing issues of the day. However, in all its many dialogues, the narrative studiously avoids offering any form of resolution. In a typical example, prompted by an American book about 'how awful the British are' (139), Celia and her cousin Caz discuss the ideological chasm that separates the 'allies'. Yet an initial outburst of patriotism gives way to introspection: 'why did we present the news so badly . . . with no word of vigour and comfort?' (140). This recollection of uncertainty prompts one of the novel's many comparisons between England and Germany, resulting in an interpretation of Englishness as a 'steady and ferocious impetus' that destroys more remorselessly than any blitzkrieg (141). There is no specific indictment here, but the fragment is acute in its condensed account of a British war machine that could not prevent the fall of France, but which acquired the ruthless 'impetus' to obliterate Dresden. Ultimately, war produces not right and wrong, but simply different modes of might. *The Holiday*'s politics, then, are allusive and troubling, breaking off from analysis into moments of comedy and counsels of despair. 'An answer suffocates' (145), asserts Smith, and this refusal of completion is exacerbated by the form of the novel. It is a tapestry of fragments – stories, reviews, anecdotes, parables, poems and snatches of conversation – that persistently resist any attempt to construct a grand (or even a clear) narrative. Rather, the effect is cumulative, and the novel's combination of formal and psychic fragmentation works to convey a sense of loss that, in other writing of the period, seems to be wholly inarticulable.

'I wish for innocence more than anything, but I am conscious only of corruption' (143) cries Celia, but this perception of an all-pervasive postwar guilt is only one dimension of her torment. In its totality, *The Holiday* presents a powerful anatomy of mourning, and at its heart is what Butler would term the 'inscrutability' of the subject. At intervals throughout the novel Celia is quite literally 'beside herself' with grief, not least because she does not know what she mourns:

> Oh what is the barrier that stands out against this happiness, and what are the wolfish words upon our lips that deny it, the words that are not our words? What is the dog within us that howls against it, the dog that tears and howls, that is no creature of ours, that lies within, kennelled and howling, that is an alien animal, an enemy? (Smith 1949/1979: 62)

Her pain emerges from both public and private loss. Throughout the narrative she questions the conduct of the war, its causes and its consequences. She confronts her own and others' investment in ideas of nation and empire, and in belief systems from Christianity to Communism. She is tormented by a sense of moral loss, demanding of her virtuous Uncle Heber: 'How can we have a revolution and make a new world when we are so corrupt?' (131). The postwar moment, for Smith, is a moment between communities, between beliefs, between selves and, as her poem inserted into the novel observes, it is 'touch and go' whether 'man will come out of the mountains' (72).

Beyond this engagement with public and political stasis, *The Holiday* also confronts the intimate pain of personal loss. In her love for her cousin Caz, Celia is confronted by the question 'Who am "I", without you?'. The two characters are depicted as soul mates – their voices often difficult to distinguish due to the absence of speech marks – but their desire must remain unconsummated on account of their parents' adultery, a past sin that, in making them incestuously one, insists on their perpetual division. To live, in this context, is to be confronted by loss (171), and this is perhaps one of the reasons why Celia romanticises death:

> It is the desire to tear out this animal, to have our heart free of him, to have our heart for ourselves and for the innocent happiness, that makes us cry out against life, and cry for death. For the animal is kennelled close within, and tearing out this animal we tear out also the life with it. (62)

To live and to love is to hold a dangerous investment in the other, to give a hostage to pain. No wonder, then, that Celia declares, 'I am happy when I am unconscious' (51). Work displaces thought and takes away the necessity of expression. It distances her from the grief work that would otherwise dominate her psyche. In this statement, Smith acknowledges the difficulty of articulating trauma, a difficulty later given semi-comical expression through a touching instance of adynaton. Describing her staunch Lion Aunt, a symbol of resilience, fortitude and archetypally British 'common sense', Celia comments on a curious postwar transition: 'Now the war is over my Aunt feels that the house must not be left; during the war it has stood so much so now it must not be left' (81). It is not surprising that, when so much has been lost, what remains will be more cherished; but more significantly, this can be seen as a displacement of the human war-survivor's anxieties onto the inanimate form of the house. It may be sentimental to personify your house, but it is easier than attempting to express your own vulnerability.

Smith's novel, then, gives us clues to enable our reading of the wider postwar context. In the sheer excess of its pain, and its refusal to avoid the melancholic tug of unresolved grief, it points out the glaring absence of these post-traumatic symptoms in other instances of postwar writing and representation. In these years, repression reasserts itself and we witness the last gasp of a stoical Britishness that would rapidly become redundant. The result is a 'literature of lost possibilities' that, in the margins of its normalising discourse, mourns a loss of life, purpose, community and change. Bowen's Preface to *The Demon Lover* constructs war writing as a tentative concept in which the writer becomes a conduit for the 'flying particles of something enormous and inchoate that had been going on' (1950: 47). In the writing of the aftermath too we find particles and fragments, or in the words of Smith, 'fits and splinters' (1949/1979: 143), the traces of something enormous and inchoate that cannot find expression. These fragments constitute a signifying absence: the uncanny residue of a briefly glimpsed but swiftly overwritten change in gender constructs and relations.

A 'delayed fuse job': Nigel Balchin's *Mine Own Executioner*

The coercive normality evident in the work of women writers also found expression in the unquestioned assumptions of much male fiction. In Nigel Balchin's *Mine Own Executioner*, already noted for its depiction of the euphemistic language of male suffering, women occupy a series of traditional roles in the private sphere. The war seems to have had no impact whatsoever on their subjectivity or aspirations. When the novel's protagonist, the lay analyst Felix Milne, asks his lover Barbara why she married the obnoxious but wealthy Peter, her answer is telling: 'I wanted to be married to somebody. And I wanted to be – safe. I mean – to have money and clothes and so on and somebody to rely on' (1945: 52). Balchin's novel – like much women's writing of the period – foregrounds the domestic over the public, examining the war only in so far as it impinges on Milne's patient, Adam Lucian. However, its focus is significantly different, as it seeks to articulate a narrative of male disorientation that emerges from the impossibility of postwar 'reintegration'.

Mine Own Executioner stands as a popular primer on psychoanalysis, its characters debating the problems caused by unresolved childhood trauma and asserting the necessity of the medical profession putting mental health on a par with physical health. Its ostensible subject, however, proves incurable: the fighter pilot Adam Lucian cannot reintegrate a self fragmented by war, and transfers his unresolved issues onto women, in the form of 'that bitch' (85–6), the spitfire that let him down, and his wife, whom he eventually murders. As the coroner summarises, this is a warning to the public to take 'mental disease' seriously (243). Yet, as Stewart has noted, for all its protestations, the novel struggles to focus on Lucian's war-induced trauma, and the real substance of the narrative is the belated *bildungsroman* of Felix Milne (2006: 146).

Diagnosing himself as a case of arrested development on account of his predilection for shop-girls (169), Milne exhibits a classic inability to reconcile culture's conflicting stereotypes of femininity. Caught between his 'pure' wife Patricia and the hyper-sexualised figure of his lover Barbara, Milne achieves an adult reconciliation with his wife only when she ceases to be the uncritical good breast and tells him to pull himself together. To Balchin's credit, neither Patricia nor Barbara are straightforward representations of virgin and whore, but it is typical of much fiction of the period that woman becomes the symbol through which male crisis is articulated. Ultimately, though, Milne's problem is that of self-deception: he complains that his patients mistakenly regard him as God Almighty, but comes close to breakdown at the realisation that he is not omnipotent, and cannot save either Lucian or his wife, Mollie.

Balchin's vision of uneasy homecoming syndrome, then, is bleak and repressive. Lucian's breakdown is attributed at least in part to a pre-existing susceptibility (165), resulting in the culturally reassuring suggestion that this is not the logical outcome of war, but the aberrant product of exceptional circumstances (Lucian has been tortured, he is wracked with guilt, he was weak anyway). In positing thus an implied norm to which Lucian does not conform, *Mine Own Executioner* almost works too hard to cover the void of male trauma. Psychoanalysis is the answer, it asserts, while simultaneously attempting to suggest that there is no problem, because normal men are not susceptible to psychological wounds. It is a notable feature of Balchin's work that he both exposes and accommodates normative masculinities, demonstrating the pressures of conformity while resisting the idea of reinscription. The resulting 'wounded' heroes fight psychological rather than physical battles as they attempt to live up to the ideal of self-contained, stoical selfhood. The cracks in the façade of masculinity are exposed, but – in *Mine Own Executioner* at least – Balchin opts to paper them over. Milne can heal himself, if not Lucian, and in a comedy ending more typical of the condensations of British cinema than of prose narrative, he brings his formidable psychoanalytic powers to bear on the next generation:

> I have a certain talent for dealing with people's mental difficulties. Sometimes I have headaches, and then I let them go away and shoot their wives and commit suicide. But at other times I treat them with skill and integrity and cure them of wetting their beds. (Balchin 1945: 251)

Balchin, then, worries about male breakdown, but puts it back in the box through the reliably British discourses of euphemism and banter. It is left to Henry Green to provide a less 'realist' and ultimately more persuasive narrative of male disorientation and the dislocations of 'uneasy homecoming syndrome'.

'Gone missing': Henry Green's *Back*

'My dear, this is the war. Everything's been a long time. Why only the other day in my paper I read where a doctor man gave as his opinion that we were none of us normal.' (Green 1946/1998: 84)

This observation by James Phillips, one of the supporting cast in the looking-glass world of Henry Green's 1946 novel *Back*, encapsulates the dis-ease of the postwar period. Green makes telling use of bathos simultaneously to assert and ridicule the perception of Britain as a wounded culture, ensuring that the novel's depiction of its characters' traumatised states is both affecting and absurd. James's resort to the clichés of the popular press comes at a moment of social crisis: he has just been introduced to Nancy, the half-sister of his dead wife Rose, by his wife's paranoid ex-lover, the newly repatriated soldier, Charley Summers, who is labouring under the misapprehension that Nancy is in fact Rose. Given that this is a novel in which everyone and everything is connected, Charley's spectacular disorientation is not entirely surprising. However, it is one of the paradoxes of the book that this emphasis on metonymic connection coexists with a profound insistence on the fragmentation of self and society. As Rod Mengham notes:

Charley's instability... augments an already-existing, general disorientation, which bears on the demobilization of troops; the idea of the text being 'back' originates with the soldier's return from war. Almost from the outbreak of hostilities, demobilization was one of the issues uppermost in the public mind; the troops would come back to a society they would not recognize, with more women working than ever before, replacing men in industries geared to a war effort whose cessation could lead to massive unemployment. ... Demobilization was in many respects the keynote to uncertainty about the future. (Mengham 1982: 157)

This sense of disorientation is, however, set in a consciously anti-melodramatic context of suburban mundanity. In the words of Green's biographer, Jeremy Treglown, the story concerns the characters' 'slow, uneven progress back to more "normal" lives, as well as an unenchanted examination of what normality consists of' (2000: 184).

One answer to the question of what normality consists of would be the wound. Nearly all the characters bear some form of damage – James is a widower, Nancy a widow, Ridley has lost his mother, Mrs Grant has amnesia, Arthur has a lost an arm – but it is Charley who serves as the central embodiment of postwar loss through his multiple injuries. A prisoner of war since 1940 he has been deprived of his freedom for four years; he has suffered bereavement through the death of his lover; and he has lost his leg to a sniper's bullet, a literal wound which turns out, ironically, to be the least of his problems. Throughout the novel, Charley struggles with memories of his incarceration that are never made explicit, and with the memory of Rose, which comes to symbolise the traumatic impact of his losses. But although a woman becomes the central symbol of his suffering, Charley is not straightforwardly figured as impotent, nor does his amputated limb function as a metaphor of castration. Rather, Charley's problems with women stem from regression. His enforced absence in the prisoner-of-war camp has de-socialised him, and brought about a regression from man to boy. The Charley who returns from war is no longer the lover of the adulterous Rose, but rather the silent boy whose sole source of intimacy in the school-like environs of the camp was a pet mouse (197). Prison, we learn, 'had made him very pure' (40), and turned the female body into a site of unease; a condition the reader can share thanks to Green's imagery. Charley's secretary Dot has breasts like 'two soft nests of white mice' (40).

The brutal return to school represented by the camp is one factor in Charley's social de-skilling, the other is the changing society to which he returns. *Back* is filled with unexplained acronyms symbolising everything from government departments to aid societies, and this surfeit of meaningless letters makes explicit the extent to which 'Britain in 1944 is literally *unreadable*' (Mengham 1982: 158). This is a society in which nothing makes sense, and Charley, in his confusion attempts to impose a variety of inappropriate readings onto his experiences. Stewart argues that these are wilful misreadings – strategies of self-preservation – designed to repress the unspeakable experience of war (2006: 152). We might also, however, read Charley's behaviour in terms of a more fundamental urge: the search for maternal plenitude. Cut off from his adult life, and forcibly returned to childhood, what he yearns for in Rose is the pre-symbolic wholeness of the maternal dyad. That the 'real' Rose would have been unlikely to fill such a role (the book suggests that she was selfish and deceitful) is of no matter to Charley, who comes to believe that the world is conspiring to keep him away from this reunion. In his delusion, he comes to exhibit the symptoms of war's archetypal pathologies: hysteria and melancholia.[1]

As I suggested above, this is a novel in which almost every character has experienced some form of loss, and even those characters who seem to have completed the work of mourning are revealed to still be subjects in process, seeking, in Butler's terms, a new 'you' to give substance to their war-disrupted 'I'. The prosaic James, for example, finds that he does not want 'to lose sight of Summers' because he represents 'the main link left with the happy days which were fast slipping into the past' (82). Charley too, on first returning from the camp, visits the grave of Rose to seek some form of resolution. He finds instead the child who might be his son, and on this slight figure builds a fantasy of resurrection:

> Finally Charles was altogether taken up by a need to see the child a second time [. . .] to see if he could find a memory of Rose laughing there, and even to look deep in Ridley's eyes as though into a mirror, and catch the small image of himself by which to detect, if he could, a likeness, a something, however false, to tell him he was a father, that Rose lived again, by his agency, in their son. (1946/1998: 10)

Yet when confronted with the 'reality' of resurrection in the shape of Nancy, Charley's recovery is fundamentally undermined. The process of reality testing, part of the normative progress of grief work, is here proved false: it is not that Charley cannot believe his eyes when he sees Nancy, but rather that he believes his eyes and nothing else, and thereafter constructs increasingly convoluted structures of explanation to make sense of the impossible. Freud suggests that even in 'normal' mourning, the subject can turn away from reality and cling to the lost object 'through the medium of a hallucinatory wishful psychosis' (Freud 1917/1957: 244), but Charley moves beyond this psychic reconstruction to a more self-destructive state, evident in the physical manifestation of hysterical symptoms. Mention of either the camp or Rose's name prompts nausea and sleeplessness, and when, eventually, he is asked directly about his experiences in the camp, his response is categorical and, the novel suggests, literal: 'Can't talk about that, Nance' (191).

Back is thus a book that presents loss through the absence of expression or explanation; it makes explicit the assertion that war defies representation through its characters' inability to articulate their suffering. While Green's intense, provocative imagery communicates powerful images to the reader, within the narrative, communication is fragile and haphazard; the flawed product of encounters in which characters speak at rather than to each other. Green depicts a world of misunderstanding in which there is no guarantee that the message of speech is comprehended by its recipient. While his previous novel, *Loving* (1945), progressed painfully through dialogues comprised of parallel monologues, *Back* situates the perpetually disorientated Charley as a silent witness to a series of grotesque encounters. In part Charley's silence conveys his dislocation from the changed world in which he finds himself, but it also creates the impression of him occupying a parallel time. He is an unwilling outsider whose presence exposes what Britain in 1944 has become. In this sense, *Back* shares the hallucinatory qualities of Elizabeth Bowen's wartime world: the boundaries between the living and the dead have become permeable, and time and space are equally subject to distortion.

Charley's frequent inability to speak is thus a traumatic symptom to set alongside the obsessional quality of those utterances he does manage. Charley returns again and again to the word 'Rose', as if engaged in a process of 'nominal reanimation' (Watkin, 2004: 5). The word is, as Mengham notes, 'ubiquitous' (169) and the incantatory patterns woven around it are part of the almost obsessive patterning of the novel. This does not simply take place at the level of syntax or wordplay, rather the whole book is built around repeated encounters and reworked events. Like the child in Freud's *fort/da* game, it seems that Charley is destined endlessly to repeat his disorientating encounters until the mastery of loss is achieved. Within this structure of repetition with variations, Green further disorientates his reader through shifting points of view. Charley's weekend in the country with Dot and James Philips receives its first brief narration from Dot. Her account of James's eventual arrival in her bed removes all suspense from the 'betrayal' of Charley, and the later narration, focalised through Charley and James, is rendered comic by the reader's superior knowledge of events to come.

The novel's most significant shift in perspective, however, comes after Mr Grant's stroke. With the problematic patriarch removed, Mrs Grant is liberated from her madness, and the narrative of Charley's return from war effectively begins again. Recognised and welcomed by Mrs Grant, Charley is invited to mourn the absent Rose and offered confirmation, not only of her death, but of the contingent fact that 'Nance was a real person' (152). Mr Grant's initial manipulative behaviour is replaced by a maternal 'truth' that facilitates not just Charley's recovery, but also the emergence of a series of wider truths regarding peripheral characters. It is debatable whether this maternal truth has any greater veracity than its paternal predecessor (170), but there is no doubt that Mrs Grant's restoration to consciousness facilitates Charley's recovery. Charley needed a mother, and in the combination of Mrs Grant's recognition and Nancy's warm attention (140) he finds his constitutive others. This, arguably, is Green's happy ending: but it is a provisional one. In the final scene, Charley's cry of 'Rose' as he finally embraces the naked Nance is both a regressive mis-recognition, and an acknowledgement that his original belief in the resurrection of Rose was not so far from the truth. Nancy's interpellation as the absent woman has shaped her subjectivity, she has come to occupy the space of Rose: by the time of her union with Charley she has moved into the Grants' house and adopted Mrs Grant as her mother.

Green tells his readers that the marriage of Charley and Nancy will be a happy one, but it is evident from the closing scene that this happiness is built over the unresolved fracture of grief. In the first consummation of their desire, it is tears not semen that run through Nancy's legs (207) as Charley bawls 'like a child'. Nancy has already expressed her desire for children, and ironically, by the end of the book she has acquired one: Charley has not replaced Rose with another lover, but with a mother. The pragmatic Nancy recognises his traumatic dependency, not least because she herself cannot forget her husband, whose death, she perceptively notes, 'finished her' (141). Yet, as will be discussed in Chapter 7, public cultures of mourning stressed the need for pragmatic continuance, a perspective ridiculed by *Back* through the glib popular psychology of Charley's boss, who tells him that 'after the bad time you've had, you want to marry and settle down' (187). In bringing together two damaged people in a pietistic union of tears, Green both acknowledges and undermines the national public solution to postwar crisis. The returning hero is rehabilitated not through social reintegration, but through a return to the maternal dyad. Ultimately, Charley's losses are only assuaged by completing the regression from adult masculinity begun by the traumatic wound of war.

'We take our wilderness where we go': Rose Macaulay's Indictment

Both Stevie Smith and Henry Green mitigate their depiction of suffering with fragmentary glimpses of human connection, suggesting at least the possibility of new beginnings, however compromised. Rose Macaulay's *The World My Wilderness* (1950), by contrast, offers an unremittingly bleak vision of the postwar. In a book that begins and ends with quotations from Eliot's *The Waste Land*, Macaulay mourns the lost possibilities not simply of women, but of civilisation itself. The wasteland or wilderness is the central trope of the narrative, referring literally to the devastated city of London, and metaphorically to the alienated state of its protagonist Barbary Denison, an English girl who has grown up in occupied France. Barbary is a figure who, like the characters of Smith's dysfunctional world, 'cannot bear not to be at war' (Smith 1949/1979: 8): having known nothing else, she simply cannot comprehend the concepts of peace or civilisation. Unable to distinguish between forms of authority, or understand the political differences dividing nations,

Barbary occupies a space beyond the social: to her, all authority is the Gestapo, and all those who live in the underworld of bombed London constitute a resistance movement. As with the Maquis in postwar France, waging war has become a 'habit' (Macaulay 1950/1983: 40). The contrast with her brother Ritchie could not be greater. After three years in the army, Ritchie's 'hangover' is 'an ardent and delighted reaction towards the exquisite niceties of civilisation' (21). While his sister constitutes herself in opposition to authority, Ritchie constructs his identity through a languid aestheticism and a horror of 'the common man' (21, 150) that comically, but not unsympathetically, evokes the preoccupations of *Brideshead Revisited*.

Ritchie and Barbary have been made by war, and the conflict's role in their parenting exposes issues of responsibility, education and moral choice. *The World My Wilderness* is a dialectical novel, setting up oppositional characters to examine each individual's complicity in the collapse of social order. The book's frequent shifts in focalisation mean that the moral values of no one character can dominate, and it is difficult for the reader to determine who, if anyone, is 'right'. As with Panter-Downes's *One Fine Day*, there is a distinction drawn between a 'feminine' disregard for law and regulation, and a 'masculine' insistence on boundaries and order; the two positions finding embodiment in Barbary's mother, Helen Michel, and her father, Sir Gulliver Denison, KC. However, any easy essentialism is undermined by Helen's academic intellect and her ex-husband's repressed passion. In this world, no character fits tidily into the boxes of class or gender, and no position survives unchallenged. Barbary's outlaw subjectivity, for example, makes her as ruthless and rigidly moralistic as her father: she simply subscribes to another law (232). In comparison, Ritchie's 'horror of ruins' (252), his reaction against barbarism and cruelty, drives him 'towards bland tolerance' (149), a position as morally relativist as that of his mother, a woman who spent the war with a 'comfortable collaborator' (240), and who would abandon her own dinner parties if bored by the guests. It is, significantly, the latter transgression that disturbs Ritchie more than the former. All, then, are both sinners and sinned against. If it is Helen whose crimes are 'greater', it is also Helen who proves able, unconditionally, to forgive the terrible crime that has been perpetrated against her (231–2).

The end of the novel offers some element of personal resolution, but little sense of the restoration of order. This is a culture permeated with violence, in which the night nurse reads *No Orchids for Miss Blandish* and children become complicit in murder, and it is unclear whether the final chapter's vision of a garden amongst the ruins (252) is enough to counter the spiritual wilderness where 'the shells of churches gaped like lost myths' (254). Helen Michel's bleak conclusion that 'the maquis is within us, we take our wilderness where we go' (210) emphasises the fragility of family, state and society, an impression heightened by Macaulay's lists of London landmarks that have been destroyed. These catalogues of destruction are supplemented by the subjective distortions of grief. All the characters mourn something, but none of them can articulate this pain. Indeed, in one of the book's many ironies, the gynophobic psychologist Sir Angus Maxwell diagnoses the extent of Barbary's trauma; but can do nothing about it in a culture that stigmatises the expression of emotion (121). Indeed, how can talking 'cure' when the war-mind asserts that to talk is to betray, demanding not just the silence of 'keeping mum', but also the stoicism of a psychological 'make do and mend'? Macaulay depicts a culture of almost pathological repression, and suggests in Barbary's alienation that the rigid structures of the British middle-class family provide little protection against the social and psychic onslaught of war.

'After the first death, there is no other': Dylan Thomas's Refusal to Mourn

Macaulay's novel is, in its lamentation for a lost world, a form of elegy: the book forms a monument to a lost way of life and a generation irreparably damaged by conflict. Yet it is poetry that more conventionally performs a commemorative role, and the Second World War, like the First, produced a poetics of grief. Anthologies of the period abound with 'laments' and 'elegies', their language biblical and their imagery sacrificial. It is difficult now to appreciate the bombastic rhetoric of Apocalyptic and neo-romantic poets, but the violent excess of their imagery nonetheless speaks powerfully to the irreconcilable demands of war. J. F. Hendry's 'Lament', for example, moves painfully through a grotesque landscape, seeming to test and reject synonyms for pain:

> This grief is a spiked plant, dabbled with dorsal fins:
> Distiller of sorrow: action grown barren: war.
> Scattering wide his tears the airman tends
> In vegetable bombs the roots of his own grief.
> He weeps wild emptiness who sheds his blood.
>
> (Tambimuttu 1942: 82)

Beyond the mixed metaphors and the bathos of 'vegetable bombs', the poem makes its point through recourse to a perverted pastoral. Only grief can grow in war's sterile landscape, and in his distanced, mechanical destruction of others, the airman also destroys himself. The distortion of a cyclical regenerative ideal through the intervention of modernity – the airman becomes the farmer of death – asserts the threat war posed to human values and the human self. In Hendry's case, an attempt is made at Christian consolation, but this comfort is undermined by the inevitability of sacrifice, and the poem ends with an apocalyptic combination of tolling bells, 'blood-beaked ravens' and prophesies of doom.

Poems such as Hendry's, with its sonorous public rhetoric, seem actively to aim for the status of memorial. Yet much of the poetry of grief to emerge from the conflict resists this representative role, focusing instead on a more intimate process of bearing witness to loss. As Linda Shires has noted of poetry emerging from the services, 'the lyric of personal experience seemed the best way to make sense of so terrible and abstract a holocaust' (1985: 68). There is, then, a problem of scale in writing about loss in the Second World War: there is simply too much to grieve for. This excess of death is, ultimately, mind-numbing, prompting a form of elegiac paralysis. 'We cannot weep/ At tragedy for millions' suggests Ida Proctor's 'The One' (Reilly, 1984: 102), while Edwin Muir reasserts the value of the individual. In his succinct cascading poem 'Reading in War Time', Muir asserts literature's function as grief work, but does not claim this status for his own poem. Rather it is the literature of the past that enshrines significant death and enables a displaced act of mourning:

> Boswell's turbulent friend
> And his deafening verbal strife,
> Ivan Ilych's death
> Tell me more about life,
> Both being personal,
> Than all the carnage can,
> Retrieve the shape of man

> (Williams 1945: 381)

Here Muir poses and responds to the question of why the war prompted a massive increase in 'serious' reading (Calder, 1969/1992: 512). In the mechanised totality of modern war, with its awesome capacity not simply to kill but to obliterate the human, the reader is drawn to the apparent certainties inherent in the literature of other centuries. Writers outside the conflict retrieve 'the shape of man', and in restoring the integrity of the self, they enable the mourning process.

Dylan Thomas was both outside and inside the Second World War. A non-combatant who experienced the Blitz, he struggled throughout the conflict to complete the poems that would form *Deaths and*

Entrances (1946). This book 'accomplished a popular breakthrough' for the poet (Lycett 2003: 262), suggesting that its combination of intensely personal and often nostalgic reflection with a powerful rhetoric of mourning was very much in tune with the emotional climate of the postwar. Thomas's grandiose, obscure and often biblical language had seen him connected by critics to both surrealism and the Apocalyptics – affiliations he firmly rejected – but his wartime work achieved a new accessibility (Shires 1985: 43; Lycett 2003: 262). In the title poem, 'Deaths and Entrances', for example, Thomas succinctly evokes the heightened sensibilities and liminal states seen in prose accounts of the Blitz:

> On almost the incendiary eve
> When at your lips and keys,
> Locking, unlocking, the murdered strangers weave,
>
> (Thomas 1998/2000: 98)

'On almost the incendiary eve' simultaneously figures sunset, inferno and desire. Both the physical body and the concrete world are going up in flames, and the interweaving of intimacy's *petites morts* with the Blitz's indiscriminate destruction creates a powerful image of the unstable, permeable boundary between the living and the dead. Beyond the intensity of 'Deaths and Entrances', but similarly suggestive of the war's distortions, is the disturbing 'Conversation of Prayers'. Composed in 1945, the poem begins with the natural order of a child 'going to bed' and a man mourning 'his dying love', but ends with the man finding his love alive and the child destined for the inarticulable horrors of the nightmare: 'And the child not caring to whom he climbs his prayer/ Shall drown in a grief as deep as his true grave' (85).

Deaths and Entrances finds its focus in the extremes of innocence and experience, youth and age: from the dead child at the centre of 'Ceremony After a Fire Raid', to the 'Man Aged a Hundred' killed in a raid, for whom, in an ironic balancing of the books, Thomas now imagines 'a hundred storks' perching 'on the sun's right hand' (112). The dead child, however, cannot be compensated for. 'Ceremony After A Fire Raid', composed after a visit to Coventry, weaves echoes of the Lord's Prayer into a depiction of endless destruction for which 'miracles cannot atone' (107). The street has been 'burned to tireless death', while the dead child's arms are 'full of fires'. Here, as in most of Thomas's war poetry, the one symbolises and is intimately connected to the many, and origins are conflated with extinction. The structure of the verse, too, moves from a private, almost hesitant, syntax to a massive rhetorical climax. The opening lines both describe and demand grief work, while the same patterning in the third stanza replaces the sustenance of daily bread with sacrificial death:

> Forgive
> Us forgive
> Give
> Us your death that myselves the believers
> May hold it in a great flood
>
> (Thomas 1998/2000: 107)

But the comfort of sacrifice is problematised by the second part of the poem which immortalises not Christ's death, but that of the 'charred' child. 'In the cinder of the little skull', a terrifying image of human vulnerability, the Edenic consolations of religion become a 'garden of wilderness' (108). The poem's ceremonial climax thus becomes a blind incantation, a potent ritual commemoration that finds no consolation in the religion it appropriates.

Similarly potent in its refusal of consolation – its paradoxical undoing of elegy – is perhaps the most famous of Thomas's war poems, 'A Refusal to Mourn the Death, By Fire, of a Child in London'. Completed in March 1945, the poem's confrontational title prepares the reader for its disturbing ambiguities, and asserts from the outset Thomas's life-long loathing of conventional pieties. 'A Refusal to Mourn' is replete with Thomas's characteristic condensed images. Here is the sterility of 'salt seed' and the hypocrisy of the 'valley of sackcloth', but the crux of the poem is its concluding line: 'After the first death, there is no other' (86). The multivalent possibilities of this statement are evident in the contrasting readings it has received. Linda Shires optimistically suggests that:

> In spite of the professed inadequacy of words to capture death, the poem finds a wealth through negation. Thomas does not really refuse to mourn, he just postpones it until all things return to their original darkness. . . . Death is not to be grieved but remains a secret part of the universal rhythm of remembrance, an entrance, not an exit. (1985: 47–8)

Andrew Lycett's reading is the antithesis of Shires's. Thomas's poem is, he argues, 'avowedly unreligious', categorically refusing the possibility of resurrection (2003: 258). William Empson, one of the poem's first interpreters in 1947, suggests a middle ground: 'the plain meaning of the last line is that the child has no more pain and is well rid of such a world; it suggests also that she lives for ever as part of Nature' (1987: 386). Yet the line is redolent with further possibilities. How many times can death be mourned? Can any death signify as profoundly as the first? Later deaths accumulate, but they cannot replicate the intensity of bereavement's first pain. In some sense, after the first death, all other deaths become meaningless; repetitions that do not have the force of an original.

These questions return the reader to the poem's title. Piette and Empson recognise here a refusal of cheap sentiment and a resistance to the public cultures of mourning that seek to make political capital out of death. This is, writes Piette, not so much an anti-elegy as a true elegy 'for the kind of common feeling that respects the difference of the dead' (1995: 245). This is undoubtedly the impulse behind the central lines: 'I shall not murder/ The mankind of her going [. . .] With any further/ Elegy of innocence and youth' (Thomas 1998/2000: 86). Yet this refusal is complicated by the problematic residue of the preceding phrase: the opening of the stanza which proclaims the 'majesty and burning of the child's death'. This is a triumphal, transfigurative image that figures the child's death as spectacle and symbol. In this awe-inspiring death the individual child is turned into a sacrificial victim, a brand searing the consciousness of the reader. We demean the child by mourning, because in performing this ritual we accept not just her death, but the cause of her death. Thomas's poem thus implicitly calls not for grief but for anger, perhaps, as Empson suggests, at 'all the men who made the world situation in which she was killed' (1987: 385). Alternatively, we might see Thomas's anger directed at the fetishisation of 'innocence'. Her death is as any other, her youth should not signify, but inevitably it does; and in drawing attention to the hypocrisy of singling out the innocent for elegy, Thomas also asserts his belief that elegy itself can never be innocent.

'Every poem an epitaph': T. S. Eliot's Grief Riddles

> We die with the dying:
> See, they depart, and we go with them.
> We are born with the dead:
> See, they return, and bring us with them.
>
> (Eliot 1944/2001: 42)

These lines, from the final section of *Little Gidding*, the last of *Four Quartets*, link Eliot's exceptionality to the recurrent rhetoric of liminality that permeates wartime and postwar responses to the war in general and the Blitz in particular.[2] Here again is the unsettling interchangeability of living and dead, and here again the paradox of Judith Butler's construction of grief. Something of us 'goes missing' with the lost object, but Eliot's faith takes him beyond loss to an imagined rebirth that transcends the limits of time and liberal humanist rationality. Indeed, in a nutshell, these four lines seem magically to encapsulate the entire framework of Thomas's *Deaths and Entrances*, rebalancing the books as the storks recalibrate the loss of the 'Man Aged a Hundred'. Yet there is something not quite right about this nifty resurrection. Its glib ease and prosaic transparency seem at odds with *East Coker*'s earlier assertion that 'to be restored, our sickness must grow worse' (1944/2001: 17, 18), or indeed, the assertion that the 'agony abides' in *The Dry Salvages*. Here, 'the ragged rock in the restless waters' is sometimes concealed, sometimes a valuable 'sea mark', but it cannot be transformed or forgotten: it 'is what it always was' (1944/2001: 27). In this context, the language of *Little Gidding*'s resurrection smacks of the magic trick, as it invites the reader to 'see' the miracle of disappearance and reappearance, to stand amazed by the final transformation of pain into a 'romance of wholeness' (Esty 2004: 8) that stands as a consolatory epitaph for wartime loss.

John Xiros Cooper links the pain of *East Coker* to the 'need for despair', a necessary state of disillusionment that is a precondition for 'the revival of meaningful personal and, therefore, social existence' (1995: 134–5). Eliot, argues Cooper, offers art as a 'safe haven of inwardness' (154), a consolatory fiction for a 'mandarinate' retreating wounded from the political engagements of the 1930s. In its entirety, then, the poem is an epitaph for a set of political beliefs, an understanding of history and a secular mind-set that the conservative Eliot believed to have been variously fruitless and damaging. In this sense, the poem grieves only in so far as it dances on the graves of its ideological others. Yet the detail of the poem, its repeated turning to images of intimacy and memory, its juxtaposition of quotidian preoccupations with searing destruction, and indeed, its introspective self-consciousness, suggest a parallel possibility. Eliot's poem consoles in spite of itself, inserting into the distinguished structures of high art the fragments of mundane loss:

> Dust in the air suspended
> Marks the place where a story ended.
> Dust inbreathed was a house –
> The wall, the wainscot and the mouse.
> The death of hope and despair,
> This is the death of air.

> (*LG* II, 1944/2001: 37)

Recording the end of a story, Eliot constructs an epitaph for ordinary lives, unexpectedly weaving the atomised mass into his meditations on eternity. Indeed, these moments are all the more potent for their embedding within the structure of paradox that dominates the poem. These lines stand out as lucid, succinct and transparent: their simple rhyme and regular rhythm at odds with the more densely woven passages that precede and follow them. They are, to put it crudely, memorable, and in their reading, the congregation comes together at a point of immediate, contemporary comprehension. If we are tempted to see *Four Quartets* as a series of variations on the Anglican service, all that is missing here is the answering 'Amen'. Eliot the vicar tells us to pray, and our journey through the text proceeds with the stately rhythm of liturgical precision. The meaning here is less important than the capacity of ingrained response to offer solace in the face of abject powerlessness. As the omnipresent village church becomes a symbol of community in films that have no direct engagement with faith – *Went the Day Well?* (1942), for example – so the sonorous form of Eliot's poem asserts an inexpressible comfort.

This vital inarticulacy is integral to the timeliness of *Four Quartets*. The search for the right words, the telling image, the glimpsed idea, that will restore the lost object (which for Eliot is an ideal of community and God, but for his reader might be anything from the personal to the abstract), turns the poem into a protracted, fragmented instance of grief work. The impossibility of articulating loss, of finding words for war, or for the nebulous spiritual revival the poet hopes it will engender, is evident in the turn to self-questioning. Throughout the poem, Eliot pauses to consider the effect of his linguistic gambits: 'That was a way of putting it – not very satisfactory' (*EC*, 15). While the poem is the friendly voice of the vicar to his flock, it is also an invitation to consider meaning in cumulative rather than progressive terms, to contemplate the impact of all Eliot's 'puttings', and to ask whether the time of reading is a healing temporality that reassures through a process of verbal trial and error. Waiting for the resolution of Eliot's riddles – the interminable suggestive paradoxes of the text – readers, despite themselves, are led to recuperation.

The time of reading is, then, another time to add to the multiple temporalities negotiated by the poem. Much has been written on this: Jed Esty, for example, argues that Eliot founds an ideal of cultural revival in the failure of 'the linear time guaranteed by modern progress and expansion' (2004: 116). Into this void Eliot inserts the anti-modern, the eternal, the time of revelation. But Esty also observes that the poem depends upon a relationship between the quotidian and the transcendent: 'an achievement of a spiritually meritorious kind of consciousness [. . .] depends upon living through moments defined by an ordinary and painful knowledge of loss' (142). In one sense this is another reason for the insertion of the exploded house into the philosophical meditation, but it is also part of the poem's paradoxical offer and refusal of comfort to its readers. This is evident in *The Dry Salvages*, where the statement that 'time is no healer' (27) is followed by a potentially redemptive parable of translation (28). The metaphor that leads us to this liminal place is the train journey, and the travellers, who might be living or dead, are jolted by the rhythm of imagined train and actual poem into a new freedom: 'Their faces relax from grief into relief' (27). This is not escape, suggests Eliot, but rather a new discontinuous selfhood:

> You are not the same people who left that station
> Or who will arrive at any terminus
> While the narrowing rails slide together behind you; (28)

This image of loss, figured spatially as distance, is also an idea of human subjectivity reimagined as endless replication. The train does not 'progress', the 'end is where we start from' (42), the dead return. If Eliot were not so ill-disposed towards psychoanalysis, listing it amongst the usual 'Pastimes and drugs' (30) drawn on in times of crisis, he too might be seen to invoke the *fort/da* game, in which the child stages loss and recovery in defiance of time and death.

Another miraculous recovery takes place in *Little Gidding* II where, in a further assertion of the permeable boundaries of self and time, the poet encounters a 'familiar compound ghost' (38). This figure, both 'intimate and unidentifiable' has been variously identified as Yeats and Dante, yet while this passage undoubtedly evokes the shades of Eliot's masters, it also begs a more personal reading as an encounter with another, earlier, self. In the twilight of the Blitz, the poet assumes 'a double part . . . Knowing myself yet being someone other' (38), and the poem reclaims the cadence of an earlier work and an earlier war. Here, in the exclamation of meeting, 'What! Are *you* here?', we hear the echo of *The Waste Land*, where Eliot imagines resurrection through a brutal absurdity:

> There I saw one I knew, and stopped him, crying: 'Stetson!
> 'You who were with me in the ships at Mylae!
> 'That corpse you planted last year in your garden,
> 'Has it begun to sprout? Will it bloom this year?
>
> (1963/1974: 65)

The ghost's speech in *Little Gidding*, then, is the voice of both self and other, and 'the gifts reserved for age' he discloses are the lessons of experience: Eliot's own, and those of another dead poet, Wilfred Owen, whose 'Strange Meeting' haunts the encounter between 'two worlds' (39).

Steve Vine suggests that the poems of Dylan Thomas 'simultaneously preserve loss by refusing to convert it into meaning, and affirm poetic articulation in the face of loss' (2001: 149). *Four Quartets*, by contrast, seems to question poetic articulation and offer consolation by way of quietude: a paring down of poetry, spectacle, emotion, into a 'condition of complete simplicity' (43). Whether or not Eliot expects the reader to follow him into belief, the poem ends with revelation and unity which, like the statement 'History is now and England' (43), begs to be read in patriotic terms. Cooper suggests that Eliot as a poet was saved by the war:

> Eliot's eminence in the 1940s was most solidly sustained, even with all his personal accomplishments, by something beyond his control, the evolution of the historical situation itself. It was a situation that had reached bottom with the war and had taken down with it the concluding aspirations of the younger generation. (1995: 108)

Given this happy union of poet and topic, it is perhaps unsurprising that just occasionally the poet's mask of dignified consolation slips to reveal a less sympathetic and more clearly polemical purpose. After all, if history is timeless repetition and man eternally imperfect, there is not much point in grieving the individual. This, perhaps, accounts for the moments of jauntiness that, like voices from the past of Eliot's oeuvre, burst into the conclusion of *Four Quartets*.

Improbably, and somewhat dissonantly, T. S. Eliot ends his epic poem with a cry of 'cheer up'. The dead will be back in a minute, and individual loss will be but a moment in eternity. *Four Quartets* record the detail of Blitz and the pain of suffering in wartime, but they simultaneously invite us to see the big picture. Suffer and be redeemed, and in the meantime, as Cooper's reading suggests, go about your business respecting tradition and celebrating a mystical, but not uncritical, combination of nation and faith. One answer to Eliot's grief riddle, then, is that despair – existential, political, personal – is necessary and ultimately beneficial. In this, and in his reliance on the rhetorical tropes of a specifically premodern Englishness, Eliot enters the mainstream. He 'reenchant[s] the English landscape' (Esty 2004: 118) in a manner remarkably similar to the propaganda films that juxtaposed rural ideal and urban reality, claiming a common purpose born of, rather than transcending, difference. In the mundane moments and personal crises, the poem is consolatory, but it is also a coping strategy remarkably similar to the ideal of 'business as usual' that dominated propagandist rhetoric. Eliot's norm might have been different to that of the mass culture he rejected, but he too found and offered comfort in a reassertion of traditional pieties and habitual repetitive phrases.

Four Quartets, then, both grieve and resist, building a New Jerusalem of the spirit as others would seek to construct a planned social utopia. Mourning, once considered, is consigned to the past in a manner absolutely typical of constructions of British national identity. Alexander Baron encapsulates the dominant psychology of the 1940s:

> . . . it did not pay to grieve for absent friends. There were too many of them; a man who let their passing hurt him would carry more unhealed wounds than he could bear; and so the riflemen of the Fifth Battalion had grown, as all soldiers grow, into a state of mind in which a friend killed yesterday became as remote in the memory as some half-forgotten schoolmate, to be talked of with the same detachment. (1948/2010: 149)

As the war drew to a close, cultural expectations demanded adjustment rather than retrospection. Whether people looked nostalgically backwards or anxiously forwards, dwelling on the war itself was, for many, impossible. Increasingly, the discourses of grief were buried under, or codified through, a range of public outward-looking texts that insisted that normality could and should be reconstituted, irrespective of its subjective cost.

Notes

1. Discussing hysteria in the First World War, Showalter notes that 'war neurosis became more common after the armistice' (1997: 73), attributing this variously to the transference of long-held resentments from the enemy to those 'at home', and the shock of encountering the difference between the idealised vision of home and its altered reality.
2. I do not mean to suggest by this categorisation that Eliot's response to the war was 'exceptional', but rather that the poet himself has been rendered exceptional by a process of canonisation which has detached *Four Quartets* from the context of their production. Marina MacKay, however, notes that 'if the cultural and political work *Four Quartets* performed in their own time has been systematically bypassed, it is not because their author was interested in concealing it' (2007: 72), and a number of critical studies have traced the relationship of the poems to war and Englishness (Knowles 1990; Ellis 1991; Piette 1995; Esty 2004; Mellor 2011). In addition, John Xiros Cooper details the process of canonisation surrounding the *Quartets* in the 1940s, explaining how the poems came so swiftly to be seen as 'art' transcending a debased political reality (1995).

Chapter Seven

Adjusting

Morally and economically Europe has lost the war. The great marquee of European civilization in whose yellow light we all grew up, and read or wrote or loved or travelled has fallen down; the side ropes are frayed, the centre-pole is broken, the chairs and tables are all in pieces, the tea-urns empty, the roses are withered on their stands, and the prize marrows; the grass is dead. ('Comment', *Horizon*, Vol. XII, No. 67; 1945: 149)

London looked horrible [. . .] Half the women looked like cheap tarts and the men like Black Market touts. There was neither dignity nor genuine high spirits. The atmosphere wasn't English, wasn't Continental, wasn't honestly American: it was a dreadful rancid stew [. . .] it was a hellish huddle of nasty trading, of tired pleasure-seeking, of entertainment without art, of sex without passion and joy, of life buzzing and swarming without hope and vision. London could take it. But how much more of this could it take? (Priestley 1946: 344)

The postwar world of J. B. Priestley's *Bright Day* is one threatened by loss, but not by grief. It is a world of lost identities, lost purpose and lost direction. The middle-aged narrator, a successful Hollywood screen writer who has returned home to spend the war years working for the British studio system, feels burnt out and disconsolate, a 'weary old ghost' (1946: 360): he knows what he does not want, but cannot begin to imagine what he needs. Reliving the past provides a compelling narrative, but no useful answers. Indeed, his absorption in his memories of the period 1912–14, when he was an aspiring writer working in the wool trade, threaten to destroy those few friendships he cherishes in the present. It takes a set of fresh faces and the intervention of a perceptive woman to convince him that looking back is 'the wrong way' (361). What must be recaptured is the energy and hope of youth, not a sentimental recollection of people who belong, very firmly, in their time and place. The dead must be laid to rest. Yet in spite of its clear moral message, *Bright Day* spends far longer in the past than the present, as if uncertain itself quite how to proceed with its vision of a new creative age in which the cinema will show 'how real people behaved in a real world' (352). Priestley depicts a world run by men without imagination: in the background of both past and present is the figure of Malcolm Nixey, a man who thinks only in terms of profit and whose fundamental character flaw is his lack of capacity for enjoyment (155). Nixey is not actively evil, not even really a villain, he is simply a banal capitalist parasite: and it is this insidious quality that makes his kind so hard to fight. He has prospered during both world wars, while the brightest and best have fallen, a gross imbalance that leaves survivors with 'an astonishing burden of memories' (11).

Implicit in *Bright Day* is a question of responsibility, a duty to the reconstruction of Britain, which must not be left to the Nixeys of this world. The same question permeates Priestley's earlier demobilisation novel *Three Men in New Suits* (1945), and finds an unexpected counterpart in Charles Williams's bizarre 'spiritual thriller' *All Hallows' Eve* (1945). *Three Men in New Suits* attacks the 'problem' of the postwar directly, by exploring the tensions of homecoming for three demobilised soldiers. Priestley creates a composite everyman to facilitate his examination of the home front: Alan Strete, representing the gentry; Herbert Kenwood, the yeomanry and Eddie Mold, the honest working man. Crucially, all three have come from the ranks, with Strete refusing promotion in order to stay with his men. The problems that confront them are the collapse of community and the resurgence of self interest; a sense of cultural invasion, manifest in a parody of Hollywood cinema (1945: 99–100); visceral divisions between town and country; the resurgence of class boundaries and the re-emergence of a pre-war mode of 'power' concentrated in the hands of an unscrupulous privileged few. This power briefly dazzles Alan and he begins to revel in a Waugh-esque abandonment of responsibility, flirting with the narcissistic Betty, seduced by the comforts of nepotism and influence:

> As easy as that. An introduction or two in the right quarters, a few chats over a few drinks, and then you were inside the ring too. And as he went off to find Betty, he felt a sudden and rather angry contempt for all the blank-faced millions who were outside, gaping and wondering, waiting to see how their lives would be shaped. (Priestley 1945: 147)

This time, the warning is explicit: the greatest threat to the postwar world is the ghost of the 1930s and the rejection of the war's embryonic meritocracy.

In marked contrast to Priestley's social realism, Charles Williams responds to the anxieties of the postwar with a contemporary ghost story. *All Hallows' Eve* imagines a battle not just for Britain but for the world, a surreal narrative in which the living and the dead unite to stop the deadly machinations of a perverse Messiah, whose growing following has led even the Foreign Office to believe in him (1945/2003: 216–17). Williams adjusts to the postwar through a symbolic focus on the dead, figuring them as restless, unresolved reminders of war's transformative power. In this he anticipates a central conceit of Elizabeth Bowen's *The Heat of the Day*, an image of liminality in which the boundaries, not just between people but between worlds, have been dislocated by war:

> Most of all the dead, from mortuaries, from under cataracts of rubble, made their anonymous presence – not as today's dead but as yesterday's living – felt through London. Uncounted they continued to move through the city day, pervading everything to be seen or heard or felt with their torn-off senses, drawing on this tomorrow they had expected – for death cannot be so sudden as all that. (Bowen 1948/1962: 91)

The aftermath of the Blitz is figured as a form of dual citizenship in which the dead inhabit the living world, and the living are drawn inexorably closer to that of the dead. In *All Hallows' Eve* this uncanny image is given character and plot, as Lester, a member of the newly dead, helps two of the living to save Betty, a woman who can miraculously inhabit both worlds. In his introduction to the book, written in 1948, T. S. Eliot suggests that Williams 'knew, and could put into words, states of consciousness of a mystical kind' (1945/2003: xvii). This preoccupation is evident in the relationship between the dead Lester and her living husband Richard, whose relationship grows in the aftermath of loss: their mourning is a process of healing through learning the truth of the lost other. But this relationship is not at the heart of the novel, nor is the muted love affair between the painter Jonathan and the semi-supernatural Betty, rather it lies in the articulation of the threat they face: Simon the Clerk, a pseudo-messianic cult figure seen by many as the saviour of a damaged world. Much of the depiction of Simon's necromancy and the spiritual forces that gather to defeat it seems wilfully opaque, but Williams's fear that a damaged world will turn to false prophets is made clear in the Clerk's perversion of Christian ideology.[1] Simon aims to have dominion over both living and dead, and his reach is global, thanks to a handy capacity for self-replication:

> The war had for a while hidden them, but now that the war was over they had reappeared, proclaiming everywhere peace and love, and the enthusiasm for them broke all bounds, and became national and more than national; so that the whole world seemed to be at the disposal of that triplicity. [. . .] There

were demands that these three teachers should meet, should draft a gospel and a policy, should fully rule the worship they provoked. (1945/2003: 113)

Williams's neologism, 'triplicity', functions simultaneously to invoke the trinity and distort it into an echo of duplicity. Not three in one, but a deceptive projection, through 'derivations and automata' (113), of a single power-hungry self. The Clerk is ultimately defeated by a combination of forces that Williams terms the 'Acts of the City', after which Lester is free to go to her death, and Betty can begin at last to live. This simultaneous death and resurrection is a symbol of renewal but, like Alan's impassioned cry that '[w]e have to make the round earth our home', as he rises, 'towering, almost transfigured' above his comrades at the conclusion of Priestley's *Three Men* (1945: 169), it offers only the vaguest of templates for the future. Adjusting to the demands of the postwar, and deciding who to trust with the future, would be a challenge to which writers responded with an uncomfortable combination of reassurance, optimism, anxiety and doubt; and their work bears the traces of this indeterminacy in a series of ambivalent prescriptions for the future.

'I'm one of the strangers too': The Art of Demobilisation

The fictions of Priestley and Williams suggest that the postwar world was fragile and endangered, and much the same could be said of its citizens, many of whom seemed unable to reconcile their wartime and postwar subjectivities. For Priestley's Alan Strete, past and present are almost irreconcilable, turning 'home' into a paradoxical space of belonging and alienation:

> The sight of the old house split Alan into two men. One, who had been born there, recognised with affection every window pane and worn brick, and simply came home. The other, who had been away for years and had fought his way from the African desert into the middle of Europe, stared at this rambling old building, huddled deep into its green island hillside, and began to wonder what this remote place meant to him. [. . .] This split, this sudden double vision, was more than confusing. He felt a deep distress. (1945: 11–12)

This perception of an uncanny duality is echoed by all of Priestley's returning soldiers, who feel in their different ways that they, or their homes, have become strange and unfamiliar. Herbert identifies himself with this otherness, rebutting a self-serving gossip with the claim 'I'm one of the strangers too' (97), but the inarticulate Eddie Mold cannot make sense of the world that greets him. His home no longer feels his own (117) and his wife looks 'like somebody else' (62). That Priestley had accurately captured the disorientation of the returning soldier is evident from accounts of demobilisation:

> the years immediately following the Second World War were a period filled with tension, anxiety and anger. Untold thousands of British families struggled with very real problems of reassimilating their menfolk after a profound, sometimes psychologically bewildering, transition from one world to another. (Allport 2009: 220)

Alan Allport's compelling study suggests that this reintegration process often ended in failure. Divorce, made newly accessible by the 1937 Divorce Act and changes to legal aid during the war years, hit an all-time high of 60,300 decrees absolute in 1946 (2009: 87). Crime was on the increase, in particular violent crime, the indictable incidences of which more than doubled between 1938 and 1948. In addition, sexual assaults rose from 5,018 in 1938 to 13,185 in 1950 (163–4). Some contemporary commentators blamed social fragmentation on a 'slackening of moral fibre': a general laxity and loss of moral compass brought about by the war (164). Others laid the blame specifically at the feet of returning soldiers, speculating that 'ex-servicemen were breaking the law not because they needed the money, but because they *enjoyed* it' (165). In the mid-1940s the returning soldier, like the mobile woman, represented a potential threat to civic society. The peace of home would be jeopardised, many feared, by a generation of men 'permanently reprogrammed . . . into killers' (173). On the one hand this evokes the spectre of the traumatised veteran, driven by unbearable memories to acts of violence against himself and others. On the other hand, it conjures up the figure of the commando. This liminal bogeyman is beyond re-domestication: a figure curiously both ancient and modern, a skilled warrior who fights outside the rules. 'The commando', writes Allport, 'was a bit of a brute. He brought gangster values to the battlefield. Would he bring them home as well?' (179; see also Stewart 2006: 153–60).

Yet the image conjured up by Allport has a domestic counterpoint: the 'spiv' or black marketeer. This figure, in some sense the antithesis of the damaged ex-soldier, ensured that 'gangster values' already flourished on the home front. More significantly, though, we might see constructions of both spiv and ex-serviceman as manifestations of a deep anxiety about masculinity and the male role. This crisis, which would percolate gradually into fiction, often in the form of disturbing misogynies, found immediate expression in the cinema, giving rise to one of the most significant trends in postwar film making: an outpouring of crime narratives loosely dubbed the 'spiv cycle'. A compelling example is provided by Cavalcanti's *They Made Me A Fugitive* (1947), in which maladjusted ex-serviceman Clem Morgan gets involved with the black market out of boredom, but the cycle is usually considered to have begun with Sidney Gilliat's *Waterloo Road* (1945). In casting emerging heart-throb Stewart Granger in the role of spiv Ted Purvis, *Waterloo Road* recognised the attraction of criminal enterprise to an impoverished and weary society. Indeed, at every level the film suggests a culture that has had its fill of restrictions. Ted Purvis pursues Tilly Colter (Joy Shelton), a young married woman made unhappy by the impossibility of beginning a conventional married life. In the absence of a baby, she is easily tempted by Purvis's promise of a good time, and this threatened seduction prompts her soldier husband Jim (John Mills), to go AWOL. In a radical departure from roles that had cast him as the epitome of dutiful English masculinity, Mills's character takes the law into his own hands, evades the Military Police and reclaims Tilly after one of the most acclaimed fight sequences in British film history. It is a happy ending, and the film – constructed in flashback – concludes with a visit to the Colter's baby, a highly symbolic signifying infant. But there is a limit to what this baby can achieve, and the levels of transgression tolerated by the narrative suggest a nation no longer willing to accommodate messages of duty and self-sacrifice (Plain 2006: 81–8).

Waterloo Road thus simultaneously encodes the drive to restore 'normality' through the re-establishment of traditional family roles, and a degree of disquiet concerning structures of authority in the postwar world. In spite of the overwhelming political mandate for change given to the new Labour government, the nation in 1945 was pessimistic, tired and suspicious (Kynaston 2007: 43–5). Consequently, fictions that sought to imagine a new future, or debate pressing moral concerns, did so in tentative terms, or through displacements to other times and places. In this, the literature of reconstruction curiously overlaps with that of escape; but the retreat of writers such as J. B. Priestley and Terence Rattigan to past times and contexts is profoundly different from that of Hartley or Waugh. As the example of *Bright Day* suggests, the past is sought as a site of regeneration, an imaginative space from which values can be retrieved, and the building of a new society facilitated. This dynamic is equally evident in Naomi Mitchison's historical epic, *The Bull Calves* (1947). Set in the aftermath of the Jacobite rebellion of 1745, *The Bull Calves* explores concepts of family, loyalty and forgiveness; it also, through its central characters' transgressions, explores the psychological impact of extreme circumstances. Kirstie Haldane's attraction to a coven of witches, and the power she imagines emanating from this outlaw subjectivity, emerges as a reaction to the oppressive patriarchal governance of her fanatical first husband, the hell-fire preacher Andrew Shaw. As part of the novel's concern with healing and reconciliation, Kirstie must confess to her dark fantasies, as must her second husband, Black William, who has taken part in a range of barbaric rituals while 'bewitched' by an Indian queen in America. Confession facilitates change, but it is significant that Mitchison does not imagine that such truths necessarily demand a public platform. Her emphasis is on self-knowledge and a mode of justice that looks 'beyond the action at the motive behind it' (1947: 386). Over the course of the novel, Mitchison's fractured family struggles to reconcile its factions, and those characters who would rigidly apply the letter of the law, or who wish to use past wrongs as a motive for revenge, are eventually defeated by the forces of a humanist and humane consensus. Mitchison, like Priestley, sees the past as means of imagining a better future and *The Bull Calves* was a creative project that sustained her throughout the war.

The concept of art as regenerative for both individual and society found vocal support from the editors of literary magazines. John Lehmann was frankly optimistic, opening the spring 1946 *Penguin New Writing* with a vision of cultural rebirth: 'with this number *Penguin New Writing* emerges at last from its wartime chrysalis, and spreads its wings into the thundery post-war day' (*PNW* 27, 1946: 7). Even Cyril Connolly's apocalyptic vision of the collapsed marquee of European civilisation gives way to faint hope: 'but what a winter this is going to be in this most favoured of European countries – no coal, though the earth is still with it; no wine, though the cellars of Bordeaux are full; [...] no trips abroad, no access to snow or sun: only art and a little politics to keep warm by' (*Horizon*, Vol. XII, No. 67, 1945: 152). It is, however, a demobilisation novel that makes most explicit the desire for national spiritual regeneration through art. In *The Shop on the King's Road* (1946), the literary critic B. Ifor Evans constructs a nameless narrator, who has lost his wife, his home and – crucially – his library. He feels numbed, unable even to recover the emotions appropriate to grief (1946: 24), and he worries that many people are in a similar state of emotional paralysis. He wants, above all, the pleasure of leisure, but that, he finds, 'is of all commodities the most difficult to purchase in the England of 1945' (102). The novel, which is simultaneously a documentary, recounts his spiritual reawakening through literature, art and music. Attending the premiere of Benjamin Britten's opera *Peter Grimes*, he records: 'I felt then that something was happening to me, that I was becoming alive again' (73), a process furthered by the Old Vic's production of Shakespeare's *Henry IV, Part II*, and the reading of Dickens and

Wordsworth. A visit to the V&A, however, is more of a challenge to his romantic sensibilities: 'the pictures of Picasso rose up and assaulted me' (166).[2] The narrator is haunted by Picasso's work from the years of the German occupation, paintings that represent not the restorative power of art, but its capacity to bear witness:

> Picasso had done something to me, and I reminded myself again that he had forced me to realise that I was living in a world of self-consoling deception. This was the age of atomic force, of the brutalising of men, of torture, and the corruption of the human spirit, and I was hiding from it all. (1946: 171)

The literature of adjustment is also, to a large extent, the literature of denial and repression. Writing earlier in the book on the relationship between the Arab world and the Jews, the narrator observes that the 'suffering of the Jewish people in this last decade is one of the things which we are all hiding from our minds. We have grown so weary of the record of evil and cruelty that our imaginations revolt' (110). This is a post-Holocaust world, but for the most part, the Holocaust defies representation: like the war that produced it, it is simply too large to comprehend. And those who must comprehend it are too exhausted and numbed to assimilate its implications. At the end of *The Shop on the King's Road*, the narrator finds solace in another woman and another library, putting grief and the acknowledgement of atrocity behind him. It is a sudden ending to an otherwise unhurried, meditative text, and its very abruptness suggests the impossibility of processing the war in its immediate aftermath. The desire for home and all it symbolises ultimately outweighs the moral obligation of thought. Art, it would seem, is capable of only so much restoration.

Evans' retreat from the questions of his own narrative is indicative of the difficulty of confronting the ethical challenges of the emergent postwar world. With the end of war comes a new demand: that of exegesis. Somehow, that which has been coped with, rendered 'normal' and accepted must now be questioned, explained and attributed. But this is no easy task. In a total war, in which the private imagination has been distorted by the inescapable rhetoric of 'public spirit' (Piette 1995: 2), what significance resides in human choice? Can the individual be separated from the mass, and if so, to what extent is he or she responsible for the actions of that national body? For most writers, the war was still too close for such interrogation, but if the already potent myths of the past proved resistant to analysis, the future beckoned as a tabula rasa: an opportunity for new beginnings and a return to long-absent modes of self-determination. Here was the welcome, but nonetheless disturbing, return of individual responsibility.

'One of the lucky ones': Humphrey Jennings's *A Diary for Timothy*

> Now that the danger's over for us . . . now that the enemy in Europe's break-ing, life is going to become more dangerous than before, oddly enough. More dangerous because now we have the power to choose and the right to criti-cize, and even to grumble. We're free men. We have to decide for ourselves and part of your bother, Tim, will be learning to grow up free. (Jennings 1946)

Filmed between 1944 and 1945, *A Diary for Timothy* – a thirty-eight minute documentary charting a new-born baby's first six months – was produced by the Crown Film Unit for the Ministry of Information. Although the voice-over narration was provided by E. M. Forster, and read by Michael Redgrave, the design of the film is entirely the work of Humphrey Jennings, co-founder of Mass Observation, poet, painter and film-maker. Jennings was responsible for some of the most influential documentaries of the war years – *Listen to Britain* (1942), *Fires Were Started* (1943) – and in *A Diary For Timothy* he assembles images of Britain at home and at war to present baby Timothy with a portrait of a nation on the brink of victory, but uncertain of its postwar objectives. In so doing, he constructs British cinema's most self-conscious engagement with the process of readjustment demanded by war's end.

Described by Lindsay Anderson as 'the only real poet the British cinema has yet produced' (1953/2004: 358), Jennings's work is a sig-nificant example of the porous boundaries demarcating art forms in the war years. Writers worked for the Ministry of Information, poets produced for the radio, and playwrights turned their hands to screen-plays (Williams 1996: 181–228). Similarly, the visual was recognised as a mode not simply of propaganda or narrative, but as a means of con-structing a poetics of everyday life:

> In his films, Jennings is concerned to explore the revelation of the symbolic in the everyday, through the use of an impressionistic style dependent on juxtapositions and association. Jennings believed that, within the collective consciousness of a people, a distinctive 'legacy of feeling' could be discerned, which could be captured symbolically through art. [. . .] the documentary film-maker is both an observer, capturing what emerges from within the legacy of feeling within the nation, and a creative artist, embodying what is observed within an image containing a multiplicity of meanings. (Aitken 1998: 216)

Anderson's tribute argues that Jennings 'had a mind that delighted in simile and the unexpected relationship' (1953/2004: 361). His films fashion conceits and they suggest, without making explicit, anxieties far in excess of their quotidian subjects. Timothy's diary, then, is far from a straightforward record of Britain in the last years of war; rather it is a poetic distillation of the 'postwar' moment. The customary features of Jennings's work are immediately evident. 'Britishness' is evoked through rural landscapes, iconic buildings and machinery: St Pauls, Big Ben, Battersea Power Station and an emblematic pithead wheel. Religion, politics and industry are supplemented by culture in the form of the National Gallery and its wartime concerts, and by symbols of British enterprise: the railways and the Spitfire. Yet these familiar stimuli are given a new direction: this is a film about recovery and revision that works specifically to reinstate the value of non-combatant masculinities.

A Diary for Timothy has five protagonists: Timothy James Jenkins, the eponymous baby, whose luck in being born into the British middle classes is stressed from the outset; Goronwy, a Welsh miner, whose luck is rather less in evidence; Alan, an English farmer; Bill, a London engine driver, and Peter, an RAF pilot. Significantly, we meet Peter, the representative fighting man, not in action but in hospital, and the film will trace his rehabilitation and return to duty. His 'battlefield', then, is as non-military as those of Goronwy, Alan and Bill, and the film stresses the integral role of home-front labour in winning the war: 'all these people, Tim, were fighting for you'. Both through the script and visually – in images of the hard labour of mining and the glory of the landscape – *Timothy* re-establishes the status of the non-combatant working man, once again rendering heroic the performance of manual labour. Women, although appearing in the margins as war workers, have only one representative figure: the mother. Mrs Jenkins, who first appears looking exhausted in a hospital bed, does not, however, attain the status of a protagonist. Her thoughts on the future are not presented; it is her son to whom the film is addressed, and on whom the future rests.

The film is constructed as a contemporary record, tracing the progress of the war from its fifth anniversary, 3 September 1944, to the crossing of the Rhine in March 1945. Set alongside the public events of war are the stories of the adult protagonists, who offer points of identification, but who also complicate the film's address to the future. Before agreeing to provide a commentary, Forster expressed concerns about the film in a letter to Basil Wright, the head of the Crown Film Unit: 'the film comes out with a social slant and suggests that Britain ought to be kept right for this one class of baby and not right for babies in general' (quoted in Jackson 2004: 304) (Figure 7.1). Perhaps in a desire to counter the incontrovertible middle-classness of Tim, the opening lines of Forster's script point out how lucky he is not to have been born 'in wartime Holland or Poland, or a Liverpool or Glasgow slum', but as Jennings's

Figure 7.1 One of the lucky ones? *A Diary for Timothy*, Humphrey Jennings, 1945. Courtesy of the British Film Institute.

biographer Kevin Jackson observes, the totality of Forster's script does little to challenge the privileges of Tim's upbringing. Rather, in seeking to find a mode of address befitting a child, the narration becomes didactic and patronising, without in any sense resolving the disjuncture between Tim's choral baptism and the difficult lives of the men who have been fighting for him (2004: 297–8; 303–4). Yet this collision of worlds is important to the overall impact of the film, and Keith Beattie defends the 'school-masterly' narration as part of the film's complex textual 'voice' which, in conjunction with the imagery, gives rise to a series of 'productive ambiguities' (2010: 110).

Beattie's emphasis on ambiguity is valuable, both for an understanding of Jennings's work, and for the wider context of postwar cultural production. Ambiguity, he argues, is a way of framing a potential future without falling into the pitfalls of 'nostalgia or utopianism' (107), and the concept offers one way of reconciling seemingly irreconcilable aspects of the film's *mise-en-scène*. Yet Beattie perhaps tries too hard when he claims that 'the film offers a range of occupations as models for the future' and that Jennings refuses to privilege any one of them as 'a viable way of engaging with the issues that will confront Britain in the coming years' (110). On one level this is evidently the case – Britain will need train drivers, miners, farmers and pilots – but on another level it seems completely at odds with the visual evidence. Whatever Timothy does when he reaches adulthood, he will not become a miner. The decision to focus on Goronwy is thus an important one, and it is here that the inarticulable anxieties of the film are most clearly evident.

A Diary for Timothy contains two narratives of repair. Peter's rehabilitation is shadowed by that of Goronwy, who is injured at the coalface and stretchered away from the mine. The immediate response of the voice-over is banal: 'there's bad luck in the world, Tim, as well as good', but as the news is broken to Goronwy's family, Tim is told to contemplate the fact that after 500 years of mining, men are still being injured everyday in the coalfields. There is a challenge here, both in words and images, suggesting that while Goronwy, like Peter, will get hospital care and physiotherapy, once peace returns, his expectations of health will bear no resemblance to those of the pilot, or indeed of baby Tim. In an unacknowledged inversion of the pragmatic wartime repair of servicemen so that they can once again be confronted by death, the miner in peacetime is patched up for short-term gain. While Gwyn Thomas made the expendability of working men in 'the terraces' the foundation of nihilistic black comedy in *The Dark Philosophers* (1946), the popular press reached for the miner as a shorthand for social crisis. *Picture Post*'s 'Plan for Britain' issue opened with the questions of an unemployed Welsh miner, and those questions are echoed by Goronwy, who asks whether the 'unemployment, broken homes [and] scattered families' that followed the last war will have 'to happen again'.[3] More disturbingly, in January 1945, *Picture Post* ran another mining feature, entitled 'The Story of a Miners' Football Team'. The subheading gives the substance of the article: 'In 1929–30, eleven young men were the pride of their South Wales village. To-day not one of them is able to work at the coal-face. Most have been incapacitated by silicosis, the dread lung disease . . .' (1945: 16). The physical toll of mining was common knowledge in the 1940s, and simply by including Goronwy amongst his representative figures, Jennings makes explicit his anxieties about the future. Nothing in the optimistic claims for new health provision, nor the story of Goronwy's recovery from injury, can undo the doubt generated by the images of underground labour, images which are juxtaposed against the withdrawal from Arnhem. Beattie suggests that within *Timothy*, the English countryside functions as a 'spectacular moment' beyond investigation, part of the rural myth. Goronwy's story is the exact counterpart to this: a set of images that resist the spectacular and demand investigation, leaving a legacy of disquiet in the spectator.

This is a film that 'aches with melancholy' and 'looks forward in deep anxiety' (Jackson, 2004: 302); and Jennings's miner, like the demobbed soldier and the spiv, becomes a spectral figure haunting the postwar settlement. Here is the threat of repetition, the First World War legacy of unemployment, disillusion and discontent. What hope is offered by *A Diary for Timothy* is invested in the figure of the child, who – like the Colters' baby in *Waterloo Road* – must bear a heavy weight of signification. This investment was equally evident in fiction, and for writers unwilling to approach the problems of reconstruction directly, the child would become a crucial facilitating symbol.

Maternal Lack: Marghanita Laski's *Little Boy Lost*

> Then he smiled, for without his desiring it, there had come into his mind a vision of himself and Pierre and the child held together by love, the ordeal surmounted, the catharsis complete. It would be wonderful beyond words, he told himself dreamily – and then he realised what he was thinking. It can never be like that, he said [. . .] The traitor emotions of love and tenderness and pity must stay dead in me. I could not endure them to live and then die again. (Laski 1949/2001: 86)

Little Boy Lost, like *The World My Wilderness*, negotiates the postwar through a consideration of the generations that will inherit its legacy. However, unlike Macaulay's bleak text that grieves for the lost innocence of the teenage Barbary, Laski's novel finds hope through a narrative of innocence regained. The key symbol here, as in *A Diary for Timothy*, is the child, but as the novel makes clear, the 'little boy lost' is equally the adult protagonist, Hilary Wainwright. Hilary, an isolated intellectual who takes refuge from emotional engagement in literature, has lost his wife in occupied France and is alienated from his emotionally inadequate mother. He knows he has a son, John, but having met the child only once, has managed to keep this relationship in the realm of the hypothetical, a dormant set of possibilities to be enacted at war's end. This safe detachment is disrupted, however, by the arrival of Pierre, who tells him that the boy is missing. Hilary's response is indicative of his emotional disassociation: 'With horror he discovered in himself only a deep wish to be spared this new phase of pain' (20). Pierre, however, has a different approach to trauma, which he encapsulates in a parable about a man with a putrefying hand:

> 'Then in the end the doctor, who was a wise old man, insisted that he should open his eyes and look at it. I can tell you it was a horrible sight because I saw it. There were white worms – But after this man looked at it – and it was some

time, mind you, before he could glance at it naturally, not just stare – then, it started to heal.' (22)

For Pierre, the wound – be it physical or psychological – must be acknowledged before it can heal, and this recognition will be crucial to the novel's redemptive trajectory.

Both Hilary and Pierre are in the emasculating position of having survived a war which killed their lovers: their search for the lost child is thus both an act of reparation that seeks to reconstitute the family, and a reconstruction of masculine agency, ironically formed through the begetting of children. Unfortunately, the symbolic trans-national union of the two men is undone by the intervention of a public father, in the form of General de Gaulle. When Pierre confesses himself a Gaullist, Hilary's left-wing intellectual sympathies are repulsed, and he politely distances himself from a man he had begun to think of as a friend. This rejection is typical of Hilary, who rigorously polices the boundaries of his engagement with others, setting unattainable ethical standards for those around him. This impossibility is particularly the case in relation to mother figures (of whom Pierre is one), making the text simultaneously a search for and a rejection of the maternal. Hilary harbours a deep resentment of his own mother; indeed, so strong is his desire to punish her for her perceived failings that he tells her his son is dead. John's mother Lisa, however, is exempt from criticism: having been murdered by the Gestapo, she exists as a memory, a lost ideal, to which Hilary clings as both lover and child.

In the rejection of his mother and the absence of his wife, Hilary is constantly searching for surrogates to comfort him. He even makes this demand upon Nelly, the French tart whose abject attractions distract him with the lure of 'immediate comfort and absolute non-obligation' (213). Attractive and repulsive in equal measures, Nelly has the maternal thrust upon her, as Hilary repeatedly insists upon his needs (191–2). This desire is figured as childish, a complete rejection of adult responsibility that is jealously possessive and pre-Oedipal in its refusal of the social. That Hilary has unresolved Oedipal issues is also made evident earlier, when he reacts violently to the suggestion that Lisa's photograph reveals a maternal expression (169). This was the one relationship in which Hilary had thought himself secure and omnipotent, not least because in death, the lover's affections are concretised into eternal loyalty. Deprived of the illusion of maternal security that his marriage had represented, he instantly becomes profoundly jealous of the imagined potency of his son. In actuality, however, his 'son' is a subject utterly devoid of power. Indeed, taken out of charity into an orphanage that can ill afford him, little Jean exists on the very limits of cultural intelligibility. He has no family and no possessions through which to constitute his subjectivity beyond 'a tiny little celluloid swan with its head broken off and a dirty piece of rag tied round its neck for a bandage' (94). The vulnerability of the toy is equally that of the boy, clinging precariously to life in a world that has no place for him.

This is the context in which Hilary must make his transition to adulthood, abandoning his egocentric desire for comfort and embracing a paternal function that has implications beyond the immediate rescue of a single child. Hilary thinks that he must determine whether this is the right child, his child, with all that that implies about inheritance within a still fundamentally patriarchal world. This private dilemma, however, is set against the perspective of the Mother Superior, and the evidence of the boy's condition. Jean has been living a bare and impoverished existence: he has nothing, and the nuns cannot afford to keep a refugee with no family and no funds, whose slight physicality ill fits him for a peasant future. The Mother Superior consequently recognises a social responsibility beyond the biological, the child must be saved in and of itself. She also recognises the needy child in Hilary – he is 'lost and in need of comfort' (177) – and suggests that he should take the boy for his own benefit, irrespective of paternity. Ultimately, it is crucial to Hilary's rehabilitation that he choose the child without certainty, and this moral obligation enables the novel to be at once a fantasy of rescue for damaged men, and a symbolic statement of social interdependency. Discussing what she terms the 'precariousness' of existence, Judith Butler argues that 'life requires various social and economic conditions to be met in order to be sustained as a life' (14):

> Precariousness implies living socially, that is, the fact that one's life is always in some sense in the hands of the other. It implies exposure both to those we know and to those we do not know; a dependency on people we know, or barely know, or know not at all. Reciprocally, it implies being impinged upon by the exposure and dependency of others, most of whom remain anonymous. These are not necessarily relations of love or even of care, but constitute obligations towards others, most of whom we cannot name and do not know . . . (Butler 2009/2010: 14)

Butler's construction is singularly appropriate for the network of gift and obligation that characterises Laski's novel, and while Jean does not remain anonymous, his precarious life impinges on Hilary, as does his uncanny status as both familiar and unfamiliar. In this context Hilary's initial inability to grieve for his lost son acquires a wider political significance. It becomes a denial of life on a much broader scale, speaking to a war-induced cultural sclerosis, a refusal of the needs of others, and a denial of the grievability of the victims of war.

Writing of later conflicts – Palestine, the second Gulf War and Afghanistan – Butler utilises a concept of 'grievability' to distinguish between those lives that signify, and those that are 'other', beyond the comprehension or care of the belligerent forces. 'Without grievability,' writes Butler, 'there is no life, or, rather, there is something living that is other than life' (14), a statement that resonates with the context of post-Second World War Europe. In Laski's novel there is an implicit insistence that if we are to live socially, we must grieve beyond the personal: we must acknowledge the suffering of the unknown other, and in *Little Boy Lost* this cultural mourning incorporates a life-affirming reciprocal dimension. Hilary's growing empathy with Jean renders both him and the child viable beings; his involvement becomes an acknowledgement of the child's significance, his value as a putative citizen of a new Europe. By choosing Jean, Hilary brings the child into the realm of what Butler would class the 'grievable': he becomes a being whose loss would be mourned.

Laski's symbolic reconstruction also demands consideration of guilt, responsibility and reconciliation. In a telling aside, Pierre observes 'I'm tired with "collaborationist" as a term of abuse; we each did under the Germans what we were capable of doing; what that was, was settled long before they arrived' (32). This seems a curiously determinist statement, reducing historical choice and responsibility to accidents of birth, but it also speaks to the need for a necessary forgetting. Hilary must forget his doubts as to the boy's origins: the child is, in a sense, born in his acceptance of the father's role. If the other children of Europe are to have a future, then nations too must find some mode of reconciliation that can offer similar hope to their citizens. The problems of imagining this global future will be discussed in the next chapter; closer to home, the paradoxical desire for both acknowledgement and forgetting found expression on the stage, where some of Britain's leading dramatists interrogated the relationship between public truth and private sacrifice.

1946 saw the première of both *The Winslow Boy*, Terence Rattigan's drama of unjust accusation, and *An Inspector Calls*, J. B. Priestley's excoriating study of middle-class hypocrisy. Two years later they were followed by Christopher Fry's *The Lady's Not For Burning*, a verse drama about a woman accused of everything and a man who will confess to anything. First performed in March 1948, this topsy-turvey indictment of the law suggested, through the distance of history, that the postwar world was not worth living in, and the play's happy endings emerged from comic convention rather than any belief in the triumph of justice. Fry's play has a carnivalistic nihilism, revelling in paradox as its world-weary ex-soldier hero demands to be hanged to free himself from a corrupt and venal world. The law that refuses to hang Thomas, though, is all too keen to burn Jennet, an independent and wealthy young woman whose mistakes include laughter, rationalism and speaking French to her poodle. The officers of the law are inept, failing to notice that Thomas claims to have killed the man Jennet is supposed to have turned into a dog, and their bourgeois hypocrisy makes them insist that 'The standard soul/ Must mercilessly be maintained' (1949/2007: 70). The end of the play sees Thomas unrepentant – 'the world sickens me still' (91) – but willing to postpone his death for the pleasure of Jennet's company. The fifteenth-century setting and the self-conscious verbal play makes it easy for the law to be an ass, but the play's contemporary relevance is underlined by its epigraph from a convict 'who confessed falsely to a murder, February 1947'. Priestley and Rattigan also retreat into history for their contemporary dramas, and this suggests that distance makes it easier to confront the law's partiality and its failure adequately to serve its citizens. The preoccupation with justice in the past of these three plays encodes the fear of its absence in the immediate postwar world, a world in which, irrespective of the anxieties of fiction, a substantial mandate for change had been given. The results of the 1945 election were a clear indication of the desire for a new social contract amongst a significant sector of the population, and of an understanding that the Conservatives, whatever their merits in time of war, were not the party of reconstruction. The Labour landslide spoke to a widespread desire that after six years of sacrifice, 'Right' should be done (Figure 7.2).

'It's the people who have triumphed': Terence Rattigan and *The Winslow Boy*

'But what's the use of being good, if you're inaudible?' (Rattigan, 1946/1994: 5)

Grace Winslow's pertinent question about the local vicar has, like many of her pronouncements, a far greater significance than she realises. *The Winslow Boy* (1946) is a play about being heard, and about the spectacular performance of 'right', far more than it is an enquiry into the catalytic question of whether or not little Ronnie Winslow stole a five-bob postal order. The play is also 'right' in its timing. Contrary to his later reputation as a conservative figure, deeply opposed to a theatre of

Figure 7.2 'And Now – Win the <u>Peace</u>' The rhetoric of war continues. The Art Archive/Bodleian Library Oxford, C. P. A. General Election, 1945.

'ideas', in the mid-1940s, Rattigan was a writer with an almost unerring sense of the public mood. His biographers, Michael Darlow and Gillian Hodson, argue that with the exception of his anti-fascist farce, *Follow My Leader* (written in 1938 and banned by the Lord Chamberlain), Rattigan 'never wrote a didactic play' (1979: 163). Such a statement is misleading, not least in the case of *The Winslow Boy*, which in its emphasis on the right to representation, and the relationship between private sacrifice and public good, is a play profoundly engaged with the anxieties of the postwar moment.

The early 1940s were good to Rattigan. Although he began the war with crippling writer's block, by the end of hostilities he was Britain's highest-earning playwright. He had written three hit plays – *Flare Path* (1942), *While the Sun Shines* (1943) and *Love in Idleness* (1944) – and the screenplays for four successful films. *The Winslow Boy* would be another success, but of a very different order. This is neither comedy nor romance, but rather something more serious and, dramatically, more unusual: a courtroom drama set entirely in a private house. The play is based on the case of George Archer-Shee, a Naval cadet whose family took action against the Admiralty after the boy's expulsion from Osborne Naval College for theft. The Admiralty's immunity from civil prosecution resulted in the family's resort to a Petition of Right, and at trial in July 1910, the boy's innocence was officially accepted (Rebellato, 1994: xx–xxi). Rattigan uses these events as the bare bones of his drama, but his approach to the narrative is complicated. In formal terms, the decision to adopt a self-consciously nostalgic dramatic form, the Edwardian four-act play, imbues the action with a sense of period; simultaneously, the period evoked – one of considerable political and social unrest – speaks eloquently to the unsettled world of 1946. As Dan Rebellato argues, the play 'has a considerably more complex relation to the new Labour government of 1945 than some critics have suggested' (1994: xxvii).

Significantly, Rattigan's dramatisation changed the focus of the story. The character we might expect to be central – Ronnie, 'the Winslow Boy' – is marginalised. He spends the first act in the garden, the second in transit, and the third asleep. His presence in the fourth act is confined to the comic admission that he has missed his own verdict because he was at the pictures. But if *The Winslow Boy* is not, in the end, about the Winslow boy, what is it about? And what was it that made the play a critical and popular success (Darlow and Hodson 1979: 147)? On one level the answer to these questions can be summarised by the concept of a Petition of Rights. This archaic dispensation permitting action against the Crown is enacted through the performative: 'Let Right be done', a phrase which in 1946 suggestively speaks both to national self-congratulation and to the optimism that had voted in the reformist Labour government. With impeccable timing, *The Winslow Boy* personalises this enormous abstract concept through a blatant abuse of institutional power. Ronnie, a child of 13, is dismissed from the Naval College after an internal hearing at which he received no representation. His family were not informed until after the tribunal, and were not permitted access to the evidence. These events cannot, in any sense, be said to constitute a fair trial, and therefore, irrespective of Ronnie's guilt or innocence, 'right' has not been done. Justice cannot be a private affair, it must be seen to be enacted, as is recognised by Ronnie's sister Catherine:

> His innocence or guilt aren't important to me. They are to my father. Not to me. I believe he didn't do it; but I may be wrong [. . .] All that I care about is that people should know that a Government Department has ignored a fundamental human right and that it should be forced to acknowledge it. (Rattigan 1946/1994: 71)

It requires a specific example to make comprehensible the abstract formulation of human rights, and Ronnie provides this. He is, thus, another of the period's signifying children. But that is the limit of his role, and it is through the rest of the family, and the structure of his 'well-made play', that Rattigan is able to expose a range of emergent concerns. The decision to confine the drama to the space of Edwardian domesticity was reputedly the result of a bet between Rattigan and his close friend Anthony Asquith, but having accepted these limitations, Rattigan had to find a way to bring news of the outside world into the private sphere of the Winslow household.[4] This is achieved through newspaper correspondence, media enquiries and court reports. The introduction of these outside 'voices' allows Rattigan to express views beyond the limits of his characters, and to air arguments as familiar to 1946 as to 1912. As Arthur Winslow reads of the 'liberty of the individual menaced . . . by the new despotism of bureaucracy' (57) he voices a genuine strand of contemporary anxiety. The fear of bureaucratic control that would be so potently exploited by George Orwell's *Nineteen Eighty-Four* was already finding expression, as Uncle Rodney's comic set piece in Priestley's *Three Men* demonstrates:

> I'm sorry for you [Alan] . . . Once a year you and your wife, who'll be as plain as a suet pudding, and all your brats, who'll have been vaccinated against everything but stupidity and dreariness, will be given a ticket to a holiday camp, along with five thousand other clerks and mechanics and their women and kids, and there you'll have physical drill, stew and rice pudding, round games, and evening talks on tropical diseases and aeroplane engines. And I'll be dead – and delighted. (1945: 26)

Uncle Rodney's sensibilities have ground to a halt in the Edwardian era, and he spends his days playing Mahler and lamenting the passing of a lost age. Rattigan, like Priestley, rejects the insidious claims of nostalgia, both in his pertinent reminders of the socio-political tensions of 1912, and in his reassuring fantasy that the individual can defeat the 'despotism of bureaucracy'. For Priestley the hope of the new world is founded upon community; for Rattigan, hope lies in the resurgence, and persistence, of the individual.

Yet *The Winslow Boy* nonetheless asks, at what cost does the individual persist? Underpinning the abstract principle of Right is the other key focus of the play: private sacrifice in a public cause. All of Ronnie's family will suffer in order to clear his name, and – ironically – it is Ronnie who will be least affected by the struggle, at least within the time frame of the drama. Given that the play's curtain falls on the eve of the First World War, it cannot be assumed that Ronnie will live to enjoy his newly-cleared name, and indeed, his precursor did not: George Archer-Shee was killed at Ypres in 1914 (Rebellato 1994: xxi). However, within the drama itself, the burden falls not on Ronnie but on his parents, Arthur and Grace, his undergraduate brother Dickie and his suffragette sister Catherine. Over the course of the play, Arthur will lose his health, Dickie his education and Catherine her marriage. Their eminent barrister, Sir Robert Morton, whose relationship with Catherine provides much of the drama's ethical substance, will also make a principled sacrifice – turning down the position of Lord Chief Justice in order to continue with the case. The detail of these family sacrifices is significant, as is the manner in which Rattigan presents them.

One of the earliest events in the play is the arrival of John Watherstone, who has come to ask for Catherine's hand in marriage. Admitted to the patriarchal presence, he and Arthur discuss salaries and settlements, a dialogue that – on first reading – seems a demonstration of Arthur's pedantic paternalism. The scene is a bourgeois financial transaction, with the younger man acquiescing to the commodification of Catherine as part of a patriarchal system of exchange. The scene though, is deceptive. Arthur will prove more complex and less comic, while John will be revealed as the one who weighs a woman's worth in purely monetary terms. It also ensures that the audience will be in a position to recognise the failure of Catherine's engagement before she can, and to see that whatever Arthur's flaws, he has greater respect for his daughter than her putative husband. In Act I, both Arthur and John agree that a man cannot live on a regular army income. In Act III, faced with Colonel Watherstone's withdrawal of support for the marriage, Catherine tentatively suggests that 'two can live as cheaply as one'. John dismisses her out of hand and Rattigan's initial, seemingly inconsequential, comedy of accounting turns out to have set the scene for one of the major private sacrifices of the play. Catherine must choose between public and private, and in prioritising the battle over her personal needs she makes a choice that is absolutely in line with the rhetorical and political demands of the Second World War. It is also radically in opposition to a literary zeitgeist that persistently depicts women as incapable of such a decision. Arguably, Rattigan's proto-feminist sympathies are facilitated by the safe distance of history: Catherine is, after all, a suffragette, a cause that hindsight has rendered respectable. Nonetheless, the centrality of Catherine's choice ensures that this play is, as John fears, as much about the 'Winslow girl' (73) as her brother.

Rattigan's sense of dramatic structure is also evident in the parallel between Arthur's request that Dickie estimate the odds on finishing his degree (34) and Sir Robert's demand that Catherine 'estimate the risk' to her marriage of Colonel Watherstone's blackmail. Implicit in these two hypothetical questions is the acknowledgement that the legal system is founded on incalculable variables. There is no certainty that Right will be done; the law for all its rationality is a lottery, and at what point is it irresponsible, rather than principled to pursue it (59)? It falls to Grace Winslow to articulate the fear that the cost of truth is 'out of all proportion' (59), and in the face of the sacrifices being demanded, she becomes an outspoken critic of her husband's choices. The breaking point for Grace is the potential dismissal of Violet, the dramatically useful half-trained parlourmaid who has been with the family for twenty-four years, and she counters this threat with the emotive reasoning that Ronnie is happy and does not need to be a judicial *cause célèbre*. If the boy is okay, what possible reason can her husband offer for destroying himself and his family (60)? The argument remains unresolved, but significantly, so too does the issue of Violet's dismissal. This is the one sacrifice that never comes to pass, and this limit to the damage that Rattigan chooses to inflict is a sop to audience sympathy. Catherine and Dickie will survive: Violet is infinitely more vulnerable, and her sacrifice might have weighed too heavily against the claims of abstract right.

After the argument with Arthur, we do not see Grace again until the final act, and the transformation in her personality is considerable. She seems to have been co-opted by the spirit of the 'people's war', and unable to stop the conflict, she – like the people of Britain – adapts to her changed circumstances. The final act finds her cheerfully mobilising her family, deflecting the media (82), and taking pleasure in the legal process as mass entertainment. And yet, in Grace's seemingly innocent enjoyment, Rattigan reiterates the critical trope of chance. The law, it becomes clear, is as much spectacular as it is forensic:

> GRACE. . . . You never saw such crowds in all your life. And such excitement! Cheers and applause and people being turned out. It's thrilling – you'll love it, Dickie.
> DICKIE. Well – if I don't understand a word –
> GRACE. Oh, that doesn't matter. They all get so terribly worked up you find yourself getting worked up, too. Sir Robert and the Attorney-General go at each other hammer and tongs . . . Nothing to do with Ronnie at all – (76)

In peace, as in war, the individual is an insignificant player in the machinery of state; but this ambivalent reality is overwritten by the play's triumphant ending. Right is seen to be done, and the play bears witness to the private sacrifices of an individual family fighting in a public cause. Arthur, who might have been Colonel Blimp, is revealed to have his heart in the right place; his feckless son Dickie joins the ranks of the workers, and – it is implied – will join the army once war breaks out; mother makes do and mends, and Catherine emerges as the ideal wartime woman, putting public need before private desire. Sir Robert Morton, the play's symbol of authority, listens to and respects 'the people', even if his reactionary sentiments are revealed in his opposition to women's suffrage. The audience knows that Catherine is right, and beyond the play will be rewarded. Such an ending is, through the comforts of history, profoundly reassuring, and Rattigan's reconstructive optimism should not be overlooked in accounting for the play's success.

Less successful at the time, and much less optimistic, was J. B. Priestley's *An Inspector Calls*. The play received its première in Moscow, in May 1945, after which it toured Europe before opening at the Old Vic. Its popularity abroad was not matched at home, and Vincent Brome describes its British reception as 'cool, almost hostile' (1988: 284). Brome suggests that this might be because the play's fusion of suspense and symbolism 'reduced its pure entertainment value' (284–5), but it seems unlikely that those attending a Priestley drama would have expected unadulterated fun. The play is, though, unremittingly bleak, abandoning even the faint hopes manifested in Priestley's fiction of the period. The story, once again set in 1912, is straightforward. As the complacent Birling family sit at dinner, celebrating the engagement of their daughter Sheila to the prosperous Gerald, an inspector calls to question them about their complicity in the death of Eva Smith. Smith has committed suicide by drinking disinfectant, symbolically 'burnt inside out' by the hypocritical society in which she lived, and as the inspector works his way around the table it is established that the whole family had a hand in her death. Arthur Birling sacked her for asking for a pay rise; Sheila Birling, disconcerted by her self possession, got her dismissed from her job as a shop assistant; Gerald kept her for a while before deciding to settle for Sheila; Eric got her pregnant, and Mrs Birling turned down her plea for charitable assistance. Eva has thus been condemned for her speech and her looks, both of which are deemed inappropriate for a woman of her class. The inspector, described in the stage directions as creating '*an impression of massiveness, solidity and purposefulness*' (Priestley 1947/2000: 169), interrogates the family until they confess their actions, but there is a notable difference between the two generations. While Sheila and Eric quickly recognise their guilt, and realise also the extent to which their class is complicit, the older generation refuse to acknowledge responsibility. Mrs Birling persists in condemning Eva for 'impertinence', while Arthur pleads capitalist necessity as his defence (173). For this generation, appearance is everything: Arthur's response to his wife's cruelty is that it will not look good if the press find out (198).

Sheila, by comparison, learns quickly, and thus becomes one of a number of young women in Priestley's work of the 1940s gifted with insight and understanding. She grasps how the plot will develop, and evolves into a Cassandra figure, attempting to warn her family, but destined never to be believed. When, in the final act, the Inspector's apparitional status is revealed – a phone call having established there is no dead girl – Sheila must articulate the symbolic dimension of this visitation (214–15). As her father angrily cries 'He wasn't an Inspector', her tart response gets to the heart of the matter: 'Well, he inspected us all right' (215). Sheila is thus a figure of hope, but only in the most limited of terms. The visionary women of Priestley's imagination need a male agent to put their ideas into practice – in *Three Men*, for example, Doris's plea to Herbert, 'Don't let 'em persuade you we can go on in the same old way, not caring what happens to other people' (1945: 113), carries hope through the prospect of Herbert's agency – but Sheila's understanding of the 'blood and anguish' promised by the inspector falls on deaf ears (220). Even Gerald, who had seemed moved by the news of Eva's death, is oblivious to the message of community, offering Sheila her engagement ring back as if nothing had happened (220). The play ends with a typical Priestley temporal distortion: the telephone informs the shocked Birling household that a girl has committed suicide and an inspector is about to call. Having spurned the redemptive possibilities of the aptly named Inspector Goole's visit, the Birlings must now face the consequences of their actions. Priestley's point is that the one and the many are inextricably intertwined. 'We don't live alone', argues the Inspector, 'We are members of one body. We are responsible for each other' (207), but not least of the bleakness of the drama is the certain knowledge that, even as the Birlings '*stare guiltily and dumbfounded*' at the final revelation, they remain protected by an impenetrable shield of class and money. With the exception of Eric's theft, they have not committed an indictable crime, and their moral failures can be explained away in the languages of respectability and capitalist necessity. The dead girl, meanwhile, is merely a composite of the countless small lives destroyed by their complacency: a symbol of 'the same rotten story' (214) being repeated time and again.

The hypocrisy exposed by *An Inspector Calls* is, amongst other things, specifically gendered: Eva is destroyed by male sexual incontinence and the potent stereotypes of femininity. Her troubling marginal presence is indicative of the problematic position of women in many adjustment fictions, and suggests the tensions within a society struggling to relearn 'normative' gender roles after their radical disruption by war. Yet such a process was never going to be straightforward for a culture that, when it came to the body, was more comfortable with repression than expression. Alan Allport observes that 'Britain in 1945 was a country quietly tormented by sexual suspicion' (2009: 85), while Ross McKibbin argues that an even more fundamental torment for the national psyche was that of guilt. Writing of the interwar period, McKibbin notes that British attitudes to sex were profoundly conflicted. Puritanism and prurience coexisted with 'a delight in pornography famous throughout Europe' (1998: 327). Somehow, over the course of the centuries, the British had undergone a transformation from a violent and unruly people to a nation characterised by an almost unnatural calm. There are various theories as to how this came about: the Victorian middle-classes are implicated, as is the First World War, which as Alison Light has noted, brought about a retreat from the rhetoric of imperialism and aggressive manifestations of 'national' masculinity (1991: 8–9; 69–70). But, however it happened, there is no doubt that by the middle of the twentieth century, repression was recognised as a particularly 'English' virtue. It came, though, at the cost of significant moral discomfort. McKibbin notes that, 'people did not believe strongly enough to behave in a "Christian" way with conviction, but they did believe strongly enough to behave in a "non-Christian" way without much pleasure' (1998: 328). Only in middle-class Britain, we can conclude, could *Brief Encounter* be regarded as an exemplary account of passion.

Brief Encounter is a key narrative of reassurance. It tells a story, ultimately, of fidelity; of the importance of home, family and the marriage bond over passion and adventure. As suggested in Chapter 3, Laura cannot bear the degradation of deceit, and the man she loves understands this. They restrain themselves out of consideration for others. Meanwhile, Laura's husband Fred, who has – the closing lines of the film suggest – intuited his wife's restlessness, triumphs by doing nothing. He weathers the storm and lets convention and duty do their work: a very British solution to a very un-British problem. This resurgence of convention is equally evident in the shifting concerns of Margery Allingham's detective fiction. Crime fiction is acutely sensitive to cultural tensions, and stands as a valuable barometer of attitudes towards class and gender: it also, as earlier analyses have suggested, recuperates violence into a reassuring narrative of order. By the end of the war, then, detective fiction had abandoned narratives of national jeopardy in favour more of domestic, comic and – in gender terms – conventional concerns.

'A stiff is still a stiff in this country': Margery Allingham's Postwar Murder

'now's not the time to be funny, neither. You've 'ad your fun abroad, I dare say. This is serious. A stiff is still a stiff in this country. There'll be a lot of questions asked.' (Allingham 1945/1987: 7)

These words, from Allingham's *Coroner's Pidgin* (1945), are spoken by Magersfontein Lugg, erstwhile manservant to the detective Albert Campion, and they take the form of a reproach. Campion, who has just returned from secret overseas war service, has emerged from the bath in his London flat to find a body in the bedroom. The dead woman was deposited there by Lugg, who was assisting a marchioness who had found the body in her son's bed. Before Campion can even begin to enquire as to the corpse's credentials, the flat is invaded by a motley collection of aristocrats, actresses and Americans whose complex inter-personal dynamics obliterate the matter of the body, turning it instead into a particularly cumbersome social *faux pas*. Finding himself in a setting reminiscent more of French farce than English detection, Campion understandably refuses to take things seriously, which prompts Lugg's affronted response. In Britain at least, Lugg implies, a line has been drawn. Standards may be under threat in every aspect of life, but a corpse is still a corpse, and the reign of law has not been challenged. It is a moment of patriotic absurdity that lampoons the national trope of understatement ('You've 'ad your fun abroad'), and asserts its claim of dignity while showing no respect for the dead whatsoever. At least to begin with, then, this is a comedy corpse, and the frivolity of its introduction situates it firmly in the postwar moment. In 1945, suicide, murder and international conspiracy are nothing but distractions preventing the patriotic detective from enjoying his well-earned leave.

The cavalier treatment of the corpse in the opening chapters of *Coroner's Pidgin* indicates the extent to which popular fictional attitudes to murder are context dependent. After the deprivations of the 'long haul', light relief was more urgently needed than fifth column vigilance, and *Coroner's Pidgin* escapes the residue of threat and the grey monotony of wartime restriction by looking forward. The novel examines the persistence of class distinction in the supposedly egalitarian 'people's war' and seeks to reassure its readership (in the face of the evidence provided by Priestley and others) that the core values of the British middle class have survived unchanged. Integral to this reassurance is the restoration of conventional masculine and feminine roles, and the reader cannot but be aware of a conspicuous absence. Amanda, a central character of the series since the early 1930s, a crucial helpmeet to the hero in *Traitor's Purse*, and a notably untypical woman in her penchant for aircraft design, does not appear until the final page. Here, she presents Campion with her 'war work': a baby (240). The hero returning to his home to be greeted by wife and child is an iconic image of the postwar, and Allingham's presentation of this tableau is indicative of the national mood. Amanda's agency is sacrificed to a nostalgic vision of gender normativity, but this is not the only way in which the novel mobilises reactionary conceptions of gender. The corpse is discovered to have been an unpopular woman given to extra-marital affairs; the capable working woman is lieutenant to a ruthless master criminal; and the innocent Susan Shering, symbol of youth, sacrifice and a new generation, is rewarded with marriage to an American officer. In a textbook instance of homosocial triangulation and woman's role as the object of patriarchal exchange, Susan's first husband, a young pilot, leaves her to his commanding officer – Johnny Carados – who in turn passes the parcel of passive womanhood onto an American who actually wants her. Explaining his actions in a letter, Carados reiterates a range of culturally powerful beliefs:

> *You, Susan, will want to know if I love you. The answer to that is, of course I do, who could help it, but (if you don't understand this, Don will be able to explain it, I think) the feeling I had for old Tom Shering was different, but very, very much stronger. Since you're the girl I know you are, Susan, you won't think me unduly ungallant for this, and as for you, Don, you'll follow me, I fancy. . . .*
> *P.S. I took the liberty of spying out Don's reputation and reputed assets. Both are impressive. There again, Don will follow me if you don't, Susan.* (208)

The priority of the homosocial bond is evident here, as is the increasingly prevalent suggestion that women cannot understand male experience. But also evident is the heteronormative assumption that men have an economic duty to look after women. Susan and Don, the new generation, are thus figured from the outset in profoundly old-fashioned terms. Postwar reconstruction finds its ideological roots in the gender paradigms of the past.

Women, their roles and their bodies are thus at the centre of *Coroner's Pidgin*, but the book also contemplates postwar reconstruction through an examination of the body politic. What is at stake, as much as any investigation of the abortive Nazi plot, is the question of who will govern Britain in the new era: who will have authority, whose words will carry weight? Like her contemporaries Nancy Mitford and Evelyn Waugh, Margery Allingham chooses to examine the aristocracy, primarily through the irrational and privileged figure of the marchioness Lady Carados, first seen assisting Lugg in the opening corpse-relocation scene. Lady Carados operates as a pertinent reminder that, in mid-century Britain, murder and its investigation are complicated by class. As both woman and aristocrat, she believes herself outside or above the law (41–2); to her, the police are 'silly and officious' (129), little men beneath her notice. For the main part, Lady Carados is figured as a symbol of the past, but her persistence is disturbing. The past has not been replaced by the present, nor by a vision of the future; rather times and generations coexist in an uncomfortable conjunction of nostalgia and modernity. 'It's not easy for us now,' observes Susan to Campion, in an unexpected echo of Priestley's demobbed soldiers, 'there are so many different worlds, you see. We each have to live in two or three' (61).

This statement in some sense encapsulates the conflicting discourses of *Coroner's Pidgin*: it is a novel that exists in different worlds. It also addresses different audiences and confronts diverse, often irreconcilable anxieties; and this generic flexibility was integral to the counterintuitive success of murder stories in wartime. In the crisis years of the war, crime fiction abandoned the private spaces of domestic murder to embrace the national concerns of spy fiction. Similarly, it proved its adaptability by deploying women as agents when politically expedient, and sending them home to reassuring gender normativity when cultural anxieties became more pressing than economic need. The formula's central business of representing death, meanwhile, needed little adjustment. Interwar crime fiction's cursory depiction of the corpse was easily translated into wartime crime's pragmatic, and at times brutal, dismissal. What had changed, though, were the stakes. Where once the corpse had been the centre of attention, it now became a distraction, its explanation subservient to higher priorities elsewhere. And here lies the ironic significance of Lugg's ludicrous assertion that 'a stiff is still a stiff in this country. There'll be a lot of questions asked' (7). For the past six years, very few questions had been asked of the body: it had become the normative fall-out of war. In reasserting the corpse's priority, however absurdly, Allingham also asserts a return to 'normality' and to such pre-war concerns as class and convention. That the form of the clue-puzzle novel never again achieved the popularity of the interwar years, though, gives pause for thought. In postwar Britain a nostalgic desire for the stability of familiar forms coexisted with a powerful will to change, and while the aftermath of the Second World War would be no less traumatic for the national psyche than the aftermath of the First, it would not be in the clue-puzzle crime novel that culture found its 'literature of convalescence' (Light 1991: 69–70).

The sheer number of 'escaping' texts considered at the beginning of this postwar section is one indication of how the nation would 'convalesce' from the rupture of the Second World War, but whether writers turned to the past or to fantasy, their works remained permeated with the conflict they sought to evade. The literature of grief is similarly embedded in war: tropes of mourning and loss would continue to find literary manifestation across the decade and into the 1950s. The transition from war to peace is an extended state of liminality, its borders porous and its preoccupations contradictory. The nostalgic pull of the past coexists with a profound desire for change, and the culture of the mid-decade period struggled to imagine a future based on a weird hybrid of planning and inspiration. The 'postwar' would persist for many years – arguably until 1979 – but before the 1940s were over, new anxieties, preoccupations and desires emerged that would, in literary terms at least, gradually displace the business of war from its cultural centrality. The final section of this book will examine the fragmented, frustrated and often reactionary writing of 'peace'.

Notes

1. T. S. Eliot, it should be noted, thought otherwise, recommending Williams's fiction as ideal for train journeys (1945/2003: xviii).
2. Evelyn Waugh was similarly challenged by this exhibition, writing to Nancy Mitford in January 1946 that 'Picasso is the head of the counter-hons' (Mosley 1996: 26). Mitford completely disagreed with him (1996: 29).
3. There is something disingenuous in *Picture Post*'s introduction of their generic 'Welsh coalminer'. The writer, B. L. Coombes, was an established

working-class author. His autobiography, *These Poor Hands*, was published by the Left Book Club in 1939 (Croft 1990: 91–2).

4. Asquith collaborated extensively with Rattigan, directing the West End productions of *Flare Path* and *While the Sun Shines*, as well as a number of films based on his work: *French Without Tears* (1939), *The Way to the Stars* (1946) and *The Winslow Boy* (1948).

III

'Peace'

III

'Peace'

Chapter 8

Atomising

After five years of the breakdown of communications through war there has never been a time when countries were so isolated within their own separate experience, and yet never a time when they shared so completely the same realities.

One might compare the countries of the world to-day to clocks. Each country registers a different time, but outside their time there is one time for the whole world, registered on one clock, with a time-bomb attached to it. Unless the countries of the world can synchronise their time and their sense of reality, that time-bomb is likely to explode. (Spender 1946: 96)

But where can one get this idea of a new world and how can one believe in it? (Smith 1949/1979: 92)

As the previous chapters have suggested, both war and its aftermath challenge conventions of representation. The new 'peace' that followed the conflict would prove similarly difficult to negotiate, as writers struggled to make sense both of past atrocity and a present that seemed, if anything, still more difficult to assimilate. Britain was exhausted and bankrupt, Europe was devastated, its infrastructure destroyed and its national and cultural legibility erased. Stephen Spender's *European Witness* (1946), an account of his travels through Germany in 1945, tries to convey this extraordinary erasure through a corporeal metaphoricity. The bombed cities of England are wounded, they are a 'scar which will heal' (22), Cologne by contrast is a 'putrescent corpse-city', its people 'parasites sucking at a dead carcase' (1946: 22). This visceral description of a physically annihilated Germany forms the introduction to a more ambivalent analysis of the German psyche: an attempt to understand how a civilised nation became not simply barbaric but actively, almost artistically, evil (240). Spender's opening descriptions of the German character posit a form of schizophrenia that permits an excess of sentimentality to coexist with extreme brutality (12): a paradox that also emerges from 'Greenhouse with Cyclamens' (1946/1955), Rebecca

West's account of the Nuremberg trials. For West, the fairy-tale world of the German cultural imagination 'was at once richly fecundated and bound to a primitive fantasy, dangerous for civilised adults' (26). Just how dangerous this fantasy might be is made explicit in West's description of the evidence produced at the trial. The French doctor in charge of the exhibits of Nazi atrocities stands bemused, unable to reconcile the nation who made lampshades of human flesh with the nation that arranges his flower-strewn breakfast tray with 'exquisite taste' (23).

Lyndsey Stonebridge draws attention to West's dependence on metaphor, suggesting that her 'brilliantly macabre descriptions' ultimately render guilt 'brittle and elusive' (2007: 102, 110). Such a crisis of representation seems inevitable, not least because, as Stonebridge concludes, West's writing reveals 'a post-war world that seems caught *between* the frames of greater and smaller tragedies' (111). Here again is the chasm between knowledge and understanding exposed by revelations of the Holocaust, and here also is the impossibility of grieving for the many or comprehending the statistics of mass slaughter. Throughout her essay, then, West juxtaposes hyperbole with an acknowledgement of the quotidian in order to demonstrate Nuremberg's conflicted status as witness to both the actual and the unthinkable: a paradox manifest in the writer's attempt to depict the astonishing face of 'the world's enemy' by describing a trial so protracted as to have become a 'citadel of boredom' (1946/1955: 3). Nuremberg is a process of accounting, a gathering of testimony and evidence. It is a collective act through which the rule of law will, in theory, be re-established, and in order to be that it must, of necessity, be evacuated of emotion. The documentary impulse so prevalent in the early years of the war should here find its most absolute subject: bearing witness in clinical fashion to the acts of Nazi brutality. Yet as the uncanny hauntings of Blitz literature and the wilful escape of sexually-heightened melodrama attest, the 'reality' of war evades the bare limits of descriptive prose. The 'neutral' recording of historical events is simultaneously powerful and inadequate, and consequently West's prose oscillates between clinical indictment and provocative distortion, cutting the 'world's enemy' down to size in images both absurd and mundane. Hess has the 'classless air characteristic of asylum inmates', Streicher is 'a dirty old man of the sort that gives trouble in parks', and Goering 'the madam of brothel' (5–6). Yet even as she writes these figures into inconsequentiality, her project is threatened by the time it takes properly to enact the process of law. It is not only that everyone present (with the notable exception of the defendants) desperately wants to go home, it is that a year in a courtroom inevitably breeds a perverse and counterproductive familiarity: 'If a trial for murder last too long, more than the murder will out. The man in the murderer will out; it becomes horrible to think of destroying him' (46).

West explains that Nuremberg's achievement was to record beyond doubt what had been done. What the trial could not do, though, was explain why these things had been done (64), and both West's essay and Spender's book are heavy with detail gathered in an attempt to piece together meaning from the incomprehensible. Spender quotes Jung, positing the possibilities of collective guilt and mass suggestibility (1946: 162), while both writers depict the disturbing persistence of myths of racial superiority (Spender 1946: 39; West 1946/1955: 56–7). Both also describe individuals working to rebuild in the face of devastation. Indeed, 'Greenhouse with Cyclamens' takes its title from the essay's striking image of German trade reasserting itself, an ambivalent symbol of regeneration and individual single-mindedness in the midst of the torpid business of effecting justice. In a landscape beyond commerce – there is nothing to buy in what few shops remain – the one-legged gardener breeds cyclamens to sell to the international community. West's description of a man absorbed in his work to the exclusion of all else, while not exactly childish, nonetheless has an obsessive quality that is child-like in its self-absorption. Implicit here, and in Spender's suggestion of Germany's adolescent quality (1946: 39), is a narrative of explication rooted in a concept of national immaturity. Intentional or otherwise, that a nation might be characterised in such a way suggests a desire to reconfigure criminal responsibility as something more excusable or, at least, something that might be rehabilitated. That this reconstitution of Germany might be imaginable for British writers, however, is largely attributable to the presence of two other anthropomorphised nations: the youthful, cocky and self-confident America, and the dangerous anarchic child-nation, Soviet Russia.

The perception of Russia as dangerously immature was widespread in the late 1940s (Stonebridge 2007: 101–2). Stevie Smith, for example, depicts the 'Comrades' as hyper-active children who arrive in Berlin to 'stare and to destroy' (1949/1979: 54–5), while Spender renders defence of the Soviet system ridiculous by putting it in the mouth of 'Boyman', an ebullient film-maker encountered during the poet's travels (219–20). Growing anxiety regarding the political threat posed by Russia was paralleled by concern about American cultural hegemony. West is not unsympathetic to America, particularly in the case of the young soldiers in exile from their small-town lives (13–14), but her depiction of American authority suggests an unsubtle absolutism and bullying inadequacy (47, 59). J. B. Priestley similarly distinguished between individual Americans – seen in his fiction as forthright and fun-loving –

and a more disturbing ideological concept, 'the American way of life', a narcotic illusion that threatens the integrity of Englishness (1945: 99–100). Priestley was not alone in his concerns. Kynaston records that the end of the Lend-Lease policy and the punitive terms of the American Loan combined with wartime resentment of GI's spending power to ensure that attitudes towards America were 'distinctly mixed': 'There was an element of gratitude, certainly, and many personal entanglements, together with a largely frustrated longing for American material goods, but at the same time resentment of a newly risen super-power that seemed unpleasantly inclined to throw its weight around' (2007: 133).

Yet while West and Priestley hinted at the resentments of a newly dependent Britain, Evelyn Waugh went further, returning to the satirical voice of his early fiction to produce *The Loved One* (1948), a cynical black comedy of Anglo-American cultural relations. The novel is set in a Hollywood world where fashion determines not just clothes but bodies. An early example sets the tone, as long-term Englishman abroad Sir Francis Hinsley is forced to reinvent his own creation, the 'sadis-tic' sexually-charged actress Juanita del Pablo (1948/1951: 10). With the League of Decency demanding 'healthy films', Juanita – originally Baby Aaronson – is forced to 'start at the beginning again as an Irish colleen' (11). Sir Francis's failure convincingly to reinvent Juanita ends his career, and he hangs himself; a convenient death that will bring his friend, former RAF officer and poet, Dennis Barlow to Whispering Glades, the spectacular manifestation of American hubris at the heart of the book. The cynical Dennis is lost in admiration for the inauthentic wonders of Whispering Glades, a funeral home that promises, in effect, to protect the dead from death:

> *This perfect replica of an old English Manor*, a notice said, [. . .] *is certified proof against fire earthquake and*　　　　　*Their name liveth for evermore who record it in Whispering Glades.*
>   At the blank patch a signwriter was even then at work and Dennis, pausing to study it, discerned the ghost of the words 'high explosive' freshly oblit-erated and the outlines of 'nuclear fission' about to be filled in as substitute. (1948/1951: 35)

Here, at this monument to denial, Dennis meets the aptly named mortu-ary cosmetician Aimée Thanatogenos. For Dennis, her infatuation with death sets her apart from the 'standard product' American woman (45), but for Waugh she is an unstable hybrid composed of a little education and a sentimental worship of false gods. Aimée is as empty and vacuous as the nation she represents, the 'sparse furniture of her mind' (105) leaving her ill equipped even for the demands of a banal love triangle.

Her second suitor is Chief Mortician Mr Joyboy, 'a true artist' in the medium of death (48), but also an organisation man, caring more about his career and his mother than Aimée, who he seduces with the smiles he fixes on the faces of the newly-embalmed dead. Dennis is little better as a lover, plagiarising British poetry's greatest hits to win the undiscerningly romantic girl. A liar, a cheat and, by the novel's end, a successful black-mailer, he is, in effect, another manifestation of the postwar disaffection and maladjustment evident in the spiv films and the fictions of 'uneasy homecoming syndrome' (Mengham and Reeve 2001: 162). Yet although the lovers are equally unappetising, and will become allies when Aimée opts to abandon them both for her true love, death, Waugh's novel suggests that far more divides than unites Britain and America. *The Loved One*'s comedy of cultural difference consequently revels in the wounds of history, as its Englishmen sip whisky in the heat, surrounded by the 'native huts' of the Hollywood colony (7).

That Waugh should have his doubts about postwar Britain and the parvenue Americans comes as no surprise after *Brideshead Revisited*, but as the decade drew to a close many struggled to maintain the optimism that had given the Labour party its mandate for change. The vivid essays in Michael Sissons and Philip French's *Age of Austerity* (1963) and the Mass Observation diaries of Simon Garfield's *Our Hidden Lives* (2004) detail the extent to which life in Britain got worse before it got better. With bread rationed and even the undesirable dried egg tempo-rarily absent from the shops, coupons and regulations proliferated, and the average citizen had less to eat than in wartime (Cooper 1963/1986: 25). The housing shortage was acute, giving rise in 1946 to a short-lived squatting movement, as desperate families moved into unoccupied prop-erties and derelict military camps (31–4). There was little to celebrate at the first anniversary of the war's end, as diarist Edie Rutherford noted: 'So the war, all of it, was over a year and two days ago. I think it passed unnoticed by most. The peace is so grim that it occupies all our time' (Garfield 2004/2005: 266). The situation would deteriorate further when the worst winter of the century hit the country. January 1947 brought an unprecedented quantity of snow that paralysed trans-port and industry. Roads stayed impassable for months, livestock died, and the domestic use of gas and electricity, when not actually cut, was restricted (Cooper 35–7). This bitter, all-encompassing cold, and the associated difficulties of daily life came to shape even the possibilities of anxiety, as Pamela Hansford Johnson's *A Summer to Decide* (1948) makes clear. The novel begins with a death, and finds its protago-nist, Claud Pickering, experiencing an unwelcome degree of pathetic fallacy:

> In a snow-locked London, reduced in fire and light, where thousand upon
> thousand of conscientious basement-dwellers lived by candlelight, the stage
> seemed set for the tragic event. . . . I was obsessed by the sense of halted time,
> of snow for ever settled and the darkness fastened for ever across a sun that
> was now no more than an idea. (1948/1954: 23)

A sense of hiatus dominates the novel, a loss of direction in a world
'outworn' (89) – yet Claud retains a degree of political optimism that
completely escapes the American Hattie Chandler. Describing how
many of her compatriots live in fear of a pre-emptive Russian strike
(174), by the end of the novel she has worried herself into a state of
near-hysterical next-war anxiety. In a decadent embrace of a collapsing
civilisation, she tries to 'cram the unforgiving minute with as much, and
more, than it could hold' (322). Claud's response, by contrast, prosaic-
ally suggests that austerity has some advantages. In Britain, the 'ordinary person' is too busy wondering how to clear up the debris of the last
war to worry about the next (174).

In this climate of frustration and political despondency, Cyril Connolly
brought *Horizon* to a close with an editorial verging on the apocalyptic.
The final double issue, featuring an essay by Maurice Blanchot on the
Marquis de Sade, a bleak American short story, an account of the atonal
composer Dallapiccola's 'Songs for Prisoners' and some reproductions
of Francis Bacon's 'horror-fretted canvases' (361), led Connolly to
suggest in his 'Comment' that the concerns of his contributors were
emblematic of the decade:

> One can perceive the inner trend of the Forties as maintaining this desperate
> struggle of the modern movement, between man, betrayed by science, bereft
> of religion, deserted by the pleasant imaginings of humanism against the blind
> fate of which he is now so expertly conscious that if we were to close this last
> Comment with the suggestion that every one who is now reading it may in
> ten years' time, or even five, look back on this moment as the happiest in
> their lives, there would be few who would gainsay us. . . . This is the message
> of the Forties from which, alas, there seems no escape, for it is closing time
> in the gardens of the West and from now on an artist will be judged only by
> the resonance of his solitude or the quality of his despair. (*Horizon*, Vol. XX,
> Nos 120–1, December 1949–January 1950; p. 362)

Malcolm Bradbury draws on Connolly's counsel of doom to argue both
for the deadening impact of war, and for a 'sense of fracture' emerging
from the decade (1987: 71). In the age of Holocaust and atom bomb, he
notes, 'it was not surprising that the arts that did emerge postwar were
marked by minimalism and muteness' (1987: 71). Bradbury suggests
that Connolly's despair was shared by *Penguin New Writing*, which
produced its fortieth and final issue in 1950. In their place emerged

'a new seriousness', epitomised by F. R. Leavis's *Scrutiny*, that was 'moving literary activity toward the academy and the provinces, and away from the metropolitan literary world with all its Bloomsbury shadings' (85). Bradbury's conclusions return us to the concept, discussed in the Introduction, of the 1940s as a caesura in the century; but while it is hard to challenge the perception that anxiety had become the dominant note of an uncertain postwar world, it would be a mistake to assume that literature did not thrive on despair, nor benefit from the collapse of the contingent concept of wartime national unity.

The literature of 'atomising', then, is that of both national and personal fragmentation. It moves away from the idea of a common purpose to respond to the psychological wounds of war and modernity, and it turns its attention once again to divisive cultural and political issues shelved for the duration of the war. The following sections trace some of the most potent strands to emerge from the uncertain landscape of 'peace'.

A Seamless Transition: From Old War to Cold War

That communism had 'arrived' as the new bogeyman par excellence and the root of a not-inconsiderable paranoia is evident from Dennis Wheatley's occult thriller *The Haunting of Toby Jugg* (1948). Although set in the war, this story of a wealthy young airman disabled in combat and held captive for his inheritance is permeated by Cold War anxiety. Toby is the victim of an elaborate plot to drive him insane, after which an evil global conspiracy will take control of the vast corporate wealth he is set to inherit. Wheatley's use of a limited first-person diary form adds to the paranoia, as does the self-doubt arising from Toby's wounded state, as he struggles to impose a rationalising narrative upon the psychic terrors confronting him. These terrors initially take the form of nightly hauntings by what seems to be a giant octopus, trembling with 'repulsive lust' (1948: 21), but as the plot progresses, it turns out that the spectral creature is in fact the Great Spider, a flesh-eating astral projection that feasts on the vulnerable (206). But behind these supernatural torments lies human agency: Toby's guardian Helmuth, a sinister foreign intellectual, who had hoped initially to indoctrinate his charge through 'advanced' schooling methods and a spot of pseudo-masonic ritual. However, Toby's unexpected patriotic urge to join the RAF undoes his guardian's plans, and it is not until the disabled pilot is physically at his mercy that Helmuth can once again proceed with – and, in the manner of all good thriller villains, explain – his fiendish conspiracy:

> Communism is the perfect vehicle for the introduction of the return of Mankind to his original allegiance. It already denies Christianity and all the other heresies. It denies the right of free-will and the expression of their individuality to all those who live under it. Communism bows down only to material things; and my real master is not Stalin but the Lord of Material Things; Satan the Great, the Deathless, the Indestructible. (1948: 249)

The message is clear. A vote for Labour is just the first step on a slippery slope that leads ultimately to Satanic dominion and a plague of astral spiders. Fortunately for Toby, he has by this point acquired a virginal hyper-English girlfriend (211) and the two are saved by a combination of her plucky agency and the power of a love so strong that it miraculously enables Toby to walk again.

Wheatley was a phenomenally popular writer in the 1940s, producing fictions to suit all moods – from contemporary espionage in the early war years to historical adventures in the mid-decade – and *Toby Jugg* cannot therefore be dismissed as the paranoid fantasy of a conservative minority. Phil Baker notes that Wheatley's 'identification of Satanism and Communism was a major innovation in [his] propaganda career' (2009: 453) – a topical response to emergent fears – but, more problematically, *Toby Jugg* also worries about modernity in general, especially as manifest through atheism, immigration and Jewish refugees (1948: 13–14, 120–7). Wheatley's readership is encouraged to invest in a potent and regressive national ideal that does much to explain why Toby's redemption should come through the twin powers of a chivalric military ideal – as embodied by the RAF – and natural English maidenhood. The British nation, its soil, substance and people are being invoked as a pure, pre-industrial force capable of withstanding the combined forces of Communism, Satanism, mechanised modernity and the relentless foreign 'other', a profoundly nostalgic and – in its pervasive anti-Semitism – disturbing myth in a rapidly changing world.

Graham Greene took a less paranoid but nonetheless bleak approach to the new world of 'peace', as is evident from the preoccupations of *The Third Man*. Directed by Carol Reed in 1949 from an original treatment and screenplay by Greene, and published as a novel in 1950, the story of the 'friendship' between Harry Lime and Holly Martins is arguably the finest film to emerge from the so-called 'spiv' cycle in British cinema. Carol Reed was the ideal director for Greene's disenchanted *weltanschauung*. Described by Rob White as 'one of the great directors of city-experience', his back catalogue, including *Odd Man Out* (1947) and *The Fallen Idol* (1948), is rich with ambiguous heroes hunted through disorientating, threatening urban environments (2003: 46). Yet while the film has roots in the British preoccupation with crime and black market culture, it is also significantly international in conception. *The Third Man* originated in producer Alexander Korda's 'inside knowledge of the emergent Cold War' (Piette 2009: 26), and was, like so much else in this period, dependent on American money. It was the financial clout of David O. Selznick that made the production possible, and which resulted in significant changes both to the original script and to the version released to American audiences. Yet both British and American versions would go on to phenomenal success, generating radio and television spin-offs that turned 'Harry Lime' into an international man of mystery and made an equally phenomenal sum of money for his creator, Graham Greene (Thomson 2009: 95–9).

Like the fiction of Raymond Chandler, to which the film is undoubtedly indebted, *The Third Man* is a quest narrative in which one good man, the American Holly Martins (Joseph Cotten), searches for a lost homosocial ideal, embodied by his pre-war schoolfriend, Harry Lime (Orson Welles). As with Chandler's fiction, the texture of the telling – atmosphere, setting, dialogue – is more important than plot, and as with Chandler's Philip Marlowe, the 'detective' is a romantic. Holly (called Rollo in the novel) is a writer of 'cheap novelettes', who believes in friendship and who has, in the words of the watching English policeman Calloway (Trevor Howard), 'never really grown up' (1950/1976: 13). Greene's debt to the romantic noir of Chandler, as opposed to the darker world of contemporaries such as Dashiell Hammett and James M. Cain, is evident in the deployment of Harry's abandoned girlfriend, Anna (Valli). Here is an unwitting *femme fatale*, whose plangent beauty and absolute unavailability will drive the detective to pursue his quest irrespective of consequence; she is the force that will motivate him when the ties of friendship finally fail. And fail they must, for this is also a coming-of-age narrative in which the naïve Martins must recognise a reality long known to the world-weary Calloway. Harry Lime is not a symbol of past securities, he is – as Vienna's foremost racketeer – an unwelcome manifestation of modernity.

For Holly, then, this is an uncanny narrative of discovery in which the familiar becomes not simply unfamiliar, but actively evil. And Greene is careful to render Lime's crimes as unredeemable: his diluted penicillin racket murders children. However, the performative dimension of the film renders such absolutes as uncertain as the Greene of *The Power and the Glory* (1940) might have wished. In this novel, his nameless whisky priest is compelling, even admirable, in spite of all his sins; similarly, Harry Lime is mesmeric, lovable even, for all his appalling crimes. The power of Lime is in large part attributable to Orson Welles' cherubic appearance – the face of a naughty schoolboy, not a murderer – but it also emerges from the character's absence. Martins arrives in Vienna to the news of Harry's death: the expected encounter is displaced, and before we meet Lime he has acquired a multifaceted identity; Martins' friend, Calloway's enemy, Anna's lover. His belated appearance is a paradigm shift in the narrative; nothing is what it had seemed, and everything tilts, as if to endorse the vertiginous camera angles adopted throughout by cinematographer Robert Krasker. Appropriately, the first sight of Welles is theatrical: framed in a doorway he is illuminated, as if by spotlight, for just long enough to offer a tantalising half-smile. Surface appearance disguises depths of corruption, and Harry's boyishness is a sign of his arrested moral development. As Martins will later muse in Greene's novella, 'evil was like Peter Pan – it carried with it the horrifying and horrible gift of eternal youth' (1950/ 1976: 104).

The decision to adopt a generic framework for a film about postwar Europe has a certain pragmatic economy of signification. The world of noir is one of deceptive surfaces in which power inevitably corrupts. The detective is an outsider, a lone figure who fights for some belief or archaic loyalty in the face of opposition from both the law and its criminal counterpart. It is also a fictional form profoundly dependent on place. The city, whether specific or generic, generates narratives that are heterogeneous, fragmentary and violent. In this context crime cannot be detected, it can at best be policed, and Calloway's role in the Four-power occupation of Vienna has as much to do with diplomacy as justice. As the occupying forces fight over territory, a criminal subculture flourishes in the literal and metaphorical sewers running beneath the city. Calloway tells Martins, a writer of westerns, that he is not the sheriff, and this is not a world of cowboys and Indians, but it is in exactly these terms that the film will end. Holly and Harry face each other for the final time, their game of hide and seek having ended in tears. In shooting his friend, Holly will, ironically, get to play the sheriff's role, but even here his agency is undermined. In the film version, an almost imperceptible nod from Harry prefaces the sound of a gunshot, giving tacit permission to his friend to save him from the authorities.

The book seems more confident of Martins' capacity for choice, or rather, without Welles's presence, the wounded Harry Lime loses much of his appeal. On the page he becomes simply a cornered rat: 'he began to whimper again' remembers Martins, 'I couldn't bear it any more and I put a bullet through him' (118). Greene's novel is narrated by Calloway, a focalising decision that, in bringing Martins and Calloway together, contributes to the dilution of Lime. For Calloway to narrate, Martins must tell him everything, and their relationship consequently becomes more intimate. The verbal sparring that shapes their screen encounters

Figure 8.1 Martins (Joseph Cotten) and Calloway (Trevor Howard) face up to the postwar world in *The Third Man* (1949). Courtesy of STUDIOCANAL Films Ltd.

becomes the tip of a hard-boiled encounter in which two dissimilar men come to a grudging appreciation of each other's virtues (Figure 8.1). This focalisation is not the only difference shaping the two versions of *The Third Man*. The novel's ending is also more upbeat. Sergeant Paine, whose unflappable politeness and enthusiasm for the western has provided a comical counterpart to Calloway, is killed by Harry in the film; the novel spares him and it spares Holly. The film's famous closing shot, in which Anna walks towards the camera and past the waiting Holly, becomes in the book the beginning of a new story: 'before they turned out of my sight her hand was through his arm' (119). The ending is scarcely any happier but, like *The Ministry of Fear* before it, it brings damaged people together into a fragile intimacy of loss.

What is shared by both versions of *The Third Man* is a conception of the black market, not simply as a microcosmic survival mechanism, but also as a macrocosmic malaise. The opening voice-over is cheerfully brisk and disturbingly ambivalent. Over shots of the black-market exchange of goods, and the floating corpse of an 'amateur', the unspecified narrator confesses his complicity with the acknowledgement that 'we'd run anything then'. When he then assumes the confiding tone of the storyteller – 'Oh, wait, I was going to tell you' – the audience too becomes part of the uncertain moral framework of the postwar. Rackets are ubiquitous – nobody minds – but the film insists that such moral relativism cannot go unchallenged. When Harry and Holly finally talk, suspended in the Prater ferris wheel above the city and its dot-like inhabitants, the scene is set for an ethical seduction:

> 'Would you really feel any pity if one of those dots stopped moving – for ever? If I said you can have twenty thousand pounds for every dot that stops, would you really, old man, tell me to keep my money – without hesitation? Or would you calculate how many dots you could afford to spare?' [. . .] 'In these days, old man, nobody thinks in terms of human beings. Governments don't, so why should we? They talk of the people and the proletariat, and I talk of the mugs. It's the same thing.' (1950/1976: 104, 106)

Sarah Street argues that *The Third Man* 'offers a critique of the slippery slope *logic* of spivvery, even linking it with totalitarian ideology' (1997: 71), and Harry's fascism is explicit both in his absolute egotism, and in his logic. 'Statistics don't bleed' was, for Arthur Koestler, an indictment of unthinking ethical complicity (1945/1983: 92); for Harry Lime, it is a simple truth. The simultaneous presence of past and present evils – fascism and Cold War politics – is evident in the *mise-en-scène* of the film. Reed's camera turns food and its consumption into grotesque spectacle, setting those growing fat on profiteering against the watching faces of the dispossessed. Surveillance is an all-pervading trope, Reed's camera lingering on the faces of the Viennese who superintend the shabby spectacular events of the narrative from windows, stairwells and streets, their gazes unflinching, their expressions unreadable. But these watchers too can be threatening. The sinister child who sets a mob in pursuit of Holly has a shrieking voice and an old/young face that turns him into a horrifying hybrid of ventriloquist's dummy and Hitler youth: a monstrous manifestation of childhood in a world unfit for children.

The Third Man, then, is both Holly's personal quest and a dissection of postwar ethics. It is also, in the conjunction of American naïveté and world-weary British experience, an attempt to assert the ongoing significance of Britain on the international stage. As suggested earlier, Anglo-American relations in the postwar period were an amalgam of gratitude and resentment, complicated by governmental anxieties regarding the status of Britain and the stability of the Empire. The film's Cold War narrative has consequently been read by Adam Piette as variously an allegory of the 'special relationship' (2009: 39); a fantasy of British Cold War influence, imagined as a third force independent of both America and the Soviet Union, and a darker set of enmities in which Freudian resentments drive a secret British 'urge to *annihilate* the rival United States' (35). In this, and in his analysis of Storm Jameson's Berlin-set novel *The Black Laurel* (1947), Piette explores the political events that would lead, eventually, to the acceptance of the UK/USA client relationship in 1949. All the manoeuvrings of this new European war, he suggests, are contaminated by the rotting corpse of the past, and the machinations of power continue to demand sacrificial victims. In the case of Jameson, this sacrifice is the unjustly executed Jew, Kalb; in *The Third Man*, it is Anna who, betrayed by Harry, will presumably disappear behind the Iron Curtain (Piette 2009: 42–4). Yet Anna's role in the film is perhaps even more depressing than this reading suggests, infected as she is by the pervasive gender assumptions of the period. Anna's loyalty to Harry is unflinching: even when she learns of his appalling crimes she will not collude in the effort to stop him. In consequence she becomes a symbol of eternal woman – beautifully framed as a weeping Pietà in Harry's pyjamas – divorced from the rational, her elemental loyalties ensuring that she will sacrifice her own safety for that of her man. Anna is, of course, also a necessary force of heterosexual legitimacy within the text. Without her as a third party, the relationship of Holly and Harry would risk exceeding the bounds of the homosocial; as it is, the economy of desire within the film plays on the comic interchangeability of lovers. Anna calls Holly 'Harry' throughout, while Holly's desires latch on to Anna as the nearest he can get to the man he seeks. They are brought together out of hunger for the uncanny residue of Harry that each embodies.

The Third Man is then both intimate and spectacular, a love triangle embedded within an emergent narrative of Cold War extremes. In Harry Lime it constructs an anti-hero whose nihilistic philosophy ironically couples the extremes of collectivism and free enterprise to produce the moral void that would be become central to the narratives of spy fiction. His analysis of the 'dots' is equally the logic of numbers that dominates the thinking of Arthur Koestler's Ivanov, the loyal servant of Communism who must interrogate his former comrade N. S. Rubashov in *Darkness at Noon* (1940). The novel explores the intellectual appeal of the Communist system, suggesting that its danger lies in its 'intellectual deformations: logical derivations from legitimate starting points rendered fatal by the failure to take into account the individual' (Judt 2008: 40–1). Ivanov's rhetoric is still more disturbing: 'Nature is generous in her senseless experiments on mankind. Why should mankind not have the right to experiment on itself?' (1940/2005: 131). The reduction of the individual to a dot, a statistic or, indeed, a laboratory experiment, links the preoccupations of Koestler and Greene to those of

George Orwell who, in *Nineteen Eighty-Four*, would follow the logic of totalitarianism and the destruction of the individual to their absolute and awful extreme.

Staying Human: *Nineteen Eighty-Four* and the Age of Austerity

> The proles had stayed human. They had not become hardened inside. They had held on to the primitive emotions which he himself had to re-learn by conscious effort. And in thinking this he remembered, without apparent relevance, how a few weeks ago he had seen a severed hand lying on the pavement and had kicked it into the gutter as though it had been a cabbage-stalk. (Orwell 1949/1989: 172)

There is perhaps no more famous book of the 1940s than George Orwell's *Nineteen Eighty-Four*. Published in 1949, it consolidated the enormous success of his first fictional study of totalitarianism, *Animal Farm* (1945), and ensured that when Orwell died in January 1950, he would be remembered as one of the most important political writers of mid-century Britain. Yet there remains a sense of critical unease around both Orwell and his fiction. Not only has *Nineteen Eighty-Four* proved appropriable across a wide spectrum of political beliefs (Bluemel 2004: 144; Rodden 1989: 6, 46–7), it has also been subject to criticism as, in Harold Bloom's words, a 'good bad book' (cited in Clune 2009: 30). Bloom's phrasing implies that Orwell's success has little to do with literary merit, a concern shared by Ben Pimlott, whose introduction to the Penguin edition of 1989 accuses Orwell of a 'lack of subtlety' and a 'crude plot' (1989: vi). In some sense, the choice of Pimlott – a political historian – to write the Penguin introduction, encapsulates the anxiety that surrounds *Nineteen Eight-Four* as a work of fiction, and indeed, the book has attracted as much attention from philosophers as from literary critics. Recent criticism has sought to complicate the assumption of Orwell's prosaic transparency, but it nonetheless seems odd that he could ever have been viewed as a straightforward writer. Orwell's 'Fairy Tale', *Animal Farm*, and its dystopian Big Brother, *Nineteen Eighty-Four*, are paradoxical and evasive texts that insist on revolution at the same time as they seem to deny its very possibility: they are also strangely funny and deeply violent books, prompting inappropriate laughter in equal measure with visceral disgust. These contradictory tensions are important, and they help to explain how Orwell's works came to be 'exactly the right books at exactly the right time' (Rorty 1998: 140).

What then makes these books so timely? *Animal Farm* is an allegory that demonstrates how power corrupts. When the animals stage their popular uprising against the cruel regime of farmer Jones, they create a site of revolutionary potential that is gradually destroyed through the pigs' assumption of the characteristic features of a despotic ruling class. With power over language, the pigs control history, and their capacity to rewrite the past enables them to legitimise their assumption of power in the present. By the end of the book, the pigs are walking, wielding whips, drinking and gambling: they have become indistinguishable from humans. *Nineteen Eighty-Four* by contrast begins after the revolution has faded into mythology, and the citizens of Oceania have no idea what 'really' happened because the past is constantly being revised to suit the needs of the present. Politics have acquired a tripartite structure that evokes the class system: a privileged elite form the Inner Party, the Outer Party comprises an anxious middle-class, and the bulk of the population is made up of 'proles', the disregarded working classes. The 'middle-class' Outer Party, where the most likely threat to the Inner Party's power is perceived to lie, lives under a regime of terror that turns the appearance of respectability into a form of torture. Subject to constant surveillance, through omnipresent telescreens and hidden microphones, no-one must utter an inappropriate comment or let their face reveal the faintest trace of non-conformity (Orwell 1949/1989: 82, 112). Unsurprisingly, this panoptical environment has bred a seething mass of repression, most evidently manifest in the violent fantasies of the novel's protagonist, Winston Smith; but such fantasies are also the logical outcome of a culture in which torture and 'vaporization' are omnipresent threats. In *Nineteen Eighty-Four*, power has 'come out' as an end in itself. As explained to Winston by his nemesis O'Brien, the party does not claim to exercise its brutal power for self-protection or the benefit of others, rather it acknowledges that power is a drug; an intoxicating investment in a collective potency: in Oceania, the 'object of persecution is persecution. The object of torture is torture. The object of power is power' (276).

It is not difficult to see the component parts from which Orwell has constructed his dystopia: Nazi Germany, the Soviet Union, and the familiar shabby milieu of postwar London. While the combination of these physical, psychic and ideological spaces does much to explain why *Nineteen Eighty-Four* was 'the right book at the right time', there are further contributing factors to the novel's timeliness. The Party is founded on three central tenets: War is Peace, Freedom is Slavery and Ignorance is Strength. All are pertinent to the propaganda context of total war, but none is more relevant to the mood of the 1940s than the paradoxical claim that war and peace are indistinguishable. This conceptual amalgamation speaks directly to the condition of the 'postwar', as do the opening pages of *Nineteen Eighty-Four*, which recreate the desolate dreariness of austerity Britain. 'War' as a strategic engagement is over, 'war' as a condition of being continues. More significantly, though, 'War is Peace' is the *raison d'être* of the Cold War and the concept of a nuclear deterrent. War as once understood is held in abeyance by a peace that is war. The redefinition of war and its frighteningly essential quality, however, goes beyond social structures: it is also, according to *Nineteen Eighty-Four*, the fundamental condition of human subjectivity. 'I do not know', writes Stevie Smith in *The Holiday*, 'if we can bear not to be at war' (1949/1979: 8), a statement which suggests the ironic security of the war mind; *Nineteen Eighty-Four* pushes further, basing cultural cohesion upon the formative need for an enemy, an 'other' through which group identity can be secured. Implicit in the operation of the Party is the understanding of the void that follows victory: the loss of collective and individual purpose, and the difficult necessity of self-regeneration. It is uncertainty, not peace, that follows from war, and Orwell imagines a world in which that liminality is removed: Oceania will always be at war, be it with Eurasia or Eastasia, and the body politic will be rendered homogenous through a 'continuous and universal' state of 'war hysteria' (193). This 'certainty' is the gift of Big Brother, and seemingly it is capable of overriding the denuding constraints of living in a perpetual war economy.

At the same time as *Nineteen Eighty-Four* reveals the inescapable structural power – and the emotional security – of 'war is peace', it also demonstrates the corrosive impact of living with such a paradox. The horror of the book is not that Winston is 'The Last Man in Europe' (as the original title for the book would have described him) trapped by an invidious system, it is that Winston himself is part of that world. How could he be other? He, the figure humanised by his retention of memory and desire, is also an embodiment of the state's formative violence, a man who writes himself and his rebellion into existence not through the predictable 'political' rhetoric of '*DOWN WITH BIG BROTHER*' (20), but with a much more vivid and infinitely less sympathetic account of a trip to the cinema:

> *Last night to the flicks. All war films. One very good one of a ship full of refugees being bombed somewhere in the Mediterranean. Audience much amused by shots of a great huge fat man trying to swim away with a helicopter after him . . . then you saw a lifeboat full of children with a helicopter hovering over it. . . . then the helicopter planted a 20 kilo bomb in among them terrific flash and the boat went all to matchwood. then there was a wonderful shot of*

a child's arm going up up up right up into the air a helicopter with a camera
in its nose must have followed it up ... (1949/1989: 10–11)

Winston begins as INGSOC's answer to Mass Observation, recording
the response of the audience, but as the passage progresses, his punc-
tuation collapses and the distance evaporates leaving the reader with
their protagonist's warm appreciation of the sight of a dismembered
child. Winston, then, is a product of his time as much as a man out of
time, and the text is riven with examples of the violence that shapes his
desires, both political and erotic. His first fantasy concerning Julia, the
woman who will become his lover, encapsulates this integral sadism:
'Vivid, beautiful hallucinations flashed through his mind. He would
flog her to death with a rubber truncheon'(17). Rather later in the text,
Winston is asked how far he will go to defend his belief in the concept of
truth and to challenge the power of the Party. His response is to agree,
unhesitatingly, to the prospect of throwing sulphuric acid in a child's
face (180). Winston is never asked to put this certainty to the test, but
it nonetheless seems hard, on the face of this evidence, to see him as the
last repository of the human; rather he seems at best to represent the last
empiricist in a land of postmodernity, insisting on evidential knowledge
in the face of O'Brien's assertion that reality 'exists in the human mind,
and nowhere else' (261). The construction of Winston as an empiri-
cal historian divides him not only from the Party, with its ideological
emphasis on 'doublethink' and the mutability of the past, but also from
Julia. While Winston clings to the illusory security of linear time, the
youthful, uninhibited Julia inhabits a serial present that is simultaneously radical in its refusal of patriarchal regulation (131–3), and reactionary in its customary association of 'woman' with an unthinking,
animal, corporeal sensuality (138–9).

Nonetheless, Winston retains some sort of conscience, and this will
be his downfall. As the lexicographer, Syme, explains, Newspeak – the
'official' language of Oceania – will ultimately ensure conformity by
abolishing conceptual thought: 'orthodoxy is unconsciousness' (56).
The full implications of this statement emerge in the description of characters such as the 'Duckspeak' man. As a stream of orthodox jargon
pours from his mouth he looks, to Winston, like 'some kind of dummy'
in which body is disconnected from mind: 'It was not the man's brain
that was speaking, it was his larynx' (57). This sense of fragmentation
is repeated in more visceral terms when Winston is tortured to a state of
subjective dismemberment in the Ministry of Love: 'He became simply
a mouth that uttered, a hand that signed, whatever was demanded
of him' (254). While the 'obliteration of the self' is constructed as a

political philosophy (205), Orwell's imagery takes the reader beyond such dry abstraction and intellectual satire, drawing instead on the abject fascinations of body horror. For all the critical energy that has been devoted to the determining the politics underpinning the book, at a fundamental and – for many readers – more memorable level, *Nineteen Eighty-Four* is an exercise in horror; a futuristic cyborg nightmare in which the human is turned, not into the gleaming hard-bodied robot of 1950s science-fiction fantasy, but into a decaying, repulsive, infinitely dowdy austerity cyborg. Mrs Parsons, for example, is not 'human', but rather a malfunctioning machine unable to finish the stock phrases of her script. She is object, not subject, and like all objects, gathers dust if not regularly cleaned; hence the grotesque and absurd transition from poetic licence to factual statement: 'One had the impression there was dust in the creases of her face' (22); 'In the better light of the living-room he noticed with interest that there actually *was* dust in the creases of her face' (25). This becoming inhuman is reinforced by the description of Winston's wife Katherine, a 'jointed wooden image' (70), whose capacity mindlessly to spout Party slogans prompts Winston to nickname her the 'human sound-track' (69).

The culmination of the book's abject fascination with the body comes at the end of Winston's sustained interrogation by O'Brien. In a very literal re-imagining of the psychoanalytic mirror phase, Winston simultaneously recognises and mis-recognises the figure in the mirror: 'A bowed, grey-coloured, skeleton-like thing was coming towards him. Its appearance was frightening, and not merely the fact that he knew it to be himself' (284). The effect of this encounter is the exact opposite of Lacanian development. Winston does not mistakenly see his inchoate self as whole; rather his ruined, scarcely recognisable body prompts an emotional collapse beyond anything yet achieved by O'Brien's torture (285–6). Winston is a laboratory experiment for O'Brien (256), a process that will see him made both monster and – in his eventual mindless love for Big Brother – machine. His reprogramming is a staging post on the way towards a future in which the human subject has become entirely instrumental, devoid of pleasure, curiosity, enquiry; transhistorical cogs in the perpetual motion machine that is 'a boot stamping on a human face – for ever' (280).

In the debate surrounding *Nineteen Eighty-Four*'s fictional status – is it science fiction or polemic, philosophy or horror? – accusations of inconsistency have accompanied criticism of Orwell's style and preoccupations. The text itself, however, suggests that neither the creation of a seamless future world, nor a coherent political philosophy, were at the forefront of the writer's imagination; rather these elements feed into a visceral engagement with the contemporary moment (Taylor 2003: 388–9). Certainly the novel is sceptical of its status as polemic: Orwell mocks his own explicatory powers when Julia falls asleep during Winston's reading of Goldstein's book, disrupting his concentration just as he reaches 'the central secret' (1949/1989: 226). Meaning is deferred: Winston will never read the answer, and the book evades the difficult business of world creation. Orwell's inconsistencies also speak to the novel's double time frame: it is a book about the future, set firmly in a recognisable present, a setting that limits the amount of alien world exposition required of Orwell and his insider protagonist. Rather, dystopian horror is made legible through a metaphoricity Orwell's audience – rather than Winston Smith – will understand. The result is a third-person narrative that fluctuates between Winston's point of view and the 'real' twentieth-century perspective of an omniscient narrator, a dual narration that results in such curious anachronisms as the monstrous prole woman who looks as 'solid as a Norman pillar' (144). This duality, and the novel's concern with the postwar present, is most clearly evident in the portrayal of Julia. Supposedly a character who remembers nothing of life before the Party, she nonetheless displays a remarkable atavistic 'femininity'. When she and Winston meet illicitly, she constructs a fantasy of domesticity, producing food, coffee and the equipment to turn herself into what she terms a 'real woman'. Clumsily painting her face with cosmetics, she announces: 'I'm going to get hold of a real woman's frock from somewhere and wear it instead of these bloody trousers. I'll wear silk stockings and high-heeled shoes! In this room I'm going to be a woman, not a Party comrade' (149). If Julia knows nothing but the world of the Party and her own physical desires, from where can this construction of femininity have come? The answer would seem to be that this is one of the many places where the novel bears a closer relationship to 1948 than 1984. Julia's lament is the cry of a 1940s war worker, not that of a frustrated member of the Junior Anti-Sex League.

Returning to the appeal of the book at the time of its publication is instructive, not least for the insight it gives into 'austerity' Britain. Writing of the war years, Adam Piette argues that a militarised culture 'does not merely incidentally invade the private imagination, but actually covets it as its own, wishes to transform it for its own uses, to make it its creature' (1995: 5). This is one of the many things that the first readers of *Nineteen Eighty-Four* would have recognised as they struggled, in the aftermath of war's 'fabricated communal feelings' (2), to reclaim their right to commit one of the novel's less commented upon crimes: *ownlife*. This transgression, encompassing such sins as a 'taste for solitude' and 'individualism and eccentricity' (1949/1989: 85), encapsulates the world of impulse, choice and self-determination devastated by the war. *Nineteen Eighty-Four*, then, is a dystopia not just fashioned from the horrific realities of fascism, communism and the BBC canteen, it is also a lament for the loss of *ownlife* and the ambivalent wartime purpose that replaced it.

There is one further contemporary element shaping the horror of *Nineteen Eighty-Four*: the atomic age. The book imagines a bomb dropped on Colchester, but avoids any exploration of the consequences beyond asserting that atomic bombs are of little use in maintaining a climate of constant conflict (202–3). In this, as with the Holocaust, it seems that Orwell is a man of his time. John Newsinger argues that although Orwell knew the facts of the Holocaust he, like many of his contemporaries, 'never actually understood either the enormity or the significance of the crime' (2007: 123); similarly, in *Nineteen Eighty-Four*, there is little sense of engagement with the long-term implications of atomic warfare or radioactivity. Mass Observation's *Peace and the Public*, discussed in the Introduction, suggests that many initially imagined the atom bomb as a miraculously condensed version of conventional bombing: Hiroshima was related in understanding to Dresden and Coventry, not recognised as a paradigm shift in annihilation. Others, however, recognised all too fully the unthinkable quality of its condensed potency. Edith Sitwell's 'Three Poems of the Atomic Age' were among the first to grapple with the scientific and ethical implications of atomic physics, and these powerful incantatory poems integrate religious symbolism, science and alchemy to figure Hiroshima and Nagasaki as 'a kind of self-inflicted leprosy' (Morrisson 2002: 609). Yet Sitwell's political engagement is an inward-looking one – a study of global threat configured as 'some primeval disaster in the heart of man' (1947: 9) – and in this she is far from exceptional. In poetry and in prose, the predominant trend of the decade's final years was a turning inward, as writers sought strategies to confront both political change and personal desolation.

'Some primeval disaster in the heart of man': The Atomised Self and Society

When the historical process breaks down and armies organize with their embossed debates the ensuing void which they can never consecrate, when necessity is associated with horror and freedom with boredom, then it looks good to the bar business. (Auden 1948: 11)

W. H. Auden's *The Age of Anxiety* begins with bathos: rhetoric and high ideals give way to that familiar symbol of despair, the lonely drinker, slumped at the bar. As idealism reaches an impasse, suggests Auden, so too do the energies of the self, and indeed, much writing of the late 1940s finds its subject in tropes of confinement and a paralysing sense of disillusionment. 'Where is the fear that warmed us to the gun' asks Louis MacNeice in 'Aftermath' (2007: 255), one of a number of poems in his collection *Holes in the Sky* (1948) that speak to the uncertainty of the postwar subject. In spite of the best efforts of the writers discussed in Chapter 7, both poetry and fiction returned to the aching emptiness of war's aftermath, a personal desolation compounded of alienation and ennui. MacNeice's 'Bluebells' epitomises this emotional void:

> She, who last felt young during the War,
> This Easter has no peace to be waiting for;
> . . .
> And though her man is back, yet feels he has brought
> The Desert with him, making her cheeks taut.
>
> (MacNeice 1948/2007: 256)

The atomised consciousness of MacNeice's poem is unusual only in its focus on female subjectivity. The majority of alienated peacetime selves were male, men unable to adjust and resentful of the women they perceived as depending on or exploiting them. The result was a refusal of the future and a 'literature of suicide', either with determined intent or through the slower but equally effective method of alcoholic excess. Elizabeth Taylor's fiction is replete with examples of this postwar malaise. *Palladian* (1946), for example, rewrites Jane Austen in the style of *Jane Eyre*, or perhaps of Du Maurier's *Rebecca*: a neuralgic hero, his alcoholic cousin, a dead wife, a gothic nanny and a little too much crumbling masonry for comfort. *A Wreath of Roses* (1949) is bleaker still, offering two suicides, a murder and a painful portrait of loneliness, cruelty and fear. Philip Larkin's novels share this underlying desolation. *Jill* is set in wartime, but its concerns have little to do with the conflict. John, the central character, arrives at Oxford from his lower-middle class provincial home, the subject of a Pygmalion-like experiment by his indifferently cruel teacher (1946/2005: 63). Expectations of *Bildung*, however, are swiftly undercut. John begins his university career a passive figure, exploited by his fellow students, and he becomes the object of ridicule in his attraction to the youthful Gillian. Nothing about his experience – the literature he studies through a process of exhaustive note-taking, or the fiction through which he creates his ideal 'Jill' – offer him either consolation or agency, and he is humiliated in his attempts to belong. The 'real' of war briefly cuts through this nightmare, taking him home in the aftermath of an air-raid, but his return to Oxford brings only the futile liberation of a drinking binge that slides into the fever of illness. Larkin described the book as an 'unambitious short story' (xvii), but this seems harsh for a novel that captures social exclusion in such excruciating detail:

> It seemed that the next few days passed quickly, but the lengthening of time only increased the pain he felt, as if each day were a weight added to a load slung from a hook in the flesh. . . . All his life he had imagined people were hostile to him and wanted to hurt him; now he knew he had been right and all the worst fears of childhood were realized. (1946/2005: 185)

Katherine Lind, the protagonist of *A Girl in Winter* (1947), is far more self-possessed, and the novel – a study of memory and desire that exposes the formations of Englishness through Katherine's outsider perspective – offers at least the possibility of intimacy, albeit fleeting. Reunited in wartime, Katherine and Robin (who met as pre-war language students) share, for one night, their radically different lonelinesses: hers the stuff of exile; his the product of war's fracturing impact. The carefree young Englishman is now a soldier, war has 'broken the sequence' and his links to the 'life' of parents, family and future have all been severed (1947/1975: 246). Snow and ice dominate the novel's present; sunshine is reserved for the past.

Absent futures take many forms in the late 1940s. In *The Dark Philosophers* (1946) and *The Alone to the Alone* (1947) Gwyn Thomas returns to the bleakness of Wales in the 1930s, making black humour out of a cast of characters who, through long-term unemployment, provide a more literal manifestation of the no-future trope. Julian Maclaren-Ross's *Of Love and Hunger* (1947) also makes dark comedy out of the economic despair of the 1930s, but offers his dissolute vacuum-cleaner salesman the prospect of escape into the homosocial world of the army. Edward Gaitens's *Dance of the Apprentices* (1948), by contrast, sees little redemption in war. The novel returns to the beginning of the century, following a group of Glasgow slum-dwellers through youthful ambition and political activism to a seemingly inescapable fate of drink, despair and self-destruction. Gaitens asserts the dignity of labour, but overall *Dance of the Apprentices* is a remorseless catalogue of hope destroyed and potential unfulfilled. There seems little to be gained through education or political action when a man's fate is inevitably to be brought low by the forces of religious hypocrisy, world war, unemployment and marriage. The failure of marriage, the impossibility of agency and the collapse of the self are also at the heart of perhaps the decade's most agonising 'suicide' fiction, *Under the Volcano*, which the peripatetic English exile Malcolm Lowry finally published in 1947. Set in Mexico at the end of the 1930s, and largely written in Canada, the book owes its enduring fame more to its success in North America than to a specifically British sensibility; but, nonetheless, its desolation – at least nine years in the making – speaks eloquently to the atomised culture of the late 1940s. The protracted death of the alcoholic British consul Geoffrey Firmin, conveyed through twelve chapters of incantatory apocalyptic prose, offers a 'solipsistic' nightmare in which the 'anxieties, alarms and aberrations [of the self] displace the "objective" reality of the world' (Schmidt, in Lowry 1947/1962: xiv).

Yet probably the most debated despair of the decade is that of Graham Greene's colonial policeman Scobie, the ill-fated protagonist of *The Heart of the Matter* (1948). Scobie, as a Catholic suicide, has been extensively discussed in terms of his relationship to God and Greene's resistance to religious orthodoxy. Yet the exploration of the novel as a site of theological debate has overshadowed its relationship to other tropes of the 1940s, not least of which is misogyny: the void blighting Scobie's existence, and the root of all his troubles, is woman. Scobie builds on earlier Greene protagonists, such as Arthur Rowe, in that he is undone by a sentimental pity that draws him first into debt and then into adultery, although both, ironically, are figured the same (1948/2004: 136–9). Scobie's major error of judgement – borrowing money from the manipulative Syrian merchant Yusef to pay for his wife's escape from the Colony – is, however, less selfless than it might seem. Aside from the repulsion Scobie feels from his wife's body (33), he also longs to be free of the psychological weight she represents. At the outset of the novel, a ludicrous image associates Louise with imprisonment: 'the danger of submarines had made her as much a fixture as the handcuffs on the nail' (7); after her departure, by contrast, Scobie relishes the 'quality of security and impregnability in the silence' of her absence (91). He is relieved to be rid of a woman he no longer loves, whose presence acts as a drain on his masculine self-sufficiency and interrupts his peaceful homosocial relationship with the houseboy Ali.

Scobie's second substantial mistake, the affair with the young widow and shipwreck survivor Helen Rolt, also perversely combines the generous and the selfish, developing as it does from a pleasure in his capacity to amuse this child-woman rather than any more familiar formulation of desire. The relationship is rendered disturbing from the outset. Helen lies gravely ill in hospital next to the bed of a dying child, who Scobie must comfort, seemingly as divine punishment for missing his own child's death (112). Helen is thus linked to Scobie's memories and when they first talk, their subjects are the stuff of childhood: school, netball and her stamp album, the only possession to have survived forty days in an open boat. Helen's rebirth in the hospital establishes her as a reincarnation of Scobie's lost daughter, before, as their relationship develops, becoming a unpleasant replica of his wife. The first kiss between them links Helen to both wife and child, and exposes Scobie as a traumatised fetishist of need, hopelessly attracted to vulnerability: 'When she turned and the light fell on her face she looked ugly, with the temporary ugliness of a child. The ugliness was like handcuffs on his wrists' (146). Louise Scobie and Helen Rolt are improbable *femmes fatales*, and the extent of their power is debatable. We are given no access to the interiority of these women, and the words they speak seem often to be wilfully misinterpreted by Scobie (145, 217). They function, though, as useful scapegoats, figures that Scobie can blame for his failure to maintain the façade of impenetrable male subjectivity in the face of a corrosive environment. The man who only wanted to be left in splendid isolation ends up as the servant of too many masters: his wife, his lover, his employers, his creditor and his God.

Scobie's desire for masculine self-sufficiency is the stuff of hardboiled fiction. Greene's debt to Raymond Chandler has been discussed earlier in this chapter, and it is equally evident here in the construction of a protagonist who fails to conform to his own self-conception as the 'one good man' of legend. The habit of distinguishing between Greene's 'major' novels and his 'entertainments', disguises the generic features at play in *The Heart of the Matter*'s preoccupation with work and the construction of masculinity. It is perhaps one of the greatest ironies of the novel that Scobie only achieves success after his fall from grace. Initially figured as 'Scobie the Just' (9), the one incorruptible man in a landscape of endemic deceit, he is nonetheless overlooked for the post of commissioner. Any thwarted ambition Scobie feels is displaced onto Louise, but the economic impact of his rejection undoubtedly unmans him (37). From this point the book tracks the consequences – in classic noir fashion – of a single criminal act. When Scobie succumbs to the sweating appeal of the fat Portuguese captain who has illicitly written to his daughter in Leipzig, for the first time he crosses an ethical line:

> Perhaps it was because his temperature had risen that it seemed to him he was on the verge of a new life. One felt this way before a proposal of marriage or a first crime.
>   Scobie took the letter and opened it. The act was irrevocable, for no one in this city had the right to open clandestine mail. (1948/2004: 43)

Whether this action is seen to emerge from misplaced pity, Catholic fellowship, or the significance of absent daughters, the fact remains that it breaks the code of 'Scobie the Just': it implicates him in a regime of secrets and facilitates his transition from the blameless man beyond temptation who can banter easily with Yusef (24–7), to the man who will accept a loan from the 'untrustworthy, sincere' Syrian (95), to the man who will – ultimately – become complicit in murder. By telling Yusef he suspects Ali, a figure who for 15 years has been his most loyal and conducive companion, Scobie signs the man's death warrant. This is the betrayal that underpins the suicide; this is the act for which there can be no redemption: 'it seemed to him that he had no shape left, nothing you could touch and say: this is Scobie' (229).

The Heart of the Matter, then, might be seen as an example of Catholic noir, the story of a just man losing his integrity in a corrupt environment peopled by ugly passive-aggressive *femmes fatales*. The story demands a powerful adversary, to whom the protagonist will be drawn in a confrontational relationship of desire and denial: it finds that adversary in God. Describing Greene's negotiation of his own Catholic faith, Murray Roston argues that Greene sees 'the world of corruption, despair and suffering as a truer challenge to the priest than attending afternoon tea at the Ladies Guild or raising funds for a new belfry' (2006: 46). Unexpectedly – and presumably unintentionally – Roston's description echoes the metaphoric framework of Raymond Chandler's 'The Simple Art of Murder' (1950). In Chandler's case, the 'flustered old ladies – of both sexes (or no sex)' (1950/1964: 196) are the readers and writers of classic, clue-puzzle narrative, derided in order to establish the virile masculine credentials of the hard-boiled protagonist, and to valorise a school of writing that 'gave murder back to the kind of people that commit it for reasons, not just to provide a corpse' (195). In Greene's world, a missionary Catholicism that confronts a specifically male world of 'corruption, despair and suffering' is set against the domesticated – and feminised – pieties embodied by Louise; religion, like work, is a man's world. For this reason, the novel ends with Father Rank's rebuke of Louise; whether Scobie is damned or redeemed, Rank understands the man's masochistic, almost homoerotic, confrontation with his God, and prefers it to the pious orthodoxy of 'woman'.

Noir fiction emerges from the pressures of an urban landscape, and in *The Heart of the Matter*, Greene replaces the conventional city with the colony, depicting this outpost of empire as enervated and decaying, a simulacra of society that absorbs sincerity and transforms it into the petty jealousies and power struggles of a carceral community. As Wilson, the ill-disguised spy with ambitions to become Scobie's nemesis, takes his leave of Louise, the narrative voice notes:

The words vibrated with sincerity: it gave them the sound of a foreign language – the sound of English spoken in England. Here intonations changed in the course of a few months, became high-pitched and insincere, or flat and guarded. You could tell that Wilson was fresh from home. (1948/2004: 32)

The sickness of the colony is also evident in the inadequacy of its administrators: Pemberton, the book's other suicide, leaves a note 'like a letter from school excusing a bad report' (78), while Harris is sufficiently desperate to contact the old boys association of a school at which he had been profoundly unhappy (135). These immature public school boys seem ill-suited to the burden of empire, and their presence situates *The Heart of the Matter* as one of many novels to emerge in the late 1940s that figure colonial cultures as claustrophobic and spiritually atrophied; replicas that rehearse at the periphery a model of British culture no longer sustainable at the centre. This instability is testimony to the imperial unrest that developed apace in the interwar years. In India, for example, the civil disobedience campaigns of the Indian National Congress had forced the British government into constitutional changes and an acknowledgement that 'sooner or later Indian self-government must come' (Darwin 1988: 82). The war complicated and accelerated this process, not only in India, but across Britain's territorial possessions. In her analysis of women writers' engagement with the end of empire, Phyllis Lassner argues that embedded in the defeat of Nazism and its project of racial extermination is a recognition of the untenable status of the imperial project 'however benign in its articulated mission' (2004: 7). Yet the knowledge that empire must change is not in itself an acceptance of the end of empire. Indeed, as John Darwin demonstrates, the colonies remained integral to conceptions of national identity and influence:

> Belief in the desirability of a strong British voice in world affairs was held just as firmly on the Left as on the Right of British politics. The colonies were not seen as useless encumbrances nor as a shameful legacy best disposed of, but as an opportunity for planned redevelopment. (Darwin 1988: 72)

In the light of these ideological and economic contradictions, it is perhaps a concept of 'unsettledness' (Lassner 2004: 11) that best describes the representation of empire in British postwar writing. Lassner uses the term to pinpoint the particular spatial and subjective relationships found in the work of writers such as Elspeth Huxley and Rumer Godden, but this state of dislocation also shapes the communities at the heart of texts as diverse as *The Heart of the Matter*, H. E. Bates's *The Jacaranda Tree* (1949) and Emma Smith's *The Far Cry* (1949). None of these novels directly addresses the end of empire – indeed both Greene and Bates set their fiction in wartime – but they nonetheless suggest, in their portraits of exiled British culture, a way of living denuded of all vitality. It is the all-pervading malaise of colonial culture that ensures that these fictions do not, to paraphrase Chinua Achebe, simply appropriate Africa or Burma as an exotic backdrop for the breakdown of the Western subject. Rather the background of these books exposes the inadequacy of colonial systems and the arrogance of the colonists' assumed superiority. The result is a literature characterised by competing discourses of annihilation and regeneration.

Bates's *The Jacaranda Tree* is the most confident in its annihilation and the most problematic in its regeneration. The novel concerns the attempt of a small British colony, based around a rice mill in Burma, to escape the advancing Japanese army. The ill-assorted community attempt to co-operate for the journey to the Indian border, but are torn apart by festering resentments focused around class, race and gender. Paterson, the manager, is the dominant male, his status ironically symbolised by his rejection of the group's values. He is a man of action and a man of few words, sufficiently self-reliant not to 'join the club' and openly keep a Burmese mistress. His reluctance to belong is unsurprising given the vampiric manner in which club society is depicted: 'other men, fresh to the town, were seized upon by the European colony as creatures bringing the stimulus of new blood to a tired stable' (1949/2006: 44). The undead quality of the colony is further demonstrated in the catalogue of its inhabitants' inadequacies. Betteson is a ditherer and Portman a coward, his superficial by-the-book correctness exposed by crisis. The women of the colony are similarly worthless, stereotypically condemned by their lack or excess of sexuality. Mrs Betteson, the 'batty' childless woman whose 'whitish, protuberant, almost albino-like eyes . . . waved about in their sockets like sterile flowers' (11), is set against the hypersexual Mrs Portman, who would rather sunbathe than take seriously the threat of Japanese invasion. Her absurdity is embodied in the narcissism that drives her to acquire from vanity, and with no sense of contradiction, the skin colour she despises in Paterson's lover Nadia (178).

It is not a pretty picture, and Bates's prose is remarkably judgemental, but as the journey progresses some redemptive possibilities emerge that suggest the complex imbrication of race and gender in this imagined community. Most of the Europeans die in a car crash caused by Portman's intemperance: but Mrs Betteson survives, to find redemption in the assumption of an almost masculine set of survival skills that suit her better than her redundant femininity. Shedding the trappings of a corrupt culture, she will join the Anglo-Burmese nurse Miss Allison in an ethic of service to the children of Burma. By becoming useful,

Mrs Betteson is forgiven her sterility. Usefulness, especially to men and children, is Bates's benchmark for women, and no woman fulfils this role more effectively than Nadia. She is the embodiment of her nation, much as 'the girl' was in *Fair Stood the Wind for France*, and her calm domesticity represents the 'simple' virtues of the uncorrupted Burmese. Bates's almost biblical vision of woman's role is encapsulated in Nadia's refusal to learn English. While her young brother, also devoted to Paterson, is described as 'passionate in a desire to amplify his English with new words', Nadia 'did not want to learn. It was as if it gave her greater secrecy with Paterson' (87). In representing Burma through the 'complaintless constancy' (168) of a subservient woman and child, the Burmese are inevitably figured as infant to the experience of Western civilisation. Tuesday, the boy, becomes a symbol of a potentially regenerated colonial Britishness, required to replace the decadent culture embodied by the westerners who have, over the course of the book, committed a form of race suicide through their crass stupidity.

Emma Smith's *The Far Cry* is more nuanced, presenting postwar India through the eyes of a poorly socialised and achingly lonely fourteen-year-old girl. Leaving England with a father she scarcely knows to escape the attentions of a mother she does not know at all, Teresa Digby begins the novel in a state of emotional numbness that is incomprehensible to her bombastic father, who disguises his own fear of change – and of his estranged ex-wife – by imagining himself as a great adventurer. Teresa's alienation is incrementally challenged throughout the novel, initially through the journey she must undertake, and then through the possibilities presented by India, a space made appealing by its absolute non-Britishness. Here Teresa 'sees' for the first time, awakening to a Woolfian epiphany of colour, and finds the anonymity of the crowd to be a space that liberates curiosity. Smith's debt to Woolf is evident in turns of phrase that echo the experiences of characters such as Lily Briscoe (1949/2002: 173) and a preoccupation with the subjective qualities of time and space. She also owes a debt to Forster, mobilising a modernised Mrs Moore in the shape of the self-contained spinster Miss Spooner, whose pleasure in the new world around her is a revelation to the inhibited Teresa. Miss Spooner offers Teresa the previously unknown experience of consistency: emotionally undemanding but intelligent companionship that permits to girl to find the anchor points of her previously inchoate identity. The clichés of colonial rule wash over Teresa, and they mean little to the other character who will provide the stability she so needs – her brother-in-law Edwin, a teaplanter. These three characters will survive the novel, each symbolising a negotiable mode of Britishness capable of encountering the otherness of India, while never assuming to understand or dominate it:

> After twelve years of living in the same part of India [Edwin] knew nothing, he sometimes alarmed his acquaintances by saying, about either India or the Indians. Nor did he want to. Nor did he expect to. He looked about him and liked almost everything he saw. He was curious, as a child is curious, about everything, only unlike a child he seldom asked why. He drew no conclusions and made no pronouncements. In this he was unusual, for even Mr Digby, after only a week or so on Indian soil, knew all about the Indian character and was quite ready to talk of it for hours. (1949/2002: 208)

Irrespective of age, Edwin, Miss Spooner and Teresa represent a new generation, while the old – symbolised by Mr Digby and his narcissistic daughter Ruth – will collapse under the contradictions of fighting an environment beyond their control. Ruth, constantly performing ideal-ised femininity, attempts to recreate England in exile. She finds herself with the perfect home and no-one to show it to, her material perfection rendered meaningless by the absence of an approving mirror. Brought up as an ideal, Ruth has no resources, and is caught in limbo; too weak to leave the colony, and too unhappy to adapt to her surroundings. Teresa is thus her antithesis: coming alive in an environment that does not notice her failure to embody English femininity, and lets her take shape as a subject capable of responding to an evolving idea of place and belonging.

In contrast to Bates and Smith, Phyllis Bottome brings the politics of colonialism centre stage. *Under the Skin* (1950) analyses the impact of racism through the narrative tropes of romance and melodrama. Lucy Armstrong, a decorated war hero who lost two lovers in the conflict, arrives on a Caribbean island to start a new life as head teacher of a mixed race school. The manipulative villain of the story, Elvira Loring, schemes constantly to get rid of Lucy, whose privileged whiteness has enabled her to take the job that Elvira believes is her due. Elvira is a classic *femme fatale* – her hyper-feminine seductive powers extend-ing, when it suits her, to pathological lesbianism – and her overblown characterisation sadly detracts from her legitimate grievances. As this unashamedly didactic novel explains, Elvira, and others who turn to the 'bad power' of Obeah, do so in order to 'overcome the evil power of their masters' (1950: 148): namely, the planter aristocracy who enjoy ownership of the island, as once their ancestors enjoyed ownership of slaves. Lucy, arriving with a patronising colonial mindset (54–5), finds her prejudices challenged by the man with whom she will fall in love, the West Indian doctor, Philip Calgary. Philip and a morally upright group of Chinese characters act as teachers to Lucy, and the book draws explicit parallels between fascism and the historical abuses of imperialism. The psychological legacy of colonialism is also made clear, as Philip explains the barriers to a mixed-race relationship:

> We dark people in countries owned and run by white ones drink in this agonizing sense of inferiority with our mother's milk. If we try to escape into the life of the mind we find you there before us! Our thoughts are coloured by your thoughts – inhibited by your restrictions. (204)

In permitting the union of Lucy and Philip, Bottome pushes further than most writers of her time against the fault-lines of colonial culture. She also makes explicit the fundamental issues of belonging and the fractured relationship between centre and periphery that would be central to debates about nation and empire in the 1950s.

As discussed in the Introduction, the events leading up to and consequent upon the arrival of the *Empire Windrush* symbolised the confusion surrounding the issue of who did and did not 'belong' to the nation. This uncertainty was also internal to the British Isles, where the events of the war had covered over, but not erased, the tensions between an imperial Englishness and its subject nations. While Northern Ireland – its protestant majority committed to the United Kingdom – had been presented with a devolved government it did not want (MacNeice 1990: 146), Wales in the late 1940s could not even persuade the government to acknowledge its difference with a government department (Morgan 1995: 194). This cultural insensitivity generated support for nationalist movements in both Wales and Scotland, and George Orwell, writing in *Tribune* in February 1947, suggested that more attention should be paid to 'the small but violent separatist movements which exist within our own island' (2006/2008: 364–5). His comment came in response to an instance of Anglophobia that had shocked him into a recognition that Scotland 'is almost an occupied country. You have an English or anglicised upper class, and a Scottish working class which speaks with a markedly different accent, or even, part of the time in a different language' (364). The languages of Scotland had been at the heart of the disagreements between two of the creative powerhouses behind the interwar Scottish literary renaissance: Edwin Muir and Hugh MacDiarmid. Did the future of Scottish literature lie in a cosmopolitan English-language literature or in the reinvigorating power of Scots and Gaelic writing? Anthologies of the time, such as Lindsay's *Modern Scottish Poetry* (1946), suggest the two were not wholly incompatible, but the conflicting claims of political and cultural nationalism were nonetheless sufficient to ensure that the war divided Scottish writers. Some, such as Norman MacCaig and Douglas Young, refused to participate; others – in particular Sorley MacLean and George Campbell Hay – responded in Gaelic; while J. F. Hendry and G. S. Fraser became part of a 'movement', the New Apocalypse, that united English, Welsh and Scottish poets. Surveying the period, Robert Crawford concludes that the cultural energies of the interwar renaissance were 'not entirely dissipated' by the conflict, and that Scottish writing would go on to develop 'in tandem a strong nationalist impulse and a corresponding cosmopolitanism', simultaneously looking inward for its subjects, and outwards past England to the fertile possibilities of European culture (2007: 606–9).

Wales too wanted little to do with English or British culture, but here the linguistic fault-lines were stronger, creating a sense of division rather than dialogue. Wyn Griffith, writing *The Voice of Wales* (1946) for the British Council, is vehement in his assertion that Welsh literature is a term that can only be applied to 'literature in the Welsh language', a claim that leads to the paradoxical categorisation of the new writers of an urban-industrial Anglophone South Wales – Richard Llewelyn, Jack Jones, Dylan Thomas, Gwyn Thomas – as contributors to 'the fund of English literature' (1946: 17). This literature, like the dominant voices of the Scottish renaissance, was 'proletarian in sympathy, socialist in conviction and internationalist in outlook' (Thomas 2003: 2), a profoundly different conception of a national ideal from that cherished by R. S. Thomas, who in the 1940s would learn Welsh 'in order to be able to return to the true Wales of my imagination' (quoted in Brown and Thomas 2003: 165). Yet whether nation is conceived in terms of land, language, history or community, what unites these writers is a fundamental antipathy to English imperialism:

> Important though it may be that writers of Welsh nationality should succeed in English, it is a thousand times more important that they should succeed in Welsh. [. . .] If the Welsh language were to die, Wales would become a geographical group of a few counties in Western England, a mere region, and the Welsh would cease to be a nation. What is particular to a people would be lost, and it would have little or nothing of its own to offer the world. (Griffith 1946: 38)

These anxieties and their colonial context might usefully be juxtaposed against the opinions of Mulk Raj Anand regarding the future of English in a newly liberated India. In *The King-Emperor's English* (1948) Anand distinguishes between positive and negative modes of cultural hybridity. There are two Englishes: the 'King's English' of Shakespeare, Milton, Wordsworth and all the other writers who have stimulated the imagination of Indo-Anglian writers, and 'brought the techniques of European literature into our country' (1948: 19); and there is the 'King-Emperor's

English', a debased language symbolising the bowdlerised education and negative hybridity of the 'Babu', a figure caught between cultures and condemned to be at home neither in traditional Indian nor colonial British culture (15). Anand is as scathing about the damage done by the one, as he is eloquent in support of the other. *The King-Emperor's English* is a succinct, witty plea for an internationalism of the mind that makes fun of the British, while embracing English as a medium for an as yet unimagined new literature. It is time, concludes Anand, for the British to 'take a few lessons in other people's languages' (50–1).

'The years that did not count'? Ending the 1940s

The years that did not count – Civilians in the towns
Remained at the same age as in Nineteen-Thirty-Nine,
                                          (MacNeice 1948/2007: 254)

Louis MacNeice's 'Hiatus' stops time in 1939, and yet this gap 'was too packed with fears and frowns' to have had no impact on those who lived through it. No wonder, the poem concludes, 'we wake stiff and older', facing an obscure future. MacNeice's description of the war years give some sense of why – psychologically and artistically – the 1940s remain so difficult to integrate into the narrative of twentieth-century British literature. As I suggested in the Introduction, the decade does not fit: its writing resists narratives of continuity and its legacy conforms to few, if any, canonical categories. MacNeice, for all his earlier associations with the Auden generation, is typical of this dislocation. Declaring he had never felt 'at home' in England (1990: 88), he nonetheless returned to Britain from America in December 1940. By 1941 he was working full time at the BBC producing more or less propagandist features and writing journalism for papers as diverse as *Picture Post* and the American periodical *Common Sense*. He became, thus, part of the documenting tradition, embracing in his reports on the Blitz 'a fantasy of destruction' he found paradoxically 'enlivening' (1941/1990: 118). He also, in his rapid adjustment to broadcasting, became part of the era's technologi-cal revolutions. The postwar saw him weary and in need of escape to Ireland, but producing innovative radio works, such as the symbolic drama *The Dark Tower* (1946), before his role at the BBC prompted a return to witness, reporting on Indian independence and the creation of Pakistan. This experience prompted more sober reflection than the Blitz. Arriving at the site of the Sheikhupura massacre, he reflects on the intimate horror of war between neighbours and warns against the presumption of judgement: 'And who were we to feel superior? Did we not come from twentieth-century Europe?' (1950/1990: 165). Yet for all MacNeice's travels, and his confident grasp of broadcasting, his poems of the late 1940s suggest the decade's characteristic inward turn. Peter McDonald argues that while 'MacNeice's Blitz poems had gestured towards a removal of the barriers between the self and others', a poem such as 'Aftermath' suggests 'unity replaced by separation' (1991: 133).

The 'atomising' of the political, then, is equally that of the private, and MacNeice's journey is emblematic of the decade's trajectory. Writers were pulled out of the familiar – whatever form that might have taken – and exposed to a 'new' both liberating and destructive. The Second World War imposed, ideologically and practically, a set of unprecedented constraints. Few writers took these lying down, and the results are all the more remarkable for the difficulties attendant on their production. But the stimulus of war was also and equally the strain of war: writers struggled to articulate their experience and turned nostalgically or critically to a more-or-less prelapsarian past. The struggle to find a language for what had been lost and to adjust to the anti-climax of victory, was in turn superseded by fear for the future. The latest war to end all wars had given rise to a wholly new war of attrition: the Cold War. And as if that were not enough, the atomic bomb now threatened annihilation beyond any previous imagining. The overwhelming nature of the Second World War had seen writers turn to the documentation of the quotidian; the overwhelming nature of its aftermath sent them instead to the personal and the intimate, and to an renewed interrogation of land, home and belonging. But, as the tentative emergence of postcolonial discourses suggest, the meanings of such concepts were far from stable, and in a poet such as R. S. Thomas, they offer little hope of regeneration. *The Stones of the Field* (1946), his first collection, captures the harshness of the 'bald Welsh hills' in sparse, pared-back language (1946: 14). That image, of an unyielding landscape figured in terms of an equally unyielding humanity, opens perhaps the most famous of the collection's poems, 'A Peasant', in which Thomas introduces the recurring figure of Iago Prytherch. This is humanity's 'prototype', eking a living from the crude earth, 'his spittled mirth/ Rarer than the sun that cracks the cheeks/ Of the gaunt sky perhaps once a week' (1946: 14). Prytherch's mind is 'frightening' in its vacancy, but, cautions Thomas, 'he, too, is a winner of wars' (14). International political struggle is distilled to the brute fact of man's battle for survival in a hostile environment. Is Prytherch's resilience a triumph or an indictment? It is hard to say, but his continuance is automatic, unconscious; a mode of being that reduces humanity to its bare – almost animal – essentials.

Thomas's peasant, like the primeval wanderers of Sitwell's poetry, the black market of Greene's Vienna, and Orwell's 'boot stamping on a human face – for ever', suggest a fundamental pessimism colouring the literature of the late 1940s. It is, in the final analysis, difficult to write when 'highly civilized human beings are flying overhead, trying to kill [you]' (Orwell, 1941/1970: 74), and not much easier when you are weary, anxious and struggling to adjust to a new world order. But Britain in 1950 was not Oceania, and *ownlife* would return to those frustrated by rationing and the restrictions imposed by austerity. The Introduction ended by invoking Bowen's state of 'lucid abnormality'. The years that followed the war could not maintain this heightened sense of alert, but they did begin a crucial process of digestion: the absorbing of almost unimaginable change and the slow, uncertain embrace of a world being reshaped by the technological legacy of war. The end of the 1940s was not only the inception of the Cold War; it was also the beginning of the jet age and the birth of the teenager. Modern Britain had arrived.

Works Cited

Aitken, Ian (ed.) (1998), *The Documentary Film Movement: An Anthology*, Edinburgh: Edinburgh University Press.

Aldgate, Anthony and Jeffrey Richards (1986/1994), *Britain Can Take It: The British Cinema in the Second World War*, Edinburgh: Edinburgh University Press.

Allingham, Margery (1941/2006), *Traitor's Purse*, London: Vintage.

—(1941/2011), *The Oaken Heart*, Pleshey, Essex: Golden Duck.

—(1945/1987), *Coroner's Pidgin*, London: J. M. Dent.

Allport, Alan (2009), *Demobbed: Coming Home After the Second World War*, New Haven: Yale University Press.

Ambler, Eric (1940/2002), *Journey into Fear*, New York: Vintage Crime.

Anand, Mulk Raj (1942/1986), *The Sword and the Sickle*, Liverpool: Lucas Publications.

—(1948), *The King-Emperor's English*, Bombay: Hind Kitabs.

Anderson, Lindsay (1953/2004), 'Only Connect: Some Aspects of the Work of Humphrey Jennings', in Ryan (ed), 2004, pp. 358–64.

Auden, W. H. (1945), *For the Time Being*, London: Faber.

—(1948), *The Age of Anxiety*, London: Faber.

Babington, Bruce (2002), *Launder and Gilliat*, Manchester: Manchester University Press.

Baker, Phil (2009), *The Devil is A Gentleman: The Life and Times of Dennis Wheatley*, Sawtry: Dedalus.

Balchin, Nigel (1942/2002), *Darkness Falls From the Air*, London: Cassell.

—(1943/1958), *The Small Back Room*, Harmondsworth: Penguin.

—(1945/1947), *Mine Own Executioner*, London: The Reprint Society.

Balcon, Michael (1969), *Michael Balcon Presents . . . A Lifetime of Films*, London: Hutchinson.

Baring, Nora (1946), *A Friendly Hearth*, London: Jonathan Cape.

Baron, Alexander (1948/2010), *From the City, From the Plough*, London: Black Spring Press.

Bates, H. E. (1944/2005), *Fair Stood the Wind for France*, London: Penguin.

—(1949/2006), *The Jacaranda tree*, London: Methuen.

—(1952/2002), *How Sleep the Brave: The Complete Stories of Flying Officer X*, London: Vintage.

Bax, Clifford and Meum Stewart (eds) (1949), *The Distaff Muse*, London: Hollis & Carter.

Baxendale, John (2007), *Priestley's England: J. B. Priestley and English Culture*, Manchester: Manchester University Press.

Beardmore, George (1984/1986), *Civilians at War: Journals 1938–1946*, Oxford: Oxford University Press.

Beattie, Keith (2010), *Humphrey Jennings*, Manchester: Manchester University Press.

Bell, Kathleen (1995), 'Cross-Dressing in Wartime: Georgette Heyer's *The Corinthian* in its 1940 Context' in Kirkham and Thoms, 1995.

Bell, Mary Hayley (1943), *Men in Shadow*, London: Samuel French (first perf. 1942).

—(1947), *Duet for Two Hands*, London: Samuel French (first perf. 1945).

Bennett, Andrew and Nicholas Royle (1995), *Elizabeth Bowen and the Dissolution of the Novel: Still Lives*, Basingstoke: Macmillan.

Bergonzi, Bernard (1993), *Wartime and Aftermath: English Literature and its Background, 1939–1960*, Oxford: Oxford University Press.

Berridge, Elizabeth (2000), *Tell It To A Stranger*, London: Persephone.

Betjeman, John (1945), *New Bats in Old Belfries*, London: John Murray.

Bluemel, Kristin (2004), *George Orwell and the Radical Eccentrics: Intermodernism in Literary London*, London: Palgrave.

—(ed.) (2009), *Intermodernism: Literary Culture in Mid-Twentieth-Century Britain*, Edinburgh: Edinburgh University Press.

Bolton, Jonathan (1997), *Personal Landscapes: British Poets in Egypt during the Second World War*, London: Macmillan.

Bottome, Phyllis (1941), *London Pride*, London: Faber.

—(1943), *Within the Cup*, London: Faber.

—(1950), *Under the Skin*, London: Faber.

Bourke, Joanna (1999), *An Intimate History of Killing: Face to Face Killing in Twentieth-Century Warfare*, No Place: Basic Books.

Bowen, Elizabeth (1945), *The Demon Lover*, London: Cape.

—(1948/1962), *The Heat of the Day*, London: Penguin.

—(1950), *Collected Impressions*, London: Longmans Green and Co.

—(1980/1983), *The Collected Stories of Elizabeth Bowen*, London: Penguin.

Bradbury, Malcolm (1987), '"Closing Time in the Gardens" or, What Happened to Writing in the 1940s?' in *No, Not Bloomsbury*, London: Andre Deutsch.

Brand, Christianna (1945/1999), *Green for Danger*, London: Pan.

Brannigan, John (2003), *Orwell to the Present, 1945–2000*, London: Palgrave.

Bridie, James (1944), *Plays for Plain People*, London: Constable.

—(2007), *The Devil to Stage: Five Plays by James Bridie*, ed. Gerard Carruthers, Glasgow: ASLS.

Brittain, Vera (1941), *England's Hour*, London: Macmillan.

—(1945), *Account Rendered*, London: Macmillan.

Brome, Vincent (1988), *J. B. Priestley*, London: Hamish Hamilton.

Brown, Tony and M. Wynn Thomas (2003), 'The Problems of Belonging', in Thomas (ed.) 2003.

Burlingham, Dorothy and Anna Freud (1942), *Young Children in War-Time in a Residential War Nursery*, London: George Allen & Unwin.

Buster, Gun (1940), *Return Via Dunkirk*, London: Hodder & Stoughton.
Butler, Judith (2004), *Precarious Life: The Powers of Mourning and Violence*, London: Verso.
—(2009/2010), *Frames of War, When Is Life Grievable?*, London: Verso.
Calder, Angus (1969/1992), *The People's War: Britain 1939–1945*, London: Pimlico.
Calder, Angus and Dorothy Sheridan (eds) (1984), *Speak for Yourself: A Mass Observation Anthology, 1937–49*, London: Cape.
Calder, Jenni (1968), *Chronicles of Conscience: A Study of George Orwell and Arthur Koestler*, London: Secker and Warburg.
—(1997), *The Nine Lives of Naomi Mitchison*, London: Virago.
Campbell, James (1999), 'Combat Gnosticism: The Ideology of First World War Poetry Criticism' in *New Literary History*, Vol. 30, No. 1 (Winter 1999), pp. 203–15.
Cary, Joyce (1940), *Charley Is My Darling*, London: Michael Joseph.
—(1941/1968), *Herself Surprised*, London: Calder and Boyars.
—(1942/2009), *To Be A Pilgrim*, London: Faber and Faber.
—(1944/1948), *The Horse's Mouth*, London: Penguin.
Cesarani, David (1998/1999), *Arthur Koestler: The Homeless Mind*, London: Vintage.
Chandler, Raymond (1950/1964), 'The Simple Art of Murder' in *Pearls are a Nuisance*, London: Penguin.
Cheyette, Bryan (1993), *Constructions of 'The Jew' in English Literature and Society: Racial Representations, 1875–1945*, Cambridge; Cambridge University Press.
Cheyette, Bryan and Laura Marcus (eds) (1995), *Modernity, Culture and 'The Jew'*, Cambridge: Polity Press.
Christie, Agatha (1941/1962), *N or M?*, London: Fontana.
—(1942/1994), *The Body in the Library*, London: Harper Collins.
—(1943/1950), *The Moving Finger*, London: Pan.
—(1975/1977), *Curtain*, London: Fontana.
Clune, Michael (2004), 'Orwell and the Obvious', *Representations*, 107, Summer 2009; pp. 30–55.
Collini, Stefan (2008), *Common Reading: Critics, Historians, Publics*, Oxford: Oxford University Press.
Collins, Norman (1945/2008), *London Belongs to Me*, London: Penguin.
Colls, Robert (2002/2004), *Identity of England*, Oxford: Oxford University Press.
Compton-Burnett, Ivy (1947), *Manservant and Maidservant*, London: Gollancz.
Connell, R. W. (1995), *Masculinities*, Cambridge: Polity Press.
Cooper, John Xiros (1995), *T. S. Eliot and the Ideology of Four Quartets*, Cambridge: Cambridge University Press.
Cooper, Susan (1963/1986), 'Snoek Piquante', in Sissons and French (1963/1986).
Costello, John (1987), *Virtue Under Fire: How World War II Changed Our Social and Sexual Attitudes*, New York: Fromm International Publishing.
Coulton, Barbara (1980), *Louis MacNeice in the BBC*, London: Faber.
Coward, Noël (1941/1999), *Blithe Spirit*, New York: Vintage International.
—(1954), *Future Indefinite*, London: William Heinemann.
Crawford, Robert (2007), *Scotland's Books*, London: Penguin.

Croft, Andy (1990), *Red Letter Days: British Fiction in the 1930s*, London: Lawrence and Wishart.

Dahl, Roald (1946/2010), *Over to You: Ten Stories or Flyers and Flying*, London: Penguin.

Darwin, John (1988), *Britain and Decolonisation: The Retreat from Empire in the Post-War World*, Basingstoke: Macmillan.

Darlow, Michael and Gillian Hodson (1979), *Terence Rattigan: The Man and His Work*, London: Quartet Books.

Davison, Peter (1996), *George Orwell: A Literary Life*, London: Macmillan.

Delafield, E. M. (1940/1984), *The Provincial Lady in Wartime*, in *The Diary of a Provincial Lady*, London: Virago.

Dickens, Monica (1942/1956), *One Pair of Feet*, London: Penguin.

—(1943/1964), *The Fancy*, London: Penguin.

—(1946/1958), *The Happy Prisoner*, London: Penguin.

Douglas, Keith (1946/1992), *Alamein to Zem Zem*, London: Faber.

—(1978/2000), *The Complete Poems*, London: Faber.

Du Maurier, Daphne (1941/1976), *Frenchman's Creek*, London: Pan.

—(1945/1994), *The Years Between*, in Morgan (1994).

—(1946/1962), *The King's General*, London: Penguin.

Dudley Edwards, Owen (2007), *British Children's Fiction in the Second World War*, Edinburgh: Edinburgh University Press.

Duncan, Ronald (1946), *This Way to the Tomb*, London: Faber.

Dyer, Richard (1979/1998), *Stars*, London: BFI.

Easthope, Anthony (1990/1992), *What A Man's Gotta Do: The Masculine Myth in Popular Culture*, London: Routledge.

Eliot, T. S. (1944/2001), *Four Quartets*, London: Faber.

—(1948), *Notes towards the Definition of Culture*, London: Faber.

—(1950), *The Cocktail Party*, London: Faber.

—(1963/1974), *Collected Poems 1909–1962*, London: Faber.

Ellis, Steve (1991), *The English Eliot: design, language and landscape in 'Four Quartets'*, London: Routledge.

Ellmann, Maud (2003), *Elizabeth Bowen: The Shadow Across the Page*, Edinburgh: Edinburgh University Press.

Empson, William (1987), *Argufying: Essays on Literature and Culture,* ed. John Haffenden, London: Chatto & Windus.

Esty, Jed (2004), *A Shrinking Island: Modernism and National Culture in England*, Princeton: Princeton University Press.

Evans, B. Ifor (1946), *The Shop on the King's Road*, London: Hodder & Stoughton.

Ferguson, Frances (1996), 'Romantic Memory', *Studies in Romanticism*, 35, pp. 509–33.

Ferrer, Daniel (1990), *Virginia Woolf and the Madness of Language*, London: Routledge.

Forester, C. S. (1943/2006), *The Ship*, London: Penguin.

Forster, Peter (1963/1986), 'J. Arthur Rank and the Shrinking Screen' in Sissons and French (eds), 1963/1986.

Francis, Martin (2008), *The Flyer: British Culture and the Royal Air Force 1939–1945*, Oxford: Oxford University Press.

Freud, Anna with Dorothy Burlingham (1974), *Infants Without Families and Reports on the Hampstead Nurseries 1939–1945*, London: Hogarth Press.

Freud, Sigmund (1953/2001) [1905], 'Three Essays on the Theory of Sexuality' in James Strachey (ed.), *The Standard Edition of the Complete Psychological Works of Sigmund Freud*, Vol. VII, London: Vintage.

—(1957/2001) [1917], 'Mourning and Melancholia' in James Strachey (ed.), *The Standard Edition of the Complete Psychological Works of Sigmund Freud*, Vol. XIV, London: Vintage.

—(1955/2001) [1919], 'The Uncanny' in James Strachey (ed.), *The Standard Edition of the Complete Psychological Works of Sigmund Freud*, Vol. XVII, London: Vintage.

Fry, Christopher (1949/2007), *The Lady's Not For Burning*, in *Plays One*, London: Oberon Books.

Fussell, Paul (1989), *Wartime: Understanding and behaviour in the Second World War*, New York: Oxford University Press.

Gaitens, Edward (1948/1990), *Dance of the Apprentices*, Edinburgh: Canongate.

Gardner, Brian (ed.) (1966/1999), *The Terrible Rain: The War Poets 1939–1945*, London: Methuen.

Garfield, Simon (ed.) (2004/2005), *Our Hidden Lives: The Remarkable Diaries of Post-War Britain*, London: Ebury Press.

Gay, Peter (1989/1995), *The Freud Reader*, London: Vintage.

Gibbons, Stella (1946/2011), *Westwood*, London: Vintage.

Glendinning, Victoria (1981/1993), *Edith Sitwell: A Unicorn Among Lions*, London: Phoenix.

Goldman, Jane (2004), *Image to Apocalypse*, London: Palgrave.

Goodby, John (2010), 'Dylan Thomas and the Poetry of the 1940s', in O'Neill, 2010.

Graham, Desmond (1974), *Keith Douglas*, London: Oxford University Press.

Green, F. L. (1945/1991), *Odd Man Out*, London: Cardinal.

Green, Henry (1940/2000), *Pack My Bag*, London: Vintage.

—(1943/2001) *Caught*, London: Harvill.

—(1945/2000), *Loving*, London: Vintage.

—(1946/1998), *Back*, London: Harvill.

Greene, Graham (1940/2004), *The Power and the Glory*, London: Vintage.

—(1943/2001), *The Ministry of Fear*, London: Vintage.

—(1948/2004), *The Heart of the Matter*, London: Vintage.

—(1950/1976), *The Third Man*, London: Penguin.

Griffith, Wyn (1946), *The Voice of Wales*, London: Longman, Green and Co.

Gubar, Susan (1987), '"This Is My Rifle, This Is My Gun": World War II and the Blitz on Women', in Higonnet et al. (1987).

Gun Buster (1940), *Return Via Dunkirk*, London: Hodder & Stoughton.

Gunn, Neil (1941/1969), *The Silver Darlings*, London: Faber.

Habermann, Ina (2010), *Myth, Memory and the Middlebrow: Priestley, du Maurier and the Symbolic Form of Englishness*, London: Palgrave.

Haffenden, John (ed.) (1983), *W. H. Auden: The Critical Heritage*, London: Routledge & Kegan Paul.

Halberstam, Judith (1998), *Female Masculinity*, Durham, NC: Duke University Press.

Hamilton, Patrick (1941/1966), *Hangover Square*, London: Panther.
—(1947/2006), *The Slaves of Solitude*, London: Constable.
Hampton, Janie (2008), *The Austerity Olympics: When the Games Came to London in 1948*, London: Aurum.
Hanley, James (1943/1990). *No Directions*, London: André Deutsch.
Harper, Sue (1994), *Picturing the Past: The Rise and Fall of the British Costume Film*, London: BFI.
Harrold, R. F. (1940), 'Peace Aims and Economics' in *Horizon*, Vol. I, No. 3, March 1940.
Hartley, Jenny (1997), *Millions Like Us: British Women's Fiction of the Second World War*, London: Virago.
Hartley, L. P. (1944/2000), *The Shrimp and the Anemone*, London: Faber.
—(1958/2001), *Eustace and Hilda*, New York: New York Review Books.
Hastings, Selina (1985), *Nancy Mitford: A Biography*, London: Hamish Hamilton.
—(1994), *Evelyn Waugh, A Biography*, London: Sinclair Stevenson.
Hayes, Nick and Jeff Hill (eds) (1999), *'Millions Like Us'? British Culture in the Second World War*, Liverpool: Liverpool University Press.
Hendry, J. F. and Henry Treece (eds) (1941), *The White Horseman: Prose and Verse of the New Apocalypse*, London: Routledge.
Hennessey, Peter (1992/1993), *Never Again: Britain 1945–1951*, London: Vintage.
Hewison, Robert (1977/1988), *Under Siege: Literary Life in London, 1939–1945*, London: Methuen.
—(1981/1988), *In Anger: Culture in the Cold War 1945-1960*, London: Methuen.
Heyer, Georgette (1940/2004), *The Corinthian*, London: Arrow.
—(1944/ 2004), *Friday's Child*, London: Arrow.
—(1946/2004), *The Reluctant Widow*, London: Arrow.
Higonnet, Margaret Randolph, Jane Jenson, Sonya Michel and Margaret Collins Weitz (eds) (1987), *Behind the Lines: Gender and the Two World Wars*, New Haven: Yale University Press.
Hill, Diana Murray (1944), *Ladies May Now Leave Their Machines*, London: Pilot.
Hillary, Richard (1942/1997), *The Last Enemy*, London: Pimlico.
Hirsch, Pam (2010), *The Constant Liberal: The Life and Work of Phyllis Bottome*, London: Quartet.
Hoare, Philip (1995), *Noël Coward: A Biography*, London: Sinclair Stevenson.
Hodge, Jane Aiken (1984), *The Private World of Georgette Heyer*, London: Arrow Books.
Hodgson, Vere (1971/1999), *Few Eggs and No Oranges: The Diaries of Vere Hodgson 1940–45*, London: Persephone.
Holden, Inez (1941), *Night Shift*, London: John Lane.
—(1943), *It Was Different At the Time*, London: John Lane.
—(1944), *There's No Story There*, London: John Lane.
Holderness, Graham, Bryan Loughrey and Hahem Yousaf (eds) (1998), *George Orwell*, Basingstoke: Macmillan.
Humble, Nicola (2002), *The Feminine Middlebrow Novel, 1920s to 1950s*, Oxford: Oxford University Press.

Irwin, Margaret (1944/1998), *Young Bess*, London: Allison and Busby.
—(1948/1999), *Elizabeth, Captive Princess*, London: Allison and Busby.
Jackson, Kevin (ed) (1993), *The Humphrey Jennings Film Reader*, Manchester: Carcanet.
—(2004), *Humphrey Jennings*, Basingstoke: Picador.
Jameson, Storm (1943/1945), *Cloudless May*, London: Macmillan.
—(1947), *The Black Laurel*, London: Macmillan.
Jolly, Margaretta (ed.) (1997), *Dear Laughing Motorbyke: Letters from Women Welders of the Second World War*, London: Scarlet.
Johns, W. E. (1940), *Biggles in the Baltic*, Oxford: Oxford University Press.
—(1941), *Spitfire Parade*, Oxford: Oxford University Press.
—(1941), *Worrals of the W.A.A.F.*, Glasgow: Lutterworth Press.
—(1943), *King of the Commandos*, Oxford: Oxford University Press.
Johnson, Pamela Hansford (1948/1954), *A Summer to Decide*, Harmondsworth: Penguin.
Judt, Tony (2008/2009), *Reappraisals: Reflections on the Forgotten Twentieth Century*, London: Vintage.
Kennedy, A. L. (1997), *The Life and Death of Colonel Blimp*, London: BFI Publishing.
Keyes, Sidney (1945/2002), *Collected Poems*, Manchester: Carcanet.
King-Hall, Magdalen (1944/1974), *Life and Death of the Wicked Lady Skelton*, London: P. Davies.
Kirkham, Pat and David Thoms (eds) (1995), *War Culture: Social Change and Changing Experience in World War Two*, London: Lawrence and Wishart.
Klein, Holger (ed.) (1984), *The Second World War in Fiction*, London: Macmillan.
Knight, Stephen (1995), 'Murder in Wartime', in Kirkham and Thoms 1995.
Knowles, Sebastian D. G. (1990), *A Purgatorial Flame Seven British Writers in the Second World War*, Bristol: The Bristol Press.
Koestler, Arthur (1940/1994), *Darkness at Noon*, London: Vintage.
—(1941/2006), *The Scum of the Earth*, London: Eland.
—(1943/1999), *Arrival and Departure*, London: Vintage.
—(1944), 'On Disbelieving Atrocities', in Koestler (1945/1983).
—(1945/1983), *The Yogi and the Commissar and Other Essays*, London: Hutchinson.
Kushner, Tony (1996), 'Anti-Semitism and Austerity: The August 1947 riots in Britain', in Panayi (ed.) 1996.
—(1998), 'Remembering to Forget: Racism and Anti-Racism in Postwar Britain', in Cheyette and Marcus (eds) 1998.
Kynaston, David (2007), *Austerity Britain 1945–51*, London: Bloomsbury.
Larkin, Philip (1946/2005), *Jill*, London: Faber.
—(1947/1975), *A Girl in Winter*, London: Faber.
Laski, Marghanita (1949/2001), *Little Boy Lost*, London: Persephone Books.
Lassner, Phyllis (1997), *British Women Writers of World War II: Battlegrounds of their Own*, Basingstoke: Macmillan.
—(2004), *Colonial Strangers: Women Writing the End of the British Empire*, New Brunswick: Rutgers University Press.
Leavis, F. R. (1948/1972), *The Great Tradition*, Harmondsworth: Penguin.

Lehmann, Rosamund (1944/1982), *The Ballad and the Source*, London: Virago.
—(1946/1972), *The Gypsy's Baby and Other Stories*, London: Collins.
Lewis, Alun (1942), *Raider's Dawn and Other Poems*, London: Allen and Unwin.
—(1948/2006), *In the Green Tree*, Cardigan: Parthian/Library of Wales.
—(1990), *Collected Stories*, ed. Cary Archard, Bridgend: Seren Books.
Lewis, C. S. (1943), *Perelandra*, London: John Lane.
—(1950/1991), *The Lion, the Witch and the Wardrobe*, London: HarperCollins.
Light, Alison (1991), *Forever England: Femininity, Literature and Conservatism Between the Wars*, London: Routledge.
Lindsay, Maurice (ed.) (1946), *Modern Scottish Poetry: An Anthology of the Scottish Renaissance 1920–1945*, London: Faber.
Linklater, Eric (1946/1992), *Private Angelo*, Edinburgh: Canongate.
Lowry, Malcolm (1947/1962), *Under the Volcano*, Harmondsworth: Penguin.
Lycett, Andrew (2003/2004), *Dylan Thomas: A New Life*, London: Phoenix.
McAleer, Joseph (1992), *Popular Reading and Publishing in Britain 1914–1950*, Oxford: Clarendon Press.
Macaulay, Rose (1946), 'The Best and the Worst: II – Evelyn Waugh' in *Horizon*, Vol. XIV, No. 84, December 1946.
—(1950/1983), *The World My Wilderness*, London: Virago.
McDonald, Peter (1991), *Louis MacNeice: The Poet in his Contexts*, Oxford: Clarendon Press.
McDonnell, Jacqueline (1986), *Waugh on Women*, London: Duckworth.
MacInnes, Helen (1942), *Assignment in Brittany*, London: Harrap & Co.
MacKay, Marina (2007), *Modernism and World War II*, Cambridge: Cambridge University Press.
—(ed.) (2009), *The Cambridge Companion to the Literature of World War II*, Cambridge: Cambridge University Press.
McKibbin, Ross (1998), *Classes and Cultures: England 1918–1951*, Oxford: Oxford University Press.
McLaine, Ian (1979), *Ministry of Morale: Home Front Morale and the Ministry of Information in World War II*, London: George Allen & Unwin.
Maclaren-Ross, Julian (1944), *The Stuff to Give the Troops*, London: Jonathan Cape.
—(1947/2002), *Of Love and Hunger*, London: Penguin.
—(1965/1991), *Memoirs of the Forties*, London: Cardinal.
McLeish, Robert (2008), *The Gorbals Story* in Bill Findlay (ed.), *Scottish People's Theatre: Plays By Glasgow Unity Writers*, Glasgow: ASLS.
McLoughlin, Kate (2009), *The Cambridge Companion to War Writing*, Cambridge: Cambridge University Press.
—(2011), *Authoring War: The Literary Representation of War from the* Iliad *to* Iraq, Cambridge: Cambridge University Press.
MacNeice, Louis (1990), *Selected Prose of Louis MacNeice*, ed. Alan Heuser, Oxford: Clarendon Press.
—(2007), *Collected Poems*, London: Faber.
—(2010), *Letters of Louis MacNeice*, ed. Jonathan Allison, London: Faber.
Marcus, Steven (1984), *Freud and the Culture of Psychoanalysis: Studies in the Transition from Victorian Humanism to Modernity*, Boston: George Allen Unwin.

Masefield, John (1941), *The Nine Days Wonder*, London: Heinemann.

—(1942), *Land Workers*, London: Heinemann.

Mass Observation (1947), *Peace and the Public – A Study By Mass Observation*, London: Longmans, Green and Co.

Maugham, Somerset, (1944/2000), *The Razor's Edge*, London: Vintage.

Mellor, Leo (2011), *Reading the Ruins: Modernism, Bombsites and British Culture*, Cambridge: Cambridge University Press.

Mengham, Rod (1982), *The Idiom of the Time: The Writings of Henry Green*, Cambridge: Cambridge University Press.

Mengham, Rod and N. H. Reeve (eds) (2001), *The Fiction of the 1940s*, London: Palgrave.

Miller, Betty (1941/2000), *Farewell Leicester Square*, London: Persephone.

—(1945), *On the Side of the Angels*, London: Robert Hale.

Miller, Kristine A. (2009), *British Literature of the Blitz: Fighting the People's War*, London: Palgrave.

Miller, Tyrus (1999), *Late Modernism: Politics, Fiction, and the Arts Between the World Wars*, Berkeley: University of California Press.

Mitchell, Gladys (1945/1996), *The Rising of the Moon*, London: Virago.

Mitchison, Naomi (1985/1986), *Among You Taking Notes: The Wartime Diary of Naomi Mitchison, 1939–1945*, London: Oxford University Press.

—(1947), *The Bull Calves*, London: Jonathan Cape.

Mitford, Nancy (1940/1961), *Pigeon Pie*, London: Penguin.

—(1945/1986), *The Pursuit of Love*, London: Penguin.

Montefiore, Jan (2009) 'Englands Ancient and Modern: Sylvia Townsend Warner, T. H. White and the Fictions of Medieval Englishness', in Bluemel 2009.

Morgan, Fidelis (ed.) (1994), *The Years Between: Plays by Women on the London Stage 1900–1950*, London: Virago.

Morgan, Kenneth O. (1990), *The People's Peace: British History 1945–1990*, Oxford: Oxford University Press.

—(1995), *Modern Wales: Politics, Places and People*, Cardiff: University of Wales Press.

Mosley, Charlotte (ed.) (1996), *The Letters of Nancy Mitford and Evelyn Waugh*, London: Hodder & Stoughton.

Morrisson, Mark S. (2002), 'Edith Sitwell's Atomic Bomb Poems: Alchemy and Scientific Reintegration', *Modernism/Modernity*, Vol. 9, No. 4, Nov. 2002, pp. 605–33.

Newsinger, John (2007), 'Orwell, Anti-Semitism and the Holocaust' in Rodden 2007.

Nicholas, Sian (1996), *The Echo of War: Home Front Propaganda and the Wartime BBC*, Manchester: Manchester University Press.

Nicholson, Norman (1946), *The Old Man of the Mountains*, London: Faber.

Noble, Barbara (1946/2005), *Doreen*, London: Persephone.

Noble, Peter (1946), *British Theatre*, London: British Yearbooks.

O'Neill, Michael (ed.) (2010), *The Cambridge History of English Poetry*, Cambridge: Cambridge University Press.

Orwell, George (1942/1970), 'London Letter to *Partisan Review*' in Orwell 1970.

—(1944/1965), 'Raffles and Miss Blandish', in Orwell 1965.

—(1945/1951), *Animal Farm*, Harmondsworth: Penguin.

—(1946/1965), 'The Decline of the English Murder', in Orwell 1965.

—(1949/1989), *Nineteen Eighty-Four*, London: Penguin.

—(1965), *The Decline of the English Murder*, London: Penguin.

—(1970), *The Collected Essays, Journalism and Letters of George Orwell: Volume 2*, London: Penguin.

—(2006/2008), *Orwell in Tribune*, ed. Paul Anderson, London: Methuen.

Panayi, Panikos (ed.) (1996), *Racial Violence in Britain in the Nineteenth and Twentieth Centuries*, London: Leicester University Press.

Panter-Downes, Mollie (1947), *One Fine Day*, Boston: Little, Brown and Company.

—(1999), *Good Evening, Mrs Craven: The Wartime Stories of Mollie Panter-Downes*, London: Persephone.

Paris, Michael (2000), *Warrior Nation: Images of War in British Popular Culture, 1850–2000*, London: Reaktion Books.

Partridge, Frances (1978/1996), *A Pacifist's War*, London: Phoenix.

Patey, Douglas Lane (1998), *The Life of Evelyn Waugh: A Critical Biography*, Oxford: Blackwell.

Paul, Kathleen (1997), *Whitewashing Britain: Race and Citizenship in the Postwar Era*, Ithaca: Cornell University Press.

Peake, Mervyn (1946/1998), *Titus Groan*, London: Vintage.

Pfau, Thomas (2005), *Romantic Moods: Paranoia, Trauma and Melancholy, 1750–1840*, Baltimore: Johns Hopkins University Press.

Piette, Adam (1995), *Imagination at War: British Fiction and Poetry 1939–45*, London: Macmillan.

—(2009), *The Literary Cold War 1945 to Vietnam*, Edinburgh: Edinburgh University Press.

Plain, Gill (1996), *Women's Fiction of the Second World War: Gender, Power and Resistance*, Edinburgh: Edinburgh University Press.

—(2001), *Twentieth-Century Crime Fiction: Gender, Sexuality and the Body*, Edinburgh: Edinburgh University Press.

—(2003), '"A Good Cry or a Nice Rape": Margery Allingham's Gender Agenda', *Critical Survey*, Vol. 15, No. 2.

—(2006), *John Mills and British Cinema: Masculinity, Identity and Nation*, Edinburgh: Edinburgh University Press.

Priestley, J. B. (1940), *Postscripts*, London: Heinemann.

—(1941), 'When Work Is Over', *Picture Post*, Vol. 10, No. 1; January 4, 1941.

—(1942), *Blackout in Gretley: A Story of – and for – Wartime*, London: Heinemann.

—(1943), *Daylight on Saturday*, London: Heinemann.

—(1944), *They Came to A City*, London: Samuel French (first perf. 1943).

—(1945), *Three Men in New Suits*, London: Heinemann.

—(1946), *Bright Day*, London: Heinemann.

—(1947/2000), *An Inspector Calls*, in *An Inspector Calls and Other Plays*, London: Penguin.

Pritchett, V. S. (1942), *In My Good Books*, Chatto & Windus.

Pudney, John and Henry Treece (eds) (1944), *Air Force Poetry*, London: John Lane.

Rattigan, Terrence (1953/2011), *Flare Path*, London: Nick Hern Books (first perf. 1942).

—(1944), *While the Sun Shines*, London: Hamish Hamilton (first perf. 1943).

—(1946/1994), *The Winslow Boy*, London: Nick Hern Books.

Rau, Petra (2009), *English Modernism, National Identity and the Germans, 1890–1950*, Farnham: Ashgate.

—(ed.) (2010), *Conflict, Nationhood and Corporeality in Modern Literature: Bodies-at-War*, London: Palgrave.

Rawlinson, Mark (2000), *British Writing of the Second World War*, Oxford: Clarendon Press.

Rebellato, Dan (1994), 'Introduction', in Rattigan (1946/1994).

Reilly, Catherine (1984), *Chaos of the Night: Women's Poetry and Verse of the Second World War*, London: Virago.

Renault, Mary (1944/1984), *The Friendly Young Ladies*, London: Virago.

Rhys, Keidrych (1941), *Poems from the Forces*, London: Routledge.

—(1944), *Modern Welsh Poetry*, London: Faber.

Ridler, Anne (1946), *The Shadow Factory*, London: Faber.

Roberts, Lynette (2005), *Collected Poems*, ed. Patrick McGuinness, Manchester: Carcanet.

Rodden, John (1989), *The Politics of Literary Representation: The Making and Claiming of 'St. George' Orwell*, Oxford: Oxford University Press.

—(2007), *The Cambridge Companion to George Orwell*, Cambridge: Cambridge University Press.

Rolf, David (1988), *Prisoners of the Reich: Germany's Captives 1939–45*, London: Leo Cooper.

Rorty, Richard (1998), 'The Last Intellectual in Europe' in Holderness et al. (eds) 1998.

Rose, Sonya (2003), *Which People's War: National Identity and Citizenship in Wartime Britain, 1939–1945*, Oxford: Oxford University Press.

Roston, Murray (2006), *Graham Greene's Narrative Strategies: A Study of the Major Novels*, Basingstoke: Palgrave.

Ryan, Paul (ed.), *Never Apologise: The Collected Writings of Lindsay Anderson*, London: Plexus.

Sansom, William (1944), *Fireman Flower*, London: Hogarth.

Sayers, Dorothy L. (1943), *The Man Born to be King*, London: Gollancz.

Scammell, Michael (2009/2010), *Koestler: The indispensible Intellectual*, London: Faber.

Scammell, William (1988), *Keith Douglas: A Study*, London: Faber.

Schneider, Karen (1997), *Loving Arms: British Women Writing the Second World War*, Lexington: University Press of Kentucky.

Seaton, Jean (1987), 'The BBC and the Holocaust', in *European Journal of Communication*, 2.1 pp. 53–80.

Selwyn, Victor (ed.) (1995/1996), *The Voice of War: Poems of the Second World War*, London: Penguin.

Sheridan, Dorothy (ed.) (1990), *Wartime Women: An Anthology of Women's Wartime Writing for Mass-Observation 1937–45*, London: Mandarin.

Shires, Linda M. (1985), *British Poetry of the Second World War*, London: Macmillan.

Showalter, Elaine (1997), *Hystories: Hysterical Epidemics and Modern Culture*, London: Picador.
Shute, Nevil (1942), *Pied Piper*, London: Heinemann.
—(1945/2000), *Most Secret*, York: House of Stratus.
Sinclair, Andrew (1989), *War Like a Wasp: The Lost Decade of the Forties*, London: Hamish Hamilton.
Sissons, Michael and Philip French (eds) (1963/1986), *Age of Austerity*, Oxford: Oxford University Press.
Sitwell, Edith (1942) *Street Songs*, London: Macmillan.
—(1945/1948), *The Song of the Cold*, New York: Vanguard Press.
—(1947), *The Shadow of Cain*, London: John Lehmann.
Smith, Emma (1949/2002), *The Far Cry*, London: Persephone.
Smith, Stevie (1942), *Mother, What is Man?*, London: Cape.
—(1949/1979), *The Holiday*, London: Virago.
Spain, Nancy (1949/1994), *Poison for Teacher*, London: Virago.
Speaight, Robert, Henry Reed, Stephen Spender and John Hayward (1949), *Since 1939: 2*, London: Phoenix House.
Spender, Stephen (1942), *Ruins and Visions*, London: Faber.
—(1946), *European Witness*, London: Hamish Hamilton.
—(1978), *The Thirties and After: Poetry, Politics, People 1933–75*, London: Macmillan.
Spicer, Andrews (2001), *Typical Men: The Representation of Masculinity in Popular British Cinema*, London: I. B. Tauris.
Stafford, David (2007/2008), *Endgame 1945: Victory, Retribution, Liberation*, London: Abacus.
Stallworthy, Jon (1994), *The War Poems of Wilfred Owen*, London: Chatto & Windus.
Stapledon, Olaf (1944/2011), *Sirius*, London: Gollancz.
Stannard, Martin (ed.) (1984), *Evelyn Waugh: The Critical Heritage*, London: Routledge & Kegan Paul.
Stevenson, Randall (1986), *The British Novel since the Thirties: An Introduction*, London: Batsford.
—(2008), 'Introduction', in Bill Findlay (ed.), *Scottish People's Theatre: Plays By Glasgow Unity Writers*, Glasgow: ASLS.
Stewart, Victoria (2006), *Narratives of Memory: British Writing of the 1940s*, London: Palgrave.
Stonebridge, Lyndsey (2007), *The Writing of Anxiety: Imagining Wartime in Mid-Century British Culture*, Basingstoke: Palgrave.
—(2011), *The Judicial Imagination: Writing After Nuremberg*, Edinburgh: Edinburgh University Press.
Streatfeild, Noel (1945/2000), *Saplings*, London: Persephone.
Street, Sarah (1997), *British National Cinema*, London: Routledge.
Struther, Jan (1939/1989), *Mrs Miniver*, London: Virago.
Sutherland, John (2004/2005), *Stephen Spender: The Authorized Biography*, London: Penguin.
Tambimuttu, M. J. (1942), *Poetry in Wartime*, London: Faber.
Taylor, D. J. (1993/1994), *After the War: The Novel and England Since 1945*, London: Flamingo.
—(2003/2004), *Orwell, the Life*, London: Vintage.

Taylor, Elizabeth (1945/2006), *At Mrs Lippincotes*, London: Virago.
—(1946/2011), *Palladian*, London: Virago.
—(1949/2011), *A Wreath of Roses*, London: Virago.
Templeton, William (writing as T. Atkinson) (1946) *Exercise Bowler*, London: Samson Low, Marston & Co.
Tey, Josephine (1946/1992), *Miss Pym Disposes*, London: Mandarin.
Thomas, Dylan (1946), *Deaths and Entrances*, London: Dent.
—(2000), *Collected Poems 1934–53*, London: Phoenix Press.
Thomas, Gwyn (1946/2006), *The Dark Philosophers*, Cardigan: Parthian.
—(1947/2008), *The Alone to the Alone*, Cardigan: Parthian/Library of Wales.
Thomas, M. Wynn (ed.) (2003), *Welsh Writing in English*, Cardiff: University of Wales Press.
Thomas, R. S. (1946), *The Stones of the Field*, Camarthan: Druid Press.
—(2000), *Collected Poems 1945–1990*, London: Phoenix Press.
Thomson, Brian Lindsay (2009), *Graham Greene and the Politics of Popular Fiction and Film*, Basingstoke: Palgrave.
Tilsley, Frank (1939), *Little Tin God*, London: Collins.
Tolley, A. T. (1985), *The Poetry of the Forties*, Manchester: Manchester University Press.
Treglown, Jeremy (2000), *Romancing: The Life and Work of Henry Green*, London: Faber.
Tröger, Annemarie (1987), 'German Women's memories of World War II' in Higonnet et al. (eds) 1987.
Vine, Steve (2001) '"Shot from the Locks": Poetry, Mourning, Deaths and Entrances' in John Goodby and Chris Wigginton (eds), *Dylan Thomas: New Casebooks*, Basingstoke: Palgrave.
Wallace, Diana (2005), *The Woman's Historical Novel: British Women Writers, 1900–2000*, Basingstoke: Macmillan.
Waller, Jane and Michael Vaughan-Rees (1987), *Women in Wartime: The Role of Women's Magazines 1939–1945*, London: Macdonald Optima.
Warner, Rex (1941/1982), *The Aerodrome*, Oxford: Oxford University Press.
Warner, Sylvia Townsend (1948), *The Corner That Held Them*, London: Chatto and Windus.
Wasson, Sara (2010), *Urban Gothic of the Second World War: Dark London*, Basingstoke: Palgrave.
Watkin, William (2004), *On Mourning: Theories of Loss in Modern Literature*, Edinburgh: Edinburgh University Press.
Watkins, Vernon (1945), *The Lamp and the Veil*, London: Faber.
Waugh, Evelyn (1942/2011), *Put Out More Flags*, London: Penguin.
—(1943/1967), *Work Suspended and Other Stories*, London: Penguin.
—(1945/1962), *Brideshead Revisited*, London: Penguin.
—(1946), 'Fan-Fare', in *Life*, 8 April 1946; repr. in Stannard 1984.
—(1948/1951), *The Loved One*, London: Penguin.
West, Rebecca (1949/1982), *The Meaning of Treason*, London: Virago.
—(1946/1955), *A Train of Powder*, London: Macmillan.
Wheatley, Dennis (1948), *The Haunting of Toby Jugg*, London: Hutchison.
Whipple, Dorothy (1943/2005), *They Were Sisters*, London: Persephone.
White, Rob (2003), *The Third Man*, London: BFI Publishing.
White, T. H. (1958), *The Once and Future King*, London: Collins.

Whitehead, Anne (2009), *Memory*, London: Routledge.

Willetts, Paul (2005), *Fear and Loathing in Fitzrovia: The Bizarre Life of Writer, Actor, Soho Raconteur Julian Maclaren-Ross*, Stockport: Dewi Lewis Publishing.

Williams, Charles (1945/2003), *All Hallows' Eve*, Vancouver: Regent College Publishing.

Williams, Emlyn (1944), *The Druid's Rest*, London: Heinemann (first perf. 1943).

—(1945), *The Winds of Heaven*, London: Heinemann.

Williams, Keith (1996), *British Writers and the Media, 1930–45*, Basingstoke: Macmillan.

Williams, Oscar (ed.) (1945), *The War Poets*, New York: John Day.

Willis, Ted (1943), *Buster*, London: Fore Publications.

Winnicott, D. W. (1984), *Deprivation and Delinquency*, ed. Clare Winnicott, Ray Shepherd and Madeleine Davis, London: Tavistock Publications.

Woolf, Virginia (1941/2000), *Between the Acts*, London: Penguin.

—(1942), *The Death of the Moth and Other Essays*, London: Hogarth.

Woon, Basil (1941), *Hell Came to London: A Reportage of the Blitz During 14 Days*, London: Peter Davies.

Wyndham, Joan (1985/2001), *Love Lessons: A Wartime Diary*, London: Virago.

Index

Note: page numbers in *italics* denote illustrations

ABCA Play Unit, 19, 22
abject, 177
  body, 61, 219, 256
  fascination, 10, 126
  horror, 120
  powerlessness, 202
abstraction
  death as, 112
  diary-writing, 42
  and femininity, 79, 88, 95
  gendered, 72
  Germans as, 25, 43
Achebe, Chinua, 265
Ackland, Valentine, 32
adjustment fiction, 213, 230
Adler, Alfred, 110n2
adventure, 27, 54, 68, 115, 119, 121
'Advice for a Journey' (Keyes), 120
adynaton, 8, 121, 187
The Aerodrome (Warner), 75, 124
'Aftermath' (MacNeice), 259, 271
The Age of Anxiety (Auden), 258–9
Age of Austerity (Sissons and French),
  243
agency, 27
  class, 129
  desire for, 151
  factory workers, 63
  as fantasy, 138, 150
  Freud, 110n2
  gender differences, 104, 232
  marriage, 110
  masculinity, 122, 140, 219, 229, 259
  removal of, 98, 137, 260–1
  suicide as, 45
  women, 54, 60, 140, 151, 154, 174,
    232, 246, 248
air warfare, 116
airmen, 123–6, 144n2, 179, 197
Aitken, Ian, 214

Alamein to Zem Zem (Douglas), 112,
  113, 117–20, 121, 129–30, 131, 132
alienation, 8, 46, 62, 64, 94, 135
  class, 52–3
  marriage, 180
  peacetime, 259
All Hallows' Eve (Williams), 207–9
Allingham, Margery, 27, 44, 45, 136,
  138–9, 231–4, 232
Allport, Alan, 210, 230
The Alone to the Alone (Thomas), 260
amateurism, 128, 136, 137, 139
Ambler, Eric, 27
Anand, Mulk Raj, 16, 26, 269–70
Anderson, Lindsay, 214
Anglo-American relations, 242, 250, 251
Animal Farm (Orwell), 252, 253
Another Time (Auden), 31
anti-hero figures, 131, 154–7, 251
anti-Semitism
  Britain, 246
  Europe, 68
  fiction, 63
  Jameson on, 71
  pre-war, 13
  propaganda, 5
  refugees, 34n4, 54
  riots, 14
anxieties, 55, 59, 83, 137, 187, 224, 245
Apocalyptic poetry, 28–9, 30, 155, 198
Archer-Shee, George, 224, 226
aristocracy, *118*, 139, 167, 175, 233, 267
armed forces
  homosociality, 114, 127, 171, 179, 260
  as machine, 114–15
  paternalism, 116, 128
Arrival and Departure (Koestler), 69, 75,
  106
art, 86, 212–13, 214
Arts Council, 19

Arts Theatre Group, 22–3
Asquith, Anthony, 4, 225, 235n4
assimilation, 13, 34n4
At Mrs Lippincote's (Taylor), 180
atomic bomb, 14, 258
atomising, 17, 245, 258–9, 261, 271; *see
    also* fragmentation
atrocities, 69–70, 240
Attenborough, Richard, 128
Attlee, Clement, 15, 17
Auden, W. H., 16, 20, 28, 31, 258–9
Austen, Jane, 12
austerity, age of, 14, 17, 154, 169, 185,
    243–4, 254, 257, 272

Back (Green), 190–4
The Backward Son (Spender), 41
Bacon, Francis, 244
Baker, Phil, 246
Balchin, Nigel, 2, 25, 74, 94–6, 179,
    188–90
Balcon, Michael, 101
The Ballad and the Source (Lehmann),
    26
Baring, Nicole, 61
Barker, George, 28, 32
Baron, Alexander, 26, 112, 113, 114–15,
    127, 129, 205
Bates, H. E., 71, 264, 265–6
'The BBC and the Holocaust' (Seaton),
    69–70
Beardmore, George, 11, 70
Beattie, Keith, 215, 216
Bell, Kathleen, 152, 153–4
Bell, Mary Hayley, 22, 101
Bennett, Andrew, 90
bereavement, 178
Bergonzi, Bernard, 28, 30
Berridge, Elizabeth, 24, 51–3, 183
    'The Prisoner', 183
    'Tell it to a Stranger', 51-52
    'To Tea With the Colonel', 52-53
Betjeman, John, 30, 170
Between the Acts (Woolf), 25, 42, 75,
    160–2
Biggles Sees it Through (Johns), 115
bildungsroman, 26, 163, 165, 175, 188–9
birdsong/nature, 45, 64, 155
Black Chiffon (Storm), 23
The Black Laurel (Jameson), 251
black market, 210–11, 246–7, 249–50
Blake, Nicolas, 27
Blanchot, Maurice, 244
Blithe Spirit (Coward), 23, 104
Blitz
    aftermath, 11, 208
    analysis of, 48, 73n2
    Balchin on, 94-95

Bowen on, 42, 92–3
in *Caught*, 96–7, 99
chaos, 58
as displacement, 93
Englishness, 186
as epitome, 10, 43, 44–5, 46
escape from, 162
euphemisms, 119
Four Quartets, 204
Green on, 42, 96–7, 99
Hanley on, 42
liminality, 200
MacNeice on, 270, 271
in *Night Shift*, 63
Piette, 3
psychological impact, 7
Sitwell on, 30
Bloom, Harold, 252
Bloom, Ursula, 78–9
Bluemel, Kristin, 3, 41, 64
Blunden, Edmund, 32
Blyton, Enid, 27
body, 110
    abject, 61, 219, 256
    female, 79, *81*, 83, 94, 98, 101, 191
    national, 9, 83, 128, 138–9, 213
    wounded, 59, 71, 95, 97, 122–3, 140,
        158, 190
Bolton, Jonathan, 28, 29
Bomber Command, 144n2
Book Production War Economy Standard,
    272
Books and the Public (Mass Observation),
    143–4
Bottome, Phyllis, 3, 55, 57–9, 69, 75,
    267–8
Bourke, Joanna, 111–12
Bowen, Elizabeth, 8, 9, 23, 92
    climate of war, 33–4, 47, 49, 137–8
    The Demon Lover, 7, 24, 92, 158–9,
        188
    desire, 75, 89–90
    The Heat of the Day, 39, 42, 90–4,
        181, 184, 208
    'Ivy Gripped the Steps,' 159–60
    'Mysterious Kôr,' 76–7, 157–60
    past/present, 55–6, 92, 93
Bowlby, John, 151
Bowra, Maurice, 33
Bradbury, Malcolm, 2, 244–5
Brand, Christianna, 27
Brannigan, John, 170
Brent-Dyer, Elinor M., 27
Brideshead Revisited (Waugh), 26–7,
    169–70, 243
    cultural dislocation, 170–1
    double narrative, 174–5
    elegiac tone, 170

evoked, 195
tone/popularity, 175–6
women's status, 171, 172, 173–4
Bridie, James, 19, 20, 21, 23
Brief Encounter (Coward), 74–5, 181, 230–1
Bright Day (Priestley), 206–7, 211
Britain, Battle of, 9–10, 44, 46
Britain at Bay (Priestley), 45, 142
British Council, 18, 269
British Expeditionary Force, 9
British Nationality Act (1948), 15
British Poetry of the Second World War (Shires), 2
British Theatre (Noble), 21–2
British Writing of the Second World War (Rawlinson), 3
Britishness, 16, 46, 179, 215, 266
Brittain, Vera, 39, 45
Britten, Benjamin, 212
Brome, Vincent, 228
Browne, Martin, 20–1
Bulge, Battle of, 11
The Bull Calves (Mitchison), 27, 211–12
Burdekin, Katherine, 40
Burgess, Anthony, 154
Burlingham, Dorothy, 54–5, 57
Burma, 265, 266
Burrell, John, 19
Buster (Willis), 22
Butler, Judith
    dispossession, 183
    gender roles, 93
    grievability, 200, 221
    mourning, 178, 179, 186, 191–2
    Precarious Life, 178, 179
    precariousness, 220

Cain, James M., 247
Calder, Angus, 2, 12, 101
Calder, Jenni, 68–9, 150
Campbell, James, 112
carnivalesque, 101, 161, 222
Carter, Dorothy, 116
Cary, Joyce, 2, 26, 85–6
castration, symbolic, 101, 191
catharsis, 52, 53, 180, 218
Caught (Green), 25, 42, 96–101
Cavalcanti, Alberto, 4, 211
Chandler, Raymond, 247, 262, 263
Chaos of the Night (Reilly), 32
Charley is My Darling (Cary), 26
Chase, James Hadley, 135, 195
Cheyette, Bryan, 13
Cheyney, Peter, 27, 134
childhood
    defamiliarising perspective, 58–9, 162
    displacement, 53–61

family disruption, 55–6, 59–60
home, 56–7
monstrosity, 250
symbolism, 218
as trope, 26
unresolved trauma, 188
children's fiction, 27, 35n7
Christie, Agatha, 27, 134, 135, 136, 137, 138, 139–41
cinema
    adaptations, 4
    American boycott, 34n3
    class, 48, 181–2
    closures, 101
    demobilisation, 211–12
    heroism, 116
    Hollywood parodied, 207
    postwar, 181–2
    spiv cycle, 210, 246–7
    transgressiveness, 181–2
    see also documentary films; Gainsborough studios
citizenship, 3, 15–16, 79, 83
class, 60, 67, 181
    agency, 129
    alienation, 52–3
    in *Caught,* 97
    cinema, 48, 181–2
    cross-class relations, 48, 65, 129, 153
    evacuation, 55, 58–60, 61
    female body, 94
    marginalisation, 64
    in *Nineteen Eighty-Four,* 253
    otherness, 99–100
    postwar trauma, 183
    respect, 153
    see also aristocracy; middle classes; working class
Cloudless May (Jameson), 71–2
Clunes, Alec, 22
The Cocktail Party (Eliot, T. S.), 23
'Cold Spell' (Lewis), 77
Cold War, 156, 247, 250–1, 254, 271
Collins, Norman, 26
Colls, Robert, 6
Colonial Office, 15–16
colonialism, 6, 263–8
combat literature, 111–13, 127
comedies, 4, 101, 104
commando figures, 132, 210
Common Sense, 270
Communism, 57, 58, 245, 246, 251–2
Compton-Burnett, Ivy, 25, 27
concentration camps, 70–1
Connolly, Cyril, 11, 28, 40, 69, 212, 244
Conrad, Joseph, 12

consciousness, states of
  alternative, 162
  atomised, 259
  child, 59
  collective, 214
  Daylight on Saturday, 65
  disrupted, 99
  double, 151
  Eliot on, 208
  erasure of death, 114
  hallucination, 158
  restoration to, 193
  Silver Darlings, 75–6
  spirituality, 202
  subjectivity, 164, 180
  and survival, 127
Constantine, Leary, 16
Coombes, B. L., 234–5n3
Cooper, John Xiros, 201, 204
The Corinthian (Heyer), 153–4
The Corner That Held Them (Warner), 150
Costello, John, 76
Cotten, Joseph, 247
Council for the Encouragement of Music and the Arts, 19, 22
Coward, Noël, 21–2, 104
  Blithe Spirit, 23, 104
  Brief Encounter, 74–5, 230–1
  In Which We Serve, 4, 116, 128
Crawford, Anne, 48
Crawford, Robert, 269
Creasey, John, 27
creativity, 3, 43
Crete, Battle of, 170
crime fiction, 27, 134–44, 231, 233–4, 247–8, 262
crime figures, 210–11
Crispin, Edmund, 27
Crompton, Richmal, 27
Crossman, Richard, 70
Crown Film Unit, 214, 215
cultural dislocation, 170–1
Curtain (Christie), 139

Dahl, Roald, 111, 124–5, 126–7
Dallapiccola, Luigi, 244
Dance of the Apprentices (Gaitens), 260–1
Daphne Laureola (Bridie), 23
The Dark Philosophers (Thomas), 217, 260
The Dark Tower (MacNeice), 270–1
Darkness at Noon (Koestler), 69, 251
Darkness Falls from the Air (Balchin), 94–6
Darlow, Michael, 224
Darwin, John, 264
Davin, Dan, 16

Day-Lewis, Cecil, 27, 28
Daylight on Saturday (Priestley), 64, 65
D-Day Normandy landings, 11, 113
De Gaulle, Charles, 219
death, 193
  as abstraction, 112
  civilian, 7, 119
  comedies about, 104
  desire, 83–4, 110n2, 137, 187
  and killing, 111
  The Loved One, 242–3
  representation of, 178
  sex, 98–9, 101
'Death of an Old Old Man' (Dahl), 124–5, 126–7
Deaths and Entrances (Thomas), 197–9, 201
'The Decline of the English Murder' (Orwell), 135–6
Delafield, E. M., 39, 40, 41
demobilisation, 190, 207, 209–13
The Demon Lover (Bowen), 7, 24, 92, 158–9, 188
Desert Highway (Priestley), 22
desert warfare, 130–1, 133
desire
  authority, 91
  Bowen, 89–90
  British mode, 103
  conventionality, 74
  death, 83–4, 110n2, 137, 187
  Freudian influences, 76
  Green, 89–90
  heterosexual/homosexual, 74, 87–8, 102–3, 106–7, 267
  literature of, 75
  love, 104–6
  marriage, 74
  repression, 164
  self annihilation, 90
  unconsummated, 93–4
  violence, 75
destruction, 43, 45, 64, 162, 196
detachment, 8, 95, 111, 120, 121, 218–19
detective fiction, 136, 231; *see also* crime fiction
A Diary for Timothy (Jennings), 214–18
diary-writing, 41–2, 72–3n1, 112, 243
Dickens, Charles, 4, 212
Dickens, Monica, 26, 64, 65–7, 66, 78, 181
disassociation *see* detachment
disease imagery, 45, 83
disorientation, 53, 188, 190, 209–10
displacement, 53–61, 93, 184, 187
dispossession, 178–9, 183, 184–5
dissonance, 45, 155
Divorce Act, 210

documentary films, 4, 47–8, 116, 144, 214–18
documentary writing, 4, 39, 43–4, 50
domesticity, 181, 182–3
  Edwardian, 225
  emasculation, 76
  as fantasy, 257
  femininity, 83, 151–2
  in peril, 67–8
  in warfare, 130
Doreen (Noble), 55, 57, 59–61, 145n4
double standards, 66, 152–3
Douglas, Keith, 32, 33, 120, 121
  Alamein to Zem Zem, 112, 113, 117–20, 121, 129–30, 131, 132
  'Aristocrats,' 118–19
  'Dead Men,' 121
  and First World War poetry, 39–40
  'How to Kill,' 121
  'Landscape with Figures,' 121
  pencil drawing, *118, 130*
  in *Personal Landscape,* 29
  'Sportsmen,' 111
  'Vergissmeinnicht,' 111–12
drama *see* theatre
Du Maurier, Daphne, 22, 150
Duet for Two Hands (Bell), 22
Duncan, Ronald, 21
Dunkirk, 9–10, 46, 168
dystopian novels, 40, 124, 252, 253, 257, 258

Ealing studios, 4, 101
Easthope, Anthony, 9, 123
Edinburgh Festivals, 20
El Alamein, Battle of, 46
Eliot, George, 12
Eliot, T. S., 33, 208, 234n1
  The Cocktail Party, 23
  Four Quartets, 28, 32, 200–5
  Murder in the Cathedral, 20–1
  The Waste Land, 5, 194, 203
Ellman, Maud, 90
emasculation, 76, 98
emotion, 9, 173, 179, 218–19, 252
Empire Windrush, 15, 268
Empson, William, 7, 32, 199, 200
English Story, 51
Englishness, 165
  and American hegemony, 242
  and Britishness, 16, 46
  pre-modern, 204
  propaganda, 168
  repression, 179, 230
  Smith on, 186
ENSA, 19
equal pay, 62–3
eros/thanatos, 96

escape literature, 12–13, 149
escapist cinema, 48, 144
escapist fiction, 157–60, 168–9, 176
Esty, Jed, 29, 202–3
ethics of warfare, 145n3
euphemism, 119, 120, 133, 168, 188
European Witness (Spender), 239–40
Eustace and Hilda (Hartley), 162
evacuation, 53, 54–5, 58–60, 61
Evans, B. Ifor, 212–13
Evans, Edith, 23
Exercise Bowler (Templeton), 22

factory work, 62, 63, 64–6, 78
Fair Stood the Wind for France (Bates), 71, 266
The Fallen Idol (Reed), 246
family disruption, 55–60, 59–60
The Fancy (Dickens), 64, 65–7
Fanny By Gaslight (Asquith), 4
fantasy fiction, 154–7
The Far Cry (Smith), 264, 266–7
Farewell Leicester Square (Miller), 13
A Farewell to Arms (Hemingway), 78
Fascism, 40, 71–2, 128, 139, 250, 268
femininity
  and abstraction, 79, 88, 95
  domesticity, 83, 151–2
  idealised, 89, 267
  lesbian, 107
  performance of, 153
  posters about, 78–9, *80, 81*
  postwar, 151–2
  stereotypes, 166, 189, 230, 265
  subversive, 150, 152
  working class, 103–4
feminisation, 95, 172
femme fatale, 79, 81, 83, 94, 247, 262, 263, 267
Ferguson, Frances, 169
Ferrer, Daniel, 161
fetishism, 76, 100
fiction *see specific titles*
Field, Sid, 22
film *see* cinema
Finlay, Ian, 18
fire as trope, 43, 63, 97–9
Fire Services, 9, 97–8
Fireman Flower (Sansom), 42–3
Fires Were Started (Jennings), 214
First World War
  aftermath, 7, 8–9, 71, 75–6, 87, 116, 137, 171–3, 218
  Freud, 76
  hysteria, 205n1
  as influence, ix, 39, 49, 173, 230
  officers/men, 115
  poetry, 111, 112–13

Flare Path (Rattigan), 88–9, 101, 224
Follow My Leader (Rattigan), 224
For the Time Being (Auden), 31
Forester, C. S., 128–9
Forster, E. M., 69, 214, 215, 266
fort/da game (Freud), 193, 203
Four Quartets (Eliot, T. S.), 28, 32, 200–5
fragmentation
  discourse/structures, 17
  The Holiday, 186
  national/personal, 100, 169, 210, 245
  Nineteen Eighty-Four, 255–6
  Spender, 32–3
  of subjectivity, 180–1
  through torture, 255
France, collapse of, 68, 71–2
Francis, Martin, 123
Fraser, G. S., 28–9, 121, 269
French, Philip, 243
Frenchman's Creek (du Maurier), 150
Frend, Charles, 4
Freud, Anna, 54–5, 57
Freud, Sigmund
  agency, 110n2
  death drive, 110n2
  fort/da game, 193, 203
  mourning, 192
  Oedipus conflict, 75
  on sexuality, 110n4
  Three Essays on the Theory of Sexuality, 76
  uncanny, 160
Friday's Child (Heyer), 152–3
A Friendly Hearth (Baring), 61
The Friendly Young Ladies (Renault), 106–10
From the City, From the Plough (Baron), 113, 114–15, 127, 129, 205
Fry, Christopher, 23, 221–2
Fuller, Roy, 32
Fussell, Paul, 49

Gaelic language, 269
Gainsborough studios, 4, 12, 17, 144
Gaitens, Edward, 260–1
Garfield, Simon, 72n1, 243
Gascoyne, David, 32, 43
Gay, Peter, 110n2
gender
  assumptions, 251
  class, 60
  fluidity, 107
  hypocrisy, 230
  identity, 109
  norms restored, 181, 230, 232
  performativity, 89
gender differences, 62–3, 83, 86, 104, 164, 232

gender roles, 22, 67, 74–5, 79, 88–9, 93, 95, 164, 166–7, 230, 232–3, 267
George Orwell and the Radical Eccentrics (Bluemel), 3
Germany, 25, 239–40, 241
Gibson, Wilfred, 43
Gielgud, John, 22
Gilliat, Sidney, 47–8, 211, 218
Gingold, Hermione, 22
A Girl in Winter (Larkin), 27, 260
Glasgow Citizens Theatre, 19, 20
Glasgow Unity Theatre, 19, 20, 23
Godden, Rumer, 264
Goering, Hermann, 240
Gold in His Boots (Munro), 23
Goodby, John, 29
The Gorbals Story (McLeish), 19–20
Graves, Robert, 32
Great Expectations (Lean), 4
Green, F. L., 25
Green, Henry, 2, 27, 75, 89–90, 194–5
  Back, 190–4
  Caught, 25, 42, 96–101
  Loving, 192–3
  Pack My Bag, 101
Greene, Graham, 2, 7, 23, 272
  The Heart of the Matter, 261–4
  The Ministry of Fear, 25, 88, 135, 136, 141–3, 249
  The Power and the Glory, 26, 247
  The Third Man, 4, 246–51
'Greenhouse with Cyclamens' (West), 239–41
grief, 178, 196–200, 221
grief work, 54, 187, 192, 198–9
Griffith, Wyn, 18, 269
grotesque, 65, 84, 86–7, 154, 192–3, 196, 250, 256
group hero, 47, 66, 114, 116, 129, 145n3
Gubar, Susan, 83
Gun Buster, 46
Gunn, Neil, 26, 75
Guthrie, Tyrone, 19, 20

H. D., 16
Habermann, Ina, 22
Haffenden, John, 31, 32
Hamilton, Patrick, 25, 26, 46–7, 83–4, 105, 162
Hamlet (Olivier), 4
Hammett, Dashiell, 247
Hangover Square (Hamilton), 25, 83–4, 162
Hanley, James, 42, 43, 63–4
The Happy Prisoner (Dickens), 181
Hare, Cyril, 27
Harper, Sue, 144
Harrold, R. F., 11

Hartley, J. P., 26, 162–4
Hartley, Jenny, 3, 12, 149–50
The Haunting of Toby Jugg (Wheatley), 245–6
Hay, George Campbell, 269
The Heart of the Matter (Greene), 261–4
The Heat of the Day (Bowen), 39, 42, 90–4, 181, 184, 208
Hell Came to London (Woon), 46
'Hello Boyfriend,' 82
Hemingway, Ernest, 78
Henderson, Hamish, 29
Hendry, J. F., 28, 196, 197, 269
Hennegan, Alison, 106, 110n3
Henry IV, Part I (Shakespeare), 212
Henry V (Olivier), 4
heroism, 115, 116, 137, 153–4; *see also* anti-hero; group hero figure; wounded hero
Herself Surprised (Cary), 85
Hess, Rudolf, 240
heteronormativity, 106, 107
Hewison, Robert, 2, 29, 46
Heyer, Georgette, 27, 151–4
Heyward, John, 23–4
'Hiatus' (MacNeice), 270
Higonnet, Margaret, 79
Hill, Diana Murray, 47, 62
Hillary, Richard, 112, 114, 122–4, 125–6, 170
Hiroshima, 14, 157, 258
historical fiction, 12, 27, 149–50, 152–4, 162
Hoare, Philip, 104
Hodgson, Vere, 70–1
Hodson, Gillian, 224
Holden, Inez, 41, 61–4
Holes in the Sky (MacNeice), 259, 271
The Holiday (Smith), 177, 184, 185–8, 254
Hollywood cinema, 207
Holocaust, 13, 14, 197, 240, 258
home, 56–7, 83, 129, 130; *see also* domesticity
homecomings, 180, 189, 207, 209–10, 243
homoeroticism, 128, 172
homosexuality, 76, 106
homosociality
  armed forces, 114, 127, 171, 179, 260
  banter, 9
  caring, 127
  in fiction, 76, 84
  and homoeroticism, 172
  priority of, 77, 232–3
  self-sufficiency, 130
  and women, 152–3

Horizon
  Bowra in, 33
  on *Brideshead Revisited*, 175
  Comment, 206
  Connolly in, 11, 28, 40, 212, 244
  Koestler in, 69
  on Sitwells, 30
  Spender in, 30–1, 39
horror, 120, 256, 257, 258
The Horse's Mouth (Cary), 85–6
housewives, 67, 152, 184; *see also* domesticity
housing shortages, 243
'How to Kill' (Douglas), 121
Howard, Trevor, 247
Hulten, Karl, 136
human rights, 225
humanity, 252, 254
humour, 142, 168, 260
'The Hunger of Miss Burton' (Panter-Downes), 105
Huxley, Elspeth, 264
hypocrisy, 85, 152, 199, 221–2, 230; *see also* double standards
hysteria, 191, 205n1

identity, 122, 131–2; *see also* national identity
immigration, 1, 6, 15, 16, 34n4, 246, 268
imperialism, 161, 264, 268
In the Second Year (Jameson), 40
In Which We Serve (Coward), 4, 116, 128
India, 15, 266–7, 269–70
Innes, Michael, 27
An Inspector Calls (Priestley), 23, 221, 228–30
insularity, 6, 13, 16
interpellation, 98, 157, 193–4
interwar years, 20, 134–5, 167
Irwin, Margaret, 27, 150
Isherwood, Christopher, 20
The Island of Adventure (Blyton), 27
'It All Depends on You,' 48
Italy, 132, 133
'Ivy Gripped the Steps' (Bowen), 159–60

The Jacaranda Tree (Bates), 264, 265–6
Jackson, Gordon, 47
Jackson, Kevin, 215, 216, 218
Jacob, Naomi, 27
James, Henry, 12
Jameson, Storm, 3, 40, 68, 71–2, 251
Jarman, Wrenne, 32, 133–4
Jennings, Humphrey, 4, 214–18
Jewish identity, 13, 54, 213; *see also* anti-Semitism
Jill (Larkin), 27, 259–60

Johns, W. E., 27, 115–16
Johnson, Pamela Hansford, 13, 243–4
Jones, Elizabeth, 136
Jones, Jack, 269
Joyce, James, 5
Jung, Carl, 110n1, 241

'Keep Mum,' 79, *81*, 196
Kemp, Robert, 20
Kennedy, A. L., 117
Keyes, Sidney, 32, 120
killing, 10, 111–12, 127; *see also* death
King of the Commandos (Johns), 116
The King-Emperor's English (Anand), 269–70
King-Hall, Magdalen, 150
The King's General (du Maurier), 150
Knight, Stephen, 134–5, 140
Koestler, Arthur, 16, 75, 125, 126, 250
    Arrival and Departure, 69, 75, 106
    Darkness at Noon, 69, 251
    'On Disbelieving Atrocities,' 70
    Scum of the Earth, 68–9
Korda, Alexander, 247
Korean War, 15
Krasker, Robert, 248
Kristeva, Julia, 159
Kushner, Tony, 14
Kynaston, David, 143, 144, 211, 242

Labour government, 6, 177, 222, *223*, 243
Lacan, Jacques, 256
Ladies May Now Leave Their Machines (Hill), 62
The Lady's Not for Burning (Fry), 23, 221–2
The Lambs of God (Scott), 23
'Lament' (Hendry), 196, 197
Land Workers (Masefield), 32
'Landscape with Figures' (Douglas), 121
Larkin, Philip, 27, 259–60
Laski, Marghanita, 218–22
Lassner, Phyllis, 3, 264
The Last Enemy (Hillary), 112, 122–4
The Last Inspection (Lewis), 49
Lauder, Frank, 47–8
Lean, David, 4
Leavis, F. R., 12, 245
Ledward, Patricia, 32
Lee, Laurie, 32
Lehmann, John, 28, 212
Lehmann, Rosamund, 3, 24, 26
Lend-Lease policy, 242
lesbianism, 106, 107, 109, 110n4
Lewis, Alun, 3, 24, 32, 39, 49–51, 77, 112
Lewis, C. S., 27

The Life and Death of Colonel Blimp (Powell and Pressburger), 116–17, 136
Life and the Poet (Spender), 41
Light, Alison, 8–9, 137, 166, 230
Lilliput, 24
liminality, 122, 167, 200–1, 208, 210
Lindsay, Maurice, 268
Linklater, Eric, 131–4
The Lion, the Witch and the Wardrobe (Lewis), 27
Listen to Britain (Jennings), 4, 214
litotes, 168
Little Boy Lost (Laski), 218–22
Little Tin God (Tilsley), 40
Llewelyn, Richard, 269
London, 2, 4–5, 10, 11, 29; *see also* Blitz
London Olympics (1948), 17
London Pride (Bottome), 55, 57–9
London Unity Theatre, 19, 22
loss
    grief, 197
    mastery of, 193
    mourning, 191–2
    mundane, 201
    public/private, 186–7
    repression, 183–4
    women, 180–1
    work of, 178, 179
love, 65, 90–6, 104–6
    loyalty, 90, 139, 152, 219, 251
Love in Idleness (Rattigan), 224
The Loved One (Waugh), 242–3
Loving (Green), 192–3
Lowry, Malcolm, 26, 261
loyalty
    archaic, 248
    assumptions, 131
    to beauty, 132
    Colonel Blimp, 117
    love, 90, 139, 152, 219, 251
    marital, 152
    national, 133–4, 168, 211
    women, 79, 83, 182
Lycett, Andrew, 199
Lyndsay, David, 20

McAleer, Joseph, 144
Macaulay, Rose, 26, 175, 177, 194–6, 218
MacCaig, Norman, 268
McCarthy, Desmond, 31–2
MacDiarmid, Hugh, 268
McIndoe, Archibald, 122
McInnes, Helen, 27
MacKay, Marina, 3, 170, 174, 205n2
Mackenzie, Compton, 26
McKibbin, Ross, 17, 230

Maclaren-Ross, Julian, 3, 24, 49, 50, 162, 260
MacLean, Sorley, 269
McLeish, Robert, 19–20
McLoughlin, Kate, 8
MacNeice, Louis, 28, 32, 43, 259, 270–1
The Man Born to Be King (Sayers), 21
The Man in Grey (Arliss), 4, 144
Manifold, John, 50
manliness *see* masculinity
Manning, Olivia, 29
Marcus, Steven, 76
marriage
    agency, 110
    alienation, 180
    companionate, 66–7, 74, 166–7
    desire, 74
    fiction, 65
    loyalty, 152
    masochism, 74
    as normativity, 109–10
    patriarchy, 226–7, 232
Marson, Una, 16
masculinity, 123, 132–3, 230
    agency, 122, 140, 219, 229, 259
    anti-hero, 131
    emasculated, 171
    Fascist, 127–8, 132
    female, 107, 108–9
    hegemonic, 108, 140–1, 172, 176n2
    heroism, 116, 137, 153–4
    killing, 111–12
    language register, 179
    non-combatant, 145n4, 215
    normative, 189
    Oedipus complex, 75–6
    paternity, 97
    self-sufficiency, 262
    spivs/ex-servicemen, 210–11
    trauma, 9, 25, 33, 54, 61, 100, 113, 156, 184–5, 187, 189, 210
    war, 113–27, 134, 189
    and women's work, 78
    wounded, 140–1
Masefield, John, 32, 46
masochism, 74, 76, 182, 263
Mass Observation, 14, 17, 72n1, 143–4, 243, 258
maternal dyad, 191, 193, 194, 219
maternity, 172, 184
Maugham, Somerset, 26, 87–8
melancholia, 184, 185, 187, 191, 218
melodramas, 12, 17, 144
Memoirs of the Forties (Maclaren-Ross), 3
memory, 3–4, 99–100, 165–6, 169–70, 171, 254
Men in Shadow (Bell), 22, 101

Men Should Weep (Stewart), 23
Mengham, Rod, 180, 190
metaphor, 240
middle classes, 8–9, 136–7, 173, 215–16
middlebrow perspective, 3, 53, 142
militarised culture, 79, 128, 257–8
Miller, Betty, 3, 13, 145n4
Millions Like Us (Lauder and Gilliat), 47–8, 65, 78
Millions Like Us: British Women's Fiction (Hartley), 3
Mills, John, 116, 211
Mine Own Executioner (Balchin), 179, 188–90
mining industry, 217
The Ministry of Fear (Greene), 25, 88, 135, 136, 141–3, 249
Ministry of Information, 47, 214
Ministry of Labour, 15–16
misogyny, 77, 83–90, 104
Mitchell, Gladys, 27
Mitchison, Naomi, 3, 27, 40, 70, 150, 211–12
Mitford, Nancy, 26, 162, 164–9, 170, 175, 176n1, 234n2
Modern Scottish Poetry (Lindsay), 268
Modernism and World War II (MacKay), 3
modernity
    Brideshead Revisited, 174
    conservative, 74, 166, 167–8
    critique of present, 159
    Freud, 76
    gender roles, 74–5
    memory, 3–4
    patriarchy, 108
    postwar, 33
    and romanticism, 165
Montefiore, Jan, 150
The Moral Basis of Politics (Mitchison), 40
Morgan, Diana, 22
Morgan, Kenneth O., 17
Most Secret (Shute), 145n3
mourning
    anatomy of, 178, 186
    cultural, 176, 221
    Freud, 192
    loss, 191–2
    national identity, 205
    nostalgia, 198
    private/public, 179, 194, 200
    readjustment, 144
    refusal of, 140, 168
Movement poets, 28, 33
The Moving Finger (Christie), 139–41
Mr Bolfry (Bridie), 21
Mrs Miniver (Struther), 24–5, 142

Muir, Edwin, 32, 197, 268
Munich crisis, 7, 83
Munro, George, 23
murder, 135–7, 139, 141, 142, 232
Murder in the Cathedral (Eliot, T. S.),
    20–1
Murrow, Edward, 16
Murry, John Middleton, 144n2
'Mysterious Kôr' (Bowen), 76–7, 157–60

N or M? (Christie), 137, 138
narcissism, 74, 265, 267
Narratives of Memory (Stewart), 3, 34n2
National Health Service, 15, 17
national identity, 14, 15, 16, 45–6, 138,
    205
Nazism, 25, 44, 50, 69, 72, 240
New Apocalypse, 2, 269; *see also*
    Apocalyptic poetry
The New Apocalypse (Hendry and
    Treece), 28
The New Commonwealth, 14
new internationalism, 134
New Statesman, 11
The New York Times Magazine, 70
Newsinger, John, 258
Nicholson, Norman, 21
Night Shift (Holden), 61–2, 63–4
The Nine Days Wonder (Masefield), 46
Nineteen Eighty-Four (Orwell), 27, 88,
    225, 252–8, 272
Niven, David, 116
No Directions (Hanley), 42, 63–4
No Orchids for Miss Blandish (Chase),
    135, 195
Noble, Barbara, 55, 57, 59–61, 145n4
Noble, Peter, 19, 21–2, 23
noir fiction, 263–4
noir film, 247, 248
normality, 143, 158, 188, 190–1, 211
Normandy landings, 11, 112, 115
Northern Ireland, 16, 268
nostalgia, 160–2, 164, 165, 169, 176n1,
    198, 226
Nuremberg trials, 240–1
nursing stories, 78

O'Casey, Sean, 20
Odd Man Out (Green, F. L.), 25
Odd Man Out (Reed), 246
Oedipus complex, 75–6, 219
Of Love and Hunger (Maclaren-Ross),
    162, 260
The Old Man of the Mountains
    (Nicholson), 21
Old Vic, 19, 22, 212
Oliver Twist (Lean), 4
Olivier, Laurence, 4, 19

'On Disbelieving Atrocities' (Koestler),
    70
On the Side of the Angels (Miller), 145n4
The Once and Future King (White), 150
'The One' (Proctor), 197
One Fine Day (Panter-Downes), 180–1,
    182–3, 195
One Pair of Feet (Dickens), 66, 78
Operation Barbarossa, 10
Operation Market Garden, 11
Orwell, George, 7, 41, 69, 134, 272
    Animal Farm, 252
    'The Decline of the English Murder,'
        135–6
    Nineteen Eighty-Four, 27, 88, 225,
        252–8
    in *Partisan Review,* 41
    'Raffles and Miss Blandish,' 135, 142
    in *Tribune,* 268
otherness, 13, 16, 43, 49, 51
    Britishness, 138
    class, 99–100
    dialect, 58
    enemy, 254
    and exile, 29
    India, 267
    and Jewish identity, 54
    and self, 127
    women, 83, 158, 164, 167, 172, 187
Our Hidden Lives (Garfield), 243
Outline of History (Wells), 162
Owen, Wilfred, 111, 203

Pack My Bag (Green), 101
pain, 122–3, 179–80, 187–8; *see also*
    suffering
Pakistan, 270–1
Palestine, 14, 15, 221
Palladian (Taylor), 259
Panter-Downes, Molly, 24, 105, 180–1,
    182–3, 195
paranoia, 140, 156, 245
Paris, Michael, 115, 116
Partisan Review, 41
Partridge, Frances, 41, 42, 44–5, 46, 70,
    72–3n1, 123–4, 144
pastoralism, 160–2, 169–70, 171, 196–7
paternalism, 116, 128
patriarchy
    gender roles, 79
    history, 150
    marriage, 226–7, 232
    mind/body dualism, 88
    modernity, 108
    power relations, 74
    violence, 162
patriotism, 58, 62, 79, 125, 186
Paul, Kathleen, 15

peace, 14–18, 132, 185, 259
Peace and the Public (Mass Observation), 14, 17, 258
Peake, Mervyn, 5, 27, 154–7
Penguin New Writing, 24, 28, 41, 212, 244–5
Penguin 'Specials,' 143
The People's War (Calder), 2
Personal Landscape (ed. Durrell, Spencer and Fedden), 29–30
Personal Landscapes: British Poets in Egypt (Bolton), 29
Peter Grimes (Britten), 212
Petition of Rights, 224–5
phoney war, 9, 44, 95, 96, 98, 170
Picasso, Pablo, 213
Picture Post, 11–12, 217, 234–5n3, 270
Picturegoer, 149
Pied Piper (Shute), 53–4
Piero della Francesca, 132
Piette, Adam
    on Bowen, 90
    domesticity in warfare, 130
    on Douglas, 117–18, 119, 121
    fire trope, 43
    Imagination at War, 3
    on Jameson, 251
    militarised culture, 257–8
    neo-romanticism, 28
    private imagination, 8
    on *The Third Man*, 242, 250
    on Thomas, 200
    on Waugh, 170
Pigeon Pie (Mitford), 170
pilots *see* airmen
Pimlott, Ben, 252
Pitter, Ruth, 32
Plain, Gill, 3, 150, 211
Ane Pleasant Satire of the Thrie Estaitis (Lyndsay), 20
Poems from the Forces, 29
poetry, 18, 28–33, 117–21, 268
    commemorative role, 196–7
    grief, 196–200
    Holocaust, 197
    postwar, 179–80
    Second World War, 29, 33, 120, 196
    Spanish Civil War, 41
    women writers, 32
    see also specific titles
Poetry London, 16
The Poetry of the Forties (Tolley), 2
Poison for Teacher (Spain), 106, 110n3
political revues, 22
Portman, Eric, 48
Postscripts (Priestley), 27, 34–5n6, 45
Pound, Ezra, x, 5
Powell, Michael, 4, 116–17, 136

The Power and the Glory (Greene), 26, 247
Precarious Life (Butler), 178, 179
Pressburger, Emeric, 4, 116–17, 136
Priestley, J. B., 4, 12, 20, 27, 241–2
    Bright Day, 206–7, 211
    Britain at Bay, 45, 142
    Daylight on Saturday, 64, 65
    Desert Highway, 22
    An Inspector Calls, 23, 221, 228–30
    Postscripts, 27, 34–5n6, 45
    They Came to A City, 22
    Three Men in New Suits, 207, 209, 225, 229
Prince, F. T., 32
'The Prisoner' (Berridge), 183
Private Angelo (Linklater), 131–4
Proctor, Ida, 197
pro-natalism, 16, 151–2
propaganda, 4, 45, 47
    Englishness, 168
    Nineteen Eighty-Four, 253–4
    war effort, 62
    women's work, 78, 79
    writing, 5, 7, 270
The Provincial Lady in Wartime (Delafield), 40, 41
psychoanalysis, 75–6, 107–8, 110n2, 110n4, 188–9, 256
The Pursuit of Love (Mitford), 162, 164–9, 175
Put Out More Flags (Waugh), 98, 170

racism, 15, 241, 267
radio programmes, 4, 101
Rae, Gwynneth, 27
'Raffles and Miss Blandish' (Orwell), 135, 142
Raine, Kathleen, 32
rape, 134, 161
rationing, 7, 9, 13, 46, 67, 243
Rattigan, Terence, 4, 101–2
    Flare Path, 88–9, 101, 224
    Follow My Leader, 224
    Love in Idleness, 224
    The Way to the Stars, 89
    While the Sun Shines, 21, 22, 102–4, 224
    The Winslow Boy, 221, 222–8
Rau, Petra, 25, 144n1
Rawlinson, Mark, 3, 95, 111, 119
The Razor's Edge (Maugham), 87–8
Read, Herbert, 43
'Reading in War Time' (Muir), 197
Rebellato, Dan, 101–2, 224
'The Recruit' (Manifold), 50
Redgrave, Michael, 214
Reed, Carol, 4, 246, 250

Reed, Henry, 18, 24, 25–6, 32
Reeve, N. H., 180
Reilly, Catherine, 32
The Reluctant Widow (Heyer), 151–2
Renault, Mary, 75, 106–10
repression, 75, 140, 180
  desire, 164
  Englishness, 179, 230
  loss, 183–4
  memory, 99–100
  Nineteen Eighty-Four, 253
resurrection, 192, 199, 201
Return Via Dunkirk (Gun Buster), 46
Reynolds, Quentin, 16
Rhine crossing, 11, 215
Richardson, Ralph, 19
Ridler, Anne, 21, 32
Roberts, Michael, 31
Robson, Flora, 23
Roc, Patricia, 47
Rorty, Richard, 252
Rose, Sonya, 7, 16, 45–6, 79–80, 83,
  151–2, 153
Roston, Murray, 263
Royal Commission on Population, 16
Royle, Nicholas, 90
Ruins and Visions (Spender), 41
Russia, 241–2, 244
Rutherford, Edie, 243
Rutter, David, 122

sacrifice, 199, 226–7
Sandauer, Artur, 13
Sandbag Follies, 22
Sansom, William, 24, 42–3
Saplings (Streatfeild), 26, 55–7
Sayers, Dorothy L., 21
Scammell, William, 119
schizophrenia, 84, 239–40
Schneider, Karen, 3
science fiction, 27
Scotland, 16, 19, 268
Scott, Benedick, 23
Scott, Paul, 50
Scott, Walter, 12
Scovell, E. J., 32
Scrutiny (Leavis), 245
Scum of the Earth (Koestler), 68–9
Seaton, Jean, 69–70
Second World War, 1, 4, 5, 6–10
  crime fiction, 134–5, 137, 234
  Germans in novels, 25
  literature of desire, 75
  memory in writing, 165
  myth of, 14
  poetry, 29, 33, 120, 196
  polemical writing, 40–1, 44
  psychological impact, 185, 271

satire, 170
  women's roles, 78, 83
  writing about war, 177–8, 197
Seferis, George, 29
self, 17–18, 127, 169, 258–9, 271
self annihilation, 90, 255–6, 260
self-consciousness
  adynaton, 8
  agonies of, 60
  Caught, 97
  Englishness, 44, 45
  introspection, 201
  lack of, 132
  and realism, 94
  rejection, 127
  repetition, 119
  subjectivity, 112
self-sufficiency, 130, 262
Selznick, David O., 247
'A Sentimental Story' (Maclaren-Ross), 50
sex, 96, 98–9, 101, 150, 184
sexual assaults, 210
sexuality, 76, *82*, 83, 86–7, 103, 191
The Shadow Factory (Ridler), 21
Shakespeare, William, 4, 22
Sheikhupura massacre, 270–1
Shelton, Joy, 211
The Ship (Forester), 128–9
Shires, Linda, 2, 197, 199
The Shop on the King's Road (Evans),
  212–13
Showalter, Elaine, 179, 205n1
The Shrimp and the Anemone (Hartley),
  26, 162–4
Shute, Nevil, 27, 53–4, 145n3
Silver Darlings (Gunn), 75
'The Simple Art of Murder' (Chandler),
  263
Since 1939 (British Council), 18, 24, 31,
  35n8
Sinclair, Andrew, 2–3
Sissons, Michael, 243
Sitwell, Edith, 30, 32, 258
Sitwell, Osbert, 30, 69
The Sixth Heaven (Hartley), 162
The Slaves of Solitude (Hamilton), 25,
  46–7, 105
The Small Back Room (Balchin), 25
Smith, Emma, 264, 266–7
Smith, Stevie, 26, 144, 194–5, 239, 241
  The Holiday, 18, 177, 184, 185–8, 254
Snow, C. P., 27
'Someone Like You' (Dahl), 111
Spain, Nancy, 106, 110n3
Spanish Civil War, 7, 31, 41
Speaight, Robert, 18, 20, 23, 29
Spender, Stephen, 11, 18, 29, 30–3, 41,
  239, 241

The Backward Son, 41
European Witness, 239–40
in *Horizon,* 39
Life and the Poet, 41
Ruins and Visions, 41
in *Since 1939,* 35n8
Spitfire Parade (Johns), 115–16
spivs, 210–11, 246–7, 249–50
'Sportsmen' (Douglas), 111
Spring, Howard, 27
spy fiction, 79, 83, 90, 141–2, 233, 251,
    263
'The Squander Bug,' 79, *80*
Stapledon, Olaf, 27
stereotypes, 95, 101, 133, 189, 230
Stevenson, Randall, vii
Stewart, Ena Lamont, 23
Stewart, Victoria, 3, 34n2, 165, 180,
    188–9, 191
Stonebridge, Lyndsey, 4, 34n2, 96–7, 100,
    240, 241
The Stones of the Field (Thomas),
    271–2
Storm, Lesley, 23
'Strange Meeting' (Owen), 111
Streatfeild, Noel, 26, 55–7
Street, Sarah, 250
Street Songs (Sitwell), 30
Streicher, Julius, 240
Struther, Jan, 24–5, 142
The Stuff to Give the Troops (Maclaren-
    Ross), 49
subjectivity
    consciousness, states of, 164, 180
    duality/death, 101
    emotion, 179
    female, 167, 259
    fragmentation of, 180–1
    function, 157
    outlaw, 195
    wartime/postwar, 209
suffering, 155, 188, 191, 194–5, 213
suicide, 45, 259
A Summer to Decide (Johnson), 13,
    243–4
Sunday Times, 31–2
Sutherland, John, 41
Swastika Night (Burdekin), 40
Sword of the Air (Carter), 116

Tambimuttu, M. J., 16, 29, 196
tank culture, 129–31
Taylor, Elizabeth, 3, 27, 180, 259
'Tell It to a Stranger' (Berridge), 51–2
'Tell Us The Tricks' (Scott), 50
Templeton, William, 22
Tey, Josephine, 27
thanatos/eros, 96; *see also* death

theatre, 18–23, 88–9, 101; *see also*
    specific titles
There's No Story There (Holden), 62–3
'They Came' (Lewis), 49–51
They Came to A City (Priestley), 22
They Made Me A Fugitive (Cavalcanti),
    211
They Were Sisters (Whipple), 74–5
The Third Man (Greene), 4, 246–51
The Third Man (Reed), 4, 246–51
This Way to the Tomb (Duncan), 21
Thomas, Dylan, 4, 30, 32, 197–9, 201,
    203–4, 269
Thomas, Gwyn, 217, 260, 269
Thomas, R. S., 30, 269, 271
Three Essays on the Theory of Sexuality
    (Freud), 76
Three Guineas (Woolf), 40
Three Men in New Suits (Priestley), 207,
    209, 225, 229
'Three Poems of the Atomic Age' (Sitwell),
    258
Tilsley, Frank, 40
Titus Groan (Peake), 5, 27, 154–7
To Be A Pilgrim (Cary), 85
'To Tea With the Colonel' (Berridge),
    52–3
Tolley, A. T., 2, 28
totalitarianism, 124, 135, 250, 252
Traitor's Purse (Allingham), 138–9,
    232
trauma, 9, 25, 33, 54, 61, 100, 113, 156,
    184–5, 187, 189, 210
Treece, Henry, 28
Treglown, Jeremy, 190
Tribune, 268
Tröger, Annemarie, 9

uncanny, 160, 209–10, 220–1
Under Siege: Literary Life (Hewison), 2
Under the Skin (Bottome), 267–8
Under the Volcano (Lowry), 261
United States of America, 34n3, 178,
    241–2, 244
Unity Theatres, 19

Valli, 247
venereal disease, 79, *82,* 83
'Vergissmeinnicht' (Douglas), 111–12
Versailles Treaty, 7
Vienna, 248, 272
Vine, Steve, 203–4
violence, 75, 76, 136, 161–2
The Voice of Wales (Griffith), 269

Wales, 16, 268, 269
Wallace, Diana, 149, 150, 162
War Like A Wasp (Sinclair), 2–3

war writing, 7–8, 25, 40, 165, 177–8,
    188, 197
warfare, 113–14, 130, 145n3
Warner, Rex, 26, 75, 124, 126
Warner, Sylvia Townsend, 32, 150
Wasson, Sara, 62, 63–4, 99–100
The Waste Land (Eliot), 5, 194, 203
Waterloo Road (Gilliat), 211, 218
Watkin, William, 178, 179
Watkins, Vernon, 32
Waugh, Evelyn, 2, 3, 23, 170–2, 233
    Brideshead Revisited, 26–7, 169–76,
        243
    The Loved One, 242–3
    on Picasso, 234n2
    Put Out More Flags, 98, 170
    Work Suspended, 174
The Way Ahead (Reed), 116
The Way to the Stars (Asquith), 116, 181,
    235n4
The Way to the Stars (Rattigan), 89
We Have Been Warned (Mitchison),
    150
Welles, Orson, 247–8
Wells, H. G., 162
Went the Day Well? (Cavalcanti), 48,
    202
West, Rebecca, 239–41, 242
Wheatley, Dennis, 26, 245–6
While the Sun Shines (Rattigan), 21, 22,
    102–4, 224
Whipple, Dorothy, 74–5
White, Rob, 246
White, T. H., 150
The White Horseman (Hendry and
    Treece), 28–9
Whitehead, Anne, 169, 175
'Why Not War Writers?', 40
The Wicked Lady (Arliss), 4, 150, 181
Williams, Charles, 207–9
Williams, Emlyn, 22
Williams, Keith, 7
Williams, Oscar, 197
Willis, Ted, 22
Wilson, Edmund, 171–2
Winkles and Champagne, 22
Winnicott, D. W., 53, 55–6
The Winslow Boy (Rattigan), 221, 222–8
Winter, Jay, 1
Within the Cup (Bottome), 75
Wolfit, Donald, 22

women
    agency, 54, 60, 140, 151, 154, 174,
        232, 246, 248
    air warfare, 116
    alienation, 64
    in *Brideshead Revisited*, 171–2, 173–4
    in Coward, 104
    desire, 87–8
    domesticity, 67
    home, 83
    instinct, 87, 88
    loss, 180–1
    loyalty, 182
    misrule, 85
    in politics, 80, 83
    postwar status, 130, 151
    as problem, 77–90
    Second World War, 78, 83
    stereotypes, 101, 189
    symbol of suffering, 155, 191
    transgressive, 181–2
    as victims, 133–4
    see also female body; femininity;
        misogyny
women workers, 64–5, 78, 79, 84–5, 179,
    181
women writers, 32, 149–50, 179, 180–5,
    188
Women's Own, 78–9
Woolf, Virginia, 3, 5, 27, 75, 266
    Between the Acts, 25, 42, 75, 160–2
    'Thoughts on Peace in an Air Raid,' 43
    Three Guineas, 40
Woolley, Rollo, 123–4
Woon, Basil, 46
Wordsworth, William, 169, 213
Work Suspended (Waugh), 174
working class, 61–2, 64, 103–4
The World My Wilderness (Macaulay),
    26, 194–6, 218
Worrals of the WAAF (Johns), 116
wounded hero, 95, 125, 126, 181, 189
A Wreath of Roses (Taylor), 259
Wright, Basil, 215
The Writing of Anxiety (Stonebridge), 4,
    96–7
Wyndham, Joan, 96

The Years Between (du Maurier), 22
Young, Douglas, 268
Young Bess trilogy (Irwin), 150